Bullies and Mean Girls
in Popular Culture

Bullies and Mean Girls in Popular Culture

PATRICE A. OPPLIGER

McFarland & Company, Inc., Publishers
Jefferson, North Carolina, and London

LIBRARY OF CONGRESS CATALOGUING-IN-PUBLICATION DATA

Oppliger, Patrice A.
Bullies and mean girls in popular culture / Patrice A. Oppliger.
pages cm
Includes bibliographical references and index.

ISBN 978-0-7864-6865-2
softcover : acid free paper ∞

1. Bullies in mass media.   2. Bullying—Social aspects.
3. Mass media and girls.   4. Girls in popular culture.   I. Title.
P96.B85O66 2013   302.34'3—dc23   2013028263

BRITISH LIBRARY CATALOGUING DATA ARE AVAILABLE

On the cover: (left to right) Yano Anaya as Grover Dill, Scott Schwartz
as Flick and Zack Ward as Scut Farkus in *A Christmas Story*,
1983 (MGM/UA Entertainment Company/Photofest);
title frame Hemera/Thinkstock

Manufactured in the United States of America

*McFarland & Company, Inc., Publishers
Box 611, Jefferson, North Carolina 28640
www.mcfarlandpub.com*

To my dear friend Ernie Spence

Table of Contents

Acknowledgments

Thanks to my stellar staff of graduate assistants: Alex Sear, Nicole Henninger, Ashley Waxman, Gabby McNevin, and Emily Lospennato. Thanks to John Ryan for getting me up to speed on the WWE. Also thanks to my colleagues at Boston University, especially Denis Wu, Deborah Jaramillo, Tammy Vigil, Mina Tsay, and Cheryl Ann Lambert, who helped me through the rough patches and talked me down when times got tough. Many thanks to my readers, who I hope are still my friends: Joe Finnerty, Becca Bennett, Lorena Prime, Susan Rosa, Denise Breault, Sharon O'Rourke, and Nancy Dow. Thanks for the grammar "hotline" help from Marsh Pelletier and her trusty sidekick Lee Urton. As always, thanks to my family for their support: Lee Ann and Al Zach, Gail and Gregg Holcomb, and Brian and Julie Oppliger. A big shout out to my parents, Walter and Gracie Oppliger, for teaching me empathy and compassion.

Preface

The numerous anti-bullying programs in schools across the United States have done little to reduce the number of reported bullying instances in the past decade. One major flaw in a majority of the programs I found is that little attention has been paid to the role of the media and popular culture in adolescents' bullying and mean-girl behavior. Today, American adolescents spend more time engaged with multiple forms of media (Kaiser, 2010) than any other activity except for sleeping. This book addresses media role models and the influence of popular culture in the realm of bullying and relational aggression.

There have been thousands of books published on bullying as of September 2012. A keyword search of "bullying" on Amazon.com yielded 6,487 books. The majority focus on helping victims deal with bullies rather than addressing the causes of bullying. The books that address causes almost exclusively target individual children's dispositions (e.g., self-esteem), the school environment, or parenting styles. In my search of thousands of books on Amazon.com, I could not find a single book dedicated to the influence of the media and popular culture in terms of bullying and mean-girl behavior. Only a few books had chapters dedicated to media. In much the same vein, books on relational aggression and mean girls ignore, barely address, or gloss over the influence of popular culture and media role models. I did find academic articles that addressed the link between media and bullying somewhat; however, they comprise a fraction of the studies compared to those dedicated to the link between media and physical and relational aggression.

To begin my textual analysis, I conducted a word search for "bully" or "bullies" in movie synopses and television episode guides. A keyword search for "bullying" on IMDb produced 1,138 results. Additional television episodes were found using the website locatetv.com. Because of the mislabeling and overuse of the term "bullying," I eliminated programs and movies that did not meet Olweus' (2010) definition of bullying: "A person is bullied when he or she is exposed, repeatedly and over time, to negative actions on the part of one or more other persons, and he or she has difficulty defending himself or herself." Mean-girl portrayals were included only if they met criteria set by Simmons (2011), which defines mean-girl behavior as social exclusion or some sort of relationship-destroying behavior that is meant to be harmful emotionally. I further narrowed the pool by only including programs and movies that addressed adolescent bullying. Adult portrayals were included if the physical or relational aggression mirrored adolescent bullying and mean-girl behaviors. I included picture and chapter books because of their popularity with small children and adolescents.

1

Introduction

Bullying among young people is a significant problem today. According to the National Institutes of Health ("NIH News Release," 2001), almost 30 percent of teens in the United States (or over 5.7 million) are estimated to be either bullies or targets of bullies. Updated statistics show comparable numbers, reporting nearly one out of three middle school and high school students reported being bullied in 2007 (National Institute of Child Health and Human Development, 2010). Advances in technology (e.g., social networking sites, cell phones) have made bullying even more pervasive. In 2010, more than 5 million American students were bullied at school, on the bus, at home, through their cell phones and online, making it the most common form of violence enacted by young people in the United States (The Bully Project, 2012).

The Centers for Disease Control and Prevention (cited in "School Bullying," n.d.) report that bullying can affect teens' self-esteem and feelings of self-worth. Bullying can also increase victims' social isolation, leading them to become withdrawn and depressed. Bosworth et al. (1999) noted that a single bullied student can create a climate of fear at a school. Adams and Russakoff (1999) reported that the climate of bullying created an atmosphere that could have helped trigger the perpetrators' extreme violence at Columbine High. According to Chang (2005), children who are bullied on a weekly basis are four times more likely to carry a weapon and 3.8 times more likely to bring a weapon to school than those not bullied.

Three-quarters of junior high school or middle school principals, 43 percent of elementary school principals, and 45 percent of senior high school principals report that bullying, name-calling, or harassment of students is a serious problem at their schools (Parent Further, 2011). Many schools have instituted anti-bullying workshops in which victims are taught how to deal with bullying. Merrell, Gueldner, Ross, and Isava (2008) conducted a meta-analysis on the effectiveness of bullying intervention. They found that bullying intervention programs appear to be useful in increasing awareness, knowledge, and self-perceived competency in dealing with bullying. Unfortunately, they found these programs were unlikely to dramatically influence incidents or victimization. More research into the causes of bullying and relational aggression is sorely needed.

According to Olweus (2010), components of bullying include aggressive behavior that involves unwanted, negative action, patterns of behavior repeated over time, and an imbalance of power or strength. Bullying can take various forms such as physical contact (e.g., hitting, kicking, shoving), taking money, damaging things, or issuing threats. In addition, bullying can be manifested in psychological forms such as verbal aggression (e.g., derogatory comments and bad names), social exclusion, or lies and rumors. Bosworth, Espelage, and Simon's (1999) definition of bullying included several dimensions: calling kids names, teasing or saying things about a kid to make other kids laugh, threatening to hit or hurt, and actually pushing, shoving, slapping, or kicking other kids. Slee (1995) argued that behavior can be classified as bullying when an imbalance of physical/psychological power exists between bully and victim, the bully's negative action toward the victim are repeated, the bully deliberately intends to hurt the victim, and the bully's negative actions toward the victim is largely unprovoked. Coloroso (2004) described the progression or escalation of bullying. First, a potential bully will survey the landscape and perhaps test out bullying strategies. Second, once he or she takes action and is successful in gaining power, he or she may become emboldened. Coloroso (2004) described the third and fourth possible steps as depression and rage (what Coloroso calls "pinnacle of pain"), and finally advancing to a damaged or criminal adult.

Bullying does not appear to be a solitary or private act. Pepler and Craig (2009) reported that in 85 percent of bullying cases, peers were involved. Of those bystanders, 81 percent reinforced the behavior (48 percent of which actively participated) and only 13 percent intervened to help the victim. Salmivalli et al. (cited in Smith, 2004) differentiated types of bullies as "ring-leaders" who initiate the bullying, "followers" who join in, "reinforcers" who watch and perhaps encourage the bully, "outsiders" who are complicit and whose lack of action perhaps reinforces the bullying, and "defenders" who help or get help from others such as a parent or teacher. Olweus (2000) categorized passive bystanders as those who do not disapprove of the bullying and those who disapprove of the bullying but are afraid to challenge the perpetrator. Olweus argued that the lack of intervention or support of bystanders increases the likelihood of continued bullying. Gini, Pozzoli, Borghi, and Franzoni (2008) found that bystanders' behavior was directly related to students' sense of safety and that when bystanders were passive in the face of bullying, peers assumed that the bystanders were supporting the bullying behavior.

The U.S. Department of Health and Human Services (2009) reported that children who bully are impulsive/hotheaded/dominant, easily frustrated, lack empathy, have a difficult time following rules, and view violence in a positive way. However, other studies have contradicted these findings. According to Slee's (1995) definition of bullying, the behavior must be deliberate, repeated, and largely unprovoked; therefore, bullying is not an impulsive act by an impulsive antagonist. Some experts (including Bosworth et al., 1999) found that bullies are not lacking in social skills; rather, they deliberately select strategies to maintain dominance and power. Gottheil and Dubow (2001) argued that bullying is not an attempt to resolve conflict but to express power and control. Rather than impulsivity and feelings of depression, bullies have a strong need for power/dominance and carefully plot their attacks. Most bullies find satisfaction in causing injury and suffering and are often rewarded for their behavior.

Another myth about bullies is that they are loners. Bullies usually have a small group of friends who support or encourage their bullying (HRSA, 2009). In addition, bullies report to have average or above-average self-esteem. Like Bosworth et al. (1999), Smith, Bowers, Binney, and Cowie (1993) found that bullies choose social strategies that perpetuate their power and dominance. Felmlee and Faris' (2011) study of bullying found that peer status or popularity increases capacity for aggression, which students may use as a way to compete for or keep their social status. Faris (cited in Hadad, 2011) reported that students appeared to be engaged in "social combat," a "verbal, physical, and cyber fight to the top of the school social hierarchy." The closer the student was to the top of the social structure, the more likely he or she was to bully and be bullied, except for the very top. Felmlee and Faris (2011) found that students in the top 2 percent and in the bottom 2 percent of their school social hierarchy were the least aggressive. They explained that the students at the bottom either do not have the social power or the means to be aggressive. Although the students at the very top might have all the power, they are less likely to feel they need to use that power since they had already achieved the highest levels of social status.

According to Olweus (cited in Espelage et al., 2000), there is a variety of contributing factors that go into making a child into a bully. Parenting style has been found to be of great significance in the development of bullying behaviors. Olweus defined bad parents as those who lack warmth or involvement, those who bully themselves or use physical punishment and emotional outbursts in discipline, or parents who permit their children to be inappropriately aggressive with other children, siblings, or adults. Felmlee and Faris (2011), on the other hand, found that bullies do not necessarily come from disturbed backgrounds or poor parenting. They warn that it is much harder for parents and teachers to identify bullies because they look like normal kids. Salmivalli and Voeten (2004) found that group norms could be used to predict bullying behavior. The culture of the school climate and the level of tolerance by the administration is a strong factor in the extent to which children bully.

Cyberbullying

With the increase in use of technology, Olweus (2010) argued that cyberbullying has become a significant problem. Cyberbullying differs from regular bullying because there can be almost limitless distribution of harassing materials and 24-hour accessibility to victims. The anonymity of the sender may create additional fear when the victim cannot identify the bully. In addition, disinhibition of bullies who can hide behind a fictitious screen name can increase the likelihood a child will become a cyberbully (Olweus, 2011). Dellasega and Nixon (2003) reported that online relational aggression can be just as damaging as face-to-face incidents, sometimes worse because the target may not know the identity of the aggressor. Carpenter and Ferguson (2009) created a typography of cyberbullying activities that included harassment, flaming, spreading rumors, posing as another and sending out negative messages in that person's name, outing personal information about another, and posting embarrassing photos or videos of another.

Lenhart (2010) reported that 26 percent of teens in the United States have been bullied or harassed through text messages and phone calls. In a survey conducted by the Cyberbullying Research Center (cited in Chan, 2010), one in five youths between the ages of 10 and 18 reported to have been victims of or participated in cyberbullying. The Center, however, estimates this number to be low because of the reluctance of victims and perpetrators to report cyberbullying. Cullen (2010), citing a report from The Massachusetts Aggression Reduction Center, put the number of kids who reported being cyberbullied at 60 percent, compared to about 25 percent who reported to be victims of traditional bullying. At the same time, the report showed that nearly 70 percent of high school teens said their parents either do not worry or rarely worry about cyberbullying.

Smith (2010) found that victims of cyberbullying are more likely to report feeling depressed than victims of traditional bullying. The perpetrator of cyberbullying is also more likely to go unpunished. Hollingsworth (2011) cited a Cyberbullying Research Center report that cyberbullying victims are almost twice as likely to attempt suicide as their non-cyberbullied peers. The researchers of the study concluded that it is not the cyberbullying that causes the suicide attempts but rather that cyberbullying exacerbates the struggles of adolescents. Carpenter and Ferguson (2009) also noted that because technology is changing so quickly, researchers are having difficulty keeping up. Parents are also having issues with overlooking or misunderstanding subtle online bullying.

Gender Differences

Studies show significant differences between boys' and girls' bullying behaviors. Specifically, gender identification has been known to influence bullying, or at least the type of bullying. According to the National Institutes of Health ("NIH News Release," 2001), males are more likely to bully and be bullied than females. Also, boys are more likely to use physical bullying and verbal threats than girls. Girls are more likely to use social and verbal tactics such as spreading rumors and excluding individuals from groups (Boulton & Underwood, 1992; Gottheil & Dubow, 2001; Sharp & Smith, 1991), a phenomenon also known as relational aggression. Felmlee and Faris (2011) found that girls used more indirect aggression, although the overall rates of aggression were equivalent by gender. Girls were less likely to bully boys than boys were to bully girls. Chang (2005) found that direct bullying is linked with depression and suicidal thoughts specifically in girls. Chang reasoned that while boys fight and get it over with, girls are more likely to become depressed.

Pellegrini and Long (2004) employed dominance theory to explain how bullying is used to gain status in a group, which is moderated by gender and age. Bullying strategies are used particularly when youth and transitioning into a new social structure such as moving from elementary to middle school. Adolescent males especially use aggressive strategies in order to gain dominance over peers. Dellasega and Nixon (2003) stated that relational aggression is quieter, more insidious, and harder to detect than physical aggression. Relational aggression is more likely to affect girls because females' identities are more often defined by their relationships. It is more likely to occur in adolescents because of the immense physical and mental changes during that period (Dellasega & Nixon, 2003). Pellegrini and Long's (2004) study showed that boys continued to exert dominant behavior even as they entered higher grades. Girls, on the other hand, reported decreases in physical aggressive behavior over time; however, they were likely to continue dominance through other means such as relational aggression. Aggression tends to dissipate somewhat in late adolescence (17 to 19 years of age) as girls become more independent (Dellasega & Nixon, 2003).

Gender identification as well as biological sex has strong influences on bullying. Gini and Pozzoli (2006) found that masculine traits predict active bullying behavior, regardless of the sex of the child. This finding is particularly true when the bullying is manifested in physical ways. For example, Scharrer (2001) found that males who rated high on hypermasculinity scales tended to respond to violent media with more callousness and aggression compared to less hypermasculine males. She identified hypermasculinity as a mitigating factor in the effects of violent television on aggression and hostility of the viewer.

Conclusion

An extensive amount of research has been dedicated to bullying. Smith (2011) defined four waves of bullying research beginning in the mid–1970s to today. He identified the first important scientific work on the topic as *Aggression in Schools: Bullies and Whipping Boys* (Olweus, 1978). Olweus launched his anti-bullying campaign in 1983. The second wave (1989 to mid–1990s) expanded the definition of bullying to include indirect and relational bullying. The third wave (mid–1990s to 2004) expanded internationally, to include cultural differences. The fourth and current wave includes cyberbullying with the differing levels of causation ranging from an individual level (e.g., temperament and personality) to a societal level (e.g., portrayals in the mass media). Bullying researchers have been slow to include media portrayals in their work, however. While it has been established that media has a significant effect on adolescents' aggressive behavior, it is unclear why equal attention has not been paid to media exposure in the realm of bullying. The next two chapters deal specifically with the influence of media portrayal of bullies and mean girls on adolescents' attitudes and behaviors.

1

Bullies and the Media

Children, ages 8 to 18, spend more time (44.5 hours per week on average) in front of computer, television, and game screens than any other activity in their lives except sleeping (Kaiser Family Foundation, 2005). Other estimates of media use are as high as 6 hours and 21 minutes a day (AAP, 2009). Because of the enormity of time spent with media and past research linking aggression to violent media use, it is vital to investigate the link between media use and bullying. Results from the few studies that have investigated the effect of media on bullying (see Barboza et al., 2009, Kuntsche, 2004, Lee & Kim, 2004) have shown that media exposure to violence, especially on television, is directly related to bullying. Zimmerman, Glew, Christakis, and Katon (2005) found that television exposure plays a role in developing bullying behavior as early as four years old. Barboza et al. (2009) argued that overall the absence of explicit research on adolescent media usage and bullying is a significant omission.

On the other hand, extensive research has been done to link violent media to aggressive behavior in children, which is a substantial factor in many bully cases. Paik and Comstock's (1994) meta-analysis of 217 studies found strong support for both experimental and survey research findings linking media violence to aggressive behavior. From their cross-cultural longitudinal study of media, Huesmann (1986) found that children who were exposed to high levels of violence on television were more likely to be aggressive as teenagers and young adults than those children who watched less violence. These results held even when controlling for IQ, social status, parental aggression, and church attendance (Huesmann, 1986). Results of Bushman and Huesmann's (2006) meta-analysis, which included violent media in TV, movies, video games, music, and comic books, showed overall modest but significant links to aggressive behaviors, aggressive thoughts, angry feelings, and arousal levels. Kuntsche (2004) argued that excessive television-viewing and electronic game-playing for boys lead to indirect violence, such as bullying, rather than to physical violence.

The American Academy of Pediatrics (AAP) (2009) determined that violent media is a likely mediating factor not only in adolescents learning about violence but learning to be violent. Bushman and Heusmann (2006) concluded that long-term media effects require the learning of scripts, schemas, or beliefs and that children can encode these new scripts, schemas, and beliefs via observational learning with less interference and effort than adults. Gentile, Coyne, and Walsh (2011) also found that violent media exposure can contribute to aggressive cognitive constructs. According to Bandura's (1986) social learning theory, media consumers can learn negative behaviors, such as verbal aggression and bullying, vicariously through media representations. A crucial variable in whether the viewer will imitate behavior they witness is motivation. Individuals assess their beliefs about the action and the consequences learned vicariously by observing external sources. Further, imitation is heavily influenced by reward and punishment of models. Viewers are much more likely to judge behavior as socially acceptable and more likely to imitate that behavior if they see that behavior is rewarded (Bandura, 1986). Much of media today includes instances of rewarded bullying behavior. For example, a content analysis of television programming showed that perpetrators went unpunished in 73 percent of all violent scenes (AAP, 2009).

In addition to social learning, another effect of the media is that repeated portrayals can normalize bullying, as explained by cultivation theory. The theory states that media effects happen slowly over time and intensify with increased exposure (Gerbner, 1998). Repetitive exposure to bully portrayals may reinforce the notion that bullying is inevitable. Media may also have a desensitization effect. Desensitization theory states that with repetitive viewing, aggressive and violent behavior become less shocking over time (see Huesmann, 2007; Gentile, 2003). Seeing a great deal of bullying on television and in video games will likely lessen the impact on bystanders when they see bullying in real life and thus make them less likely to intervene or even care about the victim.

Pepler and Craig (2009) argued that bullying is a relationship problem rather than simply a problem with aggression. Zimmerman and associates (2005) also warned that programs that include characters behaving disrespectfully toward one another could serve as a model for children and encourage them to bully. Children often learn interpersonal strategies from the media. Situation comedies such as *Everybody Loves Raymond* and *Seinfeld* are rife with mean-spirited verbal exchanges. Chord-Assad and Tamborini (2004) found that sitcoms consistently feature the most verbal aggression of all television genres. Pepler and Craig (2009) asserted that children who bully are not just modeling aggressive behavior but are learning how to use power and aggression to control their peers. Kuntsche, Pickett, Overpeck, Craig, Boyce, and de Matos (2006) found that verbal forms of bullying (e.g., calling names and spreading rumors) were more closely related to television viewing than physical forms (e.g., kicking or punching). Frequent television viewers are more likely to act and react in verbally aggressive ways rather than being physically violent.

Because of the link between media and bullying behavior, it is vital to assess the types of bullying messages portrayed in the media. The following analysis investigates the portrayals of bullies in the media chronologically and by target audience. I look at the types of bullies and victims that reoccur in television, particularly situation comedies.

Bully Portrayals

The bully characters in television, film, and children's picture books are heavily stereotyped. It appears that few movies and television shows take the time to develop bullies' personalities. Their stories are seldom as rich and complex as the protagonist of the story. Bully characters are generally one-dimensional, with the bulk of the character development dedicated to the victim or bystander. Bullies are usually physically domineering with spiky hair or shaved heads. Particular actors get typecast, often playing the bully in several works. They are dressed in leather jackets or sleeveless denim shirts with chains and bandanas. The jock bully wears a letter jacket or football jersey. Most bullies are portrayed as doing poorly in school and using poor grammar. Most of these attributes extend to the female bully, although female bullies are rare. A significant size difference between bullies and victims is a casting strategy used by producers to easily establish the bully character. The size differential between the bully and the victim may be used to intensify the conflict or elicit sympathy for the victim. When the bully is significantly smaller than the victim (e.g., *How I Met Your Mother*) or female (e.g., *Like Family*), family and friends of the victim appear to be particularly judgmental and further degrade male bully victims.

One variation of the typical bully character is the sympathetic bully who comes from a dysfunctional or abusive home. The sympathetic bully is often shown being bullied by a parent, sibling, and/or teacher. "Loveable" bullies include Nelson from *The Simpsons* and Sue Sylvester from *Glee*. Audiences appear to judge bullying behavior of a likable character as justified or humorous and therefore trivialize or excuse aggressive acts. If the bully is a jock, coaches and school officials may be reluctant to punish the bully for fear the team will lose the big game. In some cases of bullies from wealthy families, a principal or school board member at a private school may fear the loss of a donation from the parents.

Film Bullies

Perhaps the earliest media representations of adolescent bullying is *Our Gang* (AKA *Little Rascals*), a series of comedy film shorts that spanned from the early 1920s to the late 1930s. One of the recurring bullies, Butch, is a tough-looking kid with a name to match. Butch plays practical jokes on the gang and often sabotages their wacky plots. Other bullies appear in the series: Snoozer in season two, Johnny in season three, and Toughey in season five.

In the *Our Gang* episode "Glove Taps," Butch tells the other kids that starting Monday, he will be in charge of the school. He tells them he is going to "lick the toughest one" of them and demands that kid step forward. Alfalfa accidentally steps forward after backing into a nail. The boys get set to fight in a makeshift ring. Butch and the crowd of kids laugh as Alfalfa swings, misses Butch, and gets tangled in the ropes. In "Rushin' Ballet," Butch and his crony steal Buckwheat's and Porky's marbles and then smear tomatoes in their faces. "Fishy Tales" begins with an archery exhibition where Alfalfa accidently hits Butch in nose with a suction cup arrow. Butch threatens Alfalfa if there are any more "accidents." When a toddler hits Butch in the back of the head with another arrow, Butch thinks it was Alfalfa again and makes a fist. Alfalfa faints. Spanky tells Butch it is lucky for him that Alfalfa fainted because Alfalfa was going to beat up Butch. Butch has to leave when his mother calls but he vows to return. The gang tricks Butch into thinking Alfalfa dislocated his shinbone and cannot fight. Spanky makes up a story about a kid who claimed that Butch was "yella" and Alfalfa chased after him in Butch's defense. When the bullies find out Alfalfa was faking his injury, they chase him. Butch threatens Spanky with a black eye if Alfalfa shows up to a talent competition that Butch wants to win in "Framing Youth." Spanky convinces Alfalfa to pretend he lost his voice in order to avoid a beating from Butch. Butch is about to win the talent show when Spanky lets Alfalfa sing and he wins the competition instead. Butch takes Spanky outside. Spanky comes back with a black eye; however, Butch comes back with two black eyes. Spanky and Alfalfa shake hands, celebrating their victory over the bully, Butch. The *Our Gang* shorts treat bullying as a normal and inevitable part of childhood.

The heyday of the movie bully was perhaps in the 1980s comedies. Jefferson (2011) argued that bullies were an integral part of almost every successful film about teenagers during that decade. Craw (2010) also identified the 1980s as a significant time for bully portrayals. Victims were tossed into dumpsters, lockers, and pools. Craw (2010) described the wedgie as "the '80s bully's most physically and emotionally debilitating weapon." The victims were often represented by the stereotypical nerd (e.g., *Revenge of the Nerds*, *Weird Science*, *Zapped*, and *Back to the Future*). The nerds in the 80s comedies like science, were physically clumsy, and have bad hair, bad skin, and bad fashion sense. Many of these movies granted the nerd special powers to help ward off the bullies (e.g., *Teen Wolf*, *Zapped*, and *Weird Science*). The endings of these movies were almost always the same as well: the bullies get their comeuppance and the nerds get the girls.

The Breakfast Club stands out for its exploration of bullying from the perpetrator's perspective. In most films, the bullies are not given sufficient screen time to develop a backstory about why they bully. There is a sharp contrast to the two bullies in *The Breakfast Club*: Andrew, the popular jock whose father is a tyrant, and Bender, the stereotypical thug who comes from an abusive household. Romantic comedies such as *Pretty in Pink* and *Some Kind of Wonderful* often cast mean boys rather than traditional bullies (e.g., most James Spader roles). Class issues keep the lead couple apart, with the target of bullying daring to date outside his or her socioeconomic status.

The Outsiders is a bit unusual as well because it is the poor kids or Greasers who are the victims of a brutal attack. Generally rich boys are written as more devious in their bullying and less physical than the underclass. The Socs (short for Socials) in the film are the bullies even though the Greasers stereotypically look the part of bully with their leather jackets and slicked-back hair. In the "sleep-away camp" movies, it is almost always the rich kids who are the bullies. The bullies in the "fight back" movies likely belong to the exclusive gyms with top-notch trainers, whereas the targets train with the janitor or handyman-type character in a spare room or alley. In the "sports" movies, the bullies belong on the privileged team with nice uniforms and top-of-the-line equipment. The disparity in all these situations adds to the victims' underdog status and increases the audience's sympathy and joy when they overcome great obstacles to win the fight or the game.

TELEVISION BOY BULLIES

Television bullies have changed little since the golden days of television. In the episode of the 1950s sitcom *Leave it to Beaver* entitled "Lumpy Rutherford," Lumpy, an oversized and underachieving teenager, is introduced as a bully picking on the main characters Wally and the Beaver. He knocks the books out of Wally's hands and pulls Beaver's cap down over his face. Wally and Beaver resort to taking a different route home after school to avoid Lumpy. When Mr. Rutherford finds out his son has been bullying the Cleaver brothers, he gives Lumpy a "talking to." Lumpy appears to stop bullying Wally and Beaver, and over time, Lumpy and Wally become friends.

The recurring bully is most often represented in television situation comedies that either target adolescent audiences or are animated. A few exceptions are *Diff'rent Strokes*, *Malcolm in the Middle*, and *Everybody Hates Chris*. The Gooch, the bully in the 1980s sitcom *Diff'rent Strokes*, is never actually shown on camera. He is only described as being bigger than Arnold. Arnold comes home with a black eye when he stands up to the Gooch in the episode "The Fight." The Gooch reappears a year later in "Return of the Gooch." This time Arnold takes karate lessons. Four years later, the Gooch resurfaces again, this time picking on Sam, Arnold's new stepbrother. Arnold tries to defend Sam but comes home after being manhandled by the Gooch. Arnold bribes a female foreign exchange student with a date with his brother Willis if she will take care of the Gooch. She returns victorious.

Reese, Malcolm's older brother from *Malcolm in the Middle*, is a rather loveable bully. He is a "traditionalist" when it comes to bullying. He limits his bullying of smaller boys to giving them wedgies, stealing their lunches, making them eat grass, and forcing them to do his homework. The most notable episode characterizing Reese as a bully is the episode entitled "The Bully." When Reese is beaten in a school wrestling match by a girl, he reassesses his role as the school bully. When he sees the mayhem his absence as school bully has caused, he returns to bullying to restore order in the schoolyard.

The sitcom *Everybody Hates Chris* recounts comedian Chris Rock's childhood. Because it is set in the 1980s, racial discrimination is presented almost nostalgically. Joey Caruso is a stereotypical Irish and Italian American with freckles and a propensity for fighting. Caruso not only steals Chris's lunch money, but takes his bus pass, Chris's only way of getting back to his neighborhood. If Chris is late coming home from school, he will have to deal with his bully of a mother. Chris's strategy to deal with Caruso is, "I couldn't beat him, but maybe I could out-black him." At times the principal and the police look the other way when Caruso is bullying Chris. Chris knows he will get little sympathy from his father, who lived through the Civil Rights riots. In "Everybody Hates Sausage," Chris tricks Caruso into bullying him in front of the principal's office. Caruso and his cronies who are throwing batteries at Chris finally get detention. When Caruso is beaten in a fight by an Asian boy in "Everybody Hates Caruso," he resigns as school bully. Chaos ensues when all sorts of new bullies emerge, much like the *Malcolm in the Middle* episode "The Bully." In order to restore social order, Chris helps Caruso regain his title by getting the Asian boy to throw the next fight with Caruso.

There are slight variations of the bully in sitcoms specifically targeted to adolescents. These shows often appear as part of ABC's TGIF lineup aimed at adolescents (e.g., *Boy Meets World*, *Parker Lewis Can't Lose*) or on cable channels that are targeted to a younger age group such as Nickelodeon and The Disney Channel (e.g., *The Adventures of Pete and Pete*, *Phineas and Ferb*). These shows feature adolescents as the primary stars of the shows with little if any interaction with adults (e.g., parents, teachers).

Cory first encounters Harley, the bully, in "Back 2 School" on the sitcom *Boy Meets World*. Harley and other senior boys are taking freshmen's clothes and forcing them to walk around school in their underwear. Harley is a stereotypical bully in that he wears either a leather jacket or a bowling shirt (the kind that is popular with the Soprano crowd). Harley has a Brooklyn accent although they are nowhere near New York City. Harley has his cronies, Frankie and Joey, do most of his dirty work. In season three, Harley is sent away to reform school. When he returns, another bully, Griff, has taken over his turf. After a dispute between Griff and Harley, Frankie and Joey decide to quit bullying. Harley targets Cory, whom Harley nicknamed "Baboon," but not exclusively. In "The Uninvited," Harley tells Cory, "Pardon me, it's my 11 o'clock" when some even geekier kids than Cory walk by talking about chess. Harley also has a kinder, gentler side. In "Sister Theresa," Harley tells Cory he would like for Cory to take out his sister and even gives him money to take her someplace nice. When Cory asks if the two of them are "okay," Harley quickly says "no." There appears to be more bullying in the future. In "Cyrano," Cory finds Harley at Cory's house having tea with and getting girlfriend advice from Cory's mother.

In the pilot of *Parker Lewis Can't Lose*, Larry the bully does not even speak. He just grunts phrases such as, "Eat now?" He is shown eating a large turkey leg with his hands. Rumors circulate that Larry killed a nun when she misplaced his lunch. He is about to beat up Parker and his friend, Mikey, for sitting on his lunch, when his little brother comes into the room. Larry shows a softer side when interacting with his brother. Larry becomes friends with Parker within a few episodes. The transformation is very similar to Lumpy from *Leave It to Beaver*. Myron, in *Phil of the Future*, also transforms from bully to friend. Myron plays the bully in the episode "Double Trouble," however, two episodes later in "Raging Bull," Myron is friendly toward Phil and invites Phil to hang out with him and his friends.

The bully in *The Adventures of Pete and Pete*, Endless Mike Hellstrom, turns out to be more of an obnoxious acquaintance than a bully. His slight stature is not the stereotypical bully. He has little muscle to back up the physical threats he makes. In "Time Tunnel," the voiceover introduces Mike as "the most hated bully in town." Mike pulls his car up to Little Pete and his friend on their bicycles. Mike opens his car door, purposely knocking the little girl and Little Pete to the ground. Little Pete gets revenge later by playing embarrassing home movies of Mike as a baby at the drive-in theater. In the episode "Rangeboy," Endless Mike tells Big Pete's dad that when he golfs, he imagines it is Pete's head on his tee as he whacks the golf ball. The father is apparently oblivious to the threat of violence towards his son. In the show's voiceover, Pete describes Endless Mike as a "high school lifer" who is always in shop. In the episode "Tool and Die," Endless Mike has a boy's head trapped in a vise. The shop teacher, Mr. Slurm, pays no attention. Mr. Slurm appears to be a bully himself. Mike teases Pete about his shop ineptness and sarcastically calls Pete "saw boy." Endless Mike and Pete appear to be friends in later episodes. Mike tries to help Pete out with Ellen, Pete's love interest. Mike gives him advice in "Yellow Fever" how to stop another boy from flirting with Ellen. Mike talks Pete into flicking geeky Mark's ear, which stick out. A flashback shows a series of boys who have flicked Mark's ear. Pete seems horrified and apologizes to Mark for the ear flicking.

The bully from *Salute Your Shorts*, Bobby Budnick, was played by Danny Cooksey. Cooksey also was the voice of the bully Victor in *Ren and Stimpy*, the voice of the bully big brother Brad in *Kick Buttowski*, and the voice of the Stoop Kid in *Hey Arnold*. Bobby is not very big physically. Cooksey played the young bullying victim, Sam, in *Diff'rent Strokes*. (Note: Cooksey played Sam at age 9 and Bobby at age 16.) In season one of *Salute Your Shorts*, Bobby uses his friend Donkeylips as his muscle. Although Bobby does some typical bully tricks, he seems more like a mean boy than a bully. Bobby mainly plays pranks and manipulates people with exclusion and blackmail rather than threats of physical harm. Bobby appears to annoy the other kids more than scare them. "The First Day" begins with Michael being greeted by Bobby and Donkeylips when he arrives at Camp Anawanna. Bobby and Donkeylips steal Michael's bag and run his underwear up the flagpole. The kids laugh and assume there must be a new kid at camp. Bobby holds Sponge, the smart kid, in a headlock and orders Michael around the cabin. Bobby and Donkeylips rig the bed so when Michael lies down, the bed collapses. Bobby and Donkeylips offer to leave Michael and Sponge alone for the rest of the summer if they raid the girls' cabin. Tired of being pushed around, Sponge squirts ketchup on Bobby and all the kids laugh.

Each episode of *Ned's Declassified School Survival Guide* opens with Ned's voiceover describing middle school as "full of bullies and insane teachers." The premier bully, Loomer, is bigger than the other kids, wears black clothes and a thick silver chain, and has spiky hair. In the first episode, "First Day," Ned runs into Loomer. Loomer nicknames a small boy with a new haircut "coconut head" and orders his cronies to "get him." The episode "Guide to: Cheaters and Bullies" opens with Loomer and two of his cronies terrorizing the school. One small boy walks by with his clothes on backward and his hair messed, presumably a Loomer victim. In the meantime, Ned and Simon devise a trap to get back at Loomer. When Loomer sees the traps, he threatens greater revenge. In "A New Grade," Ned keeps accidently injuring Loomer. For example, as Ned is swinging his backpack to swat a bug, he mistakenly hits Loomer in the face. Ned bends down to tie his shoe and Loomer trips over him. Loomer becomes afraid of Ned and no longer bullies. Like other sitcoms when the primary bully is removed, a host of other bully wannabes emerge to take his place. Order is restored when Ned's female friend Moze hits Ned and convinces Loomer that Loomer hit Ned. Feeling confident again, Loomer takes charge of the school's bullying.

Animation series appear to be a popular venue for the recurring bully. In the Disney Channel series *Phineas and Ferb*, Buford focuses most of his bullying on a small Indian boy named Baljeet. Buford has the stereotypical flattop haircut and wears a black t-shirt emblazoned with a skull. In "Bully Bromance Breakup," Buford actually misses Baljeet when Buford goes to work for a mad scientist. When Buford returns, Baljeet gives Buford a wedgie. Buford apologies, saying he did not realize how uncomfortable wedgies are. Buford is from a broken home and gets nicer as the series progresses. Buford also appears to bully out of habit rather than meanness. Similar in looks to Buford, Francis is the school bully in *The Fairly OddParents*. Francis gives wedgies to Timmy and his friends. He is stereotypical in that he wears ragged clothes, shoplifts, and does poorly in school. He bullies both boys and girls. In "Kung Timmy," Francis beats up Timmy and Timmy's father. Francis then steals the deed to the family house and kicks them out.

Although in animated form, *The Ren & Stimpy Show*, *South Park*, and *The Simpsons* are intended for a more adult audience. In "A Visit to Anthony," the bully, Victor, beats up Ren and Stimpy. Victor's dad, who is waiting in the car, just watches. When Anthony tries to defend Ren and Stimpy, Victor beats him up, too. Victor's dad compliments Victor on the beatings and gives Victor, who looks like he is in middle school, a cigar. In "No Pants Today," Victor cuts down the tree where Stimpy is hiding. Victor, seeing that Stimpy is naked, offers Stimpy his underwear if Stimpy will let him hit Stimpy in the stomach. Victor proclaims himself a professional bully and shows his badge. He hits Stimpy but instead of giving him his underwear, he and his father take Stimpy on a drive to the country. Victor's father gives Stimpy his ill fitting underwear and throws Stimpy out of the car. As they are driving away laughing, their car goes off a cliff.

Cartman, from the animated series *South Park*, has bullying qualities; however, he does not make the list of bullies often produced by media critics. Cartman perhaps does not have the physical ability nor the social standing to create a power difference as called for in the definition of a bully. Cartman is racist, sexist, homophobic, and anti-Semitic. In "The Death of Eric Cartman," Cartman has Butters make a list of all the bad things Cartman has done. The list includes Cartman pretending to be retarded and joining the Special Olympics, trying to exterminate all the Jews, taking a crap in the principal's purse, and talking a woman into an abortion. Cartman reminisces about things he does to Butters when Butters spent the night at his house in "Cartman Sucks." Cartman made Butters a mustache out of cat poo, put a tampon in Butters' mouth, and put his bare behind in Butters' face. The next day, Cartman brings a picture of Butters' wiener in his mouth.

He chuckles that the picture makes Butters gay until the boys tell Cartman that it means Cartman is gay. The boys convince Cartman the only way to reverse it is if Butters puts Cartman's wiener in his mouth. Cartman blindfolds Butters and pulls down his pants. Butters' father walks in on them just before Cartman can put his wiener in Butters's mouth. Cartman appears to be excused because of his ineptness and that he is as likely to be the victim of bullying as the perpetrator.

Scott Tenorman is described as the school bully in the *South Park* school system. In "Scott Tenorman Must Die," Scott tricks Cartman in to buying his pubic hair. Scott makes Cartman beg for his money back by oinking like a pig. Scott humiliates Cartman by showing the video of Cartman oinking. Cartman devises a plan to have Scott's parents killed. Cartman tells a farmer that pony killers are coming so the farmer shoots and kills Tenorman's parents when they get to the farm. Cartman then grounds up the bodies and puts them in chili. He tricks Scott into eating his own parents. In episode "201," Scott returns after spending some time in a mental institution. He reveals to Cartman that they are half-brothers and that Cartman had his own father killed. Cartman cries, not over the death of his real father, but because he discovers he is "half ginger."

The Simpsons is famous for its cast of bullies, the most notable of whom is Nelson Muntz. In "Bart the General," one of Nelson's first appearances, a group of Nelson's bullying victims plots get revenge on Nelson. They bomb Nelson and his gang with water balloons. They take Nelson prisoner after his cronies flee. They force Nelson to sign a peace treaty. Nelson is allowed to remain a figurehead of a menace of the neighborhood. This early episode establishes Nelson's role on the show. Almost as bad as his physical bullying is Nelson's ridicule of others. He makes his victims hit themselves, adding insult to injury. Nelson prances around saying Bart is going to marry Milhouse, a precursor to homophobic bullying.

In "Sleeping with the Enemy," information about Nelson's background establishes some sympathy with the audience. Marge feeds Nelson a sandwich after she finds him eating tadpoles from the public fountain because he has nothing else to eat. Nelson confesses to Marge that his mother works at Hooters and his father never came back after going out for cigarettes. When Nelson gets home that night, his mother is entertaining the local bar owner, Moe. She says she thought Nelson was sleeping in the park that night. Marge takes Nelson in after Nelson's mother leaves him in the middle of the night to go to Hollywood. Nelson punches Bart the next morning when Bart takes his good life for granted and does not clean his plate at breakfast. Bart catches Nelson crying and singing for his father to come find him. When Nelson comes back from school the next day, he finds his father there. His father explains he was gone because of a long story about a peanut allergy and a circus. Nelson's mother comes back as well. The family structure does not last and Nelson resumes bullying.

Nelson's character is very insightful into how bullies are portrayed. His appearance and sad upbringing make for a stereotypical but likeable bully. With Bart being neither the hero nor the anti-hero, Nelson balances out Bart's bad side. It appears Nelson's role as a bully is inevitable. Bart asks Nelson if he wishes he is not a bully. Nelson answers that it is not up to him. When Nelson's parents come back, Bart asks if, since Nelson is happy, he will stop bullying. Nelson says he wishes it was that simple. Nelson appears to have a few redeeming qualities and moments of niceness. Nelson is an ongoing project for Lisa. The audience gets a glimpse of the good in Nelson through Lisa's eyes. In "Lisa's Date with Density," Nelson stands up to the other bullies for Lisa. In "The Haw-Hawed Couple," Nelson tells Bart that Bart is his new best friend since Bart is the only one to show up at Nelson's birthday party. Bart is unsure of Nelson's sincerity until Nelson defends Bart against the other bullies, Dolf, Jimbo, and Kearney. Bart gets special treatment from his classmates as he walks down the halls with Nelson. Nelson, however, begins to get possessive of Bart and jealous of Bart's friendship with Milhouse. Nelson comes to apologize for threatening to hit Bart and offers to take him back as "best friends forever." When Bart calls him a "whack job," Nelson tells Bart that he is a "bad friend" and warns Bart to get his "affairs in order." When Nelson saves Bart's life on a school field trip, Nelson says they are "field trip buddies" and nothing more.

While Nelson is the primary bully character on *The Simpsons*, Jimbo, Dolf, and Kearney make up a gang of bullies that terrorize Springfield. Jimbo is the leader of the bully gang. While they most often serve minor roles in episodes, Jimbo is featured in "New Kid on the Block" and "Beware My Cheating Bart." In "New Kid on the Block," the new girl, Laura, starts dating Jimbo because he is a rebel. Bart, who also has feelings for Laura, makes a prank call to Moe's and gives Moe Jimbo's name and address. An angry Moe goes to Jimbo's house, threatens him with a knife, and makes Jimbo cry. Seeing Jimbo's sensitive side, Laura rejects Jimbo and shows him the door. In "Beware My Cheating Bart," Jimbo makes Bart look after his girlfriend, Shauna, who develops feelings for Bart. When Jimbo finds out, he goes after Bart. Lisa helps Shauna realize both Bart and Jimbo are bad for her. Shauna decides to find a "dysfunctional older man" to help her figure out her life. As soon as Shauna leaves, Jimbo cannot remember why he was going to beat up Bart. Dolph and Kearney are generally written into the storyline to persecute Bart as part of a bullying gang rather than individuals.

TELEVISION GIRL BULLIES

Girl bullies are rather unusual in mass media representations. Producers are more likely to write girls as mean, perpetuating stereotypes of females. Murderess females are depicted in movies such as *The In Crowd*, *The Craft*, and *Confessions of Sorority Girls*; however, the girls are deemed insane rather than bullies. In the world of television, girl bullies are more likely to appear in comedies than in dramas, specifically young girls who are physically bigger and more mature than their male peers. Examples of reoccurring girl bullies on children's programming are nine-year-old Helga from *Hey Arnold* and three-year-old Angelica from *Rugrats*. Helga is one of the girls who is mean to Arnold because she secretly likes him. Helga has named her fists "O'Betsy" and the "Five Avengers." Angelica appears to be mean to the younger babies because she can. Whereas Angelica is overly spoiled by her parents, Helga's parents are neglectful. Most of the older mean girls in television and movies are spoiled with unlimited credit cards and raised by nannies.

There are examples of girl bullies in televisions shows such as *Ned's Declassified* and *iCarly*, shows targeted to tweens and girls in their early teens. Moze from *Ned's Declassified* is a "clueless" bully. She describes herself as "aggressive" rather than a bully. Flashbacks show her shoving another student in gym class, pushing another student's face into his lunch, and putting Ned into a headlock. She takes the criticism from her friends who tell her she is a bully at heart and helps organize a peer conflict resolution organization at school. Sam from *iCarly*, on the other hand, is a bully and relishes the fact. There is a vast contrast between Sam and her best friend Carly, who sweet and kind. Sam is loud and mean and especially cruel to Carly's friend Freddie. Sam is also mean and disrespectful to adults such as Carly's older brother and the principal at her school. It is difficult to see why someone as nice as Carly would have such a mean friend. In the episode "iSam's Mom," it is clear why Sam is the way she is considering her mother is portrayed as equally mean and obnoxious as Sam. For example, they stick their tongues out at each other. Carly tricks them into going to therapy. They are so bad, they make the therapist cry. Not only do they say hateful things to each other, Sam and her mother physically fight. Sam and her mother are shown pulling each other's hair and fighting on the floor. A frustrated therapist puts them in the therapy box and locks them in together until they resolve their differences. Carly tells them they are both "horrible." Carly forces Sam and her mother to admit they are both a mess but that they love each other. The mother states, "I guess I could have had a worse kid." They hug.

TELEVISION VICTIMS

Most bullying appears to be a one-time/one-episode occurrence on television, especially on situation comedies. This isolated portrayal of victimization fits Pepler and Craig's (2009) findings that bullying problems for 70–80 percent of kids is temporary. The following sitcom characters are not only bullied over more than one episode, there is often more than one bully victimizing them. In some cases, audiences might even enjoy the bullying because it appears the character partly deserved the bullying for standing out or being annoying. For example, Urkel (*Family Matters*) is the quintessential target. He has a high-pitched, nasally voice. He buttons his shirt up all the way and wears suspenders, a pocket protector, and large glasses that fall down his nose. Audience members are likely to be more understanding of bullies' attraction to Urkel. Viewers may even enjoy seeing Urkel get bullied because they feel he deserves it for standing out from the norm.

Sue, from the sitcom *The Middle*, is a perpetual victim of bullies and mean girls. Sue is a very likeable character who is also clueless about how mean others are around her. Instead of making her a pathetic character, the victimization somehow makes her endearing. The audience perhaps envies her in that she appears unaffected by what others say or do. Oversized glasses and braces are only a small part of her quirkiness. She is bold in her misfit character. Even her parents cringe at times, although they are very supportive in general. Her brother scolds her for her behavior at school but it does not seem to faze her. In one episode "The Test," she mistakenly is told that she made the cheerleading squad. Instead of being humiliated and devastated when she finds out it was a mistake, she negotiates a compromise where she gets to cheer at one game and get her picture with them in the yearbook. When the camera pans to her cheering at her one game, she is flailing about with great pleasure and disregard to what others think. She is clearly aware of the social structure at school and tries to climb the social ladder as any average kid. Sue, however, is seldom discouraged by her failings. She glorifies in the small victories. She is so excited to make the cross-country team that she wears her sweatshirt every day to school, even in extremely warm temperatures. Her dream of participating in the big school assembly as part of an athletic team is compromised when she collapses from the heat in her sweatshirt. The next day, her mother tries to hide the newspaper story about the incident. The headline reads, "Overheated student ruins pep rally." Instead of being humiliated, Sue is thrilled that she got her photo on the school website. The parents in *The Middle* are much more sensitive and patient than other shows (e.g., *Home Improvement*).

A girl in Sue's class, Shannon, invites Sue's best friend, Carly, to a slumber party but not Sue in the episode "Errand Boy." Sue's father, Mike, overhears Shannon discussing the Sue-less slumber party. He asks his wife what she is going to do about the slight. Sue's mother says there is nothing she can do. She calls it "junior high school drama." The dad is confused. He refuses to accept "that's just the way things are." Mike decides to make a special movie night for Sue the night of the slumber party. When Shannon calls, Mike is relieved thinking she is inviting Sue after all. Instead, Shannon just wants to borrow Sue's sleeping bag. Mike takes the bag over to Shannon's house himself. He confronts Shannon's father about Shannon excluding Sue. Shannon's father tells Mike that he allows Shannon to do what she wants. Mike lectures him that it is a father's job to make daughters do what they do not want to do. In "The Prom," Sue and her best friend often walk around eating their lunch so they will not have to suffer rejection of sitting at the wrong table. They commit to trying to break into the "B" table in the middle school cafeteria. When they finally think they made it to the "B" table, the kids at the "B" table leave, taking their chance at getting to the "A" table.

Meg Griffin is the target of the popular kids at school, especially Connie DiMarco, in the animated sitcom *The Family Guy*. Unlike Sue from *The Middle*, Meg is very aware of others being mean to her. For example, Connie tells Meg she has a "ginormous ass." When Meg tries on a new pair of jeans at the mall in "Don't Make Me Over," the sales clerk sets herself on fire. In "Stew-roids," Meg shows Connie the scars from cutting herself when Connie has been mean to her. Meg is so obsessed with being popular and desperate to rise in social status that she keeps coming back for more punishment. In "Let's Go to the Hop," the principal scolds the cool kids for getting Meg's hopes up by letting her hang out with them. Meg's family can at times be very supportive and particularly vicious in their revenge. Meg is sent into the "makeout" closet with a boy at Connie's sixteenth birthday party. When Connie opens the door, Meg is kissing a pig that the boy is holding. Meg's mother tells her not to worry. She sends a pedophile over to Connie's house. When Connie asks Meg if she can put her extra books on Meg's ginormous ass, Peter, Meg's father, bashes Connie's head into the fire extinguisher glass. Brian, the Griffins' talking dog, agrees to take Meg to the dance when she cannot find a date. Connie tells Meg that there are no dogs allowed so Meg will have to leave. Brian calls Connie a "bitch." He tells everyone that Connie developed early so she used to be popular but now she is a whore and cannot stand herself so she picks on Meg. Connie runs off crying.

Lisa Simpson at times has fallen victim to bullies and mean girls. Lisa is "book smart" and plays the saxophone. In "Bye Bye Nerdie," when Lisa is nice to Francine, a new girl in school, she is rewarded with a black eye. Lisa does some detective work and determines the bully is only bullying the smart kids. Francine leaves Lisa alone after Lisa disguises her smart smell with salad dressing. When Lisa fails an exam in "Stealing First Base," all the kids want to be her friends. When it turns out to be a mistake, they taunt her with chants of "gifted, gifted, gifted." Even the teacher is incredibly sarcastic to Lisa. When Lisa posts her sadness on her blog, First Lady Michelle Obama posts a positive and supportive comment. Mrs. Obama tells the students at Lisa's school that when she was young, she was a high achiever, got all A's, and was a nerd. She warns them that the nerds may be running the world soon. In "Sleeping with the Enemy," Lisa is teased by mean girls in her class for having a "big butt." She starts to excessively exercise and refuses to eat. Nelson, who is usually a bully, helps Lisa by giving the mean girls a box with a skunk in it. They then laugh at the girls for stinking.

Butters is a character in *South Park* who is desperate to fit in and make friends. He is another character who is fairly clueless to the poor treatment from others, especially his clueless parents and Cartman (see the description of Cartman in the Television Boy Bullies section of this chapter). Cartman does some nasty verbal, physical, and sexual things to Butters over several episodes. Butters is desperate to have friends, he puts up with the abuse. The other boys do little to help him, appearing to accept this treatment as inevitable. The gang realizes Butters is getting bullied in "Butterballs." Since Butters does not want to be considered a snitch, the boys convince him to confide in his family. However, it is Butters' own grandmother who is bullying him. The grandmother comes to school, traps Butters in the boys' room, and tries to make him put the urinal mint in his mouth. She threatens Butters if he tells anyone. Grandma stabs Butters in the leg with a fork under the table and does disgusting things to his food at home. Butters gets back at his grandmother by reminding her that she will die soon.

Conclusion

Because adolescents spend an inordinate amount of time with media each day, it seems imperative that parents and educators know what their children are watching and possibly learning from the portrayals of bullying. Historically little has changed in bullying portrayals in either television or film. Stereotypical bullies are still physically larger than their victims, wear leather jackets, and have spiky hair. Many bullies still steal lunch money and shove geeky kids in lockers. Black eyes are still the injury of choice.

Reoccurring bullies found primarily in situation comedies often have a lovable quality about them. Generally overtime the bullies become friends with their past victims. Over the course of one or more seasons, writers give insights into why bullies bully and therefore perhaps make the bullies more sympathetic characters. The following chapter goes more in depth into how bullies are represented in different genres and mediums.

2

Mean Girls and the Media

According to O'Donnell (2011), the term "mean girls" has become synonymous with relational aggression. Gentile, Coyne, andd Walsh (2011) defined relational aggression as spreading rumors, talking behind someone's back, and ignoring and excluding others. Coyne et al. (2008) argued that relational aggression often escapes scrutiny because it is subtler than physical and verbal aggression. According to Bjorkqvist, Lagerspetz, and Kaukianen (1992), researchers often overlook indirect aggression in favor of physical aggression, which is more easily identifiable. Bjorkqvist and his colleagues (1992) reasoned that girls use indirect strategies, such as gossip and exclusion, to make it appear as though they do not intend to harm others. Simmons (2011) identified indirect aggression as a way for the perpetrator to avoid confronting the target directly. Simmons also argued that girls often express their aggression indirectly or covertly because female aggression is often labeled as deviant behavior. Because of social expectations that girls be "nice" and not be physical or raise their voices, girls may use strategies that are more subtle and less visible to adults and their peers.

In Bjorkqvist and his colleagues' (1992) seminal study of indirect aggression, the researchers found that aggression begins to appear once children have the verbal and social skills necessary to manipulate other children. Because girls develop verbal skills earlier than boys, they may be more likely to understand the impact of words and have them available as a weapon ("Relational Aggression," 2011). Harrison reported frequently seeing girls as young as eight excluding and victimizing their peers (cited in Hill & Helmore, 2002). He speculated that relational aggression develops further when children are forced to switch from a smaller primary school to a large, impersonal middle school. Bjorkqvist et al. (1992) found that boys and girls have similar levels of indirect aggression before age 11 and similar levels of direct verbal aggression after age 15. They reasoned that girls use more indirect methods between ages 11 and 15 because developmentally they are forming tight social groups. After age 15, Bjorkqvist reasoned that girls may be turning their attention beyond friendships to dating.

Like bullying, relational aggression has been linked to media exposure. Gentile et al. (2011) found that children who watched more media violence reported increased relational aggressive behaviors and decreased prosocial behaviors in addition to physical aggression. Coyne, Nelson, Lawton, et al. (2008) found that females who viewed physically violent media were more likely to show relational aggression toward a confederate. They also found female participants who viewed media that portrayed relational aggression were also more relationally aggressive. They described the results as a "crossover" effect between physical violence and relational aggression. Further research by Coyne, Linder, Nelson, and Gentile (2012) found that females who viewed media containing physical aggression showed evidence of activation of both physical and relational aggression cognitions while women who viewed relational aggression content also showed activation of relational aggression cognitions.

Theories such as social learning theory (see Bandura, 1986) may explain how representations in the media can be instructive to viewers about relational aggression, social hierarchies, and the treatment (or mistreatment) of peers. Even though the intent of the producers of mean-girl media portrayals may be to expose the mean-girl phenomenon, the glamorous portrayals of the mean-girls could actually increase its attractiveness when mean girl behavior is rewarded. Dellasega and Nixon (2003) added that these stereotypes work to normalize the behavior. Nixon (cited in Watson, 2011) argued bad behavior can be linked to media images that frame cruel behavior as humorous such as in the movie *Mean Girls*. The humorous context may lead viewers to take the phenomenon less seriously. Swearer (2008) also credited stereotypical media depictions for the oversimplification of relational aggression. In an experiment by Behm-Morawitz and Mastro (2008), results showed that exposure to mean-girl teen movies is associated with "negative stereotypic beliefs about female friendships as well as unfavorable attitudes about women in general" (p. 141) particularly for male viewers.

This chapter explores how media representation and resolutions of relational aggression link to mean-girl perpetrators, bystanders, and victims. Harrison (cited in Hill & Helmore, 2002) argued that while bullying tactics have not changed much over time, girls have become more cruel and manipulative, using extraordinary sophisticated tactics.

Television Mean Girl Portrayals

Bully portrayals appear to be rather straightforward in comparison to mean girls. Physical bullying and threats are usually direct. Representations of bullies are often formulaic so that audience can quickly identify the bully. Instances of relational aggression or mean-girl representations are often more complex. Part of the effectiveness of being mean is the ambiguity both for the victims and the adults who are supervising them. Four types of mean girls emerged from my analysis: standard, snobby, sexpot, and stealth. Although I later discuss mean girls in film, my primary focus is on television characters because of their ongoing presence week after week.

"STANDARD" MEAN GIRLS

Using the movie *Mean Girls* as the benchmark, there is a very stereotypical mean girl represented particularly in the movies. In his review of the movie *Sleepover*, film critic Roger Ebert (2004) stated, "I take it as a rule of nature that all American high schools are ruled by a pack of snobs, led by a supremely confident young woman who is blond, superficial, catty, and ripe for public humiliation. This character is followed by two friends who worship her, and are a little bit shorter." A simple disapproving facial expression such as an eyebrow furrow, sneer of the upper lip, or eye roll establishes the standard mean girl's distain of her less popular peers. She is not only mean to strangers but also to close friends.

She manipulates the girls around her, often pitting one against the others partly for sport and partly to maintain control over her clique. Much of the reason why the other girls put up with the mean girl is because they do not want to become the target. In most films and television shows, the mean girl gets her comeuppance in the end. Often the protagonist uses the same methods to take down the mean girls as the mean girls used to control others. The mean girls are very attractive, generally rich, and dressed in designer fashions. Class is often a factor in the social hierarchy. At times one of the girls comes from a less wealthy family and hides the fact from the other mean girls because of shame and fear she will be rejected.

Brooke Davis is the queen bee of the high school, cheerleading captain, and later president of the student body on the series *One Tree Hill*. With wealthy but absent parents, Brooke appears to be able to do what she wants. She is best friends with Payton; however, there is an unspoken rivalry as they are both in love with the same boy, Lucas. Brooke is a snob who puts down others she deems are beneath her. In the first few episodes, she is condescending to Haley, nicknaming her "Tutor Girl." She tries to break up Haley and Nathan, but later tries to make up for it. She is especially mean to Mouth, a geeky boy who is desperate to get her attention. Brooke often uses his infatuation for her to boss him around. She is a rather sad character at times, with an evil mother and unlucky in love. Brooke's character develops and she becomes friends with Haley and Mouth.

Gilmore Girls' mean girl Paris Geller is Rory's major nemesis at Chilton. Having stolen Rory's file on Rory's first day of school, Paris sees that Rory is a threat to her dominance as the school's highest achiever. Paris heckles Rory and puts her down for her modest home life. Paris' parents are incredibly wealthy and powerful, although Rory's grandparents are also high on the social ladder. Paris's parents are absent but, at the same time, very demanding of Paris in terms of academic achievement. At one point, Paris laments to Rory about growing up with nannies as her only social support. Paris bullies her two friends, Madeline and Louise, who are more attractive than Paris and get more boys' attention. They are less intelligent although they do not seem too concerned about grades. They follow Paris more out of fear or perhaps laziness rather than a desire to be her friend or be like her, which is more common with mean-girl plotlines. In order to win a speaking competition, Paris picks on her competitors' shortcomings such as braces and clumsiness. She calls them "losers" and "stupid" in an effort to destroy their self-esteem.

Blair Waldorf, the consummate mean girl from *Gossip Girl*, rules Constance Billard, a posh private school on the Upper East Side of Manhattan. Blair's mother is a high fashion designer and takes every opportunity to critique Blair. In the Gossip Girl book series by Cecily von Ziegesar, Blair is bulimic. The television pilot only hints at an eating disorder. Blair has an intense rivalry with her best friend, Serena, although Serena does not actively participate. Success and attention come easily to Serena, while Blair desperately acts out for acceptance. Blair rules her minions by following a rigid social structure. They even have designated steps to sit on, with Blair on top of course. Jenny is a new freshman at Constance Billard. She attempts to join Blair's minions and climb the social ladder despite her lack of socioeconomic status. She is desperate to overcome the shame that comes from living in Brooklyn. Jenny can be equally as cruel as Blair. She spread the gossip that Blair lost her virginity to Chuck, rather than her boyfriend, Nate. With the news of her betrayal to Nate, Blair temporarily loses her Queen Bee status to Jenny.

While the two lead characters, Brooke and Sam, in the series *Popular* are mean girls in their own way, Brooke's friend Nicole Julian is the most stereotypical mean girl. Nicole picks on Carmen, a slightly heavier girl and friend of Sam's, and rejects her from the cheerleading squad because Nicole considers her "fat." She nominates Carmen for homecoming queen as a joke. When Brooke chooses Sam's friendship over Nicole's, Nicole runs down Brooke with her car. Throughout the series, Nicole struggles to be second to Brooke, who is not even sure she wants the popularity, driving Nicole even crazier.

Naomi Clark, from *90210*, is a typical wealthy mean girl. Her parents go to the school board to get Naomi an extension on a paper because she needs time to plan her 16th birthday party. Naomi lies about a teacher sexually harassing her. When Naomi thinks Annie is sleeping with her boyfriend, Naomi circulates a topless picture of Annie via text message. On the other hand, Naomi can be a sympathetic character at times because most of her schemes to get guys backfire. She seems to be the one who is always cheated on by her boyfriends rather than the usual mean girl sleeping with other girls' boyfriends. Her sister betrays her by sleeping with one of her boyfriends and tricks her out her trust fund money. By the third season of the series, Naomi has shed her mean girl image.

In the first episode of *Wizards of Waverly Place*, Alex describes Gigi as her enemy since kindergarten. Gigi spilled juice on Alex's mat during naptime and told everyone Alex had an accident. Gigi is almost always accompanied by her two underlings, whom Alex and Harper call the "Wannabes." The girls even got nose jobs to look more like Gigi. Gigi again spills a drink in front of Alex and tells everyone Alex had an accident. The girls in the hall all laugh. When Gigi gets a drink spilled on her, her friends run away thinking she had an accident. Gigi is at her most cruel when she invites Harper to a fancy tea in order to win the "who can bring the biggest loser" competition in "Alex's Choice." Gigi gets her comeuppance when Alex casts a truth spell. Gigi reveals her mean-girl thoughts. One of her underlings shoves Gigi's face into a cake while the other one pours punch on her head.

In the sitcom *Suburgatory*, the rich mean girl, Dalia Royce, is assigned to be Tessa's "buddy" at school. Dalia explains to Tessa that she is only doing it for extra credit. She asks Tessa if she is a lesbian in a very judgmental tone. As Tessa is hanging out in the bathroom having lunch in one of the stalls, she overhears the mean girls, lead by Dalia, picking on another girl, Lisa. They ask if Lisa's brother is jealous because Lisa can grow a mustache and he cannot. Tessa comes out of the stall see if Lisa needs help only to have Lisa call Tessa a "lesbian." Lisa later apologizes to Tessa, explaining that she did it because she did not want to get made fun of anymore. She and Tessa become friends.

In the MTV series *Awkward*, Jenna's nemesis is a girl named Sadie Saxton who is slightly overweight. Sadie's mother is quite critical of her daughter's appearance. Sadie's mother warns her that she will be unloved unless she loses weight. Unlike other mean girls, Sadie has few sympathetic qualities other than her mother's judgments. Jenna's friend accuses Sadie of buying her way onto the cheerleader squad because Sadie "can't even jump two feet off the ground." Sadie acts like a mean girl when she excludes Jenna and says terrible things about her such as, "She should go to Thailand. Only a pedophile would screw her...maybe." In "Knocker Nightmare," she tells Jenna, "Maybe people would stop staring at you if you could just finish the abortion your mom botched." Sadie takes a picture of Jenna when she is changing and circulates it around school. Sadie is also disrespectful to the adults in her life, especially the school principal and guidance counselor. Sadie, feeling invincible, admits to sending out the picture of a topless Jenna. She states that the administration cannot do much to punish her, likely because they fear her.

In real life, mean-girl behavior tends to peak in adolescence and dissipate somewhat in late adolescence (17 to 19 years old) as girls become more independent (Dellasega & Nixon, 2003). In media portrayal of mean girls, however, the peak appears to extend into later adolescence and even adulthood when the actresses playing the roles of teenagers are actually in their twenties. Viewers are seeing adult women playing high school sopho- mores (e.g., Leighton Meester from *Gossip Girl* was 21 and Dianna Agron from *Glee* was 23). The older actresses are more physically developed, which creates a false social com- parison for the teen viewer.

"Snobby" Mean Girls

The snobby girl is generally rich and spoiled. She tries to control all of those around her. The character is not portrayed as someone to be feared but rather someone who is an obstacle in the way of the "good" characters' happiness. She has no true friends, just lack- eys. She is very upfront about her power grab. She cares more about getting what she wants than making friends or getting people to like her. She is very Machiavellian. Her parents are often absent in her life so she seeks attention from others. She also bosses around adults, particularly adult males who serve a subordinate position. She also often bosses around teachers and principals.

Nellie Oleson's family owns the general store in a small rural farming community in the drama series *Little House on the Prairie.* Mirroring her snobbish mother, Nellie looks down on the other girls in town, especially the Ingalls girls. She controls the playground and dictates who gets to play and who has to stand and watch. She often uses her parents' store and her access to unlimited candy as a bribe to get other children to play with her. She makes fun of other children with disabilities like limps and stutters. Nellie is also dis- respectful to her teachers. She holds her mother's position on the school board as a threat.

Sharpay Evans, the mean girl in the *High School Musical* series, is thin, attractive, and comes from a wealthy family. Sharpay connives and lies to try to break up the dream cou- ple Troy and Gabriella so she can have Troy to herself. She uses her family's wealth and social connections to bribe Troy with a college scholarship to get his attention. In *HSM 2*, she badgers and bosses around a grown man, the manager of the country club that her parents own. She is bossy and condescending to the waitstaff. She is also bossy with her mother. Her mother is rather airheadish and ignores her for the most part. Sharpay plays "daddy's girl" with her father. In *HSM 3*, Sharpay is matched against an even more con- niving girl who wants to take her place as leader of the drama club. The turn of events elicits some sympathy for Sharpay since she is betrayed by the canniving girl. One redeem- ing quality Sharpay has is her affection for her brother, although even that is rarely seen. Although she often bosses her brother around and uses him in her schemes, at the end of *HSM 2*, she gives him her talent show prize. Unlike standard mean girls, Sharpay does not have a flock of girls following her at all times like other queen bees. Often her only ally is her brother. In *HSM 2*, she is shown to have a group of three adoring girls. They do not appear in *HSM 3*.

Despite her wealth, London Tipton from *Suite Life of Zach and Cody* had a tough childhood because her father was busy with business and marrying many women. Lon- don fills the emptiness with shopping. She oscillates between shrieking and pouting. In "Poor Little Rich Girl," London makes sure the cleaning lady has the correct thread count in her sheets. Then she reprimands the bellboy for bringing her the wrong kind of marsh- mallows in her hot chocolate. When her father loses all his money, London's rich friends make up excuses why she cannot stay with them. They are getting back at London for all the times she was not nice to them. At first, London is not very appreciative of Maddie when Maddie lets her stay in her room. She criticizes Maddie for the small room and shabby décor. During a heart to heart, she discloses to Maddie that she spent most of her time growing up having dinner with her nanny and flying back and forth between her divorced parents. At the end of the episode, London gets her money back but stays nice to Maddie. In "The Suite Life on Deck," her father sends London to Seven Seas High School because his new wife wanted London out of the way. She has a new best friend, Bailey, whom she insults; however, Bailey does not seem to mind.

Holly J. Sinclair begins at *Degrassi* under the shadow of her older sister, Heather. Heather, although never shown on camera, is considered the mean girl of Degrassi High School. Their family is well off; however, they lose their money, forcing Holly J. to have to wait tables. Holly J. has a list of enemies whom she carefully schemes to take down. While many mean girls use sex to gain power, Holly J. is a prude. She is very harsh in her criticism of Mia, who is a teenage mother. She is often mean to her best friend, Anya. At one point Anya asks Holly J. why she is mean to her. Holly J. replies, "Because you let me." Holly J. does not like to see weakness in anyone. Most of Holly J.'s meanness comes from putdowns and gossip.

Summer Roberts comes from a wealthy family and looks down on others in lower income brackets in the series *The O.C.* She makes snide little comments; however, she does not sleep with other girls' boyfriends, blackmail, or spread vicious gossip. It appears her only female friend is Marissa; therefore, she has no queen bee status. Summer's character elicits some sympathy when it is revealed that her mother abandoned her when her parents got divorced.

"Sexpot" Mean Girls

Borrowing from the tradition of the daytime soap opera, the sexpot uses her sex appeal to manipulate and blackmail. She not only steals boyfriends, she takes great delight in hurting their girlfriends. She is likely to have few if any female friends and therefore differs from the standard mean girl who is battling for social status. This type of mean girl may or may not exist in the real world, but she makes for good scandals particularly on serial television shows. This mean girl tends to be older, or at least is played by an older actress. When a new mean girl is introduced to the cast, she is likely to be the "boyfriend-stealing" type of mean girl (e.g., Rachel from *One Tree Hill*, Georgiana from *Gossip Girl*). If the social structure is already established, there is little room for a mean girl to step in and take over as the "traditional" mean girl.

Valerie Malone was added to the cast of *Beverly Hills 90210* in the fifth season to breathe new life into the stale storyline. Valerie is a mean girl in the sense of lying and stealing boyfriends. She lacked the money or power over others to be that kind of mean girl. She also did not have social status with a group or lackeys to play queen bee. She went after Brenda's ex-boyfriend, getting him to sleep with her without him knowing who she was in a game to one-up Brenda. She continued to sneak around with Dylan even after she started dating Steve, who genuinely cared about her. Later, she seduced Donna's boyfriend, Ray. She gets involved with a married man and blackmails him with a fake pregnancy. The writers tried to make her sympathetic in that her father had sexually abused her when she was a child. To stop the abuse, Valerie kills her father and is sent to Beverly Hills. Later, Valerie was also drugged and date raped, although other characters had a hard time believing her after all her lies in the past.

Rachel Gattina becomes a regular in season four of *One Tree Hill* after a recurring role during season three. She and Brooke immediately become intense rivals, battling over cheerleading captain and boys. Rachel is the type of character to pop up naked in the back of boys' cars. Over time, Rachel and Brooke become friends. Rachel, however, becomes addicted to drugs and steals Brooke's money. Years later, Rachel returns to seduce and marry Dan Scott, the show's antagonist. Dan eventually divorces her, but not before he gives all his money to charity, leaving her broke.

Adrian Lee is an example of the promiscuous mean girl on *The Secret Life of American Teenager*. In the beginning of the series, her character is established as the mean girl who cares little about other girls' feelings and has no qualms about sleeping with their boyfriends. She eventually becomes friends with Grace even though she seduced Grace's boyfriend, Jack. Adrian's home life explains why she acts the way she does. Her mother works as a flight attendant and is rarely home. She only meets her father when she is a teenager. It is evident that rather than sleeping with boys to spite their girlfriends, Adrian is looking for love she is missing from her parents.

"STEALTH" MEAN GIRLS

The often overlooked mean girl is the cute girl who is usually the main character of the Disney Channel/Nickelodeon type sitcoms. Simmons (2011) noted that children's programs feature a new group of "snarky, sarcastic girl characters" (p. xvii). To the untrained eye, the stealth mean girl appears to be very generous in that she likely befriends a less attractive, less popular friend. On closer inspection, it is clear that she targets her jokes toward others, including her less popular friends. There is a standard in these shows where making fun of adults (parents, teachers, principals) both in front of their faces and behind their backs is funny—the laugh track tells the audience so. The stealth mean girl is generally a likeable character. She is not the prettiest, but is pretty. She may not be at the top of the social ladder but she has significant control over her companions. She protects her less popular friends from outsiders' teasing, a role she saves for herself.

In shows such as *The Wizards Place*, *A.N.T. Farm*, *Saved by the Bell*, and *Full House*, the sidekick endure the stealth mean girl's bad behavior toward them. Harper, Olive, Screech, and Kimmie are rather oblivious to their poor treatment by their supposed friends because of a lack of street smarts. They are easy targets for ridicule. It is also easier for the audience to laugh at them since it appears their feelings are not hurt or they appear to deserve their friends' putdowns. In *iCarly* and *Hannah Montana*, on the other hand, the characters are more equal and therefore there is less mean treatment.

The first episodes *The Wizards of Waverly Place* introduces Alex's feud with Gigi and establishes Alex's superiority to and dominance over her best friend, Harper. In one episode, Harper is wearing one of her standard quirky outfits, a sunflower shirt with rainbow socks. In a disparaging tone, Alex says, "You're not wearing that, are you?" Harper is oblivious to this slight. When Harper thinks she got invited to a slumber party because of her snickerdoodles, Alex tells Harper that no one can finish her snickerdoodles. Instead of a gesture trying to protect Harper, it appears as one of many examples of Alex putting down her friend for a laugh.

Occasionally a show will address this stealth meanness of the main character. In an isolated episode, the friend might finally stands up for herself. In the 23 minutes it takes to air an episode of a sitcom, the problem is resolved as the main character feigns a simple misunderstanding or inadvertent oversight. The episodes end with a hug, indicating that all is well...until the next episode when it starts all over again. The best example of a stealth girl getting outed is in *The Wizards of Waverly Place's* "Third Wheel." Harper finally stands up to Alex. Harper is jealous that Alex has starts spending time with another girl wizard. When Harper finally tells Alex how she feels, Alex is the one who gets upset. Alex becomes very defensive, declaring she is allowed to hang out with other friends besides Harper. Harper, who fears conflict, tells Alex that Alex will continue to do what she wants to do and Harper will continue to forgive her. Alex asks Harper if that is the way she thinks their relationship works. Alex gets upset and tells Harper that Harper is the one not acting like a very good friend. Harper replies, "You can call me a lot things, and you have, but a 'bad friend' is not okay." In a sarcastic tone, Alex tells Harper she forgives her. When Harper asks Alex for what, she says she does not know in a snarky tone, she is just being a "good friend." The principal catches them destroying the school float Harper had been working on while Alex was off with her other friend. When he threatens to expel Alex, Harper takes the blame. Alex in turn claims she did it. The principal believes Harper because, as he says, Alex is a "liar." During Harper's detention, Alex sneaks in the window. She tells Harper that she feels bad. Alex tells Harper that she is not her "friend," she is her "sister." They hug and declare their love for each other. The scenario follows material straight out of the book *Odd Girl Out* (Simmons, 2011). The resolution is to bury the feelings and go back to being best friends without resolving the anger felt by Harper.

The Disney Channel show *A.N.T. Farm*, which stands for Advanced Natural Talents, is the perfect setting for bullying or meanness. Not only are the kids middle-school age students in a high school, but they are gifted. Chyna is a cute, sarcastic 11-year-old girl. Chyna is hooked on a show called *High Heels High*. It stars a classic mean girl who is surrounded by four lackies. Chyna says, "Wow, Justine is a horrible person. I love her!" Her friends in the A.N.T. program, Olive and Fletcher, however, are stereotypically nerdy and awkward. Chyna is a tough girl with a sassy mouth even with adults; therefore, she is not a very sympathetic character. Olive and Fletcher, who are often Chyna's targets of teasing, are also annoying. The audience may in fact feel apathetic toward them as victims. In the second episode, entitled "ParticipANTs," Fletcher wears a suit of armor to the school activity fair, which he thinks will protect him against the mean kids. When Chyna makes the cheerleading squad, she immediately dumps Olive as a friend.

The cast members of *Saved by the Bell* are collectively, minus Screech, a stealth mean girl. Screech is nerdy, with a high-pitched, lispy voice. Screech has the privilege of hanging out with the popular kids. It is difficult to see why Screech would be included in their clique other than so the gang could have someone to make fun of and manipulate into doing what they want. In one scene, Screech picks up a puzzle and says "Does this really have a million pieces?" He then accidentally spills the puzzle on the floor. Lisa replies, "No, but I think your head is short a few pieces." Producers hit the laugh track button as Screech seems oblivious to the insult. In the opening of "Zach's War," Screech tells Zach he is going to get a girl that he likes. Zach asks Screech how he is going to get her, "shoot her with a stun gun?" Screech is oblivious to Zach's comment. When the girl's boyfriend approaches him, Screech locks himself in a locker. Zach opens the locker and asks what happened. Screech says, "The usual, the bully gets the girl and I get the locker." Zach says, "Oh," and shuts the locker door on Screech. In one sentence Zach will call Screech a "sucker" and then next his "pal." When Screech accidentally touches Lisa, she tells him to get off or she will have to burn her clothes.

Film Mean Girl Portrayals

In films targeted to tween and teen girls, mean girls are almost exclusively stereotypical, one-dimensional characters. The cookie cutter mean girls in *Mean Girls*, *Mean Girls 2*, *The Clique*, and *Confessions of a Teenage Drama Queen* are nearly indistinguishable from one another. They are the standard spoiled, attractive, and wealthy girls who are obsessed with social status. Most of their meanness is expressed through social exclusion and disparaging comments about others' lack of fashion (clothing, hair, and makeup) and socio-economic status. Mean girls mostly attack when they are threatened by a new pretty girl. One mean girl that stands out is Stacey in the made-for-TV-movie *Odd Girl Out*. Based on the nonfiction book *Odd Girl Out* by Rachel Simmons (2002), Stacey is very stealth in her cruelty toward her "BFF" Vanessa. Stacey allows her cronies to do the dirty work (e.g., spreading rumors, calling names, and creating a "Hating Vanessa" website) so she can smile and claim innocence. The character Nikki is more than happy to attack Vanessa in order to gain a higher status with Stacey. Stacey is also very successful at making Vanessa feel like it is Vanessa's fault the other kids are talking about her. Stacey often criticizes Vanessa for being too sensitive. Stacey, on the outside, is quite likeable. She is not immediately identifiable as the mean girl as in most film versions.

There are slight variations, particularly in films, starring younger actresses and targeted to younger audiences. In light, family films such as *Sleepover*, the mean girls' tactics are quite mild. The goal is to be able to sit at the prestigious table at lunch, while the "losers" have to sit near the dumpsters. The worst thing the mean girl Stacy does is disparage a slightly overweight girl, telling her to sue the diet company for not working. Tara, the 10-year-old mean girl in *American Girl Chrissa*, is quite sophisticated and conniving in her methods to torment Chrissa and a homeless girl, Gwen. Tara turns "good" in the end, but does a brilliant job of manipulating other girls to turn against Chrissa. She plays the teacher's pet and is covert in her attacks. She anonymously posts a disparaging message on the swim team's electronic message board about Chrissa.

Films tend to portray darker characters than television. In the movie *Thirteen*, Evie is also very sly and manipulative. Evie and Tracy's relationship is more like an abusive dating relationship, where Evie tells Tracy she loves her and then takes advantage of and is abusive toward Tracy. There are some variations in comedies as well. In some of the darker comedies, the mean girls feel little if any remorse when they unintentionally kill (e.g., *Heathers*, *Bad Girls from Valley High*, and *Jawbreakers*). They manipulate and blackmail in order to not get caught. Toward the other extreme, movies also portray staunch Christians as the mean girl (e.g., *Saved*, *Easy A*).

Conclusion

Four classifications of mean girls emerged in my analysis. To the standard mean girl discussed by most researchers and critics, I added the snobby, the sexpot, and the stealth. The stealth mean girl could potentially do the most harm because the mean behaviors often go unidentified. Most of the stealth portrayals appear in media targeting adolescent girls. Television mean girls appear to have more dimensions than either mean girls in film or books and significantly more depth than bullies in any medium.

Additional chapters in this book look more closely at the development and representation of the mean girl. One variable to note throughout the book is that venues play a significant role in establishing motivation and opportunity for bullies and mean girls. Sleep-away camp and boarding schools offer round-the-clock access to victims, sporadic adult supervision, and no chance for the victim to escape. Mean-girl portrayals often take place in hierarchical structure like sororities, which are stereotypical models that exploit the competitive, exclusionary nature of the Greek system. The homecoming dance or prom is a prime setting for mean considering voting for queen is truly is a popularity contest. Particularly for females, entry into cheerleading squads is justification for bad behavior. Competitions for something innocuous as a part in a school musical or a singing competition becomes a breeding ground for mean.

3

Film Bullies

Bullying behavior appears to be the domain of boys, particularly the world of film. Movies with bullying themes almost exclusively featured male bullies and victims. The bullying ranged in "age appropriateness" from mild comical bullying, which was not too scary for a younger audience, to extreme bullying and revenge a la the horror genre, which was geared for a more adult audience. Unlike many television representations, these movies generally have similar outcomes, with the bullies getting their comeuppances. What the movies do have in common with television shows of the same genres is that, in most of these cases, adults are absent and the kids are left to fend for themselves.

I classified movies according to genre (e.g., comedy or drama) and the following subgenres, including a breakdown by setting and age of the bully, etc. Comedies featuring younger boys often focused on settings such as camp (e.g., *Meatballs*), sports (e.g., *Bad News Bears*), and crime solving (e.g., *Sky High*). Comedies featuring older boys often included themes such as nerds (e.g., *Back to the Future*), special powers (e.g., *Zapped*), and boy makeovers (e.g., *Can't Buy Me Love*). I also included movies that featured adolescent bullying but involved an adult, for example kid victims helped by adults (e.g., *Billy Madison*), adult bullies with kid victims (e.g., *Mr. Woodcock*), and adult bullies with adult victims who acted like adolescents (e.g., *Joe Somebody*). In the drama genre, films with bullying portrayals broke down into subgenres such as coming-of-age movies (e.g., *Stand by Me*), fight-back movies (e.g., *The Karate Kid*), fantasy (e.g., *Harry Potter*), special powers (e.g., *Carrie*), revenge (e.g., *Heart of America*), and thriller (e.g., *The New Kids*).

Comedies

While the settings of the comedy movies vary, the portrayals of bullies and victims do not differ greatly. Critics warn that comedy may trivialize physical and verbal aggression; however, there is a rather high level of violence. Graphic depictions of violence are not only found in the horror or thriller drama subgenres but in comic portrayals as well.

TWEEN COMEDIES

The Diary of a Wimpy Kid is more about social status and cliques in middle school than bullying. Greg is thankful for a smaller boy who can act as a "buffer" between him and the older boys who are taunting the boy by playing keep away. The PE teacher makes the smaller boys play on the "skins" team, accenting their underdeveloped physiques. The teacher also has them play a game called "Gladiator" where the bigger boys' mission is to tackle the smaller boys. Greg spends much of the movie running from teenage bullies. Another theme of the movie is social status. The more Greg tries to gain popularity, the more he becomes an outcast and loses his best friend, Rowley. At the end of the movie, Greg gives a speech in which he laments his absurdity of the social structure of the school and the lunch tables. Greg goes back to his original friends, no longer caring about social status.

In *Shredderman Rules*, Nolan jokingly runs through the different bullying behaviors: noogies, purple nurples, the fishhook, goober yoyo, the donkey dance, the finger snaps, and the atomic wedgie. Naming the offensive behaviors may not only normalize them but may give them a playful tone. Nolan also runs through a list of nicknames of kids in the school. The bullying tactics and nicknames are mentioned in the first four minutes of the film, which quickly establishes the bullying climate at the school. In order for Nolan's former best friend to avoid being bullied, he teams up with Bubba. Bubba, the bully, is shown getting physically bullied by his father. The principal calls the bullying a "tiff" and a "good life lesson." She goes so far as to tell Nolan he should be thanking Bubba. Since it looks as though nothing will be done about the bullying, Nolan plots to expose the bullying on a larger scale. He anonymously creates a website: not to cyberbully but to get Bubba to stop. After Nolan posts a video of Bubba giving the team mascot a swirlie, pushing a kid down the stairs in a cello case, and destroying another student's project, the principal is left with no choice but to suspend Bubba.

Max Keeble's Big Move is one big lesson on bullies. The bullies ranged from an abusive principal, a harsh teacher, an overbearing boss, and a deranged ice cream truck driver to a stereotypical physical bully, Troy, and a slick bully, Dobbs, who steals lunch money and charges to use the bathroom. Troy used to be Max's friend in early childhood. He is a stereotypical bully with spiky red hair and wears leather with chains. After being dragged through the mud and thrown in a full dumpster by the bully, Max gets in trouble with the principal for being a "troublemaker." The principal, who is a bully himself, will not let Max explain what happened. Max gains confidence to get revenge on the bullies when he thinks his family is moving away and there will be no opportunity for the bullies to retaliate. When Max finds out his family is not moving after all, he has to devise a new plan so he will not get tortured in the future. His final solution is to get the bystanders to stand up to the bullies. The movie ends with the crowd wanting to treat the bullies like they treated them. Max tells them all if they do, they will be no better than the bullies. The big football players, who are normally portrayed as the bullies, are the ones who pick up the bullies and drop them in the dumpster.

In *How to Eat Fried Worms*, the bullies immediately single Billy out as soon as he arrives at his new school. They make fun of him for riding his bike on the sidewalk and hassle him for putting his bike in a certain spot on the bike rack. The bullies take his lunch from his cubby and put worms in his thermos. The kids start to call him "worm boy." Billy, makes a bet with Joe, the leader of the bullies, he can eat 10 worms. When Joe's brother bullies Joe and calls him a "loser," Billy and the rest of the boys stand up for Joe. By the end of the movie, all the boys appear to be friends. They declare the bet a tie; therefore both boys have to walk though the hallway with worms in their pants.

Luke, the main character in the movie *The First Kid*, is an unusual bullying target because he starts off as unlikeable. Luke is dressed in suit and tie, has slicked-back hair, and is obnoxious to secret service staff. The first agent gets fired for being too rough with Luke. The bully, Rob, is also obnoxious to adults, including Luke's bodyguard, Sims. During class, Sims is napping so Rob spits a spit wad at Sims. Later Sims retaliates with a really big spit wad to Rob's face.

Kenny & Co. is an older film from 1975 about two 12-year-old friends, Kenny and Doug. Kenny's dad explains to him that Kenny is going to meet bigger bullies so he should learn to shove back. Kenny's mother disagrees. The boys devise a rather dangerous plot to get the bully, Johnny, in trouble and sent back to reform school. They lure him into an old woman's house. She is armed with a shotgun. Doug's father, a secret service agent, approves the plan. At the same time Kenny is being bullied by Johnny who makes him pay protection money, Kenny and his friend are mean to Sherman, a smaller boy who follows them around. They throw dirt clods at Sherman and set a mousetrap to snap his hand. However, when the bullies pull off Sherman's underwear, Kenny jumps on one of the bullies in Sherman's defense.

CAMP COMEDIES

Camp offer a prime setting for bullying. Most camps have a distinct pecking order, especially for campers who have seniority, extensive resources, or athletic abilities. There are also many more opportunities for bullying to occur since bullies have 24-hour access to their victims. Camp counselors are generally inept in the comedy movies as well, leaving victims defenseless.

A Pig's Tale is an example of a camp movie where the camp coordinator is inept. The kids are disrespectful to the counselors. The adults allow the rich boy, Troy, and the wolves run of the place. The less popular boys, the "Pigs," are relegated to the rundown cabin. One of the counselors comes down to the cabin with the group of popular boys to give the Pigs demerits and calls them "slobs." Because of the demerits, the Pigs have to clean the bathroom with toothbrushes. The rich boys, meanwhile, get served steak and a candlelit dinner. The Pigs slowly gain confidence and begin standing up to the Wolves. In the end, the Pigs win the camp's flag and are cheered by the campers who have previously been intimidated by the Wolves.

Meatballs is another camp movie that preceded *A Pig's Tale*. *Meatballs* has a more adult theme, focusing on the sexual and romantic relationships between the staff members. The competing camp is significantly wealthier. Their counselors pick on Spaz, the stereotypically nerdy staff member from the less popular camp. They pull childish pranks such as taking Spaz's milkshake and dumping it on his head. The kids are very disrespectful to the counselors. They need to be threatened with physical punishment in order for them to behave. Rudy, a new shy boy, is bullied out of his bunk. He is called "totally useless" when he accidentally scores a goal in his own net. One of the counselors, Tripper, played by Bill Murray, takes Rudy under his wing. Even though the rich camp cheats at the inter-camp Olympiad, Rudy wins race at the end, giving his camp the victory. The other boys cheer Rudy when he comes into their cabin that night. In this case, the bullies are more interested in beating the rival camp than picking on one of their own.

Heavyweights is about a fat camp that is taken over by a sadistic and former fat kid, Tony Perkis. There are two sets of bullies, Tony and the kids from the jocks' camp across the lake. The jocks verbally abuse the heavy kids and graffiti their dock. Tony, wanting to show his campers they are losers as long as they are overweight, invites the jocks to come play them in baseball knowing the heavy boys will lose. Even though the jocks are more athletic and appear to have more resources, the heavy campers beat them in the camp competition. He also invites a girls' camp to a dance to motivate the boys to lose weight, thinking that the girls will reject the heavy boys. When the girls warm up to even the heaviest of the boys and start to dance with them, Tony ends the dance early. The campers ban together to get rid of Tony and his crew. They tie up one of Tony's henchmen, Lars, and cover him in honey and leave him to be attacked by bears. One boy then punches Lars in the crotch. The campers plot to take over the camp and get rid of Tony so they can go back to the fun activities and junk food of which Tony has been depriving them. When Tony falls in a pit, the kids tie him up and bring him back to camp. He is put in a cage wired with electricity so he cannot escape. The campers taunt Tony with negative messages such as he is a "loser" with no friends. They become the bullies. It becomes a bit of *Lord of the Flies* as the boys gorge on food and dance around the campfire knowing Tony is powerless to prevent them. Tony eventually goes crazy when the boys destroy his self-esteem and is taken away by his father. Because it is a comedy, there are no ramifications for the boys' criminal actions. Although the victims triumph in the end, their actions are worse than the bully's.

Sports Comedies

Comedy sports movies have similarities to the *Karate Kid*–type movie that have fighting competitions. The conclusion of the movies often reveals that it is the adult coach that has been inciting the aggression. Often the boys learn a lesson about sportsmanship at the end of the movie, whereas the coach will continue to hold a grudge and be a poor role model.

Bad News Bears is a collection of rejects from other teams because the players appear to lack talent and social status. Because they lose so badly on opening day, the Bears get teased and picked on in school. One of the smaller players on the team, Tanner, gets into a fight with the entire seventh grade. Some bullies from the Bears' rival team, the Yankees, take one of the Bears' hats. They put ketchup in the hat and put it back on his head. Tanner comes to his teammates' defense and smashes his burrito in one of the bully's faces. The bullies put Tanner in the trashcan. At the end of the last game, the Yankee team apologizes for treating the team so badly. Tanner tells them to shove up their apology and the Bears celebrate their second-place finish.

D2: Mighty Ducks is another movie of misfits that takes on a more developed team from Iceland with a mean coach. The team first must deal with some local bullies who challenge them to a game of street hockey. The bullies join the team and now use their physical skills to help the team win. During the competition, the Iceland team plays dirty. The referees appear to favor the bullies. When two of the Iceland players sexually harass the Ducks' female goalie, she hits them in the crotch. Not only do the harassers go unpunished, the goalie gets ejected from the game. Iceland's coach, Wolf, plays dirty, but the US coach, Gordon, maintains his composure and good sportsmanship. When the US team wins, the Iceland players disobey their coach and go shake hands with the Ducks. The Iceland coach eventually comes around and shakes Gordon's hand.

The Benchwarmers is yet another movie with a group of underdogs who stand up to bullies. There are three sets of bullies in the movie, both adults and adolescents: Jerry, the coach of the privileged team who bullied Clark and Richie in high school and continues to bully them as adults; Gus, a former bully in high school who now defends bully victims; and members of the privileged team who bully a group of misfits boys.

The bully victims in the movie are stereotypical nerds. For example, Richie works at a video store and Clark is still a paperboy. Clark talks about when he was young, kids used to spit lugies on his forehead. Brad, who was also bullied in high school but now owns a multimillion-dollar sporting goods store, tells Clark and Richie he does not recognize them without their underwear on their heads. Brad's son, Nelson, is now being bullied by the players on the privileged team. Nelson has curly hair, is slightly overweight, and wears khakis and sweater vests. The bullies pin Nelson to the ground, break wind in his face, and force him and the other geeky boys off the baseball field. Later, Nelson appears with dog feces on his face. Gus, Carl, and Richie come to the boys' rescue. They offer to coach the Benchwarmers in a tournament. Even the legendary baseball player Reggie Jackson helps the underdogs. He proclaims that he hates bullies. Gus gets back at the boy bullies by hitting one of them in the chest with a line drive hit. Problems arise when it is revealed that Gus had bullied a boy, Marcus, so badly in high school, Marcus had to be institutionalized and now lives in his mother's basement. Clark, Richie, and the Benchwarmers feel betrayed. Gus apologizes to Marcus. Marcus gives a speech during the championship game defending Gus and tells the crowd that bullies can be forgiven.

The bullies on the privileged team realize that when one of the nerdy kids gets hit in the head with a ball, their coach did not yell at them. They agree that not getting yelled at for making a mistake was "pretty cool." Jerry yells at his players for even smiling before the game is finished. He tells his team to beat "those losers." The privileged players revolt against their coach. Members of the team purposely allow the Benchwarmers score a run. Richie and Carl get revenge by picking up Jerry and hanging him by his underwear on the fence.

Kids Crime-Solving Comedies

In the movies where kids solve crimes, there is usually a bigger issue to be solved than bullying. Generally it is the adults who are doing something unethical that must be stopped by the kids. Bullies are simply there to complicate matters and slow down the real work of saving the day.

In *P.U.N.K.S*, the bullies wear standard letter jackets. They shake down a boy for protection money. The bullies, headed by Ronnie, come and take Drew's comic book. When Drew's friend Lanny tries to get involved, he gets pushed down, too. Drew forms a club to combat the bullies and "protect the underdog." Later at school, the bullies in football jerseys are putting a boy in the trash can. Drew tells them to put the boy down. Lanny, who gains confidence from his crime fighting, throws the bullies across the school yard. Drew's father works at a lab that is conducting crazy experiments and is too weak to stand up to his bully boss. The kids expose the bad guy and save the day.

Shorts is a movie that combines crime-solving and super powers. Toby, a rather geeky kid with a mouth full of braces who talks to imaginary friends, is chased by a group of five bullies. They pelt him with dirt clods. One boy hits him with a rock and makes him fall out of a tree. He hears a voice that tells him to make a wish on the rock that hit him. He wishes for friends and is sent little spaceships, which attack the bullies. He is able to stand up to Helvetica, the female leader of the bullies. Helvetica's father, Mr. Black, yells at her to do whatever it takes to get the wishing rock back after she loses it. She reminds him that he told her not to be a bully. He says, "It's not bullying if you win." Mr. Black wishes on the rock that he will be the most powerful thing in the world and turns into a giant. The children, however, are able to team up and stop him.

Sky High is about a high school for the children of superheroes. Fourteen-year-old Will is the son of two superheroes. The freshmen are greeted by two boys who appear to be bullies. They harass the boys for money until the student body president, Wendy, makes them stop. Later the bullies are shown holding a boy upside down in a trash can. The coach assigns the freshmen to "hero" or "sidekick" track. He mocks the students who are sidekicks. The bullies play keep-away with the bus driver's hat. They throw it in the mud. They steal Will's pudding at lunch and trip him so he dumps his tray on Warren. Warren, Will's archenemy since Will's parents put his father in prison, throws fireballs at Will. A teacher runs for the principal but falls like a klutz. The other sidekicks stand up to Warren. Will suddenly develops super-strength and fights back. The principal puts both boys in detention for misusing their powers. The sidekicks do not want their heads dunked in toilets anymore so they make a bet with the bullies that Will can beat them at a challenge. Will breaks up with the popular mean girl when she mistreats his friend, Leila. When the bullies trap everyone in the homecoming dance, Will and the sidekicks save the day.

TEEN COMEDIES

Teen comedies appear to be a prime subgenre for bullying themes, especially those films released in the 1980s. *The Breakfast Club* is a classic '80s movie that examines the various cliques and social structure in a typical middle-class high school. The initial voiceover identifies them as "a brain, an athlete, a basket case, a princess, and a criminal." The group is united by a common enemy, the principal. Principal Vernon is a bully in his own right with his harsh treatment of and threats to the kids in detention. More than most other movies, *The Breakfast Club* adds depth to the characters. Unlike movies with action plots, the unrushed dialogue of the Saturday, all-day detention allows the characters more disclosure of their motivations and reactions to their experiences.

Perhaps the most poignant story of bullying in the movie was when Andrew, the jock, admitted he was in detention for taping another boy's butt cheeks together. When they ripped off the tape, hair and skin came off. Andrew claims he tortured the boy, Larry, because he wanted his father to think he was powerful. Andrew's friends also laughed and cheered him on. Afterwards, Andrew felt remorse and laments about how humiliated Larry must have felt when he had to tell his father. In the context of the movie, viewers might have expected Brian, the brain, to talk more about his own experiences getting bullied by classmates. Brian's bullies appear to be his parents and the intense pressure they put on him to succeed. Claire, the princess, has the makings of a mean girl. Although she offers no specific stories, she talks about being exclusionary. She laments how difficult it is to stay popular and hates having to go along with everything her friends say. She does not receive much sympathy from the others. Her experiences pales in comparison to the cigar burn scars Bender, the criminal, received from his abusive father. Allison, the basket case, has no friends and is so desperate for inclusion, she attends detention without being required. The moral of the movie is mostly about the evils of exclusion, judging, and cliques.

Dazed and Confused includes initiations of younger students by older students, both male and female. Members of the football team bring a paddle to the junior high school. Jodi asks them to take it easy on her little brother Kramer since he's "kind of little." They promise, although as soon as she's out of earshot, they say they are going to kill him. They drive up and announce over a loud speaker they have mounted on the back of a truck that if they freshman boys come out after school and get their one licking, they won't bug them all summer. They announce they are targeting Kramer. The teacher just smiles as if it is a rite of passage. Several cars of high school boys with paddles approach the school. The junior high boys make a run for it. One the boy's mothers scares off the perpetrators by brandishing a shotgun. Two of the other boys talk about how the adults seem to condone the tradition. The guys show up at Kramer's baseball game with paddles. His friends leave him to his "destiny." The movie footage shows him getting paddles in slow motion. He is cringing in pain. As part of their initiation, the high school girls put pacifiers in the female freshmen's mouths. They make them lay down on the ground and call them "sluts" and "bitches." They cover them with ketchup, mustard, eggs, and flour. They force the girls to go through the car wash in the back of pickup trucks and then let them go.

In a series of scenarios in the movie *Better Off Dead*, a depressed teen, Lane, tries a variety of ways to committing suicide. He messes each one up. The rich jerk, Roy, cheats to make sure Lane does not make the high school ski team. Then he steals Lane's girl-friend. Lane is hassled by a much younger paperboy. When he accidentally rips the uni-form off of a cheerleader, he gets attacked by the basketball team. Lane is even bullied and humiliated by his boss, who makes him wear a pig nose. Lane is inspired by a foreign exchange student, Monique, and beats Roy in a ski race. It is interesting that Lane is con-trasted with characters who are physically geekier and more awkward than he is; however, Lane is the only one who does not seem to be able to win.

In *The Prankster*, a group of misfits anonymously battle the bullies who victimize the innocent. The varsity lettermen pants freshmen and give them wedgies and swirlies. In PE class, the jocks pick basketball teams they name "the heroes" and "the zeroes." The dean of the school plays favorites with the jocks and doesn't call fouls when the jocks start to cheat. When the bully, Blotto, calls Larry, one of the pranksters, a "woman," Larry pushes back. The dean breaks it up and punishes Larry. The pranksters set out to disrupt Blotto's driving exam and embarrass the dean. Larry flips Blotto off so the bullies drag him in the boys room and give him a swirly. The dean walks by and asks Larry what he did to provoke the lettermen. At the end of the movie, the entire senior class stands up against the dean for his treatment of Chris, one of the pranksters. Blotto comes out as a cross dresser and stops bullying. Larry's ex-girlfriend, who treats others badly through-out the film, realizes she has been a fake and gets back together with Larry.

Jerry is the slightly geeky lead character in *Three O'Clock High*. When he arrives at school, the camera quickly establishes the different cliques: the preppies are wearing their sweaters around their necks, the nerds with red hair and freckles are wearing glasses, the stoners are wearing leather jackets, and the jocks are wearing jerseys. A large, leather-jacket-wearing bully named Buddy comes to their school. There are rumors about him taking a swing at a teacher and breaking the teacher's neck at his last school. When Jerry unthink-ingly touches Buddy, Buddy picks up Jerry and flushes his feet in the urinal. He then slams Jerry against the mirror which shatters. He sets up a fight after school in the parking lot at 3 o'clock. He warns Jerry not to run or tell a teacher. In order to get Jerry out of the fight, Jerry's friend plants a knife in Buddy's locker to get him expelled. When they don't retrieve the knife in time, Jerry fears retribution. Jerry makes a run for it but he finds a note on his mother's car steering wheel stuck there with a knife. The note reads, "There is no escape. The bell rings at 3:00. Be there." Jerry lifts the hood of the car to see the wires of the engine have been pulled apart. The security guard catches Jerry with the knife and sends him to the principal. Jerry enlists a bigger bully named Craig to take on Buddy. Craig finds Buddy in the library and pokes his finger in Buddy's chest. Buddy breaks Craig's finger and punches him, sending him into the stacks of books, knocking them over like dominoes. Craig is a bloody mess. Jerry offers the money he was going to pay Craig to Buddy directly. Buddy asks him how it feels to be the "biggest pussy alive." Jerry comes back later and demands the money back and the fight is on. Jerry somehow manages to hit Buddy unconscious with Buddy's brass knuckles. By the time the police show up, Buddy has escaped. *Three O'Clock High* is full of incompetent and overzealous adults who make matters worse for Jerry as he tries to battle the bully. The law enforcement officials allow Buddy to disappear while focusing on Jerry. It isn't clear what sort of punishment Buddy will get caught. It appears he was in fights in his last school so they simply transferred him to another school. In the last line of the movie, Jerry gives the impression that bullying will continue in the school and in his life.

While many of the bullies call their male victims "faggot" or "pussy," *The Curiosity of Chance* is the only comedic movie in the analysis that features a gay character who is bullied. The title character, Chance, shows up to his first day of a new school in a bow tie, coat, leather pants, and top hat. A group of jocks in letter jackets walk by. Their leader, Brad, calls Chance a "fag." Chance stands up to them and tells him he won't comply to their standards. Brad grabs his head and slams it against the locker. A couple of girls come by and calmly try to talk Brad down. In the locker room, Brad tells Chance the girls' locker room is on the other side. He orders the team not to talk to Chance fearing he'll write an article for the school newspaper that makes them look like girls. Brad hits Chance in the head with a soccer ball and tells Chance to leave his school because Chance makes him "want to puke." Chance's father tells Chance when he is called names he should stand up for himself. He tells his father he has been called names since he was nine. His father tries teaching Chance jujitsu from a video tape. The vice principal tells Chance he must find a way to get the students to accept him or he won't make it there. The final straw for Chance is when Brad posts a photo he stole of Chance performing as a drag queen. The whole school stands around laughing at copies of the picture, which are posted all over the school. Levi, also a jock, stands up for Chance and knocks Brad to the ground. Although Chance has evidence of Brad taking steroids, he does not use it to get revenge. The vice principal later finds out about the steroids anyway and expelled Brad. Chance appears to be okay in the end.

House Party is one of the only minority comedies that made the list. Generally, movies about minorities and inner cities are gang related. Gangs are portrayed as ultra violent and therefore do not meet the definition or standard of bullying especially in Hollywood terms. Kid, one of the protagonists of *House Party*, accidentally bumps into a bully and spills his milk. The bully's friend encourages him to kick Kid's ass. Kid bumps into him a second time. The three bullies mock him and assess how to beat him up. Kid picks up some gelatin and throws and misses. The bullies call him a "pussy" and hit him repeatedly, but in a comedic, slapstick fashion (i.e., no hard blows, no blood or bruising). The rest of the kids in the lunch room cringe but do nothing to help. The supervising teacher ducks as someone throws food. Finally, a teacher comes over and sends Kid to the principal's office. She tells him not to fight. She asks the bully why he called Kid's mother a gardening tool.

She is clueless as to what a "ho" is. Later, the bullies chase Kid into a fancy party. The bully starts to strangle Kid while his two cronies hold back the crowd. While the bully is distracted, Kid hits him the crotch and runs again. They call Kid a "faggot" and a "pussy." The bullies go to the car and get a gas can and a bat. Two of them warn against setting a fire but go along. The police catch them pouring gas on the outside of the house. Later, they all get arrested. The thugs in the jail cell draw straws to see who gets to rape Kid. Kid distracts them with a rap until his bail comes. As they lock the door, Kid mocks the prisoners.

The key figures in teen comedy movies are often stereotypical nerds, both in outward appearance and love of science. *Revenge of the Nerds* features stereotypical nerds, Gilbert and Lewis, with glasses, ties, pocket protectors, and annoying laughs. When the football team accidentally burns down their own fraternity house, they kick the freshmen out of their dorm who are forced to stay on cots in the gym. The dean lets the coach and the athletes run the school. To get back at the jocks, the nerds soak their jockstraps with liquid heat. The Alpha Betas burn a "nerd" sign on their yard. After the nerds win the homecoming carnival, the football coach orders his team to trash the nerds' house. When the coach manhandles Gilbert, the dean finally stands up to him. Gilbert gives a speech about nerds. Lewis asks anyone who has ever been picked on to step forward. Almost the entire crowd steps forward. They all chant "nerds." The dean tells the coach the nerds will live in the dorm while the Alpha Betas fix their house and the team will have to stay in the gym. What is particularly disturbing about the movie is that the nerds, having been the targets of abuse by the Alpha Beta fraternity, are abusive to sorority members. Booger calls the women from Omega Moos "a bunch of pigs." When the nerds invade the Pi house for a panty raid, they catch some of the sisters topless. To make money for their charity event, the nerds sell topless pictures of the Pi president, Betty. In the most outrageous act, Lewis puts on a disguise and has sex with Betty, who thinks he's Stan, her boyfriend. When she learns the truth instead of crying "rape," she tells Lewis he was wonderful.

Back to the Future is set in a more nostalgic time before diet sodas and designer underwear. Currently, Marty's father, George McFly, is still the target of his high school bully, Biff. When the movie begins, Biff crashes McFly's car and blames him for not telling him the car has a blind spot. Biff grabs McFly's tie and taps on his head. He roughs him up for not finishing the work reports Biff is going to take credit for. McFly tells his son he is not good at confrontations. Even Marty is mean to his father and scolds him about the car because Marty wanted to use it to go camping with his girlfriend that weekend. When Marty is sent to the past, he sees Biff bullying his father in high school. Biff is hassling McFly about not getting Biff's homework finished. At school, McFly gets kicked in the hallway because someone has put a "kick me" sign on his back. The principal calls McFly a "slacker" and does nothing when he witnesses the bullying. McFly finally stands up to Biff when Biff forcefully grabs Lorraine's arm after she turned him down. (Lorraine is McFly's wife in the future and Marty's mother.) When Biff goes to retaliate against McFly, Marty trips him and punches him when he is not looking. Marty gets away and Biff vows revenge. To protect Marty and Lorraine, McFly finally gets the courage to stand up to Biff and knocks him out. Because McFly finally stood up to Biff, the roles reverse in the future. In the present day, Biff is submissive while McFly is confident and economically successful.

The title character in *Napoleon Dynamite* is an odd kid who wears glasses and moon boots in warm weather, and has red curly, frizzy hair. One of the bullies at school, Don, has him in a headlock and is banging his head against the locker. A couple of girls walk by without seeming to notice or care. Napoleon is eating tater tots he hid in his pants pocket earlier at lunch. When he won't share, a boy kicks him in the pocket, smashing all the tots. Don once again shoves Napoleon into the lockers and walks away. When Trisha's mother makes her go to the dance with Napoleon, she immediately ditches him. One of the bullies asks a smaller student for pop money. When the student refuses, he jerks his head up and down. Napoleon asks the boy about his neck and tells him that Pedro offers him his protection. The bully then tries to take the boy's bike. Two gang members, friends of Pedro's, drive up in a low rider and scare the bully away. The movie ends with no resolution with the bullies.

SPECIAL POWERS/SCI-FI COMEDIES

Comedies employ similar techniques of using supernatural powers to protect against and get revenge toward bullies as do dramas and action movies. Generally it is the self-confidence that the powers give the victims and not the powers themselves that stave off the bullies. *Weird Science* opens as two nerds, Wyatt and Gary, who are lusting after the practicing gymnasts, are pantsed by two bullies. Later at the mall, the bullies dump a slushy on them. The bullies' girlfriends initially plan to break up with the bullies but reconsider when they assess the potential drop in their social status if they do. Wyatt and Gary, using their science skills, create the perfect woman, Lisa. They use her to elevate their status and make the bullies jealous. Lisa invites the bullies, Ian and Max, to a party at Wyatt's house as her way of making Wyatt and Gary popular with the rest of the kids at school. Ian and Max offer Wyatt and Gary their girlfriends, Deb and Hilly, in exchange for Lisa. Lisa creates a group of bikers to disrupt the party in an attempt to get Wyatt and Gary to stand up for themselves and show everyone they are not bully victims. When the bikers accost Deb and Hilly, Wyatt and Gary force the bikers out. The biggest bully is Wyatt's older brother, Chet. Chet beats him up if Wyatt does not do what he tells him and gives Wyatt a wedgie. Lisa uses her powers to turn Chet into a creature. She makes him apologize to Wyatt. Secure with girlfriends and a gentler Chet, Lisa leaves the boys with their new self-confidence.

Barney, a science geek with glasses and a white lab coat, is the lead character in the movie *Zapped!*. He accidentally inhales some chemicals in the lab and gets telekinetic powers. To get back at Robert, one of his bullies, he spins Robert around until he vomits. Barney also uses his powers to make it look like his best friend, Peyton, is beating up the bullies. The female bystanders are impressed with the boys' powers. When a group of boys moon Barney, he makes them float up a tree with their pants still down. To retaliate against Robert, Peyton shows him a picture he has taken of Robert's girlfriend topless. In a series of comical scenes, Barney uses his powers to make girls' blouses pop open. When one girl retaliates and throws a watermelon at Barney, he makes her skirt come off, too. Soon whole groups of innocent bystanders' clothes are blown off. Barney and his girlfriend, Bernadette, laugh. Although Barney's initial goal was to get revenge on bullies, he now appears to be a bit of a bully himself.

During a basketball game in the movie *Teen Wolf*, Scott gets harassed by a player on the other team, Mick. Mick tells him he is "terrible" and calls him a "dork." Another player on an opposing team trips Scott. Teams foul Scott on purpose because of his inability to make free throws. When Scott begins to turn into a werewolf, his father warns him about turning into the wolf out of anger. Instead of being ostracized, Scott becomes popular. As Teen Wolf, he can now dunk the basketball. He is now a hero and gets straight As. Even Mick's girlfriend, Pamela, is smiling at Scott. When Mick catches Scott with Pamela, he calls him a "freak" and calls Scott's female friend, Boof, a "tramp." Scott turns into the wolf out of anger and rips up Mick's shirt. The bystanders start to laugh. Scott decides he wants to be himself. The crowd, fearing that Scott will lose the championship game, chants "Wolf." Scott, not the wolf, takes the final free throw of the game and makes it to win the game. The fans carry him off the floor. He rushes past Pamela and kisses Boof. Scott no longer wants to rely on special powers to be popular and get back at his bully. He gains the confidence to make the free throw and get the girl.

Boy Makeover Comedies

Boys experience similar plot lines in the make-over movies as girls. In *Can't Buy Me Love*, Ronald pays the most popular girl in school, Cindy, to go out with him. She changes his look and he becomes popular. When he confronts Cindy about how she ignored him the previous 17 years, she tells everyone at the New Year's Eve party about their arrangement. The popular kids turn on him. Ronald later stands up for his friend who is being bullied. Ronald reminds everyone how they used to all be friends when they were younger before they broke off into cliques. Kids from all the different cliques applaud him. Ronald gets the girl in the end without having to pay her.

A bullied teen, Dizzy, in *The New Guy* purposely gets expelled from school so he can start over at a new school. He gets advice from some prison inmates on how to be cool. Dizzy is a hit at the new school. He stands up for other victims of bullying. The bully from his old school outs him as a former wimp. Just when the crowd is going to turn on Dizzy, the inmates stop the bullies. Dizzy explains that he cared more about what people thought of him than who he was.

Just One of the Guys is a reverse makeover movie. Terry, an extremely popular girl in her high school, goes undercover as a boy and attends a different school to report on gender discrimination in order to win a journalism competition. As she approaches her new school, she sees a group of three bullies yank up the underwear of a passive underclassman. The leader, Greg, calls Terry a homophobic slur and throws her in the bushes. Greg walks through the cafeteria stealing food. Greg and the other bullies pick up another new kid, Rick, in the locker room and carry him to the shower as everyone chants. Terry helps to make-over Rick, not only his appearance but his self esteem. With Terry's moral support, Rick stands up to Greg in the cafeteria. He uses his pinky to show Greg's penis size. Everyone cheers. Because of Greg's behavior, his girlfriend Deborah goes to the prom with Rick. At the dance, Greg starts a fight with Rick; however, Terry gets thrown into the ocean. Terry's younger brother and Rick go after Greg. Rick is triumphant over Greg and ends up with Terry who has revealed herself as a girl. Greg hands his trash to a teacher who stands there rather helpless. He lifts up the nerd's table, pretending to turn it over. Instead he picks up the bench, causing three nerdy kids to fall. Another teacher looks on but does nothing to stop the bullying. The nerds in the movie are very stereotypical. They sit in the front row of class and speak in their own strange language. One is in a shirt buttoned up all the way with curly hair and the other has thick glasses and is wearing a velour sweat suit zipped up to his neck and a cowlick in the back.

ADULT INTERVENTION COMEDIES

Although the adult leads in these movies are likely frozen in adolescence themselves, they lend assistance to kids who are getting bullied by their peers. The immature adults' understanding of the adolescent mind allows them to create effective anti-bullying strategies. Billy in *Billy Madison*, Dickie in *Dickie Roberts*, Will in *About a Boy*, and Drillbit in *Drillbit Taylor* are clever in the way they help their young friends overcome the bully, presumably because they are not far removed from that mind set.

In the movie *Billy Madison*, the title character has to redo school in order to inherit his father's company. The audience sees school bullying through an adult's eyes. In some instances, Billy is the bully. He propositions a third-grade boy to trade him his banana for his pudding. The boy says no. When Billy tells him he could beat him up, the boy still refuses. In the third grade, Billy mocks a boy who stutters. The teacher reprimands Billy and he runs out of the room crying. The next day Billy feigns sickness not to have to go to school. As he advances grade by grade, Billy develops empathy. When Ernie accidentally pees his pants, Billy splashes water on his own pants to show the other kids that it is cool to pee one's pants. Instead of teasing him, one boy high-fives Ernie. When Billy gets to high school, he starts to get bullied. His smart-aleck comments don't work like they did in the earlier grades. In the cafeteria, a bully pours liquid on Billy's head at lunch. The bullies fill Billy's locker with horse manure. The other boys at the lunch table warn him that the bullying is going to get worse for Billy. They recount their experiences getting bullied. One boy recommends cutting his underwear ahead of time so the wedgies rip easier. The boys are rather happy that there is someone else to pick on now. Another boy tells how he was in denial about bullying until the lacrosse team stuck a parking cone up his behind. Billy calls them losers and says it's just hazing of the new guy. He doesn't understand because he was popular the first time he went to high school. Veronica, his teacher, asks if maybe he treated others badly in school. Billy goes home and calls Danny, a boy he used to pick on in high school, to apologize. It is clear that Danny has suffered from what appears to be years of bullying. Danny crosses Billy's name off a long list of "people to kill." Another dimension of the movie is the adult bully. Eric, a businessman who wants to take over Billy's father's company, bullies Billy. He blackmails the principal into telling everyone that Billy only got through grade school because he bribed him. Billy challenges Eric to an academic decathlon. When it looks like Eric is going to lose, he pulls a gun but is stopped by Danny.

In *Dickie Roberts: Former Child Star*, David Spade plays a former child star trying to make a comeback in show business. As an adult, he stoops to appearing in a celebrity boxing match where he is humiliated by Emmanuel Lewis, the former star of the television show *Webster*. Even the referee kicks him when he's down. His girlfriend calls him a "moron" and tells him there won't be comeback. She drives off with another man, leaving him stranded in the middle of nowhere. To get a part in a movie, Dickie has to experience a normal life so he hires a family. The son, Sam, is being picked on by a boy at school. The daughter, Sally, experiences a rich mean girl Heather who steals other girls' boyfriends. When the bullies are picking on Sam at school, Sally calls them "creeps." One of the bullies calls her a "bitch." Dickie steps in and starts to make fun of one bully for having red hair and the other bully for being chubby. The crowd of kids cheer and the bullies walk away.

Drillbit Taylor is a homeless scam artist who is hired by bully victims who are just starting high school. The bullies attack the boys in the boys' room and make them urinate on each other. They pour soda on one boy's laptop and put pictures of men up in another boy's locker. When the boys go to the principal, he sides with the bully. Even the bullies' victims' parents are charmed by Filkins. Drillbit trains them in fighting techniques; however, the advice backfires. Drillbit dresses up like a substitute teacher and picks on the bullies. When the bullies discover Drillbit is a fake, Filkins punches Drillbit in the nose. When Filkins insults the girl Wade likes, Wade stands up to Filkins. During the big fight, Drillbit shows up. When he finds out that Filkins is 18 and a legal adult, he beats Filkins up. The kids who have been standing by watching the fight congratulate the boys on getting rid of the bully.

Hugh Grant's character in *About a Boy*, Will, is described as "immature" but is not goofy like the other characters in this group of movies about adults helping children overcome their bullies. Will befriends a fatherless boy, Marcus. After walking him to school, Marcus' mother tells him she loves him. All the kids mock him with "I love you, Marcus." When Marcus absentmindedly sings in class, the whole class laughs at him. They continue to laugh at him at recess. One of the bullies hits Marcus in the head with a ball. Marcus's two friends tell him they don't want to hang around him because the bullies pick on them when he is around. When Will buys Marcus an expensive pair of sneakers, the bullies steal them. He is forced to walk home in the rain barefoot. Will loses his temper and yells at Marcus's mother for aiding in Marcus's bullying because of her emotional problems. Marcus signs up for the school concert because he thinks it will help his mother be happy even though he is warned that the other kids will "crucify" him. When Marcus begins his song, his friend backs out of playing the recorder with him for fear of what the bully will do. The crowd of students and their parents laughs when Marcus dedicates the song to his mother. As he starts to sing, someone shouts out, "You're rubbish." The crowd starts to boo and jeer. Will comes out with a guitar and sings along. In the end, they get a moderate amount of applause. Will continues to sing and be goofy. He gets hit in the head with an apple. The crowd starts to laugh with Marcus and no longer at him as Will diverts their attention.

In *Bad Santa*, a heavy boy with curly hair, Thurman, gets harassed by bullies. The nameless bully calls him "loser" and throws a can at Thurman when he won't turn around. Thurman is determined to go see Santa. Thurman stops a crazy man from attacking Santa, or rather Willie, a small-time criminal who plays Santa. Willie takes him home and robs the house. When Thurman gets off the bus, a gang of bullies surrounds him, call him a "retard," and give him a wedgie. The sound of underwear ripping can be heard. Thurman shows up at the department store with his underwear under his armpits. He asks Santa for a gorilla to beat up the skateboard kids. Willie, tells him when he was a boy and went home after getting beat up by bullies, his father beat him up, too. A depressed Willie is trying to commit suicide when Thurman interrupts him. When Willie discovers Thurman has a black eye, he goes and beats up the bully. He slugs him and throws him against a tree. Willie feels like he accomplished something, that he did something good for the first time in his life. Willie tries to teach Thurman how to fight. At the end of the movie, the bully comes back and taunts Thurman when Willie is not there to save him. The bully is getting ready to steal Thurman's bike. He calls Thurman a "fat ass." Thurman kicks him in the groin. He rides off on his bike, flipping off the bully.

ADULT BULLY COMEDIES

Mr. Woodcock is another movie that flashes back to the past. This time, however, it is an adult who physically bullies and humiliates kids in gym class. Mr. Woodcock is a sadistic gym teacher. He hits one boy, Nedderman, with a basketball and makes him do laps. He hits Nedderman a couple of more times with the ball as he runs. He makes another boy who is wheezing with asthma run laps as well. He makes Farley, who had his gym clothes stolen, change into rental clothes in front of the other boys. He also makes him do chin-ups in his underwear. When the boy struggles, Woodcock says sarcastically, "Not even one chin-up, Farley? You are a disgrace to fat, gelatinous, out-of-shape little kids the world over." In another flashback, Mr. Woodcock makes the boys spread their legs so he can check to see if they are wearing their cups by hitting them with a bat.

A grown Farley comes back 13 years later. He is a successful author about a book on overcoming painful memories. He visits gym class where Mr. Woodcock is making the boys do pushups. He puts his foot one of the boys' back as he does it. He also makes another boy do pushups because the boy stutters. Farley also witnesses Mr. Woodcock berating the elderly people in a water aerobics class. The problem is, the more Farley tries to get people to see Mr. Woodcock for the bully that he is, the more they stand up for him. His mother, who was engaged to Mr. Woodcock, sees him arguing with her son and breaks off the engagement. Farley sees how happy Mr. Woodcock has made his mother so he coaches Mr. Woodcock to be a nicer person. Farley realizes Mr. Woodcock made him who is today and condones the bullying.

In the movie *Heavyweights*, overweight adolescents are bullied by the camp director, Tony Perkis. Unlike other camp movies, the kids from the opposing camp play a minor role in the harassment of the campers. Tony's mission is to demonstrate the boys losing weight so he can sell his weight loss program. He uses humiliation tactics such as setting up the campers for failure with their normal weight peers. He brings the jocks from a nearby camp to humiliate the overweight boys on the baseball field. Next, he arranges a dance with a girls' camp, expecting the heavy boys to experience romantic rejection in an attempt to motivate the campers to lose weight. Tony also bullies and threatens the adult camp counselors who were hired by the previous owners. He brings in his own staff members who also bully the campers. One staff member, Lars, is a rather sterotypical German with no sense of humor. The adolescent campers take Tony hostage, keeping him in an electric cage. They call Tony a "loser" and tell him he has no friends. Instead of disciplining the boys and creating positive role modeling, the counselors join the campers in exacting revenge against their persecutor. Even when Tony goes crazy from the mental cruelty, the campers and the counselors are not held accountable for their bullying of Tony. Victims' bad behavior often gets excused or seen as justified if the bully's action is sufficient, especially if the bully is an adult.

Joe Somebody is the story of a grown-up bully. It's included here because the bully is juvenile and his tactics resemble adolescent bullying. *Dodgeball* and *The Waterboy* also fit this description. In *Joe Somebody*, a coworker in a black SUV, McKinney, cuts Joe off in the parking lot at work and steals his spot. McKinney is a real jerk and threatens to "kick Joe's ass" in front of Joe's daughter. When Joe tries to reason with him, McKinney slaps Joe twice. It makes matters worse when the daughter stands up to the bully instead of her father. She calls McKinney a "dirt bag." A crowd of employees watching the scene does nothing. Joe submissively drives to a different parking lot far from the building's entrance.

Instead of taking action to stop bullying in the workplace because it is unacceptable as a behavior, the boss acts out of fear that Joe will sue for emotional distress. He sees Joe as a loser whose wife is divorcing him, who got passed over for a promotion, and got "bitch slapped" in the parking lot. McKinney gets suspended and must attend sensitivity training. Joe is ashamed and begins missing work. Joe has a panic attack. To get back his confidence, Joe challenges McKinney to a fight. He begins physical training and takes special martial arts classes. A couple of other employees encourage him to "kick the guy's butt." More and more employees shake his hand. Only his daughter, Natalie, tells him fighting is not the answer. It appears almost everyone at work has a new-found respect for him. Joe gets a promotion with his own parking spot. He starts playing squash with the high-level bosses and gels his hair. Joe ends up not fighting McKinney. McKinney apologizes. The boss continues to insist Joe fight someone, so Joe hits his boss in the windpipe. Joe reasons he doesn't need to fight to gain others' respect. Joe "gets the girl" and lives happily ever after.

Ben Stiller plays similar characters is *Dodgeball: A True Underdog Story* and *Heavyweights*. He is a formerly overweight person who is now thin and incredibly arrogant. In *Dodgeball*, his character, White Goodman, uses his wealth to try to shut down the gym of his rival, Peter. He calls the bank and gets Kate, whom he wants to date, fired so there will be conflict of interest for her to go out with him. Peter and a gang of misfits from the gym enter a dodgeball tournament to win money to save the Average Joe's gym from foreclosure. White spies on Peter's team and tries to cheat his way to a victory. White tries to bribe Peter into throwing the game and betraying his teammates. When Kate chooses Peter over him, White hits her in the side of the face with a ball in the dodgeball tournament. Peter's team wins the tournament. He used the money White bribed him with to bet on the game. With his five-million dollar winnings, Peter buys controlling interest in Globo-Gym and fires White. White spirals into depression and eats his way into a slovenly blob of a man.

The Waterboy, played by Adam Sandler, is 31 years old and still working as a water boy. He appears mentally slow but is a wizard at water purification. The players on the college team he is working for throw a football at his head and spray him with his own water hose. Bobby scolds the player, not about mistreating him but about wasting water. The coach rolls his eyes when the players put the water jug on Bobby's head. He does nothing to the players and fires Bobby. The players on Bobby's new team purposely tackle a player into Bobby, sending him crashing into his water table. Another player spits in his water jug. Bobby flashes back to when he was little and a player spit in his jug. The coach at the time stood up for the player. The new coach advises Bobby to stand up for himself. The quarterback mocks him and pretends to be retarded. Bobby loses his temper and tackles the quarterback so hard he gets a spot on the team. The players continue to mock him, except for the field goal kicker who befriends him. When one of the professors is mean to Bobby, Bobby tackles him, claiming that the coach told him he could fight back. When Bobby wins the big game against his former team, his quarterback apologizes for mistreating Bobby.

Big Bully begins with a flashback of a chubby boy, Fang, chasing David, a kid with glasses. David begs Fang not to hit him. David is later shown in his class picture with a black eye and fat lip. After the bully pees in David's juice, David vows that Fang will regret it one day. David's father gets transferred and the family moves away. Years later, David returns to his hometown to teach a course at his old middle school. The tables have turned and David's son Ben is bullying Fang's son Kirby. David appears to do nothing to stop Ben, even though David was in Kirby's position as a child. When Ben sees some older boys bullying Kirby, he has a change of heart. He and Kirby become friends. Fang, now the shop teacher at the school, has become a timid, henpecked man who lives in a trailer with his bossy wife and five unruly sons. After David's return, Fang resumes bullying David, slashing David's car tires. By bullying, Fang claims he gained back his confidence and manhood. When a boy acts out in class, Fang forces the student's head near the power sander to scare him. When David reports Fang to the principal, the principal puts David on probation. Fang blames David for never standing up for himself. The bullying intensifies. When David climbs a rope to hide from Fang, Fang sets the rope on fire. In the end, Fang reforms after a near-death experience. The movie is another example of how the kids are often portrayed as more mature than the parents.

Dramas

Films in the drama category vary wildly from sentimental dramas to horror movies. Bullying appears to be an effective plot point that fits into a wide range of subgenres. Often the movies with bullies are touching coming-of-age stories rather than the raucous comedies described above. These movies are often set in the past to intensify the sentimentality of a more innocent time.

Lucas is a sweet story about an undersized boy trying to get the girl of his dreams to like him as more than a friend. Lucas uses humor when the older kids pick on him. They call him "Puke." Even the coach calls him "Piss Ant." When one of the football players brings him up on stage during a pep rally with the rest of the team, Lucas does a goofy dance. When Lucas tries out for the football team to impress the girl, the jocks hold him down in the showers and apply heat cream to his genitals. They kick him out of the locker room in only a towel. Cappie is the one boy who stands up for Lucas, but later dates the girl with whom Lucas is in love. Lucas is allowed in one play in the football game but gets seriously hurt. When he returns to school, the bully starts a slow clap for him, which the rest of the crowd joins in. The movie ends with Lucas raising his arms in victory.

Clifford is the new student in *The Bodyguard*. Clifford encounters usual "new kid" treatment as he looks for a seat and students tell him they are all saved. When Moody, the school bully, walks into class, some of his classmates cheers. When Clifford refuses to give up his desk, Moody makes another boy move. Clifford makes fun of Moody so Moody tells him they are going to have a "talk" later. Clifford's friend, Carson, tells him that he doesn't go to the bathroom because he is afraid to go into the boys' room. On his way out of school, couple of boys stop Clifford and take him in the boys' room where Moody is shaking down another kids for money. Moody holds Clifford against the wall and demands a dollar a day. They start to throw wet toilet paper balls at his head. Moody tells Clifford to drink urine from the toilet. Clifford's dad finds out about the boys and calls the principal. The principal lets Moody off with detention because "no harm was done." The inept principal warns Clifford not to cry wolf. In gym class, Moody elbows Clifford in the stomach. The gym teacher does nothing. Clifford's gym locker is full of trash. He washes his clothes in the sink. He hides in the stall when Moody comes in but he gets caught. A large boy named Linderman comes out of one of the stalls. Rumors are running that Linderman went psycho and shot a kid in the head. Clifford offers Linderman money to be his bodyguard. Linderman is not interested at first. When the bullies lock Clifford in a locker, Linderman walks by at first but then turns around and lets Clifford out. At the snack shop, Clifford squirts ketchup and mustard on the bullies. As they chase him down, Linderman shows up. The kids crowd around to see a fight. Moody's cronies refuse to join Moody in taking on Linderman. The kids cheer. Moody gets an even larger goon, Mike, to push Linderman around but Linderman walks away from a fight. Mike takes a baseball bat to Linderman's motorcycle and pushes it into the lake. Linderman runs away. With Linderman gone, Moody is back to taking Carson's money, flushing his lunch, and calling his mother names. Linderman finally has enough and fights back. As Moody is holding Linderman back so Mike can hit him, Clifford jumps on his back. Linderman finishes off Mike. Clifford stands up to Moody and breaks Moody's nose. Moody's cronies walk away at the end, leaving Moody crying about his nose.

Field of Vision is a made-for-TV movie that resembles a mean girl movie rather than the standard bullying movie because of the "after-school special" message. The target of the bullying is Cory, a new student with curly red hair and living with a foster family. He shows up one of the jocks, Nick, in class with the correct answer. Cory makes the football team and beats Nick in blocking. Nick and some of the other jocks take Cory's clothes from the locker room, leaving him only a towel. Later, another boy steals Cory's backpack and puts it in a garbage can. Tyler, the captain of the team, gets a lecture from his parents and his coach about his responsibilities to stop the bullying. Tyler's sister has a magic camera through which Tyler witnesses Nick and Alex's bullying. He tells the coach and the bullies are kicked off the team. By the end of the movie, Nick gives Cory advice about how to win the game. Tyler's family also finds Cory's long-lost father and they live happily ever after.

The movie *Footloose* is unusual in that it has elements of a drama but it is not quite a comedy. The movie demonstrates that using homophobic remarks, bullying, and fighting back define masculinity. In *Footloose*, Ren is the new kid in a small rural town. His boss warns to him that people are going to give him trouble because he is new and different. Chuck and his cronies jump Ren outside the town's convenience store and hold him by the throat. They call him a "faggot" and a "pansy." A bystander helps Ren. Later, Chuck confronts his ex-girlfriend, Ariel, for breaking up with him because of Ren. When she hits Chuck, he hits her back, knocking her to the ground. Chuck and his crew show up at the town dance. They beat up Ren's friend Willard but he fights back with Ren's help. Ren uses his gymnastic skills and dance moves to knock out Chuck and win the support of the town.

COMING-OF-AGE DRAMAS

In many of the coming-of-age boy stories, the bullies are generally secondary to the plot. They present roadblocks to the main character and are instrumental in shaping his character. Except for *Lifted* and *The Fat Boy Chronicles*, the films in this category are set in the past. Each movie opens with a voiceover narration of one of the bullying victims reflecting back on the past.

Henry, the lead character in *Lifted*, gets teased in school about his mother's drug problems. Henry is helped by appearances by his father although the father was actually killed in the war in Iraq. Henry hides in a church when four boys chase him home from school. The minister is compassionate toward Henry but does nothing to stop the bullying. He simply tells the boys who are chasing Henry to go home. The teacher at school also does nothing after witnessing Henry being threatened. Henry's ticket out of the bullying situation, as well as escaping from an abusive grandfather, is to win a singing competition and moving with his mother to LA.

In *The Fat Boy Chronicles*, a bully dumps Jimmy's, an overweight boy, chocolate milk on his lunch tray on the first day of high school. Jimmy barely reacts and keeps eating. He describes sitting in the back of class because if he sits in front the other kids complain they cannot see around him. Jimmy is hesitant as gets on the bus, looking as though he fears being bullying. The quarterback of the football team, Robb, calls Jimmy "stupid" when Jimmy accidentally sits in the wrong spot. Robb comments on Jimmy's chest and asks if he is a "D cup." The rest of the boys laugh. Later at a party, Nate pulls Jimmy's shirt up, exposing his chest. The boys trick him into running through the gym in his underwear, telling Jimmy it is an initiation. Jimmy, in nothing but his underwear, slumps in front of the door of the locker room and cries when he finds he had been locked out. Jimmy begins to take action and begins running and eating better. When he is assigned to tutor Robb, Jimmy and Robb eventually become friends. Robb sticks up for Jimmy when Nate is bullying Jimmy. Robb apologizes for his past behavior. The movie is a sweet representation of how a boy who was bullied gains self-confidence. In the end, Jimmy kisses his first girlfriend in the cafeteria. Everyone, except Nate, stands and claps.

Simon Birch begins with Simon's friend, Joe, visiting Simon's grave. The movie then flashes back to the early 1960s when Simon and Joe were boys. Simon was born tiny with an undersized heart. The kids in class liked to pick Simon up who is half their size and pass him across the classroom. Simon gets heckled by the pitcher on the opposing baseball team, but Simon just smiles. Pitchers get frustrated because Simon's strike zone is so small he always walks.

In *Hearts in Atlantis*, bullies hassle Bobby and his friend Carol. The ring leader, Harry, goes so far as to touch Carol's young breasts to see if they are developed yet. He then tells his cronies to beat up Bobby, calling him a "queer." Ted, who has some psychic and telekinetic powers, blackmails Harry into leaving Bobby alone. Harry is sexually confused and has been dressing up in his mother's clothes. When Harry retaliates by dislocating Carol's shoulder with a baseball bat, Bobby goes after Harry, chasing him off.

That's What I Am is about a boy, Stanley, who is a foot taller than everyone else in school. He is teased because he has large ears and orange-colored hair. His nickname is Big G for "ginger." Andy is conflicted about having to work on a class project with Stanley. He is worried about his own social status and has difficulty understanding why Stanley fails to stand up for himself. One of the bullies, Ricky, sprays Stanley's crotch with a squirt gun to make it look like he wet himself. Stanley does stop a boy, Jason, from hitting an awkward girl with his jacket. Mary, Andy's love interest, stands up to Ricky for making fun of Stanley. Andy kicks Ricky in the crotch as he is about to throw a tomato at Stanley during the talent show. The theme appears that some of the kids are willing to stand up for others, but only individually. Groups of bystanders are mostly unhelpful. The movie teaches young viewers to be confident in who they are.

In the movie *The War*, a family of evil children torment Stu and his sister. The father is very abusive and it looks as though the children do not have enough to eat. It is an example of a nostalgic time in a rural place where bullying is inevitable.

There is a variety of physical sizes among the boys in the movie *The Outsiders*; however, the two gangs appear evenly matched physically. The Socs have the economic advantages. If there is bullying in the story, it could be when the Socs chase down Pony Boy and Johnny. The boys are smaller and outnumbered. Throughout the movie, there are fights and skirmishes between the different social classes.

Ace, from the movie *Stand by Me*, is a perennial favorite in lists of movie bullies. Kiefer Sutherland, who plays Ace, has a certain swagger. He leads a team of cronies. Beyond taunting the younger boys, he plays chicken with a logging truck, forcing the driver off the road. The bullying escalates to Ace pulling a knife. He is temporarily thwarted when one of the younger boys fires off a gun. Ace backs down but vows he will get them.

In *A Christmas Story*, Ralphie and his friends are the victims of resident bullies Scut Farkus and Grover Dill. The names themselves are quite humorous and nonthreatening. They push boys down and twist their arms behind their backs until they say "uncle." They tease and hit their victims with snowballs. There are Keystone Cop type chases with lively music to denote an air of comedy rather than a dire need for escape. Flick comes into class after his bout with the bullies with a black eye but the movie does not show how it got there. Ralphie in *A Christmas Story* finally snaps and attacks Scut Farkus. After his mother comes to pull him off Scut, Ralphie fears the wrath of his father when he gets home to see that Ralphie has been in a fight. The mother cleverly steers the conversation to football to distract the father from inquiring about the specifics of the fight. Even without the diversion, it looks unlikely that the father will have much of a negative reaction. He is a man's man character who would seemingly be proud that his son stood up to bullies.

There is a distinct difference between movies set in high school such *The Chocolate War* and *School Ties* and those set in middle school discussed previously. *The Chocolate War* and *School Ties* are also similar in that they both take place in the past and in all-boy boarding schools. Much like the teen television shows, adults are cast to play the role of teenagers in these movies. (For example, in *School Ties*, Brendan Fraser was 23 and Matt Damon and Chris O'Donnell were 21. In *The Chocolate War*, Wallace Langham was 23 and Doug Hutchinson was 27. Adam Baldwin was 26 in *The Chocolate War* and 18 in *My Bodyguard*). The themes are definitely darker and at times contour more violent behavior. Movies such as *Lucas* and *My Bodyguard* have a mix of younger and older boys. The physical size of the victims is a factor in addition to their age. Corey Haim was 14 when he played Lucas and Chris Makepeace was 16 when he played the lead in *My Bodyguard*.

The Chocolate Wars is set in an all-boys religious school. The religious nature of the setting creates a strict hierarchy and code of vengeance rather than a loving, spiritual environment. Many of the religious brothers are abusive to the students, further setting up a culture that tolerates bullying. The bullies belong to a secret group called the Vigils. The bullies have others do their dirty work. When Jerry refuses to sell chocolates and otherwise disobeys the Vigils, he is called a "faggot" and is beaten up by a gang of a dozen smaller boys. In the final confrontation, Jerry loses control and beats one of the Vigil leaders unconscious. The rest of the boys watching the fight from the grandstands cheer and chant Jerry's name. While the Vigils remain as a group, it is unlikely they will yield the power they once did.

School Ties is one of the only movies that deals with ethnic or religious bullying. When the other students at an exclusive boarding school find out that the new student brought in to win football games, David, is Jewish, they hang a "Go home Jew" sign and a swastika above his bed. When David witnesses Dillon, one of his persecutors, cheating, it is Dillon who accuses David of cheating. When another classmate finally speaks the truth, Dillon gets expelled. On his way off campus, he tells David he'll still get into Harvard and David will still be a dirty Jew. David tells him he'll still be a "prick."

FANTASY DRAMAS

There is a group of movies that include the fantasy of having a special power in order to defeat enemies. For example, Lucas, in *The Ant Bully*, develops his inner strength to stand up to the bully after a fantasy adventure. He learns how small victims can band together and use their wits to overcome larger and more powerful foes.

In the Harry Potter series, Draco Malfoy is described by one fan on IMDB as snobbish, rude, and "the ultimate bully." Malfoy is oftentimes more like a mean girl, using relational aggression and his family's wealth to make others miserable. He puts other boys down for having hand-me-down robs and for being fat. He usually gets his cronies, Vincent and Gregory, to do the bullying. Malfoy appears to be an annoyance to Harry as he has more important problems to solve. In *Harry Potter and the Prisoner of Azkaban*, Harry finally retailiates, turns invisible, and swings Malfoy around by the scarf.

In *Neverending Story III*, Bastian must escape the Nasties, when they lock him in the boiler room at school. As they are chasing him, Bastian uses a magical book to escape. When he gets water poured on him as he opens his locker, he vows revenge. He uses a magical oran to turn the Nasties into nerds.

In *Adventures of a Teenage Dragonslayer*, Arthur and his friends Natalie and Tim are confronted by a gang of bullies. The leader of the bullies is the principal's son, Metz. Arthur and his friends rescue a troll who zaps Metz with a stun gun. Arthur has more important things to worry about than the bullies because he must stop an evil dragon from destroying civilization. Metz drinks a potion that he thinks will make him stronger. Instead, Arthur finds Metz hanging from the basketball rim by his underwear.

FIGHT BACK DRAMAS

The plot line of the "fight back" movie is more uniform than any other category. The teacher is often of lesser status than the bully. The disparity adds more excitement at the end but it also establishes that those in the higher class have fewer scruples. It is the more grounded strategy that wins out in the end. These movies also give hope to the underdog and expose the evils of corrupt power. They teach the lesson of discipline and hard work. Even if the victim cannot overpower the bully physically, the training can increase the self-confidence of the victim. In *Karate Kid*, Mr. Miyagi quietly teaches Daniel about karate but also life. In *Showdown*, Billy has Ken scrub toilets. Ken assumes there is a rationale for the repetitive practice, but Billy tells him it is to learn humility. Mr. Lee makes Barry do practice tactics in the restaurant's kitchen in *Sidekicks*. In almost all these movies, the final fight is a sanctioned event where the bully and victim appear on equal footing.

In the 1984 original *The Karate Kid*, the first of many fight-back movies, Daniel movies from New Jersey to California, where he is unfamiliar with the culture. Daniel is harassed not only for being new but for talking to the bully's ex-girlfriend. Johnny and his friends beat up Daniel. When Daniel retaliates against the bullies for tripping him during a soccer game, the coach kicks Daniel off the team. The mild demeanor of the teacher also demonstrates that power is to be used quietly and only for good. At the flashy karate studio, Kresse is abusive to his students. Johnny takes his intense training to heart. When the other boys tell Johnny that Daniel has had enough, Johnny continues to beat on him. He echoes the words of his sensei and shouts "no mercy." In the remake, the bully also has learned "no mercy" from his instructor. Even though Kresse cheats, Daniel is triumphant, good winning over evil.

In the 2010 remake of the *Karate Kid*, Dre's single mother moves him to Beijing. He too talks to the wrong girl at schools and draws attention from bullies. The teacher does nothing when the bully knocks Dre's lunch tray out of his hands. Mirroring the original, Dre trains with a maintenance man. Dre defeats the bully in a tournament.

Although the movie *Rocky V* was primarily about his father, Rocky Jr. was forced to deal with a bully at school. Although his father had been the heavyweight champion, Rocky was too busy investing his time in a new protégé. Junior turned to his uncle Paulie for training. Junior's mother was against the idea, wanting her son to use his mind to solve his problems. Junior gets in some good kicks during the next fight with the bully. The kids watching cheer and the bully's friends run away. Junior and the bully eventually become friends.

The lead character, *Luke in The First Kid*, is rather nerdy. He is dressed in a suit and tie and has his hair slicked back. He is also a rather unsympathetic character since he is obnoxious to the staff and rather rude to his mother. The bully, Rob, calls Luke a "dork" and his dad a "draft dodger." He throws Luke's backpack down and pushes him. The boys fight as the crowd looks on. Rob hits Luke in the mouth, drawing blood. Against his mother's wishes, Sims, the bodyguard, sneaks Luke out to a gym for boxing lessons. In the next fight, Luke gives Rob a bloody nose. The movie ends with Luke and his new friends playing street hockey outside the White House.

In *Knockout*, the new boy, Matthew, incurs the wrath of Hector when he asks out Hector's girlfriend on a dare. Matthew's mother is against him boxing because her father was a great boxer. The boxing coach in the movies is not a bad guy but he does try to protect the bully because he is the club's best boxer. Matthew bonds with his stepfather when the stepfather supports Matthew's lessons. A janitor, Dan, helps train Matthew to box. Dan is later fired because of it. Although Matthew does not beat Hector in a decision, he does get invited to join the boxing team. Hector congratulates him after the match.

In *Sidekicks*, not only does the gym coach not stop the other boys from calling Barry names such as "retard," he calls him a "lady." Barry's teacher's uncle teaches him karate in his restaurant. Mr. Lee looks small, but he beats up a group of bikers who come in threatening to hurt Barry's dad and destroy his restaurant. Barry's father is a single parent. He has a very mild demeanor and is not very helpful when Barry gets bullied. When Barry starts to fight back against Randy, the coach is encouraging. With the help of the spirit of Chuck Norris, Barry is able to beat Randy in a karate tournament.

Cal's mother is also a single parent in *Legendary*. Billy, a bully in a letter jacket, throws a rock at Cal. Cal stands up to him and makes a comment about Billy's mother. Billy punches Cal, knocking him into the water where he hits his head. Tired of getting picked on, Cal checks out wrestling practice. Cal's deceased father and his brother were wrestling stars at the school. The coach pairs up Cal with Billy for a practice drill. Billy picks up and slams down Cal hard. The coach scolds Billy for being too aggressive. During the next round, Cal elbows Billy and they fight. The coach does not seem too concerned. There is a little trash talking between Cal and Billy at practice. Over time Cal starts winning his matches. Billy hassles Cal's date Luli at the school dance. When Cal unzips Luli's dress, Cal wrestles him to the ground. There appears to be no resolution beyond Cal getting the best of Billy.

Ken, in *Showdown*, likewise talks to the wrong girl and starts a feud with her boyfriend Tom. The vice principal in *Showdown* is rather incompetent. He is always showing up at the wrong times or somehow missing the bullying and other bad behaviors at the school. He instead focuses on littering and graffiti. In many of these movies, bystanders are part of a crowd at a sanctioned tournament. In *Showdown*, a crowd at school watches Ken and Tom fight. One boy in the crowd encourages Ken to stay down after he is knocked to the ground. The crowd backs away when Tom threatens them. Ken's instructor Billy is a former police officer who is now working as a janitor at Ken's school. Billy accidentally killed a man while making an arrest years before. Tom's karate instructor, Lee, is the brother of the man that died; therefore, he has a vendetta against Billy and tries to have him killed. When Billy defends Ken against Tom, Lee hits Tom for getting beat up by Billy. Ken ultimately beats Tom in a fight. After the fight, Lee steps in and punches both Ken and Tom. Billy beats Lee. The boys in Lee's school ask Billy to be their new sensei. In the end, Ken gets the girl.

Like *Showdown*, *The Sensei* is more violent than the other fight-back movies. In *The Sensei*, Mic is forced to study with a female sensei when the regular studio will not accept him as a student. Karen is the sister of the karate school owners. She has been denied her black belt because she is a woman. Mic is gay and an outcast as well. The bullying gets progressively worse. In *The Sensei*, the bullies put a noose around Mic's neck and start to drag him, stopping only when Karen comes to his defense. There is also a scene where the bullies go after Mic with a mop handle. The scene flashes to Mic in a hospital bed. A couple of Mic's friends begin to stand up for him against Craig, the main bully. Eventually, Craig's friends turn on him, too. As a final defeat, Mic chokes Craig until he was unconscious. During a court appearance, Craig insults the new judge and is sent away to a correctional facility.

THRILLERS

Thriller movies are for a more mature audience portraying extreme bullying, including gratuitous violence at times. The thrillers begin like regular bullying portrayals but quickly accelerate into mayhem, even murder.

The New Kids is a gruesome tale of extreme bullying. In a way it is a revenge-type movie because of the violent ways the bullies die. The tormenting begins when Abby rejects one of the bullies. He grabs her but she jabs him in the stomach. The boys then bet who can have sex with Abby first. When she continues to turn them down, they spit on her computer screen, destroy her uncle's property, and break in while Abby is taking a shower and throw a dead rabbit in the shower. Abby's brother, Loren, tries to stand up for her. He even breaks into one of the bullies' houses and holds him at knife point. He warns him to leave his sister alone and takes money to cover some of the damages they have caused. The bullies retaliate and beat up Loren and urinate on him. They eventually kidnap Abby. One of the guys drops his pants as though he is going to rape her. They pour lighter fluid on her and taunt her with matches. She fights back and runs away. They go after her with a gun. When they catch her again, one of the bullies starts to unzip her pants. The gang ties up Abby and Loren's uncle, threatens him with a pit bull, and eventually shoot the uncle, but not fatally. One of the bullies goes after Abby with a flaming gas hose, which Loren turns on the bully. The other bullies are killed by such gruesome means as falling off a Ferris wheel and decapitation by the roller coaster.

In a similar movie entitled *Bullies*, the Cullen family terrorizes a small town. The film was included here only because of the use of the term "bullies" in the title, which is a gross exaggeration. Mr. Cullen beats his daughter when she dates the new boy in town, Matt. One of the sons rapes Matt's mother. When the sheriff tells the Cullens they have gone too far and asks them to come along peacefully, they shoot the sheriff. In the end, Matt and his stepfather kill the father and sons in self-defense.

The In Crowd is set at an exclusive country club. The spoiled rich kids back from college are giving one of the staff, Adrien, a hard time. Adrien is on leave from a psych ward. The boys temporarily trap Adrien in the elevator as a prank. Brittany becomes jealous of Adrien and Matt, the tennis pro. When Brittany invites Adrien to a party, Kelly comments that they are drinking with the "help." Later, Kelly tries to warn Adrien about Brittany. Someone unscrews the bolt on the wheel of Kelly's scooter so she crashes. Brittany takes her sailing and pushes her overboard. Because Kelly hurt her leg in the accident, she drowns. Brittany also kills Adrien's psychiatrist and frames Adrien. Adrien escapes from the psych ward and tricks Brittany into confessing to the murders. The movie portrayed a little bit of mean but mostly evil. The story was set in a country club, pitting the rich against the poor and meeker members of the group versus the strong.

Confessions of Sorority Girls also begins with mean treatment and ends in murder. The main character, Sabrina, has a cold mother who preferred Sabrina's sister who is dead. At her sister's sorority house, Sabrina starts trouble. She steps on a mousy girl's toga sheet, leaving her in her bra and underwear. She blackmails her French professor into giving her a passing grade with a photo of her seducing him. She gets her roommate Rita's boyfriend, Mort, to sleep with her after she tells everyone her roommate's mother is in prison. Sabrina tells another boy that Mort raped her to turn the friends against each other. When the truth comes out, Sabrina goes after Mort and Rita with a baseball bat. She locks them in a bar and sets it on fire. The two get out alive and Sabrina is arrested.

REVENGE DRAMAS

Mean Creek is a slightly different kind of revenge movie in that a group of kids accidently kill a boy, George, who has been bullying the younger kids. The kids only plan on embarrassing George by taking his clothes and making him walk home naked. George, the bully, has learning disabilities and appears more socially awkward than a bully. George is so delighted that he was invited along with the rest of the kids, one of his victims, Sam, calls off the plan to humiliate George. When George finds out about the plan, he lashes out and says he hopes their fathers all get diseases and die. He also taunts one of the boys, Marty, about how Marty's father committed suicide. As the kids hold Marty back from attacking George, George accidently falls in the water and drowns.

In *Twelve and Holding*, Jacob and his twin brother, Rudy are being bullied by a group of boys, lead by Kenny. When the bullies chase them up into their tree house, Rudy pours urine on them. The bullies later set fire to the tree house, not realizing Jacob and Rudy are in there. Rudy is killed in the blaze. Jacob goes to visit Kenny who has been sent to juvenile detention. After many visits, the two appear to be civil. When Kenny is released, Jacob shoots Kenny and buries his body to avenge his brother's death.

The 2001 movie *Bully* (not to be confused with the 2012 documentary of the same name) is a gritty story about a group of victims who plot to kill their tormentor. What is unusual about the two main characters is that the bully, Bobby, is physically smaller than his victim Marty and from a higher economic, intact family. Bobby somehow coerces Marty into dancing at a teen amateur night at a gay club and performing phone sex with men. In a typical abusive relationship, Bobby hits Marty and then tells him he is his best friend. While Marty is having sex with his girlfriend, Lisa, Bobby comes in and hits them both with a belt and presumably rapes Lisa. While Bobby is having sex with another girl, Ali, he makes her watch a video of Bobby having sex with Marty. When Ali resists, he hits her and rapes her. Marty, Lisa, and Ali decide the only way to stop Bobby is to kill him. They collect money to hire a hitman. The movie takes so long to get the killing set-up that the effect of the bullying and rape has cooled. Marty and Lisa also include some teens who do not even know Bobby. While they plot the attack, the gang dance and joke until the hitman lectures them that killing is serious business. By the time of the killing, Bobby has almost become a sympathetic character.

Heart of America chronicles a Columbine-style revenge killing. A 23-year-old thug, Frankie, comes back to the school bleachers to reminisce with his brother and the rest of the younger punks about how he bullied and beat up other students, shown in black and white flashbacks. Frankie's younger brother has now become the bully. One of his victims, Daniel, talks about getting beat up, starting in the first grade. The scene flashes back to a couple of weeks earlier. The punks hit Daniel and his friend, Barry, with rocks and fists and kick them. They make Barry eat dog excrement. They pull the victims' pants down and force them to touch themselves until they get erections. While Barry's mother is concerned for him when he comes home with bruises, Daniel's father laughs and calls him "Danielle" and "pussy." Daniel begins to plot his revenge. He begins to collect guns. He enlists the help of Daura, who has also been picked on at the school. Daniel gets one of the punks alone in the bathroom. He pulls out his gun and makes him get on his knees. The punk laughs so Daniel shoots him. Frankie's younger brother tells his friend to leave Daniel alone just as Daniel shoots them. Daniel commits suicide. Daura shoots her overly critical teacher and the girlfriend of the boy she is sleeping with. Barry cannot go through with the plan and stays away from school that day. After the shootings, a news reporter assesses that violent movies, video games, parental neglect, the availability of weapons could all be factors.

In *Stephen King's It*, bullies are used to bond a group of kids together that will battle Pennywise, a demented clown. Henry and his gang of bullies chase the kids into places where Pennywise can isolate them. In the end, the bullies are brought to justice by another evil spirit.

In the movie *The Final*, a group of popular kids torment a group of unpopular kids. The mean girls make fun of a Goth girl, Emily. They point out that she was not invited to a party. When she asks them why they are being mean, they respond that they are just being honest. They mock her when she cries. Some other bullies mock an Indian student, Ravi, for his accent. They smash his camera and call him a "terrorist." When another student, Dane, confronts the bullies, they tell Dane that he cannot stop them. Dane gets the bullied students together to plan revenge. They drug the popular kids at a party and take them to a secluded location. When the popular kids wake up, they are chained together. Dane lectures the mean kids and bullies. He and some of the other bullied kids begin sadistic games. Emily orders Bridget to cut off all Bradley's fingers to save herself. Then she gives Bradley the option to cut off her fingers. He does it. When Bridget still won't cut of Bradley's fingers, Emily puts acid on her face. Dane vows that Bradley will never have sex or play football again before he stabs him in the back. Emily shoots Dane when he is about to kill Kurtis, a bullied kid who is trying to help the bullies. Emily and Jack say they have had enough. Emily announces they are all responsible. Sirens are heard in the back. Jack shoots Emily and then himself.

Learning Curve follows the experience of a substitute teacher, Mr. Walmsley. One of the bullies, Tony, threatens a boy, Joey, who overhears them talking about stealing Mr. Walmsley's wallet. Tony forces Joey to urinate in his pants. In order to save face, Mr. Walmsley breaks the plumbing so they are both completely wet. Joey gets detention rather than the boys who bullied him. An art teacher, Louise, is threatened by a boy, Davey, with a gun. She surmises that if she reports him, he will simply get detention. On the other hand, she is likely to get fired and or sued by Davey's parents. Even though she does not report the incident, Davey's parent sue her. Davey's girlfriend, Maria, gets jealous of Louise and beats her with a belt and kicks her. The teachers conclude that they are helpless against the mean kids and bullies. Mr. Walmsley plots a sophisticated revenge. He tricks the worst and most violent students into thinking they are getting grants to a summer program. He drugs their breakfast and takes them to a secluded place. He strips them naked and put them in electrified cages that play the song "Mickey" over and over. After a few days, they get blisters from the sun. He forces them to learn and to think about the consequences of their actions. Mr. Walmsley and Louise stage their deaths in a gas explosion. The students manage to escape and become famous. They are shown on a television talk show. They get agents and book deals.

HORROR OR SUPERNATURAL DRAMAS

In *Let Me In*, the bully, Kenny, calls Owen a little girl and snaps him with a towel. When Owen tries to fight back, Kenny and his cronies give him a wedgy until his underwear rips. Owen wets himself and the boys call him a "freak." Owen befriends a neighbor girl, Abby, who is a vampire. She advises Owen to fight back and tells him if that does not work, she will help him. Kenny threatens Owen that he is going to stick his hockey stick up his behind and throw him in frozen water. Owen hits Kenny in the side of the head with the stick instead, splitting his ear and sending him to the hospital. Owen gets in trouble in the principal's office. In retaliation, Kenny's brother, Jimmy, traps Owen in the gym. He holds Owen's head under the water in the pool. Suddenly the bodies of the other boys are being thrown into the pool. Apparently Abby has come to Owen's rescue.

Sometimes They Come Back centers around a flashback to bullies who cause the death of Jim's brother, Wayne. The bullies chase Jim and Wayne into a train tunnel. They demand money and steal Wayne's sneakers. When Wayne tries to fight back, one of the bullies pulls out a knife. In the scuffle that ensues, Wayne gets stabbed in the stomach. Just then a train is coming. Wayne tells Jim to run. Jim runs away with the bullies' car keys and the bullies are trapped and killed by the train. Decades later, the bullies come back from the dead to get even with Jim. Jim is now a schoolteacher who has a bully, Chip, in his class. When Jim tells the football coach that Chip is failing, Chip threatens Jim. The bullies begin to kill off Jim's students. They attempt to recruit Chip into their revenge plan but Chip warns Jim instead. The bullies kidnap Chip and chop him into pieces. Wayne's ghost comes back and is able to take the bullies to the other side where they can no longer harm Jim or his family.

Carrie is the classic revenge movie. Carrie's classmates and even some of her teachers are cruel to her. For example, when Carrie misses the winning point in volleyball, her classmates turn on her. One hits her in the head with her hat. Another tells her to "eat shit." In the shower, Carrie thinks she is dying because she is bleeding. She was never told about her period. When she asks her classmates to help her, they chase her back into the shower and throw tampons and napkins at her. When the mean girls, Chris and Sue, get in trouble for mistreating Carrie, they plan to retaliate. They convince Sue's boyfriend, Tommy, to take Carrie to the prom as a joke. They get Carrie elected prom queen only to dump a bucket of pig's blood on her during the crowning. Carrie locks all the doors with her mind. She begins to spray the crowd with the fire hoses. The principal gets electrocuted when he tries to grab the microphone. A teacher gets impaled with a window frame. The gym starts on fire. Two boys, who have escaped from the gym, are driving away. Carrie makes their car flip and explode into flames. When Carrie's abusive mother tries to kill her, Carrie sends knives to kill her mother. The house collapses in flames.

Lester is a tormented boy in the movie *Scarecrow*. A bitter teacher mocks him for having a drunk mother and living in a white-trash mobile home. At lunch, a bully pushes him and knocks his tray out of his hands. The rest of the kids moan and heckle him. They trip him in the hallway and call him a "little bitch." After getting humiliated at a party, Lester goes home and gets into a fight with his mother's boyfriend. Lester is killed and his body is left hanging in a cornfield. He comes back from the dead to get revenge on the teacher who mocked him by stabbing her repeatedly. He rips the heart out of one of the bullies and beats his mother's boyfriend to death with a frying pan.

The Toxic Avenger is a low-budget cult classic. Mop boy Melvin is tormented by the clientele at the gym where he works. The main group of bullies runs down people in the street with their car using a point system. There are extra points for kids under 12 and the handicapped. When they hit a boy on a bike, they back over his head to make sure he's dead. The bullies run out and take pictures. One of the women lures Melvin down to the pool with the promise of sex. When the lights come on, he's hugging a sheep. The whole gym is laughing at him. They chase him down the hallways. Melvin jumps out the window into toxic waste to get away from them. He turns into the Toxic Avenger. To save a police officer from thugs, the Toxic Avenger rips off their scalps and beats them bloody. He attacks a pimp who is trying to sell a 12-year-old. He goes back to the gym to get revenge on the woman who lured him into the pool. The crowds are conflicted. Even though the Toxic Avenger is killing, he appears to only kill bad people. The corrupt mayor, who is planning to put a toxic dump near the city's water supply, sends instructions to kill the Avenger. When the police and National Guard hunt the Avenger down, a group of kids stands in their way to protect him. The Avenger pulls the internal organs out of the evil mayor. The crowd cheers.

Even though *Tormented* is a British film, it fits into this subgenre of revenge bully movies. Darren was a bullied student who was driven to suicide. There is a website with footage of the bullies harassing Darren in the lunchroom and the shower. They push him on a girl. They play keep away with his inhaler. They laugh while he gasps. Darren comes back from the grave to get revenge. The bullies begin to argue and blame each other for

Darren's death. Darren stabs and kills one of the bullies and frames another bully who gets caught by the police holding the knife. Darren is about to get revenge on the abusive gym teacher when the movie ends.

Amidst the sci fi, *The Craft* is a revenge plot against the mean girls and mean boys in the school. The mean boys, Chris, Mitt, and Trey, and mean girl Laura pick on others' most vulnerable attributes. They make fun of Bonnie's scars. Laura describes Rochelle's "nappy" hair as pubic hair. When Sarah won't have sex with Chris, he tells everyone that she was a horrible lay. To get revenge, Bonnie makes Laura's hair fall out. Sarah casts a spell so that Chris will fall in love with her. The spell begins to backfire. Bonnie starts to regret making Laura's hair fall out. Chris gets so overwhelmed he nearly rapes Sarah. Nancy kills Chris for revenge. When Sarah tries to stop the other girls from doing more violence, they turn against her and try to get her to commit suicide. Sarah's powers win out in the end.

Conclusion

Bullying portrayals in film vary by the standard genres of comedies and dramas. Within the subgenres, bullies in movies targeted to younger viewers were represented in a range of venues from camp to sports teams to crime solving. Teen comedies tended to have stereotypical victims in addition to stereotypical bullies, neither of which require great effort to develop. Movies in this analysis lacked ethnic diversity and had few roles for females.

It was not the variation in bully portrayals in dramas that stood out; rather it was the range of subgenres of films that included bullying themes that was striking. Bullies were found in the sweetest coming-of-age stories and the most violent horror movies. Overall, the resolution of the films had a common theme. Generally the male victims fought back or got someone else to fight back against the bully. The bully was often bullied as strategy to get the bully to stop. Very little time was taken to problem-solve or reform the bully. Time restraints of a two-hour film may be a factor in developing complex storylines. Perhaps books and hour-long television series are better suited for more thoughtful resolutions.

4

Film Mean Girls

Mean girl portrayals in film span from comedies to dark dramas. While there is a noticeable dearth of mean girl portrayals in television situation comedies, mean girls are well represented in film, comedies in particular. While bullying behavior can be established quickly, the relational aggression of mean girls tends to develop more slowly over time and with more nuances. Platforms such as feature-length films and television serial dramas are perhaps better suited for portraying mean girls rather than the fast pace of a half-hour sitcom.

Comedies featuring mean girls include romance (e.g., *Pretty in Pink*), makeover (e.g., *She's All That*), and dark comedies (e.g., *Heathers*). An interesting subgenre of movies that emerged includes competitions, specifically musicals (e.g., *High School Musical*) and cheerleading (e.g., *Bring It On*). Overall, comedy and competition-themed movies appear to be more popular than dramas. Straight dramas in this analysis include both feature films (e.g., *Thirteen*) and made-for-TV movies (e.g., *Odd Girl Out*). The cable network ABC Family, for example, has taken the lead in producing television programs and movies addressing different aspects of the mean girl, from weight (e.g., *Fat Like Me*) to cyberbullying (e.g., *Cyberbullying*). I also included movies that featured adult mean girl behavior in this analysis. The most common theme for adult mean girls was wedding or class-reunion themes.

Mean-Girl Comedies

Comedies varied by age of the target audience. Younger mean girl movies include *Sleepover*, *Holiday in the Sun* starring Mary-Kate and Ashley Olsen, and *The Clique*. Comedies for older teens and adult audiences include the Lindsay Lohan movies *Mean Girls* and *Confessions of a Teenage Drama Queen*.

TWEEN COMEDIES

In *Sleepover*, Julie is getting ready to enter high school. Her best friend, Hannah, is moving away and wants to set up Julie in the social structure before she leaves. The mean girl in the movie, Staci, is rather mild in her attacks. Staci tells the overweight girl, Yancy, that her lawyer father can help her sue the diet company for not working. Staci comes up

56

with a scavenger hunt as an initiation for the new school year. The winning group gets the "cool lunch spot" next year. The positive outcome of the movie is that Yancy gets an attractive boyfriend in the end. Staci does go out with one of the geeky boys because he thinks she's a goddess. Flash forward to high school where Staci, Liz, and the other popular girls are having lunch by the dumpster because they lost the scavenger hunt. Overall, the mean girls do not learn much of a lesson and will likely to continue to be mean.

Holiday in the Sun is a Mary-Kate and Ashley Olsen production. The twins' father flies the family to the Bahamas for a vacation. Brianna, another rich daughter, butts in front of the girls in the hotel. Brianna proudly informs the twins that she gets whatever she wants. She sets her sights on a cute boy, Jordan, who is interested in one of the twins, Alex. Brianna manipulates Jordan into being her personal assistant since he works at the hotel. The girls and their friends are playing in the pool when Brianna complains about excessive noise, getting them in trouble. Jordan turns down Brianna in favor of Alex and justice is restored.

The movie *The Clique* is based on a popular teen novel of the same title by Lisi Harrison (2004). A distinct class structure is set up for this movie since Claire's father works for Massie's father and Claire's family lives in Massie's family's guest house. Massie and her friends give mean looks to Claire at school. They make her ride in the back of the car by herself. One of the other girls puts red paint on Claire's new white pants. The girls tease her about getting her period. Aleesha asks her if she's a bird because her clothes are so "cheap." In a similar theme as many other mean girl movies, Claire's dream is to be part of the mean girls. When Massie's mom invites Claire to a sleepover on Friday, Claire lies to her new friend Lane with whom she has made plans. Lane finds out and ditches Claire to become friend with Massie. Massie only wants to befriend Lane to be mean to Claire and to get to Lane's older brother. Claire gets on Massie's computer, assumes Massie's identity, and trashes the other girls in order to cause Massie to lose her friends. While temporarily at the top, Claire is shunned by the popular girls when they find out she tricked them. Claire makes up with Lane. Claire later saves Massie from public humiliation. In the end it is not clear if the truce will last. The one bright spot of *The Clique* is that Massie's mother is aware of her daughter's mistreatment of Claire. She at least tries to remedy the situation; however, meanness can be stealthy and difficult to detect.

TEEN COMEDIES

In the genre classic *Mean Girls*, the main character, Cady, begins at a new school as in many other movies and television shows. The Plastics, headed by Regina, dominate the school. Cady is shunned in the cafeteria and resorts to eating lunch in a bathroom stall. She bumps into Tina Fey's character, Ms. Norbury, making Ms. Norbury spill coffee on herself. Ms. Norbury pulls her sweater off, exposing her bra, quickly establishing her as rather incompetent. Cady is befriended by Goth Janice and gay Damian. The Plastics have spread rumors that Janice is a "dyke." Janice turns out to be mean in her own way. Examples of mean behavior include the Plastics calling a girl's mother and telling her it is Planned Parenthood and they have results for her daughter's pregnancy test. Regina baits Cady into a three-way call to say bad things about Gretchen, another one of the Plastics, as Gretchen listens. Cady works to dethrone Regina, while she herself is becoming more and more of a mean girl and rejecting her friends Janice and Damian. The one touching scene in the movie is when Ms. Norbury asks the girls raise their hands if they have ever had a girl say something bad about them behind their back. Then she asks if they have ever been the one to say those things. Everyone raises their hands. Ms. Norbury has everyone write out apologies. The exercise backfires when Gretchen writes that she is sorry that people are jealous of her. Janice also takes the opportunity to expose Cady.

A similarity between the book *Queen Bees and Wannabees* and the movie *Mean Girls* is that the meaner Regina is to Gretchen, the harder Gretchen tries to stay in the group. The one redeeming line in the movie was Cady's speech: "Calling someone else fat won't make you any skinnier. Calling someone stupid doesn't make you any smarter. And ruining Regina George's life didn't make me any happier. All you can do in life is try and solve the problem in front of you." However, at the end of the movie the new junior class Plastics walk by, a clear indication that social structure is inevitable and the gains were for nothing.

Mean Girls 2 is a made-for-TV movie sequel to *Mean Girls*. The actresses playing the roles are much younger and closer in age to their characters than the original. The premise of this movie is that tomboy Jo finds that her father has spent her college money. In order to pay for college, she makes a deal with Abby's father to befriend the socially awkward Abby. The mean girls, led by Mandy, drench Abby in food in the school cafeteria. They then take photos of Abby and post them on the web. They hit her car with paint balls. When Jo refuses Mandy's offer of "friendship," they put glue on Jo's scooter seat and play the video of Jo falling off her scooter on the school's television screens. Mandy also broadcasts Jo's first kiss and sabotages the science project Jo needs for a college scholarship. The Plastics put sugar and coffee in Jo's father's gas tank, thus ruining his engine. Mandy later tells Jo they did it so he would lose his job and house and they would have to move. Mandy plots to poison Abby's guests when she holds a party the same night as Mandy's birthday party. The final straw is when Mandy steals the money for homecoming and frames Jo. Thanks to a security camera, Mandy is caught and arrested.

Lindsay Lohan also stars in *Confessions of a Teenage Drama Queen*. Lola moves to suburban New Jersey from Manhattan. She does not appear to have the usual difficulty adjusting to a new school. Lola chooses a plain girl, Ella, over the popular girls, to be her friend. Lola feuds with one of the popular girls, Carla. Lola gets the lead in the school play, which is normally reserved for Carla. The two compete to see who can go to a sold-out concert. Carla convinces everyone in the school that Lola lied about attending the concert and after party. Lola goes into a drama depression. After a pep talk from Ella, Lola returns to the play. When Lola proves she was at the concert and left after the party, Carla slinks away and falls into a fountain. Everyone laughs but Lola gives her a hand to help her out. Lola and Carla's relationship is one of competition rather than mean girl and victim. The movie is slapstick and nowhere near reality. Ella keeps talking about the evil things Carla has done but there is little evidence. Lola is unusually confident and has little trouble adjusting to her new school. The movie presents a chance for the rich mean girl to demonstrate her superiorities by attending a sold-out concert and party for their favorite group.

Super Sweet 16: The Movie was based on the MTV reality show, *My Super Sweet 16*. It is the story of two lifelong friends with the same birthday. As they plan their 16th birthday party, they get increasingly competitive. A popular senior, Taylor, befriends Jacquie because her father is famous and can put the party on the cover of one of his magazines. She drives a wedge between the two friends. After a great deal of conniving behind each others' backs, the friends make up. They have their parties together. One point of the movie is that they use their party to raise money for charity. On the other hand, they both get expensive new sports cars for their birthdays. Sarah, who the movie portrays as environmentally conscious and worried about her father taking out a second mortgage for the party, appears to have no problem accepting the gift. The movie is nearly as superficial and morally bankrupt as the reality show.

Similar to the reality show, *Super Sweet 16: The Movie* continues the portrayal of the indulgent, weak father. Sarah's father cringes when he sees the bill but tells her there is nothing he would not do for her on her 16th birthday. Sarah overhears her father talking to someone on the phone about taking out a second mortgage. For the party, the dads make a video introducing themselves as the "checkbooks."

She Gets What She Wants is a comedy about a girl who claims she is a foreign exchange student from France and moves in with a family from Texas. "Genevieve" is really Clarissa, an old classmate of Starla's who is out for revenge. In the third grade, Starla talked Clarissa into kissing the back of an ice sculpture in the shape of a cow for good luck. When Clarissa's tongue got stuck, Starla ridiculed her. In the present, Starla is a cheerleader and pageant queen. She calls her two best friends "sluts" behind their backs. At school, Starla makes fun of a girl, calls her a lesbian, and asks if her perfume is C.K. Spam. In order to get revenge, Clarissa plays a tape where Starla calls the kids at school "losers" and "posers." She frames her by putting drugs and a knife in her purse. To counter Clarissa's revenge plot, Starla publicly apologizes and reveals Genevieve's real identity.

In another movie where the popular girl gets put in her place, *The Hot Chick* is a story about how Jessica gets switched into the body of a petty criminal. Jessica had previously pulled a cruel joke on an overweight girl. After the switch, Jessica apologizes to the girl for humiliating her. The girl helps to switch Jessica back. When she does switch back, it appears Jessica learned her lesson and will be nicer in the future.

The movies *Saved* and *Easy A* feature Christian mean girls who use their religious beliefs as a place of judgment rather than a spiritual belonging. *Easy A* and *Saved* spoof religious intolerance and celibacy clubs. The movie *Easy A* begins with a popular girl bumping into Olive, dumping her books. Marianne, the head of the celibacy club, spreads rumors about Olive having sex. Olive, instead of denying the rumors, decides to embrace them. She wears an A on her chest in homage to Hester Prynne from the *Scarlet Letter*. When Marianne's boyfriend lies and says that Olive gave him chlamydia, Marianne and her Christian group harass Olive in an attempt to get Olive to quit school. Marianne laments how hard it is to follow God's order to "love the whores and gays." *Easy A* also includes a subplot about a gay character, Brandon. Brandon is leaving the principal's office, bleeding after an apparent fight with the school bully. Brandon gets detention for calling the homophobic principal "fascist" after the bully goes unpunished. To avoid further bullying, Brandon gets Olive to pretend to have sex with him so he appears straight. While he is high-fived, she, however, is called a "dirty skank."

In *Saved*, it is the most religious girl that causes the most harm. The main storyline in *Saved* is that a girl named Mary has had sex with her boyfriend in an attempt to turn him "not gay" in the name of Jesus. When Mary becomes pregnant out of wedlock, Hilary Faye shuns her. At one point, Hilary Faye throws a bible at Mary and accuses her of being "jealous of my success in the Lord." Hilary Faye is also very judgmental of Cassandra, a rebellious Jewish student at the Christian school. Hilary Faye gets revenge on Mary and Cassandra for distributing pictures of when Hilary Faye was fat. She spray paints bad words on the school and frames Mary and Cassandra. When Hilary Faye is exposed, she claims she did because Jesus told her to.

ROMANTIC COMEDIES

Pretty in Pink plays on the issue of class differences. When the popular girls make fun of Andie's clothes, the teacher stops class and asks if there is a problem. Andie does not want to make trouble so she denies there is a problem. The teacher apologizes to Andie for the popular girls' behavior and assigns them special homework. In gym, Andie's friend tells the popular girls she hopes their breasts shrivel up and fall off. The gym teacher kicks her out of class. The popular girl then tells Andie to "eat shit." The next scene is of Andie in the principal's office. She tells the principal she is fed up with the way they (i.e., poor kids) get treated. He advises her that if she puts out signals that she does not want to belong, people will make sure she does not.

When Andie turns down Steff, the mean rich boy, he calls her a "bitch." Blane, Steff's friend, takes an interest in Andie. He even enters the section of the school grounds where the unpopular kids are relegated to talk to Andie. Steff confronts Blane about going "outside" and talking to Andie, whom Steff calls a "mutant." Andie's awkward friend, Duckie, gets thrown into the girls' restroom by the popular boys. When Blane takes Andie to a party, a popular girl tells her in a snarky tone, "Nice pearls; this isn't a dinner party." Blane stands up for Andie when another girl looks at her and asks if she is having a nightmare. The girl calls Blane a "faggot" and an "asshole." He apologizes to Andie and says he overestimated his friends. Steff calls Andie "trash" and warns Blane about how Blane's parents would react to him dating her. He also threatens Blane that if he keeps seeing her he is not going to have any friends. Even the salesperson is rude to Andie when she goes shopping for a prom dress. Under pressure from his friends and family, Blane backs out of his prom date with Andie. Later Blane figures out that Steff does not like Andie because Steff could not buy her. At the prom, Blane apologizes and tells Andie he loves her. She follows him to the parking lot where they make up and kiss.

In *Some Kind of Wonderful*, Keith falls in love with a popular girl named Amanda Jones. He later finds out that she is also from "the wrong side of the tracks." She has achieved higher social status because of her rich, popular boyfriend, Hardy, who drives an expensive car and treats her badly. As Keith is pumping gas for Hardy, Hardy honks the horn to be annoying. Hardy drops the money for the gas so Keith has to pick it up off the ground. Keith gets revenge by not putting the dipstick back after being made to check Hardy's oil. When Amanda breaks up with Hardy and accepts a date with Keith, her friend pressures Amanda to back out of the date. Hardy threatens Amanda that he will ruin her reputation if she does not take him back. Amanda tells Keith she does not want to be alone so she is willing to be with the wrong people. Hardy calls Amanda "trash" and orders his friends to take Keith outside to beat him up. Some biker friends of Keith's crash the party and take care of Hardy. *Valley Girl* has the reverse storyline of *Pretty in Pink*. Randy, a "hood" from Hollywood, falls for Julie, a "preppy" girl from the Valley. Julie's ex-boyfriend Tommy sees them together and gets Julie's friends to turn against her. Julie's friends tell her she will not be able to go to any more parties or be class representative if she stays with Randy. Julie is torn between popularity (Tommy) and love (Randy). Randy punches out Tommy at the prom. Randy and Julie run off together.

FEMALE MAKEOVER COMEDIES

The goal of the classic Hollywood makeover movie is to turn the ugly ducking into a beautiful swan so she can attract her Prince Charming. This makeover theme is also fodder for mean and bullying movies. It would appear that a simple makeover, creating a new look for the victim, would often reduce the teasing and exclusion; however, these movies do not always follow that plotline. The makeover in fact can intensify meanness if the target becomes more attractive than the mean girl and, therefore, a threat.

In *Never Been Kissed*, Josie, whose nickname in high school was "Josie Grossie," gets a chance at a redo when her editor assigns her an undercover job at a high school. A full-time reporter and college graduate, Josie is still shunned in high school, even when she elevates her look. Wrongs she endured in her first high school experience are still there when she returns. She only becomes popular when her brother goes undercover and joins her at the school. When she stops the mean kids from pulling a prank on a less popular girl, Aldys, the crowd shuns her. She confesses her identity and lectures them about being mean. In the end she gets her first kiss as the crowd cheers.

At the beginning of *The Princess Diaries*, Mia has frizzy hair, thick eyebrows, and nerdy glasses. When she gets up to speak for the school debate, she stammers. The popular kids giggle and whisper about her hair. She runs out the room to get sick. The crowd roars in laughter and applause. The cheerleaders make fun of her throwing up the next day. Mia gets a makeover after her fraternal grandmother reveals to her that she is a princess. Instead of becoming more popular after her makeover, things get worse. Her best friend tells her she looks ridiculous. She calls her an "a crap wannabe" and a sellout. The mean girls ask if her hair is a wig and accuse her of trying to fit in. A cute boy asks her to a beach party but sets her up to kiss her in front of the paparazzi. The girls in her class pretend to help her, but instead put her in yet a more compromising position for paparazzi by pulling down the tent while she is changing clothes. When a popular girl makes fun of Mia's friend, Jeremiah, Mia rubs an ice cream cone in her face. Mia gets her ultimate revenge by getting a boyfriend and becoming a princess.

In *She's All That*, Laney is the motherless, artsy, plain girl in school. On a bet, Zach, a popular boy from a well-off family, must make Laney into the prom queen. Laney is contrasted with Zach's former girlfriend, Taylor, who is the stereotypical popular girl who makes fun of Laney because her father cleans Taylor's family's pool. Zach begins to develop feelings for Laney and stands up for Laney's brother Simon against the bullies in the school cafeteria. The bully is going to make Simon eat pizza covered in pubic hair. Zach is so popular he does not have to bully and is not afraid to confront bullies. Zach makes the bully eat the pizza. Even after her makeover, Laney is not accepted by the popular crowd. Taylor tells Laney, "To everyone around here who matters, you're vapor, spam, a waste of perfectly good yearbook space. Nothing is going to change that." In the end, Laney does not become popular but she gets her Prince Charming.

In the movie *Teen Spirit*, mean girl Amber stuffs the ballot box to become prom queen. As she grabs the crown, she is electrocuted in a freak accident. In order to get to heaven, she must make the least popular student in school into prom royalty in one week. Lisa is already quite attractive, so Amber teaches her popularity tricks. Lisa sends out a fake email to take down a popular girl Carlita. Like most of these movies, Lisa gets swept up in her new social status and loses her old friends temporarily. She let her friend Raj take the blame for the fake email she sent out changing the date of Carlita's party. When Lisa gets to the prom with the help of her old friends, she confesses that she is the one who sabotaged Carlita's party. She then gives a speech about being popular. She asks the crowd how many of them felt excluded or did something stupid or insensitive to get in with the "in" crowd. She suggests they all be popular and get along with everyone. She then gets everyone to vote Raj, now the least popular kid in school, for prom king so that Amber can get into heaven. Crowds of kids are shown mingling together at the prom.

Cher, the lead character in the movie *Clueless*, is an endearing character because even if she is vain and classist, she does not appear to be aware of it. She describes her friend Dionne as being her friend because they both know what it is like to have people be jealous of them. Cher does mean girl things like manipulate her teachers into better grades and criticizes others' fashion senses. Cher and Dionne take on the new student Tai as a project. Tai starts to get lots of attention and is too busy to hang out with Cher. Tai is even mean to Travis, a nice boy who liked her before her makeover. In the end, Cher learns to not judge others and gets Tai and Travis back together.

Dark Comedies

Welcome to the Doll House is a dark comedy about an awkward seventh grader, Dawn. Generally, dark comedies feature a male lead, likely because it is very uncomfortable to see a girl bullied or there is an expectation that she will be the victim of mean girls. The film opens with a lunch room scene. Dawn scans the room looking for a place to sit. She goes from table to table. She finally finds another girl who is sitting alone. The cheerleaders come over and ask her if she is a lesbian. She says no but the girl she is sitting with calls her "a liar" and tells the cheerleaders that Dawn made a pass at her. The girls walk away laughing and chanting "lesbo, lesbo, lesbo." Lolita corners her in the bathroom and tells her she has to defecate before she will let her leave. Dawn asks Lolita why she hates her. She replies because Dawn is ugly. Above Dawn's locker someone has written "wiener dog sucks" and "woof woof." For many viewers, these scenes may be very difficult to watch.

Dawn overhears some boy bullies harassing a boy named Troy, trying to get him to admit he is a "faggot." They are physically holding him against his locker. Dawn stands up to the bullies and tells them to leave Troy alone. They laugh at her and call her "weiner dog" and ask her if she likes faggots. They punch Troy in the stomach and take off. Even Troy calls her "weiner dog" and tells her to leave him alone after she stood up for him. When Dawn asks an older boy about high school, he tells her it is better than junior high. He says, "They'll call you names but not as much to your face."

Brandon, yet another bully, harasses Dawn and her only friend, Ralphy, at the convenience store. He calls Ralphy a "faggot" and warns him that next year when Ralphy gets to junior high he is going to beat him up. Dawn stands up for Ralphy and walks out after Brandon knocks the slushy out of her hand. Later at school, Brandon warns her that at 3 o'clock he is going to rape her. He finds her in the library at 3. She tries to sneak out of the school but he grabs her. He holds a knife to her face and tells her to strip. They are interrupted by a janitor. He calls her on the phone and warns her she better meet him the next day. When she shows up, her takes her to an empty lot. He kisses her but then tells her he does not think there will be enough time to have sex. He threatens her that if she tells anyone that he really will rape her. A normally violent scene, it appears rather pathetic. Dawn does not appear scared of his rape threats. Perhaps she has been beaten down so many times that she is compliant. She may also interpret Brandon's actions as attention even when he pulls a knife on her.

Movies such as *Heathers*, *Bad Girls from Valley High*, and *Jawbreaker* involve the death of mean girls in dark comedic fashion. The plots here are unrealistic and create a comic effect that draws attention away from the real problem. *Heathers* begins with the mean girls playing a practical joke on an overweight girl, Martha. They write Martha a note pretending it is from a boy. When Martha goes to talk to the boy, everyone laughs at her. When Veronica, who is part of the Heathers, feels bad about the prank, Heather tells her it is an example of what it means to be a member of the most powerful clique in school. The geek squad is very stereotypical. Three out of four geeks are wearing glasses and one sneezes, spraying milk all over the table. When one of the geeks stands up to the bullies, they make him say, "I like to suck big dicks." When Veronica talks to a loner, Jason, the jocks get jealous and decide to try to scare him. One jock puts his finger in Jason's food and asks him if he's going to eat it. They tell him about the school's "no fags" policy. Jason pulls a gun and shoots. The gun is loaded with blanks. To get back at the jocks, Veronica and Jason kill them and make it look like they were lovers who shot each other in a suicide pact. Veronica wants out of the Heathers. When she fantasizes about killing Heather, Jason takes her seriously and slips Heather drain cleaner. They forge a note and make the death look like suicide. When Martha tapes a suicide note to herself and walks into traffic, the remaining Heathers joke that the suicide was just another example of a geek trying to imitate the popular kids and failing miserably. The new Heather and Martha were childhood friends, but now Heather claims that the world would be a better place if "every nimrod would off themselves."

In the movie *Bad Girls from Valley High*, the Huns rule the school. A Hummer driven by tough guy Gavin smashes into the back of a nerd's car to take his parking space. He tells the nerd he is parking in the wrong part of the lot and walks off unapologetic. The Huns volunteer at a nursing home to make themselves look better to outsiders; however, they are mean to the patients and steal from them. The Huns are harboring a dark secret. In a flashback, Charity is confronted by the Huns because she was dating the wrong boy, Drew. They tie her hands and put a pillow case over her head. As she is running away, she accidently falls off a cliff. When the new exchange student, Katarina, is also interested in Drew, they invite Katarina shopping so they can gently tell her not to date him. Danielle begins by pressuring Katarina to spend lots of money even though Katarina is poor. As a counterattack, Katarina switched credit cards with Danielle and runs up ridiculous totals. The Huns determine that Katarina is really Charity's ghost. They plot to kill Drew so Charity's ghost will be at peace. One of the women at the nursing home is actually Charity's grandmother. She poisoned the chocolates the Huns stole from her. The movie ends with two of the Huns', Danielle and Tiffany's, funeral. Danielle and Tiffany wake up in what they think is heaven. One of the nerds shows up as the devil, assuring them they are not in heaven.

Jawbreakers is about a stunt gone bad. On her seventeen birthday, the other girls kidnap Liz as a practical joke. Courtney, the leader, puts a jawbreaker in Liz's mouth and tapes her mouth shut so she cannot scream. Liz ends up suffocating to death in the trunk of the car before they can get to their destination. The girls are not remorseful, except for Julie. Julie decides to leave the group. When an unpopular girl named Fern finds out about the coverup, Courtney offers her popularity in exchange for her silence. They change Fern's name to Vylette and give her a makeover. Vylette stands up to Courtney, thinking that she now has the power. When Courtney outs Vylette as Fern, the kids at the school torment her. Julie comes to rescue Fern. The mean girls call them "carpet munchers." A recording of Courtney admitting to killing Liz is played just as Courtney is getting crowned prom queen. Courtney is heard saying, "I killed Liz. I killed the teen dream, deal with it." The crowd turns on her and call her "murderer," "whore," and "bitch."

Overweight-Themed Comedies

Movies that use a character's weight as an object of ridicule are most likely meant to exaggerate the mean behavior. Not only are the overweight characters in movies such as *Queen Sized*, *To Be Fat Like Me*, and *Heavyweights* struggling with self-acceptance, they are confronted by some not-so-nice characters who feel superior. Because weight is seen as something someone can control, it makes an easy and acceptable target for bullies and mean girls. The notion that it simply takes self-control to stay thin makes those without weight problems feel superior. A long history of laughing at heavy comedians has perhaps conditioned viewers to find laughing at fat jokes acceptable. The audience member then participates guilt-free in the bullying.

The issue of weight is handled in interesting ways beyond the obvious punch lines. For example, the television show *Huge* features kids at fat camp. Unlike camp movies where the heavy character is the exception, these characters are all struggling with their weight. In the battle of hierarchy, the objects of ridicule in the outside world become the perpetrators of the same meanness they have likely experienced. One of the female characters, Amber, who has a pretty face and is nearer a "normal" weight, is the object of ridicule by other jealous campers. Wil, the main character who is heavier and thus jealous of Amber, steals Amber's shorts at night and puts them in the dryer to shrink them to make Amber think she is gaining weight.

In *Queen Sized*, an overweight Maggie overcomes the odds and is elected homecoming queen even though some kids nominated her as a joke. Maggie gets swept up in her new popularity. She angers her friends by not acknowledging their help in her getting elected. However, even getting voted as homecoming queen does not stop the teasing at school. In the end, Maggie triumphs over her persecutors giving a heartfelt speech at the homecoming football game telling everyone that labels are not meaningful.

To Be Fat Like Me is a made-for-TV movie in the after-school-special tradition. Alyson is a thin and popular girl headed for college on a softball scholarship until she gets injured. To win a journalism scholarship, Alyson wears a fat suit and attends a different school to get reactions from other students. She is surprised to find out how cruel and insensitive people can be. She scolds her friends for their behavior and gives a speech about her experience being treated poorly because of her weight.

In *Heavyweights*, the boys at a weight loss camp joke that since they are all fat, there is no one to pick on them. The popular, athletic kids from a nearby rich camp sneak across the lake at night and graffiti "Camp Hopeless" and "Fat Tub of Lard" on the dock. One of the rich kids yells at a heavy camper who gets hit by a pitch, "Don't blubber chubber." The heavy campers get revenge by beating the rich kids in the camp relay. Although the biggest bully in the film, Tony the camp director, proclaims to care for the health of the boys, he is only trying to promote his weight loss program info-mercial. Having been a fat kid himself, Tony should have had more empathy. In retaliation for the bullying, the boys work to destroy Tony's self-esteem. The campers reenact the cruelty Tony experienced as a fat kid. Tony eventually has an emotional breakdown and is relieved of his duties.

The Fat Boy Chronicles follows Jimmy as he tries to survive high school. The other boys tease Jimmy about having a "D cup." Through hard work, Jimmy starts to lose weight and gain confidence. His bully actually becomes his friend after Jimmy tutors him. The story is sincere and uplifting while maintaining some realism. The kids in the cafeteria cheer as Jimmy has his first kiss.

SORORITY-THEMED COMEDIES

The Greek system is often used as a venue for meanness and exclusion. Entrance into the group is used to compel otherwise nice people to do mean things to others. Sydney, the title character in *Sydney White*, is a motherless girl heading to college. Rachel, the student body president, is a stereotypical blonde driving a sports car. Rachel gets jealous when Tyler, the cool fraternity president, becomes smitten with Sydney. Rachel vows to make pledging very difficult for Sydney. Rachel, in stereotypical mean sorority girl fashion, goes through each pledge and points out their flaws. The other girls say very little and look at Rachel with fear. Rachel warns Sydney that she is last person Sydney wants to mess with. Rachel gets the sorority pledges to get the geeky boys to strip for what they think is a hot tub party. They turn on the lights exposing them to the rest of the party. The popular fraternity members are equally as shallow and mean. One of the brothers at the cool fraternity throws a football at the head of a geeky boy. Sydney has to snatch it before it hits him.

Sydney gets kicked out of the sorority for lying about her father being a plumber. However, she gets all the disenfranchised groups on campus to back her against the oppressive Greeks. One by one, everyone stands up and proclaims themselves "dorks." Everyone from band geeks, ROTC, Goths, Hasidic Jews stand with her. In the end, Rachel is stripped of her sorority status.

Sorority Wars is a less comical, more dramatic, movie about the daughters of former Delta sorority sisters, Lutie and Summer. The grown women are still concerned with being selective to make sure the legacy of their sorority is preserved. Katie, Lutie's daughter, and her friend Sara are pledging Delta. Katie decides she fits in better with another sorority, Kappa, which is less shallow. Katie overhears Gwen, Summer's daughter and head of pledging for Delta, talking about freezing out a pledge and putting down Katie and Sarah behind their backs. Gwen threatens Katie if she pledges Kappa. Other students overhear Katie accusing Gwen of breaking rush rules. Katie gets called to testify to the Greek counsel about the allegations. Sara, wanting to be a Delta, lies and contradicts Katie's testimony. The counsel cancels Delta's big house formal. Someone writes "ugly slut" and "lying bitch" on Katie's door and makes threatening phone calls to punish Katie. Instead of taking Katie's side, Katie's mother scolds Katie for tainting herself and making the mother look bad. The Deltas tamper with the food at Kappa's formal and make everyone vomit. Eventually Lutie comes around and supports her daughter in the trivia portion of the sorority competition. The Kappas beat Deltas. While Summer berates Gwen for losing, Gwen congratulates Katie on the win.

Competition Movies

Competitions are prime arenas for mean tactics and relational aggression. Cheerleading, musicals, dance, sports, and Greek organizations appear to lend themselves to bad behavior. Having a limited number of available spots on a team or cast often makes competitions personal. There is also a great deal of status in the captain position or lead role so the stakes are high to the players. Class may be an issue since the more well off girls can better afford lessons and training to improve skills. In the Greek system, it appears that status and wealth are particularly important. Much like the sports movies referenced in the bullies in film chapter, these movies use competition as the catalyst for bad behavior. Television chapters also include analysis of competition shows such as *Glee*, *Make it or Break it*, *Hellcats*, and *Greek*.

MUSICAL-THEMED COMPETITIONS

The basis of *High School Musical* is the romantic relationship between Troy and Gabriella. Sharpay, the spoiled girl, is determined to break them up and get Troy all to herself. Sharpay uses her family's wealth and connections to get what she wants. Her twin brother, Ryan, participates in her plots; however, he comes across as a more sympathetic character who is more likely to turn good. Unlike other new kids in school, Gabriella appears to have no problem, aside from Sharpay, fitting in. Sharpay appears to have influence with the school administration and rigs it so that the musical callbacks are at the same time as basketball game and scholastic decathlon so Troy and Gabriella cannot try out. Her plan fails. In the musical number at the end of the movie, Sharpay and Ryan join in the singing and dancing even though Gabriella got the lead.

In *High School Musical 2*, Sharpay uses her family's influence with the manager of the club where Troy and Gabriella are working for the summer. She tries to get Gabriella fired while trying to manipulate Troy with promises of a college scholarship. In *HSM 2*, she badgers and bosses around a grown man, the manager of the country club her parents own. She is bossy and condescending to the waitstaff. The lesson is perhaps that if someone with such wealth and power can bring a grown man to his knees, what chance does a girl have in fighting back? She is also bossy with her mother, who is rather airheadish and ignores Sharpay for the most part. Sharpay plays "daddy's girl" with her father. In *High School Musical 3*, Sharpay has met her match. She is challenged by an even more conniving girl who wants to take her place as leader of the drama club. The turn of events elicits some sympathy for Sharpay with the audience. The one redeeming quality of Sharpay is her affection for her brother, although even that is rarely seen.

Sharpay's character in *Sharpay's Fabulous Adventure* is no longer in high school; however, I included the movie because of the chance for fans to see her evolution from mean spoiled girl to a young woman. She thinks a New York casting agent is interested in her. Later she finds out that they are just interested in her dog. After promising her parents that she will come back home if New York does not work out, she works as an assistant to a big star, Amber Lee, who is mean to her. In the end, Amber Lee's true colors emerge and Sharpay gets the lead role in the production.

Musical competitions appear to be a favorite subgenre for young girls. Competitiveness appears to bring out the mean in even nice girls. In *Cheetah Girls*, four best friends are trying to get a record contract. The girls quarrel as they work on decisions about their first demo recording session. They accuse Galleria of hogging the spotlight and being bossy. When Galleria leaves the group, the record producers tell the other girls that she is easily replaced. After a wild chase of Galleria's dog, the girls make up and win the school talent competition. While the movie does not contain the stereotypical mean girl, it does demonstrate how female friends can turn on each other.

Camp Rock is a Disney movie featuring their teen music recording artists such as the Jonas Brothers and Demi Lovato. Lovato, who plays Mitchie, gets to go to Camp Rock at a discount since her mother is going to be the cook. Mitchie feels embarrassed for being the cook's daughter. The implication is that Mitchie's family is poor; however, funds are stretched because Mitchie's father is expanding his store and her mother is starting a cater-ing business. Tess, the diva who "runs the camp," is the daughter of a famous singer. Tess berates her backup singers/friends. Tess and her cronies appear to look down on Mitchie when she tells them her father owns a hardware store so she lies about her mother's career. Tess invites Mitchie to sit with her in the VIP section of the dining room. Tess talks Mitchie into being a backup singer. Tess dictates to the other girls what to wear although she wears something different to make herself stand out. Tess sings, "I'm too cool to know you. I'm too cool for you." Everyone cheers when she finishes. Caitlyn is the independ-ent girl who tries to warn Mitchie about Tess and the price of popularity. She gets into a squabble with Tess, who dumps her spaghetti on her. When the two get into a food fight, Caitlyn gets in trouble. Mitchie does not stand up for Caitlyn. During Caitlyn's perform-ance, Tess screams, pretending to see a snake. When Tess pantomimes, "Whatever, major loser" to Caitlyn, Mitchie puts Tess in her place. Tess gets jealous when she sees a cute boy talking to Mitchie. She smiles deviantly when she discovers that Mitchie's mom is the cook for the camp. Tess outs her. When Mitchie stands up to Tess, Tess frames Mitchie and Caitlyn for stealing her charm bracelet. Tess's backup singers have had enough and leave her. One of them performs a solo act, singing about being a "nice girl" who does not speak out for herself. Tess becomes nice to the girls after her mother disappoints her and takes a cell phone call during Tess' performance. Tess makes up with her friends and Mitchie gets the cute Jonas brother.

CHEERLEADING-THEMED COMPETITIONS

Bring It On and subsequent sequels have many similarities although the first was the only one to be released in theaters. The rest were released straight to video. In the origi-nal movie the cheerleaders from the urban team are crass; however, they are portrayed as honest and straightforward. There is name calling back and forth. The minority girls call the preppie team members "Raggedy Ann" and "Buffy." There appears to be no outwardly meanness toward the non-cheerleaders at the school. Perhaps ignoring them completely is quite mean. The aggression is directed at the other team as well as the girls' own team-mates. Two of the football players hassle the male cheerleader but it is fleeting. The mean girls, Courtney and Whitney, are in a constant struggle to overthrow Torrance as captain. They call her a slut when it is announced that she will be the captain.

In *Bring It On Again*, there is an internal rivalry between members of the same squad for head cheerleader. Although this version takes place in college, I included it because of the series. There is also little difference in the way the characters act between college and high school. The squad rules out potential cheerleaders, describing them as "too fat, too dorky, psycho, snaggle tooth, eczema, too gay, and not gay enough." The head cheerleader, Tina, berates the squad for their eyebrows and rear ends. Tina tells Whittier she could be head cheerleader some day but she has to dump Monica as a friend. Because they are so mean, Monica starts her own squad. The two squads must compete to see who will rep-resent the school at the big competition. Tina and Monica have a cheer off, which leads to hair pulling and slapping. The team of misfits wins over the mean girls.

In *Bring It On: All or Nothing*, a few of the cheerleaders talk about Brittany getting captain over Winnie. Amber calls Winnie "a bitch from hell." The next scene they are walking arm in arm. Winnie makes fun of Brianna's weight. She said if there was ever a case for bulimia, it's Brianna. Brittany's father moves the family from Beverly Hills to Crenshaw Heights, a less than desirable place. When Brittany sits at a lunch table with the other white girls at her new school, they all get up and walk away. Brittany works her way in and makes the cheerleading squad. When Amber calls out Winnie for making racist remarks about the Crenshaw Heights team, Winnie calls Amber "Crouching Tiger" because she is Asian. Crenshaw Heights ends up winning the competition.

Bring It On: In It to Win It takes place at cheer camp, combining two standards of mean girl and bully movies—competition and sleep-away camp. Campers are divided between those whose parents can afford camp and those who are on scholarship. When several members are injured, the two teams must merge. They quickly begin to turn their attention to another rival squad. In the end, they pull together and beat the other team.

In *Bring It On: Fight to the Finish*, Lina has to change schools when her Latina mother marries a rich white man with a daughter. Unlike Brittany in *Bring It On: All or Nothing*, Lina is going from a poor school to a rich school. Cheerleader Avery has broken off and started a new squad because her school did not make her head cheerleader. Avery calls Lina "Dora the Explorer." Avery makes reference to drive-bys and chickens in the yard and many other Latino stereotypes. When Avery calls Lina's stepsister Skyler a "sea monkey," Lina stands up to her. Lina proposes they compete in the spirit championship as an all-star squad. When Lina's squad wins the competition, the only thing Avery can do is cry.

Teen Mean-Girl Dramas

Although most of the examples of mean girls have some element of comedy, there are some dramatic movies showing relational aggression by adolescents. In *American Girl Chrissa*, ten-year-old Chrissa is the new girl at school. The head of the mean girls, Tara, purposely bumps into Chrissa and stabs her with her pencil. Tara steals Chrissa's permission slip so she has to sit out of swim practice. After practice, Tara steals Chrissa's clothes and puts them in the trash. Tara also targets a poor girl named Gwen whose father died and who is temporarily living in a shelter with her mother. Tara pretends to be nice and offers to cut Gwen's bangs but purposely cuts them too short. She then insults Gwen by telling her, "Now you really think look like a homeless person." The mean girls send Gwen a valentine reading, "Roses are red, Violets are blue, You're the loser girl and no one likes you...ha ha just kidding." When the bullying becomes evident, the principal and teacher devise a plan. The teacher rearranges the seats, splitting up the mean girls. This action only makes Tara more angry. The trio of mean girls is perfectly nice in front of the teacher. Tara posts an annonymous message on the swim team website speculating about Chrissa having a contagious disease. The swim coach confronts the team and makes them all clean when no one confesses to posting the comment. He threatens to cancel the season if it happens again.

At school, Chrissa suggests to the teacher that they do their fourth-grade project on bullying. Slowly almost everyone in class raises their hands when asked if they have ever felt bullied. Even Tara raises her hand. After Chrissa beats Tara at the swim meet, she tells her that if they work together, their relay team can win. Tara suggests to the coach that Chrissa swim anchor since she is the fastest swimmer, for the good of the team. Tara gives her some tips to be faster. After they win, they hug. The movie ends with a message about how to deal with bullying, how not to keep it a secret. The class posts words in a "friendship arch" around the school such as "courage," "forgive," and "strength." Tara chose "acceptance." Even though the adults intervene and punish Tara, she keeps doing bad things. There is lesson after lesson in this movie. Each solution doesn't automatically work, although the actions are kept pretty civil. The girls in this movie are still fairly young, fourth grade, but the message of relational aggression is very strong. Generally, television shows are set in middle schools and movies in high schools for mean behavior. This film marks a difference in social status than other young-girl-bully movies. The girls are starting to flirt with boys as well as care about hair and clothing. They are also using more indirect methods of meanness and exclusion.

Odd Girl Out is the story of an unhealthy friendship between two old friends Vanessa and Stacey. Stacey gets a new friend, Nikki, who is jealous of Vanessa. Nikki and Stacey pressure Vanessa to shoplift. When Nikki sees Vanessa talking to a boy who Stacey likes, Nikki tells Stacey that Vanessa was flirting with him. The girls gather around and call her a "slut." They start talking about how hideous her clothes are. They refuse to allow her to sit at their lunch table. One girl says "slut" under her breath. Stacey stays silent and tells Vanessa they will talk later. At soccer practice, Nikki calls Vanessa a "slut" and a "whore." The relational aggression begins to escalate. Vanessa gets a text that says, "V thinks she is all that...but EVERYONE really HATES her." More girls laugh at her at lunch as she sits by herself. One of the girls shows them an online video of Vanessa eating and getting fat. When Vanessa asks Stacey if she is mad at her, Stacy tells Vanessa she is being too sensitive. When Vanessa goes to email Stacey her English homework, she sees that she is no longer on Stacey's "buddy list." A popup appears, taking her to a "Hating Vanessa" website. Vanessa hides in a bathroom stall at school. The mean girls see her bag so they make fun of her hair and weight, knowing Vanessa can hear them. Nikki tells everyone Vanessa shoplifted and that Vanessa is poor. Stacey stands by and lets it happen. Vanessa starts skipping school. Eventually Vanessa has a breakdown and takes some pills. A neighbor boy takes video as the paramedics take Vanessa out in a stretcher to an ambulance and uploads the video to the Internet. The girls at school watch at the video and call Vanessa a "loser." Stacey continues to keep up the "still friends? Best friends" farce with Vanessa. Later, Nikki and Tiffany read out loud the transcript of the conversation Vanessa had with Stacey online. Vanessa finally stands up to Stacey and calls her fake. She tells Stacey that she is even worse than Nikki because they are supposed to be friends. The bystanders, who have been silent the whole movie, now clap.

Vanessa's mother talks to Stacey's mother about the trouble the girls are having. At first, they decide that it is just something that happens at that age. Vanessa finally shows her mother the printout of the bad things the girls are saying about her. Her mother goes to the principal who tells her there is nothing she can do since it is only verbal. After Vanessa's suicide attempt, the principal begins to take the matter seriously. *Odd Girl Out* is an adaptation of the book of the same name by Rachel Simmons. It is a much truer representation of the book than *Mean Girls* is to *Queen Bees and Wannabees*. The movie is a mix of face-to-face and online bullying. It came out the year after *Mean Girls*. *Odd Girl Out* was a made-for-TV movie with younger, less well-known actresses.

Cyberbullying, another ABC Family movie released in 2011, is about the cruelty of online postings. Taylor's school has an online site named "cliquesters." Someone hacked into Taylor's account and posted her status as "I'm a naughty bad girl. Someone should spank me." Taylor's mother tells her to shut down her profile. It turns out it was Taylor's brother and his friend who changed her profile as a practical joke. A school on Monday,

Lindsay and the popular girls start spreading rumors that Taylor has gone all the way and was with 10 guys over the weekend. A sympathetic poster with the screen name James defends Taylor. Thinking James really cares about her, Taylor discloses all kinds of personal information like her dad cheated on her mom. Later, James posts that Taylor slept with him and gave him the clap. Taylor's friend Samantha confesses she set up the account because she was mad at Taylor. Although Samantha closed the account, others continue to post hurtful things. An anonymous source posts a video of someone with a mask of Taylor's face calling Taylor a "dirty whore." The person has a pillow stuffed under her dress to make her look pregnant. A distraught Taylor posts a video of herself saying that she is done and "goodbye." Taylor is about to take pills when Samantha, having seen the video, and Taylor's mother arrive to stop her. Lindsay posts a message that if Taylor did kill herself she would not cry. Someone calls the video hilarious. Now Samantha is also getting harassed online for posing as James. When Taylor confronts Lindsay in the lunchroom, most of the bystanders clap.

In a vast majority of television and movie representations, adults are unhelpful or actually make things worse. In this case, Taylor's mother takes the problem seriously and discusses it with the principal. The principal tells her he cannot figure out what to do since he cannot control what kids do at home. He explains that he needs guidelines from the school board. The movie features a support group for kids who are being cyberbullied. The moderator of the group gives advice to the participants (and to the audience watching at home) what to do if they are victims of cyberbullying. The senator in Taylor's district declined to get involved at first. After Taylor and Samantha tell their story to a reporter, the senator reconsiders and introduces a bill about cyberbullying.

In the movie *Thirteen*, Tracy gets involved with a girl named Evie, which spirals into a very abusive relationship. Tracy is so desperate for Evie to like and accept her, she shoplifts and smokes pot. The two become inseparable. Evie tells Tracy she loves her. Evie tries to pressure Tracy into a threesome with an older guy, but Tracy refuses. When Tracy's mother sends Evie home, Evie starts telling rumors about Tracy. Another girl believes the rumors and threatens to beat up Tracy. When Tracy's mother finds Evie's stash of drugs and money in Tracy's room, Evie turns on Tracy and her mother and tells them their house stinks. It is a sad story of an abusive relationship. Evie treats Tracy badly but tells her she loves her. Tracy is so desperate, she endures the abuse. Tracy's mother learns that Tracy needs a mother and not another best friend and begins to pay more attention to Tracy's behavior.

On a bet, Greg has sex with a virgin and videotapes it for proof in the Lifetime movie *Betrayed at 17*. Greg begins to actually like the girl. His vindictive ex-girlfriend, Carly, finds the recording on his phone he made as proof for the bet and sends it out to the whole school. When the girl finds out, she runs into the street to her death. Greg records Carly confessing that she sent the video. Before he can turn in the recording, Carly gets her father's gun and confronts him. He tries to wrestle the gun away but is shot and killed. Carly is eventually caught. What could have been a cautionary tale about cyberbullying turned into a psycho drama.

Cruel Intentions is an even darker drama that takes place at an elite prep school. Catherine is the student body president. She manipulates her stepbrother, Sebastian, offering him sex in return for doing her dirty work. She works to destroy Cecile when Catherine's boyfriend falls for Cecile. Catherine then makes a bet with Sebastian to have sex with a virginal girl named Annette. When Sebastian falls in love with Annette, Catherine gets jealous and sets out to destroy them. To save Annette from Catherine, Sebastian breaks up with her. Catherine lies to Ronald, Cecile's boyfriend, telling him that Sebastian has had sex with Cecile. Ronald and Sebastian fight. As Annette tries to break it up, she is pushed into the street. Sebastian pushes her out of the way of an oncoming car and is killed. To get revenge, Annette distributes copies of Sebastian's journal outlining all of Catherine's bad deeds.

Adult Mean-Girl Comedies

The movies featuring adult bullies were chosen because they use childish tactics to bully or be mean. The adult movies included are all comedies, likely because comedy implies a silliness of adults acting like children for humorous effects. Weddings and class reunions appear to be popular venues for exposing past mean girls. These events are reasons for people from the past to get together and reminisce. Opportunities for revenge are ripe for comedy.

In *My Best Friend's Wedding*, Julia Roberts' character, Julianne, sets out to break up her best friend Michael's engagement to Kim. She devises a series of devious mean-girl plots to get the couple to fight. She even threatens Michael's career in her schemes. The one good thing of about the movie is that it does not reward Julianne for her bad behavior in the end. Julianne apologizes to the couple, Michael marries Kim, and Julianne has to settle for a dance with her gay friend at the wedding reception.

Bride Wars is an example of the insanity around weddings and the emergence of the bridezilla. Two lifelong BFFs, Emma and Liv, are mistakenly scheduled to have their weddings on the same day. They plot to sabotage each other's ceremony. Emma tampers with Liv's hair dye. Liv starts a rumor that Emma is pregnant. The movie ends with the two making up but not until after they have a girl fight in the aisle of the wedding venue. Fletcher, Emma's fiancé, is the one person who tries to bring the women to their senses and criticizes their behavior. He is rewarded by being left at the altar. Emma decides she is no longer the woman with whom Fletcher fell in love.

In *Revenge of the Bridesmaids*, a group of women, Abigail, Rachel, and Parker, plot to get back at Caityn, the rich mean girl who bossed them around as children. Olivia, Caitlyn's mother, is particularly mean to the women. When Abigail and Parker come back to town for an anniversary party, they find Caitlyn is engaged to Rachel's love Tony. In order to destroy Caitlyn's wedding, Abigail and Parker worm their way into Caitlyn's wedding party. They make space by telling two of the bridesmaids to comment on Olivia's drinking. When they do, the women get kicked out of the wedding party, leaving room for Abigail and Parker. Abigail and Parker change the flower order to flowers Caitlyn is allergic to and put her dress in a wood chipper. To make the bridesmaids look less evil and vindictive, producers of the movie included a subplot that Caitlyn is faking a pregnancy to get Tony to marry her. The bridesmaids manage to record Caitlyn confessing to the plan. Caitlyn is primarily marrying Tony because her family needs Tony's family's money. Tony, who is suspicious that Caitlyn is marrying him for his money, lies to her and tells her his family lost their fortune. Caitlyn leaves him at the altar, freeing him up to marry Rachel. Caitlyn's level of meanness and duplicity needs to be at a certain level for the retribution to be acceptable and thus comical.

The phrase "The claws are about to come out" was used to promote the movie *You*

Again. The film begins with a flashback. The main character Marni is being carried down the hallway of her high school as a massive group of popular kids sing, "We are the Champions." They deposit her outside the school and lock the door as they are chanting "loser" at her. As a freshman, she is shunned, as no one will let her sit with them at the lunch table. To make matters worse, her mother, Gail, was prom queen and head cheerleader in high school. Eight years later, Marni is gorgeous and a successful PR vice president. Gone are the stereotype characteristics of the nerd girl: bad hairdo, glasses, unstylish clothes, blotchy skin, and braces. Now, one of the girls responsible for her high school misery, Joanna, is engaged to Marni's brother, Will. Marni sets out to break up the couple. At the rehearsal dinner, Marni invites Joanna's ex-boyfriend. Marni also shows a video of Joanna bullying her in high school. Will breaks off the engagement. After a heart-to-heart talk with Joanna, Marni talks Will into giving Joanna another chance. *You Again* also demonstrates meanness that spans generations. As they get older, these women to not let go of past feuds. The women are all shown in a ridiculous light: petty, vengeful, and competitive. The two younger women are scolded by Marni's older brother and the mother and daughter are not only scolded but "grounded" by Marni's father. The two young male leads are also shown in an incredible caring light; however, neither of them helped Marni with the bullies when they were in high school. Charlie and Will simply smile at Marni as she is being harassed by bullies. The director of the film appears to purposely establish this fantasy of the all-good men and their all-nasty women.

In flashbacks in the movie *Romy and Michele's High School Reunion*, Christie, one of the popular girls, comes over to Romy and Michele's table. The girls are naïve and think Christie is being nice. Instead, she puts magnets on Michele's back brace and takes Romy's hamburger. Romy asks one of the popular boys, Billy, to dance at the prom. He agrees but then stands her up, leaving her standing on the dance floor by herself while the popular kids laugh at her. At their class reunion ten years later, Romy and Michele decide to make up stories about their lives to impress their classmates. When the crowd figures out that Romy and Michele are lying, they ridicule them even more. In a chain reaction of mean, Romy and Michele call Sandy a geek. He then puts down Heather and she puts down Toby. Romy, Michele, and Heather lament about how they get excluded but then make others feel bad as well. Romy and Michele confront Christie. They tell her she is a "bitch" and a bad person and they do not care what she thinks. When Lisa disagrees with Christie's assessment of Romy and Michele's outfits, Christie calls Lisa "a shriveled up business woman." In the end, Christie's life is exposed as a sham. Her husband, Billy, is a construction worker and cheating on her. Romy gets her chance to stand up Billy when he asks her to come to his hotel room after the reunion.

Since You've Been Gone is another high school reunion movie that looks back at past bullying and meanness and how it has shaped the victims' lives. The committee is surprised that Kevin showed up to the 10-year class reunion after getting beat up on graduation day by Pat Prince. Kevin's name is actually listed on the "in memoriam" board. Pat shakes Kevin's hand and apologizes for the fight. Pat is in homeopathy, which Kevin, a medical doctor, calls "a crock of shit." Pat asks Kevin's wife if she knows about the time they gave Kevin a chocolate swirly, embarrassing Kevin once again. In return, Kevin is very mean and condescending to many of his classmates. Kevin and Pat come into the ballroom wrestling and arguing about clinical trials. The class crowds around them as one of the bystanders pushes Kevin into Pat. Kevin gets the wind knocked out of him. Pat apologizes and Kevin walks out. Kevin learns to laugh and let go of the past. The movie ends with the annoying organizer of the reunion gagged and trapped in the balloon netting hanging above the ballroom.

Conclusion

In Behm-Morawitz and Mastro's (2008) study of a small sample of mean girl movies, they found that girls displayed social aggressive behavior and were often rewarded for it. Mean girls in the films included in this analysis were likely portrayed as thin and beautiful and leading charmed lives, so much so that it would be likely that young girls would leave the theater wanting to be the mean girl. For example, what teen or preteen girl would not want to be the beautiful and poised 26-year-old Rachel McAdams playing a high school senior in *Mean Girls*? Made-for-TV movies appeared to capture a more realistic view of the average mean girl. The movies featured less well-known actresses who were closer to the age of the character they were playing.

The mean-girl films generally end in one of two ways. Either the mean girl repents and becomes good or she is abandoned by her cronies and is left alone, miserable and without power. Few film representations take time to resolve the issue of mean girls in productive and realistic ways. The goal of most of the films is clearly entertainment rather than education.

5

Television Bullies

Researchers argue that television has the greatest impact of any medium on viewers because its themes are repeated day after day, program after program. Gerbner (1998) described television as a "centralized mass-production of a coherent set of images and messages produced for total populations, and in its relatively non-selective, almost ritualistic, use by most viewers" (p. 178). The continuity of the programming across genres creates a common concept of reality among heavy viewers. He described television programming as being more than mere entertainment; rather but as mythology, which is "highly organically connected." Barboza and associates (2009) found that television viewing was related to increases in bullying behavior, more so than other media. This chapter looks at the different portrayals of bullying in television. Because of the extremely large number of bullying portrayals in situation comedies, a separate chapter is dedicated to that subgenre. Bullying is prevalent in many teen television dramas (e.g., *One Tree Hill, Degrassi: Next Generation*). Bullying among adolescents is also found in individual episodes of adult dramas (e.g., *Picket Fences*). Bullying is occasionally used as a storyline in procedural crime shows (e.g., *Law & Order*) and fantasy shows (e.g., *Smallville*). I also included analysis of several adult bullying episodes in crime-solving shows (e.g., *The A Team*) and Western genre shows (e.g., *The Rifleman* and *Gunsmoke*).

Teen Dramas

The teen drama is the most obvious place to see portrayals of ongoing adolescent bullying. Specific representations focusing on gay (e.g., *Ugly Betty*) and lesbian teens (e.g., *Pretty Little Liars*) are analyzed as well.

When Ryan's alcoholic father kicks him out of the house on the series *The O.C.*, Sandy, a public defender, takes him into his family's affluent home in Newport Beach, CA. Ryan gets into a fight defending Sandy's son, Seth, when some guys are bullying him at a party. Ryan then becomes the target of bullying. Luke, a popular jock, especially resents Ryan because his girlfriend, Marissa, is obviously attracted to Ryan. In the second episode, Luke and his friends go after Ryan. Ryan is secretly staying in a house that is under construction to avoid being put in a foster home or group home. The jocks accidently knock over candles, setting the house on fire. They leave Ryan behind until Luke goes back and carries him out of the burning house. Ryan does not dare report the bullies since he was in house illegally. Ryan is charged with the arson and is sent to jail where he gets hassled by other prisoners. During lunch, one of the thugs knocks Ryan's tray out of his hand. He pushes Ryan down on the table and puts a fork to his neck and warns Ryan to watch his back. When the thug starts talking dirty about Kirsten, Sandy's wife, Ryan snaps and goes after him. Trouble seems to follow Ryan even after he gets out of jail. When Luke hassles Ryan and his coworker, Donnie, at a party, Donnie pulls out a gun. Luke accidently gets shot. Ryan is a sympathetic character because of his past. He is also likeable because of his fierce loyalty to his friends. Luke later becomes a likeable character as well.

In the television series *Everwood*, Ephram has moved to a small town in Colorado from Manhattan. He immediately falls in love with a popular girl named Amy. Bright, Amy's brother, bullies Ephram in the beginning of the series. Bright and his friends do not appear to bully anyone else but Ephram. The bullies trick Ephram into thinking Amy left Ephram a note on his locker to meet her after school. When Bright punches Ephram, Amy gives Bright a matching black eye in Ephram's defense. Bright's father, Hal, is a rival physician of Ephram's father, Andy. Hal is resentful of Andy who left a brilliant career as a brain surgeon to set up an office in the small town. Hal is much more passive aggressive in his bullying of Andy. The boys eventually become best friends and the doctors eventually learn to coexist.

One of the shows that presents characters who are bullied or excluded is *One Tree Hill*. Lucas is shunned by his half-brother Nathan. Their father abandoned Lucas's mother when she was pregnant and married Nathan's mother when he got her pregnant shortly after. Nathan is growing in up a wealthy two-parent home while Lucas's mother is struggling as a single parent. Lucas and Nathan eventually become best friends. While there continued to be sibling rivalry at times, the bullying lasted for only part of the first season. Nathan hazed Lucas when he first joined the basketball team in an effort to make him quit. First the team stole Lucas' clothes from the shower and poured water in his locker. The team members kidnap Lucas, take him out of town with his hands tied behind his back, and throw him in a puddle. Lucas has to walk miles back to town. The coach warns the players that they will be suspended if they do not get along. In the sixth episode of the first season, Lucas and Nathan get into a fistfight during a game. On the way back, the coach stops the bus and makes the two of them walk back from the game. Players from the opposing basketball team that night pick them up. They make Lucas and Nathan fight each other as they watch. Lucas and Nathan start to fight but then work together to get away from their captors.

One Tree Hill included a storyline of a school shooting in retaliation to bullying in season three. The episode "Just Watch the Fireworks" reintroduces the character of Jimmy. Jimmy was in the show's pilot and in the background of a few early episodes. He confronts Lucas and another classmate Mouth about no longer talking to him since they are now hanging out with the popular kids. When the class' time capsule is opened after one year instead of 50, it exposes a video of Jimmy calling his classmates "losers." Some of the boys he talked about beat him up. In the following episode, "With Tired Eyes, Tired Minds, Tired Souls, We Slept," Jimmy finds the same boys vandalizing his locker. Having had enough of the bullying, Jimmy pulls out a gun and fires a shot. He seems surprised when the gun goes off. No one is injured by the shot other than Payton who is hit in the leg with shattered glass from the gun shot. Jimmy runs and hides with other students who do not realize he is the shooter. When he hears another student call the shooter "psycho," Jimmy questions the student. The student calls Jimmy "fat ass." When they try to leave the classroom, Jimmy pulls out the gun. Jimmy wants them to ask themselves if they have ever treated someone like crap, left someone out, or talked behind someone else's back. Jimmy talks about the past and about getting spit on. He discloses that his dad saw him getting beat up and called his son "a loser." When the students try to get him to talk about his problems, he tells them, "This ain't *Breakfast Club*." He describes his best day as the day that no one noticed him at school. He had gone home and took several anti-depressants. When he came back to school a couple of weeks later, he realized that no one noticed he was gone. Before Jimmy took his own life, he said he just wanted the bullies to leave him alone. He just wanted the other students to like him.

In contrast to the severe bullying of Jimmy in season three, the bullying of Nathan and Haley's son Jamie was cute and easily resolved in "Messin' with the Kid" in season six. A bully is teasing Jamie for wearing a superhero cape. Haley tries to reason with the bully's mother. The mother justifies her son's behavior and puts the blame on Jamie. Nathan resolves the bullying by putting on his own cape and putting on a basketball dunking show for the cheering kids. The kids swarm Nathan to get the capes that he has brought the kids. Even the bully wants one. Later the bully asks Jamie to play.

Freaks and Geeks also showed bullying but in a light, comical way. The show is intended to take the perspective of the less popular kids in school. Although critically acclaimed, *Freaks and Geeks* only aired one season. It was a departure from the "pretty people" casting of other shows about teenagers from wealthy families. In the pilot, Lindsay, the older, bigger sister, rescues her brother, Sam, from a bully. The bully comes back in the cafeteria and smashed Sam's Twinkies. He asks Sam if his sister is going to come save him again. The bully calls Sam a "woman." When Sam asks the teacher for help, the teacher helps temporarily by telling the bully to get him more Twinkies. The teacher then tells Sam to "be a man." Sam scolds his two geek friends for not backing him up. The other boys confess they fear the bully will go after them next if they interfere. Later in the pilot, the kids have to play dodgeball in gym class. All the athletic boys seem to be on the other team. The geeks cower against the wall as balls fly by them. The gym teacher yells at the boys, "Ladies! Put down the mascara and get in there and play." When one of the geeks makes a run for it, a large boy hits him in the head. He then hits another geek in the crotch. The coach kicks the bully out of the game, but affectionately calls him "knuckle-head" and chuckles. The freshman geeks ask some of the older geeks for advice about handing the bullies. One advises, "If you fight your bully, they tend to leave you alone." He recounts that his tailbone was broken but the bully got expelled. Sam's plan is to get the bully's schedule and avoid those places. The three geeks fight the bully in what turns out to be a comical wrestling match. They only manage to rip the bully's shirt but walk away bragging about their accomplishments. Sam is happy his friends stood up for him. In episode four, "Kim Kelly Is My Friend," it is a girl, Karen, who bullies Sam. She calls him names and embarrasses him by checking his armpits for hair. She writes "geek" on his locker. Sam stands up to her and tells her he does not want to have to fight her since she is a girl. Karen later writes "pygmy geek" on his locker. In retaliation, one of the freaks, Kim, writes "slut" on Karen's locker and tells Karen she is going to beat her up after school. Karen backs down and no longer appears in the series.

In ABC Family cable show *Lincoln Heights*, a police officer, Eddie Sutton, moves his family back to his old neighborhood, a rather dangerous part of Los Angeles. In the episode "Bully for You," some boys from the high school are picking on junior high boys. A young

African American boy is shown with bruising on his face. He refuses to tell his friend Tay what happened. The beating is caught on tape and posted it on the Internet. Tay's father, Eddie, advises his son to tell an adult if he witnesses bullying. When pressed by the son for further advice, Eddie says, "When all else fails, a man has a right to defend himself." The boy who was being bullied shows Tay a knife he keeps for protection. They argue when Tay takes the knife away from him. Eddie warns the bullies that when a victim does come forward, the bullies will be going to juvenile hall. In a classroom discussion on bullying, some of the students blame the victim for looking different, dressing funny, or acting "uncool." Tay gets jumped in the boys' bathroom after the session in retaliation, thinking Tay snitched on them. Eddie finds Tay tied up in a storage room at the school. The bullies are arrested. At first no one shows up for the second discussion of bullying. One by one students file into the classroom. Eddie tells the class that bullies expect their victims to stay quiet. By telling, victims take away the bullies' power. The students slowly agree that they would tell an adult next time.

The series *Degrassi: The Next Generation* stands out because of its longevity and specific storylines dealing with bullying issues. The show cycles through multiple casts as the characters graduate from high school and move on to work and university. The multitude of characters allows for the storylines to remain fresh. *Degrassi* is a Canadian production that airs on TeenNick, a cable channel targeted solely at teen viewers. *Degrassi* has a "lesson" structure that is different than most US-produced programming. Storylines develop over several episodes, even over several seasons. The bullying incident with Rick, who brings a gun to school ("Time Stands Still"), aired in 2004. More recent episodes where Fitz bullies Eli ("Try Honesty") aired in 2010. *Degrassi* also includes a storyline of a transgendered teen, Adam, who is bullied again by Fitz and his gang when they discovered he is transgendered ("My Body Is a Cage"). *Degrassi* has covered mean-girl scenarios as well. "Heat of the Moment" addresses cyberbullying when Alli creates a hateful website about Holly J. in 2009.

The episodes "Mercy Street," "Anywhere I Lay My Head," "Islands in the Stream" and "Time Stands Still" lead up to the school shooting in "Heat of the Moment." In "Mercy Street," Rick returns to school after getting treatment for his anger issues. Earlier in the series, he had been abusive to his girlfriend, Terri. Rick meets icy stares in the hallways. The kids make it clear they do not want him at the school. When Emma physically removes him from the local hangout, the popular kids think she is cool. Boys bump him in the halls, knock his books down, and kick them. They prevent him from sitting at lunch and all clap when he is forced to leave the cafeteria. Later, Emma trips Rick, making him spill is coffee. Jay takes him out to the alley. He punches Rick in the stomach and stomps on his glasses. Alex goes to hit him, too, but Emma realizes things have gotten out of hand and stops her and the others. In "Anywhere I Lay My Head" and "Islands in the Stream," the bullying continues. Jimmy calls Rick a "psycho." Jay puts Toby in the locker as punishment for being friends with Rick. In "Time Stands Still" the bullying comes to a head. Spinner and Jimmy throw Rick into a dumpster. When he goes to the principal with his harassment complaints, the principal tells him he cannot do anything at this point. The kids rig it so that just when Rick wins the trivia competition, a bucket of paint lands on his head followed by feathers. Ricks runs home humiliated. He comes back to school with his father's gun. Jay and Spinner notice Rick is in a bathroom stall so they make up a story about how it was Jimmy who orchestrated the whole prank, knowing that Rick can hear them. Thinking Jimmy betrayed him, Rick later shoots Jimmy in the back. Sean wrestles Rick for the gun and it goes off, killing Rick. A police detective asks Toby if Rick ever got bullied. Toby responds, "Every day."

Another bullying storyline *Degrassi* takes on is a feud between Fitz and Eli. In "Try Honesty," Fitz blocks Eli's car. Fitz takes off the hood ornament and throws it away. Later Fitz pushes Adam up against a wall. Just as Fitz is about to hit him, Eli intervenes. A voice is heard saying, "Guys, teacher!" Fitz walks away warning, "It's not over." When Eli asks Fitz for an apology, Fitz kicks him in the groin. To get revenge, Eli sets Fitz up with a fake ID with the name of a convicted arsonist. He gets Fitz into a fight to attract the police's attention. When they run the ID, they arrest Fitz. A couple of episodes later, Fitz bullies Adam for being transgendered. In "All Falls Down," the feud between Fitz and Eli continues. Fitz gets Eli in a headlock in the hallway. A teacher sees them. Fitz lets go and the teacher keeps walking. Eli plots to put a drug in Fitz's drink that will make him vomit. When he hears about the plan, Fitz gets a knife and goes after Eli. After the police arrest Fitz, Eli explains to his girlfriend, Clare, that he got bullied when he was nine so that is why he is intent on standing up to bullies. Fitz returns from a stint juvenile hall in "Jesus Etc." He tells Clare that he found Jesus and apologizes to Eli. Fitz later shows up, covered in bruises. His stepbrother had beaten him.

Adult Dramas

The family series *Life Goes On* featured an actor with Down's Syndrome. Rarely if ever does a television show feature life as experienced through the eyes of someone with a disability. The show explored his trials dealing obstacles such as keeping up with academics in a regular high school and integrating into the social structure. On Corky's first day of school, one of the cheerleaders, Rona, smiles and flirts with Corky. Later Rona asks how they can let "cretin" like that in their school. When Rona's boyfriend, Tyler, defends Corky, Rona claims she was talking about Becca, Corky's sister, not Corky. Rona gets caught cheating off of Corky. Rona tells Becca that no one would believe that she was cheating off her "dummy brother." Becca dumps Rona's lunch tray all over her. In the second episode, Rona nominates Corky for class president. The teacher tells her he does not think it is very funny. The class seconds the nomination. Becca is worried that it is all a joke and Corky will get hurt. The jocks chant "Corky" and say they have not had this much fun all year. The popular kids invite Corky over to their lunch table. Tyler scolds Rona for her part in it. Her friend advises Rona to be nice to Corky if she wants to keep Tyler. Russo, one of the jocks, is about to pop a paper bag during Corky's speech but Tyler stops him. Surprisingly little time was spent exploring bullying and mean treatment by other students. Russo is one of the few students who has called Corky names such as "a goof ball" and "brainless." Corky gives an impassioned speech about bullying. He asks that the kids who tease handicap people could put themselves in their shoes. Most of the class gives him a standing ovation. Corky narrowly loses the election but wins the respect of many of his classmates. As the series progresses, the storyline turns more toward Becca and her romantic relationships. Although Corky experienced challenges throughout the run of the series, it appears he overcame the bullying in just two episodes.

The series *Veronica Mars* features a high school girl who works part time with her father as a private detective. In the pilot episode, Veronica's voiceover explains the social structure at her school. She states there are two types of students, "children of million-airs and children of those who work for them." When she discovers a new student, Wallace, duct-taped to a flag pole in the courtyard in his underwear, Veronica rescues him. The other students do nothing to help, and in fact take pictures of him with their camera phones. When a jerky rich boy gives Veronica a hard time, she sets him up by planting a bong in his locker. As payback, he smashes the tail lights on her car. Some biker friends of Veronica's come to her rescue. Veronica makes the rich bullies apologize to Wallace for taping him to the flagpole.

In *Ringer*'s "The Poor Kids Do It Everyday," bullying is used for character development of Juliet, the daughter of one of the main characters. The exchange perpetuates the stereotype that rich girls are mean and poor girls are bullies. Juliet is confronted by a girl Tessa in her class. When Tessa demands five dollars, Juliet gives it to her and tells her, "Now your family can eat for a whole month." Tessa slams her into the lockers later when Juliet confronts her about bullying her. Juliet lunges at her just as the principal is coming down the hallway. The principal believes Juliet's story because of Tessa's record.

Picket Fences and *Doogie Howser, M.D.* have stand-alone episodes where bullying is treated as a rite of passage. In the *Picket Fences* episode "Rites of Passage," Matthew fights the bully that has been picking on his little brother and his small friend. Matthew's father, the town's sheriff, advises Matthew first to talk it out but also to remember to breathe and not drop his hands. When Matthew and the bully begin fighting, bystanders gather to cheer. Matthew wins, breaking the bully's jaw. In stereotypical fashion, the mother is upset at the son and the father. There is a parallel storyline with a standoff with the Native Americans who want to stop a golf course being built on their burial ground. They take over the courthouse. The tribe loses in the end, but it signifies a bully forcibly taking something away from a less powerful target.

The title character in the show *Doogie Howser, M.D.* is a child genius who becomes a medical doctor at the age of 14. He is socially awkward, not having a normal childhood. When he is bullied while giving a presentation on sexual health to his local high school, he takes the opportunity to stand up for himself. He first tries using his superior intelligence to deal with the bully, but since that does not appear to be effective, he turns to a more base solution, fighting.

Soap operas are often a venue for addressing social issues, from date rape to breast cancer. Occasionally, soap operas tackle bullying. Because of the limited numbers of adolescents in the casts, there are limited opportunities to address bullying. Also, bullying is not a very sexy storyline. Because the audience for daytime soap operas skews older, it is not surprising there are not more bullying plots. Soap operas generally tend toward the older mean character who steals husbands, fakes pregnancies, or takes away company control. *One Life to Live* is one of the few soap operas that dedicated an extensive span of time to develop a bullying storyline. ABC Daytime teamed up with Stomp Out Bullying campaign. It is one of few television shows that addressed cyberbullying as well. While few adolescents, especially male adolescents, watch soaps, parents of the adolescents do.

Jack and his friend Brad play keep away with Shane's inhaler in the hallway at school. They mock him for having asthma. When Shane asks for the inhaler back, Jack pushes him against the wall and says, "Make me, bitch." The other kids in the hall do nothing to help. Shane takes a swing at Jack and accidentally hits Brad just as the principal walks by. Shane refuses to tell his parents about the bullying. Shane finds a note in his locker that reads, "It gets worse, Wheezy," which makes reference to the "It Gets Better" campaign. Jack and Brad take school raffle money that Shane was in charge of and play keep away with it. When the principal asks Shane about the money, Shane tells him that Jack took it. Jack planted the money in Shane's locker and Shane ends up getting suspended. Shane gets a text from Jack warning him that if he tells again, he is "dead." The bullying escalates to posts on Shane's MyFace page. One boy writes, "Shane M. little snitch or little bitch?" They continue to harass Shane online. Jack steals Shane's towel in gym class and some kids take pictures of Shane naked with their camera phones and upload them. Jack tells his mother that Shane is a "loser" and asked for the abuse. Shane steps out on the roof of the school. Shane's parents find him in time. Jack's mother blames herself for not checking his social networking site to see the awful things her son posted. She does not know which is worse, that Jack did not know it was wrong or that he did not care. Jack remains defiant even after he finds out Shane was on the roof. He reasons that he was not the only one, that they were just having fun, and that he did not realize Shane was "so screwed up." The storyline is realistic in the sense that it shows the progression and the escalation of the bullying. The storyline began around the middle of February 2011 and continued several months. Jack and his friends continue to bully Shane online. They pretend to be a girl and try to lure Shane to a house. The plan is to trap Shane in the basement. When Shane's mother sees the online message, she goes to the house instead. The bullies lock her in the basement, thinking it is Shane. Shane's mother goes into a coma after there is a gas leak in the basement.

Cyberbullying

While vast majorities of bullying portrayals in media are traditional face-to-face encounters, some media are beginning to include technological methods of bullying. Cyberbullying portrayals range from movies to sitcoms. The made-for-TV movie *Cyberbullying* is the most detailed portrayal of how cyberbullying can spiral out of control. The problem starts when Taylor's brother and his friends post a fake status update on Taylor's page. The subsequent negative comments spiral out of control. The movie also demonstrates how giving personal information to a stranger can backfire. In addition, there is an element of mean-girl phenomenon when one of Taylor's best friends uses the information against her because she is angry at her friend. She is able to post her comments anonymously. Even when Taylor puts up a video announcing her suicide attempt, users are posting negative comments and saying they wish she had succeeded. Even one of her neighbors records and posts footage of Taylor being taken by ambulance to the hospital. While the movie includes an after-school-special style of dialogue, *Cyberbullying* makes a much stronger statement about the problem than the comedy portrayals of bullying and mean girls. The jump to the suicide attempt is perhaps excessively dramatic and unnecessary to telling the story.

The teen show *Degrassi: The Next Generation* deals with one girl's revenge using social media. Holly J., the school's mean girl, embarrasses Alli about her boyfriend. The boy breaks up with Alli. Alli gets back at Holly J. by creating an "I hate Holly J." page. Alli writes, "Holly J. is a dirty ginger virus infecting Degrassi. She needs to be eliminated. I'D LIKE TO STRANGLE HER WITH MY BARE HANDS." The comments from some of the four hundred and eleven members of the group, however, spiral out of control. Someone writes, "Want to strangle her? I'll bring the rope." As Holly J. walks through the cafeteria, kids in the cafeteria chant, "I hate Holly J." Although Alli gets caught and is suspended from school, she thinks it was totally worth it because now she is popular. Holly J.'s parents call the police. Alli is still defiant and upset that Holly J. is causing her so much trouble. Alli's father makes Alli apologize to Holly J. in person. Alli finds Holly J. crying in bed. Holly J. says she is not coming back to school. Alli finally realizes the pain she has caused. Even though Alli takes down the site and issues a public apology, a boy still walks by and makes a joke about bringing a rope to strangle Holly J.

Harry's Law looks at the issue from the perspective of the perpetrator and addresses the legal responsibility of cyberbullies. The defendant, Sela, outed a classmate, Hannah, on her blog and used words like "tuna" and other derogatory words to describe lesbians. Hannah later commits suicide. Sela is charged with negligent homicide. Producer David E. Kelley is known to make political and social statements in his court cases. Here Kelley looks not only to the blogger's comments but to other factors contributing to the suicide such as her parents' disapproval and the religious intolerance of the Catholic Church.

The *Law & Order SVU* episode "Babes" mirrors two stories "ripped from today's headlines." The initial story is about four girls who enter a pregnancy pact. One of the girls commits suicide after being cyberbullied. The cyberbully turns out to be the victim's classmate's mothers who is pretending she is another teen.

In the episode of the Disney sitcom *Jessie*, one of the nannies is using her website to bully the other nannies by posting photos taken out of context that make them look bad to their employers. To get the bad nanny to take down the site, one of the mothers threatens to send a tweet to her many followers about the nanny. Because the mother is a famous personality, she has a significant number of Twitter followers to make her threat significant and thus effective.

The sitcom *Bent* addresses cyberbullying in the episode "HD." Thirteen-year-old Frankie begins to make excuses why she does not want to go to school. She eventually confesses she wants to skip school because a girl in her class, Nicole, is harassing her because Frankie's father is in prison for insider trading. Nicole is posting pictures of Frankie in an orange jumpsuit on Facebook. Other kids have been texting and posting Frankie messages such as "jail bird." Frankie's aunt and grandfather recommend getting back at Nicole using conventional methods such as cutting off her hair. Frankie's mother, Alex, disagrees and advises Frankie take the high road, although she does not define what that means. When some kids from Frankie's school spray paint "jail bird" on their lawn, Alex's family and friends egg Nicole's house. Alex eventually joins in. The episode ends with Frankie's aunt sending Nicole a picture of Nicole's house covered in eggs, as uplifting music plays in the background. The behavior of the adults is also quite immature and may in fact escalate the bullying. The bullying in the episode is quite mild, and Frankie only demonstrates mild distress.

LGBT TEEN PORTRAYALS

Some of the most intriguing bullying storylines feature gay boys and girls as the target. The bullying is intensified because of the cultural stigma regarding homosexuality. The characters are also dealing with internal struggles of coming out to family and friends. I found a variety of shows that emphasis the bullying of young gay males: Justin on *Ugly Betty*, Justin on *Queer as Folk*, Rickie on *My So-Called Life*, and Kurt on *Glee*. *Glee* and *Ugly Betty* are on the comic side while *Queer as Folk* and *My So Called Life* are much more dramatic and gritty.

The main storyline in the series *Ugly Betty* is Betty, a recent college graduate who trying to break into the fashion magazine industry. A second storyline is about Betty's nephew who has rather feminine characteristics associated with stereotypical gay behavior. Justin loves show tunes and the iconic celebrities who are embraced by gay culture, such as Madonna and Barbara Streisand. As he gets older and begins to explore his feelings for other boys, he gets teased and bullied by his classmates at school. Even though he has a supportive family, coming out is difficult for him. When Justin and his parents get stuck on a train on their way to *Hairspray* on Broadway, Justin sings and dances some of the scenes. When a gruff passenger calls him a "fairy," Justin's father gets in the man's face. The rest of the passengers on the train clap in support. Justin smiles and continues.

In season four of the series, Justin begins high school and experiences a new level of bullying. The boys laugh at him when he puts up a picture of Madonna in his locker. At lunch, they drink his soda and compliment his "pretty" shirt before they spill his tray on it. Almost everyone in the lunch room laughs. Other kids line the halls and laugh at him as he walks out with his soiled shirt. He comes home in a school sweatshirt. Anxious to know how his first day went, Justin tells his family he is tired and goes to his room. Justin goes to see Betty's coworker, Marc, who is out as a gay man and former bully victim. Marc provides Justin with the secret to fitting in at school, which is to befriend a gang of mean girls. Justin takes his advice and becomes friends with the cheerleaders by offering to choreograph their dances. When a boy makes fun of Justin, one of the cheerleaders stands up for Justin. Kids at the school vote Justin as Homecoming Queen as a practical joke. There is a smattering of laughter and jeers when Justin's name is called. Taking Marc's advice to not let the bullies think they are getting to him, Justin walks to the stage. He smiles and takes the flowers and crown. He thanks everyone. He turns attention to his mom and gives her his crown since she did not get to be queen because she was pregnant with him in high school. The bullies look a little annoyed that their prank failed. A few people in the crowd give Justin a standing ovation. Justin tells his mother he was playing along and denies that he is gay. When Justin gets his first boyfriend, he hides the relationship from his family. His mother plans a big "coming out" party to show her support. Marc stops the party, telling them that when Justin is ready, he will let them know. Justin decides to bring Austin, his boyfriend, to his mother's wedding. Justin's future at school is not clear but he is in his first relationship and has the support of his family.

Where the average teen drama departs from other dramas such as *My So-Called Life* is the intensity of the outcomes for the characters. There is no sugarcoating of issues with a happy ending in this series. Angela's neighbor, Brian, is often bullied in the hallways. Angela sees some bigger boys pushing Brian up against a locker. She keeps walking. In every class, Brian appears to be the only student raising his hand. Brian walks with his tray in the cafeteria as a faceless boy pushes the tray on to his chest. One storyline includes Rickie Vasquez, an out teen boy. He dresses on the extravagant side and wears eyeliner. He hangs out in the girls' bathroom with little or no notice from the girls as they come and go. In episode three, Brian sees Rickie getting hassled in the hallway. A gun goes off and Rickie and another boy run. Rickie returns with a ripped shirt. Later, Angela sees a couple of boys hassle Rickie on the stairs. Two boys, one in a bandana and one with his hat on backwards, approach Rickie. They put their arms around him. When one boy calls him a "fag," Rickie tells him to "go to hell." They push Rickie against a locker. Rayanne intervenes, but Rickie tells her he could have handled it. Later, Angela finds Rickie hiding in a car. He tells her he has trouble making it through the day in school. Rickie wants people to think he is dangerous. He explains that his cousin brought the gun into school to sell it to him, and the gun accidentally went off.

Later in the season, Rickie is shown with a bloody lip in a snowy street. His aunt and uncle have kicked him out of their house for being gay. Angela is concerned when Rickie goes to school with a black eye. He lies about it. Rayanne tells Angela that Rickie "has this tendency to get beat up and doesn't love talking about it." Having nowhere else to go, Rickie shows up at Angela's house. He sneaks out the back when he overhears Angela's parents asking questions. Jordan picks up Rickie and takes him to a warehouse where other homeless teens are living. Jordan tells Rickie his father used to hit him, too. Angela goes to the warehouse to bring him back to her house but he pushes her away. Angela's parents report the warehouse to the police, which then gets raided. Angela's mom finds Rickie in a church and brings him to their house on Christmas Eve. After a few days, Rickie begins to feel uncomfortable about staying at Angela's so he tells them that he worked it out with his family. One of Rickie's teachers, Mr. Katimski, catches Rickie sleeping in class. Rickie confesses to Mr. Katimski that he is homeless. The guidance counselor wants to put him in a facility, which is a scary shelter. The next night he calls Mr. Katimski from a phone booth in the pouring rain. When Rickie shows up at his door, Mr. Katimski and his partner take Rickie in. Life appears to become stable for Rickie at last.

Although *Glee* has a dedicated chapter in the book, it is important to look at the treatment of homophobic bullying in the context of other shows that address the issue. While the character Karofski bullies Kurt because Kurt is gay, Karofski is secretly conflicted about his own sexuality. While the bullying of glee club members is treated quite humorously, a la slushies in the face, the treatment of this topic was presented in a serious manner. When Karofski switches from bullying Kurt with his buddies to making personal threats when the two are alone, the intensity rises. The story comes full circle when Karofski gets bullied by his teammates for being gay. He also gets cyberbullied on what looks like his Facebook page. In a montage of video clips overlaid by Emo music, he tries to hang himself. Luckily his father catches him in time. When Kurt visits him in the hospital to offer him his friendship, it gives Karofski new hope. Kurt has an extremely supportive father, as does Karofski. Karofski's mother, however, appears to be very religious and is trying to pray away his sins.

Queer as Folk, although anything but a teen drama (i.e., highly sexual and mature content), featured an important storyline about a teen boy coming out. As Justin enters a classroom at school, some of the boys call out "fag." The teacher ignores the name calling. When the teacher says Justin's name for roll call, one boy shouts out "queer" instead of "here," Justin asks the teacher if he is going to do anything about it. The teacher refuses and threatens to send Justin to the principal's office. Justin confronts the teacher and tells him to go "F" himself. Justin is suspended for two days. The principal is of little help as well, claiming that it is a private school and therefore they are under no obligation to accommodate "certain" students. Justin has specific problems with one of the jocks, Chris. The jock makes Justin's life miserable in school. Justin loses his temper and outs Chris, telling a large group of people that he gave Chris a hand job. In retaliation, Chris nearly beats Justin to death with a baseball bat in the parking garage after the prom. The homophobic judge ruled that Chris was provoked by Justin and his boyfriend Brian's kiss at the prom. After Justin recovers, he joins a vigilante group to avenge homophobic attacks. Justin later gets a gun and confronts Chris. He makes Chris get on his knees and puts the gun in Chris's mouth. After Chris apologizes, it appears Justin is able to move on with his life.

Portrayals of lesbian bullying range from the teen dramas *Pretty Little Liars* and *One Tree Hill* to the soap opera *All My Children*. In the ABC Family series *Pretty Little Liars*, there is a brief storyline where a girl on Emily's swim team, Paige, makes remarks about Emily being a lesbian. Paige taunts Emily about "playing for the other team" and swimming the breast stroke. One of Emily's friends informs the swim coach. The coach calls the two girls together. She reminds them the school has a zero-tolerance policy. Emily explains that it was a misunderstanding. Paige is excused. The coach says she cannot help Emily if she does not report the incident. While Emily is swimming alone, a hand pushes her head under the water. It is Paige. She does it a couple more times before she warns Emily not to show her up in swim practice and take her spot on the relay team. Later, Paige comes to Emily's house at night in the pouring rain. Paige looks distraught and tells her that she does not know why she is there. She apologizes and rides off on her bike. Paige has an accident on her way home so Emily gets to swim in the relay. After the meet, Paige tells Emily about the accident. Paige thinks she is done with swimming but Emily gets her to swim for fun. While they are spending time together, Paige kisses Emily, revealing that Paige is also a lesbian. Paige no longer bullies.

One Tree Hill features a girl named Anna, who is a lesbian and left her old school because of the rumors she was having a relationship with another girl. It appears she left not so much because she was bullied but because she did not want her parents to find out. When her brother Felix sees Anna talking with Peyton, Felix spray paints "dyke" on Peyton's locker. Anna admits to Felix that she is gay and is only friends with Peyton. Anna begins to come out to the other characters one by one. It appears her brother is the only one who had a problem with her sexuality. The problem quickly goes away. The storyline is interesting because Peyton, who is not a lesbian is the character who gets bullied for being gay.

In 2000, Bianca Montgomery, daughter of the legendary Erica Kane on the soap opera *All My Children*, came out as a lesbian. Out of spite for Bianca telling Greenlee that Greenlee's boyfriend does not love her, Greenlee outs Bianca to a local reporter. Greenlee taunts Bianca by calling her LesBianca. Over time Greenlee and Bianca become friends.

Less Than Kind is a Canadian show featuring an overweight teenager named Sheldon. In "Fatso Loves Lebso," a mean girl teases Sheldon for being fat. She also calls his friend, Miriam, a lesbian. The mean girl is dyslexic so she writes "fasto" instead of "fatso" and "lebso" instead of "lesbo" on their lockers. In the school locker room, the mean girl accuses Miriam of checking her out when they are changing for gym class. The gym teacher yells at the mean girl. She tells Miriam to ignore the girl because she is a "bitch." Sheldon and Miriam pretend to be dating so the other kids, particularly the mean girl, will leave them alone. There is a confrontation with the mean girl after school. Sheldon goes to hit her but stops himself. The other kids just watch, except for Sheldon's friend, Danny, who urinates on the mean girl's book bag. When they come to school the next day, the mean girl has spray-painted "fasto loves lebso" on the front of the school. Miriam and Sheldon smile at each other as they walk hand in hand down the hallway.

Degrassi includes a storyline with a transgendered teen. In the episode "My Body Is a Cage," Adam is bullied by a gang of boys led by Fitz when they discover Adam is biologically a girl. Another girl calls Adam a "freak." The bullies follow Adam into the boys' room and pressure him to use the urinal in front of them. They carry him out and throw him down, breaking the glass door. Adam's brother, Andrew, stands up to Fitz. The other kids just watch as they fight. Adam, Andrew, and their mother meet with the principal. The mother talks about how transgendered kids get bullied and harassed and receive death threats. The principal suspends Fitz. Adam is assigned an adult who will accompany him to class. He will have to use the handicap restroom.

Procedural Crime Shows

In many of the crime-solving or "procedurals" shows, bullying is used as a plot line for a single episode. The crime is generally a murder by a bully or murder of a bully as revenge. The law enforcement officials try to figure out the motive, why the bullying happened or how it influenced the crime. These exaggerated portrayal have very little to do with average viewers' experience with bullying.

The *Law & Order SVU* episode "Mean" features the case of an over-the-top group of mean girls who are severely bullying an overweight student. At the beginning of the show, one of the mean girls has been murdered. The brother of one of their bullying victims is the initial suspect. He gets in trouble for trying to defend his sister when the school does not take action to stop the bullying. The mean girls write "pig" on the girl's locker. They also take photos of her changing in the locker room and send them out on their cell phones. The police eventually discover that it was the mean girls who killed one of their own because she was threatening to leave the group. As the bullies are arrested and taken out of the school, a shot is fired. The girl who was being bullied by the mean girls shoots and kills another student who is now bullying her. In the closing scene, she cries, "It was never going to stop."

A popular girl, Blair, is found murdered on an episode of *CSI: Miami*, "Stoned Cold." Someone tied Blair to the goalposts and stoned her to death. Investigators found that she was being forced to listen to a recording of students talking about how she bullied them. Blair even bullied the principal and blackmailed him against taking action against her. Blair tricked a boy, Nate, into running naked through the halls in front of the whole school. He later attempted suicide as a result of Blair's bullying. Another one of Blair's victims was Megan, a shy new girl. Wanting desperately to be friends with Blair, Megan had sex with three football players at a party. Blair was murdered by Nate and Megan's parents. They confess they only wanted to scare her; however, when Blair continued to insult their son and daughter, they lost their tempers and began hitting her with stones.

In the *Law & Order* episode "Loco Parentis," a bully, John, is arrested for ultimately killing his bullying target, Chris. The other kids identify Chris as a "dweeb." Detectives find dangerous weapons hanging on the wall in John's room and a collection of hardcore video games. John's father had previously threatened to sue another boy's father if he reported John for bullying his son, Leo. The district attorney arrests the father in an attempt to hold him responsible for his son's bullying. John's mother eventually agrees to testify against her husband for "ruining" her son. John explains that he was just going to steal Chris's money. When Chris hit him in the stomach, John reached for his weapon and killed Chris.

In *CSI*'s "Bully for You" the bully, Barry, is found in the boys' room shot in the back three times. Flashbacks show him punching one victim and pushing him off his skateboard. A variety of other victims share how Barry bullied them and stole their food. The murderer turns out to be a guidance counselor who was the assistant principal at a school where there was a mass shooting by a bully victim. She reasons that she was saving many lives by killing the bully herself before one of his victims became violent.

Eric leaves the room to go to the bathroom at school and goes missing in *Without a Trace*'s "Wannabe." In a flashback, Billy, an older bully, is shown picking on Eric. Billy gives Eric a swirly. Eric's friend Darren tries to help Eric, but Billy's cronies hold him back. There is surveillance footage of another boy, Frank, hassling Eric at a video arcade. Frank claims he was just warning Eric about calling his sister Lisa a "dog." Eric was trying to impress a girl, Brandy, in his class by picking on Lisa. Brandy lures Eric to a horse barn. She and her friends get him to take off his clothes and tie him up. The mean girls throw manure on him and call him a "dog." Lisa takes a picture and sends it around the school. Emily admits to orchestrating the plan out of jealousy because she likes Eric but Eric likes Brandy. Eric was actually not kidnapped but was embarrassed and ran away. Eric calls Darren threatening to kill himself. The detectives find Eric hanging from Brandy's backyard swing. They get to him in time.

"Painless," an episode of the show *Criminal Minds*, features a reunion of survivors from a school shooting that happened a decade earlier. The shooter, Randy, killed himself with a bomb in the initial attack. Ten years later, the principal is murdered when a bomb goes off in his apartment. Robert, an even less popular boy than the original shooter, is now getting his revenge. Robert traps the popular kids who were involved in the first shooting and holds them at gunpoint. Robert is angry that another boy stole his story by telling reporters that he was the one who stared down the first shooter. FBI agents offer Robert a chance to tell his story. Robert makes a run for it and is shot and killed by Agent Hotch. As a side story, Hotch's young son is getting bullied at school. The son's solution is to invite the boy over to play. Hotch decides not to get involved. A coworker advises him that he can let the son know he is not alone.

In *The Mentalist*'s episode "Ruby Slippers," a burned body identified as 19-year-old Archie Bloom is discovered. The suspects are the victim's father and a coworker. Archie's father is homophobic and rather mean to his son. There is video footage of his father handcuffing Archie to a chair so he would do his homework. The coworker, Rick, bullied Archie and made homophobic remarks. Once he locked him in a dumpster. Archie was also in an abusive relationship with an older man, Gabriel, who is also a drug dealer. It turns out that Archie staged his own "murder." As revenge to his abusers, he set them all up to look guilty. The dead body thought to be Archie's was taken from a funeral home and the dental records were switched. Archie is allowed to live happily ever after in his new identity as transgendered.

"Perfect Storm" is an episode of the series *Flashpoint* where Billy, the victim of bullying, is holding the school hostage. Flashbacks show an incident where Billy stands up for his friend, Ella, when her football player boyfriend, Scott, is being rough with her. Scott knocks Billy down. Billy tries to fight back by kicking at Scott from the ground. Scott says, "I didn't know gay boys could fight." One of Scott's friends records it on his cell phone, presumably to post on the Internet. Scott chokes Billy, puts garbage in his mouth, and makes him say, "I'm gay" and "I'm a piece of garbage." The bystanders do nothing. Even Ella, whom Billy was defending, just walks away. Billy later goes home to a drunk father who abuses Billy's mother. Tired of being bullied, Billy brings his father's gun to school. Billy fires the gun when a student calls him a "loser" but he does not hit anyone. Ella is upset that she did not do anything to help him. She tries to talk him down.

One of the police officers shoots Billy, thinking that he harmed his son, Tony, who has also been bullying Billy.

The *Commish* episode "Sons and Guns" features a storyline of the lead character Tony's son dealing with bullies. Tony witnesses the bully, Brad, roughing up a boy and extorting money. The principal gives Brad detention. She later tells Tony she has tried to suspend Brad but his father threatened her. She thought he might even hit her. The father is a stereotypical thug with a chip on his shoulder. One of David's friends, Jason, brings a gun to school for protection. Brad had put Jason's head in the toilet so long that Jason thought he was going to drown. Brad gets shot but refuses to tell who pulled the trigger. Brad's friend, Russ, tells the police Brad had it in for David. Brad's father shoots Jason's father for revenge.

The "Wooly Bullies" episode of *21 Jump Street* includes the usual undercover operation at a local high school. The show has a more comical side than the other procedural shows. Doug is investigating a group of nerds who are breaking into the school's computer system. Because he is undercover as a nerd, Doug becomes a victim of the school's bullies. He wears thick glasses, a tie, and pocket protector. The bully wears a white T-shirt and jeans. At lunch, the bully pours milk into Doug's shirt pocket. Like a superhero, he cannot blow his cover and disclose his powers to stop the bullying. In the end, Doug has had enough and confronts the bully. He squeezes the bully's hand until the bully backs down and walks away. The nerds invite him into their world.

There is a pattern with other crime shows and bullying. The adults appear to use the opportunity to discuss and process their own experiences of being bullied as adolescents. For example, during a discussion of high school and bullying on *Criminal Minds*, Spencer, the geeky guy, assumes JJ, the pretty blonde investigator, was a mean girl in high school. He reasons, "Valedictorian, soccer scholarship, corn fed, and still a size zero. I think you might have been a mean girl." She denies the allegation, saying she was one of the nice girls...even to guys "like him." The male detective in *Without a Trace* similarly accuses the pretty blonde female detective of being a queen bee. She corrects him and tells him she was one of the "dweebs." The *21 Jump Street* "Wooly Bullies" episode is an opportunity to features flashbacks to each character's past bullying experience. The show is on the lighter side of drama and crime shows. Doug tells his boss, Captain Fuller, the school bully reminds him of a kid that made his life a living hell in school. The bully would shove his lunch in Doug's face and knocks the books out of his hands. Doug had to sneak his entry into the science fair to school. He almost made it to the door when the bully threatened him. He got scared and dropped the project. Five years later he was still bullying Doug by putting tacks on his seat and giving him wedgies. On the way to the prom, the bully jumped into Doug's uncle's car and skidded in the snow and wrecked it. The bully moved away before Doug could get revenge. Eight years later, Doug goes to see his bully. When he gets to the bully's rundown house, he sees that bully has a miserable life. Doug walks away, smiling.

Fantasy and Sci-Fi Dramas

There is a range of shows in the category of fantasy or sci-fi. Unlike movies, the similarities were less clear among the bullying portrayals. The common theme of the episodes was the handling of bullies using special powers. There is a revenge element to these episodes as well with a mix of adolescent and adult bullies.

The episode "Mean Ghost" of *The Ghost Whisperer* begins with cheerleaders being injured one by one. The injuries are being caused by the spirit of a vindictive cheerleader, Tais. Tais was killed when she was burned to death by a pipe when her friend Rana accidentally locked her in the school's boiler room. Maddie, a former cheerleader and former friend of Rana, is part of a witch coven that is fueling Tais's revenge. The popular girls befriended Maddie, got her to disclose her secrets in a journal, and then turned on her when they found out she was lying about her family's wealth. Melinda, the ghost whisperer, gets Tais to give up her revenge plot and forgive Rana. During the episode, Melinda flashes back to her school days when the other girls called her a "freak." These bully-themed episodes give the adult characters a chance to explore their own past bullying experiences.

A boy, Aaron, is being chased by two bullies in *Fringe* "Alone in the World." One of the bullies yells, "You're dead!" Aaron runs into a tunnel, followed closely by the bullies. The bully is angry because he thinks Aaron told a teacher about the bully's "stash" in his locker. A fungus attacks the bullies and kills them. Aaron tells Walter, the doctor treating him, that he feels like the organism in the tunnel protects him. Aaron confesses that he purposely led the bullies into the tunnel. A subplot of the episode is that Aaron feels isolated and unloved, which feeds the organism. When Walter shows Aaron affection, the fungus dies. The theme of the story is the triumph of good over evil. There is a fantasy that bullies will get what is coming to them and there are "magic tunnels" that can protect the bullied.

In the episode of *Supernatural* entitled "After School Special," Sam flashes back to when he was bullied in school by Dirk. When Dirk knocks Sam down in the hallway, a teacher sends Dirk away without any apparent punishment. Sam's older brother Dean offers to step in but Sam declines his help. Later, Dirk is picking on Sam's friend, Barry. Sam comes to his defense and stops Dirk with his superpowers. Sam calls Dirk "Dirk the Jerk." The rest of the students, who have been passively watching the fight, laugh and join in on the name calling. The bully becomes the victim. Kids begin to make fun of Dirk for being poor and stupid. Dirk dies at 18. In the present day, Dirk is possessing bullied kids in the school and forcing them to take revenge on their persecutors. When a cheerleader approaches the popular kids' lunch table, another cheerleader calls her a "slut" and tells the group rumors about her. They refuse to let her sit with them. The jocks join the cheerleaders in chanting "slut." She is forced to sit at a table with an overweight girl who is sitting by herself. The overweight girl tells the cheerleader she is sorry she is being bullied. Instead of being grateful for her compassion, the cheerleader calls her "a fat ugly pig." The next day, the overweight girl confronts the cheerleader in the bathroom, banging her head into the mirror and drowning her in the toilet. Another bully demands homework from a geek. The geek loses his temper and puts the bully's hand in a food processor. Sam and Dean rescue the students from Dirk's ghost.

Smallville's episode "Reunion" flashes back to Lex Luther's days at boarding school. Oliver, the lead bully, takes Lex's comic book. When Lex demands the comic book back, Oliver rips it in half. Lex tries to fight him with no success. During the scuffle, Lex's hat falls off and the bullies make fun of his bald head. The bullies also make fun of Lex's friend Duncan for being on scholarship. Lex vows to get revenge one day. When Lex catches the bullies cheating, he wants to blackmail them into accepting himself and Duncan into their group. Lex and Duncan get into a fight when Duncan wants to turn them in to school authorities. During the fight, Duncan gets hit by a car and suffers brain damage. Years later, at the school reunion, Duncan's spirit begins to kill the bullies one by one. Oliver now regrets how he treated them. Lex regrets that he ever thought he needed friends like the bullies.

I also include an episode of *Adventures of Superman* "Bully of Dry Gulch" as a contrast to the other fantasy television shows. The episode aired in 1955. Jimmy and Lois's car breaks down in a Western town that appears to be stuck in time. A cowboy named Gunner is making an old timer dance as Gunner shoots at the man's feet. When Jimmy interferes, Gunner warns Jimmy to be gone by sunset. Gunner flirts with Lois. Gunner brags about putting men in the local cemetery. Later, Gunner bullies his men into gambling, convincing them by waving his gun around. Gunner somehow comes up with five aces in his hand. Jimmy accuses Gunner of cheating. Pedro, Gunner's sidekick, forces Jimmy out of the bar at gunpoint and locks Jimmy in a jail cell. Lois calls Clark Kent. Clark plays down the threats made on Jimmy's life, but changes into Superman and springs into action when Lois tells him that Gunner has been "making goo goo eyes" at her. When Clark refuses to play poker, Gunner gets angry and shoots up the bar. Clark sets Gunner's marked deck of cards on fire with Superman's laser vision. Clark gets a new deck and comes up with five aces. Clark gives the winning to the bartender to cover Gunner's damages. Outside the bar, Pedro draws a gun on Gunner and is shot. Gunner's other henchman drags Pedro to the cemetery. Pedro was faking it because Gunner pretends to kill men to look important. Superman finds Pedro and proposes to work together to teach Gunner a lesson. When trouble appears to be brewing, Lois taunts Clark that he is going to hide in his room. Pedro comes back and challenges Gunner to a draw. A cowardly Gunner backs down. Superman has replaced Gunner's bullets with blanks just in case. Gunner admits he has never killed anyone. Pedro shoots at Gunner's feet and makes him dance. As Gunner accidentally falls in the water trough, the bystanders laugh. They all leave as friends. Lois laments that all bullies are the same, they are just scared. Although the bully was all talk, he was none-the-less still carrying a gun.

Adult Bullies

The shows in this category tend to treat severe bullying, even murder, in a nonchalant, matter-of-fact manner. Although the perpetrators are all adults, the synopses of the episodes classify them as "bullies" because of the way they treated multiple targets and the fear they created in bystanders. In *A-Team*'s "A Nice Place to Visit," the team is in town for their friend Ray's funeral. Ray's pregnant wife explains that everyone in the town is scared of a group of bullies, the Watkins brothers. Although it appears obvious that the brothers are responsible for the accident that killed Ray, the authorities do not dare charge the brothers. The brothers harass the A-Team members, threatening them unless they leave town. The gunfight at the end of the episode is rather comical, complete with humorous dialogue. The team delivers the bullies into town with their hands tied behind their backs. The music in the background is rather lighthearted as well.

Walker, Texas Ranger also had a less than serious tone. In between the scenes, there are comical interactions among the Rangers. One of the bullies throws a rope and lassos the rodeo arena's daughter. One of the Rangers throws him in a watering tank. One of the bad guys lets out a bull while the daughter is practicing barrel racing. Again, there is peppy music in the background. In *Murder She Wrote*'s "Powder Keg," a group of drunken men stumble into the local bar. They intimidate a couple, making the couple give up their table. The leader Ed's sister is sweet on the lead singer of the band, Matt. Ed heckles Matt while he sings. The bar owner goes for his gun but one of the cronies, Billy, stops him by threatening him with a knife. The small town is reminiscent of the Wild West. Ed tells Matt to leave town and calls his own sister "a tramp." Matt lunges at Ed but Ed beats him and pours beer on Matt's head. Ed is later found dead, for which Matt is framed. A large posse of men led by one of Ed's cronies, Andy, comes to the jail to get Matt. When the sheriff refuses to release Matt to the vigilantes, Andy calls the sheriff a "colored boy." The sheriff takes off his badge and prepares to fight Andy. Ed's father comes and breaks up the scene. Angela figures out that the bar owner killed Ed because Ed was blackmailing him. The *Law & Order SVU* episode "Bully" is about an abusive boss who bullied her partner and her employees. Hidden video shows her screaming and hitting her partner. The bully victim is later found murdered. Because "Bully" is the title of the episode, I included in the analysis even though both parties are adults. There is a clear power differential between the partners that resembled childhood bullying beyond the assault.

Historic-Themed Bullying

While many of the films about bullying are nostalgic looks back at a simpler time (see Chapter 3), television shows about the recently settled West are based on a more lawless time. Few arrests appear to be made for crimes other than murder and horse thievery. Even in cases of murder and assault, the harmed party was allowed to take matters into their own hands. The Westerns are based on traditional masculinity, which included gun possession. The historic-based shows included in this analysis, *Little House on the Prairie*, *The Rifleman*, and *Gunsmoke*, feature characters who follow codes of justice and compassion for others.

The Little House on the Prairie episode "The Bully Boys" has two bully storylines. In one line, two adult brothers are terrorizing the town of Walnut Grove. In a separate story, their younger brother, Bubba, was causing trouble at the town's school. First, Bubba pushes Willie off his seat in class. Then at recess, Bubba throws a ball at a little girl knocking her down. When Laura stands up to him, she gets pushed down as well. Mary has to hold Laura back from fighting Bubba. The bigger boys are not in school because they are still in the field. When Mary stands up to Bubba, he gives her a black eye. The Ingalls' girls tell their parents it was a dodgeball accident. Nellie bribes Bubba with candy to be her friend. When Bubba steals Laura's marbles and Mary's tablet, Nellie takes Bubba's side. Mary hits Bubba with her lunch pail. Soon Laura, the rest of the school girls except for Nellie, and the smaller boys join the fight and are able to defeat Bubba as a team.

In "Troublemaker," the school board, headed by Mrs. Oleson, threatens to fire Miss Beadle if she cannot control the older boys who have come back to school after the harvest. When the trouble continues, Miss Beadle is replaced with a stern male teacher. He also has a difficult time with the boys who look like full grown men. When the teacher hits one of the older boys with a ruler, the boy laughs and tells the teacher that it tickled. The teacher singles out Laura to harass. One of the boys, telling Laura that he will help her get back at the teacher, puts ink in the teacher's case. Charles witnesses the teacher demanding Laura hold out her hand so he can hit her with a stick. Charles breaks his stick. During a school board meeting, the teacher has a meltdown and resigns. When they offer the job to Miss Beadle, she has doubts about her ability to control the older boys. Upon her return, one of the older boys drops a book, but this time no one laughs. The class stares at him until he apologizes. The moral of the episode is a combination of having a bully for a teacher and having everyone stand up to the bully to take away his power and make him stop.

In "The Werewolf of Walnut Grove," Bart, a large boy who has been working in the fields, returns to school. He makes the smaller boys move to take their seats. When asked to help with a papier mache project, Bart puts the wet paper on a little boy instead. He tells the boy he will give him a dollar if he makes him something. When the boy delivers, Bart refuses to pay. The teacher, Miss Wilder, tells Bart he has to apologize. When Laura refuses Bart's offers to carry her books, he grabs them anyway. Because Laura's brother, Albert, came to Laura's defense, Bart starts to pick on Albert. Almanzo, who is an adult and bigger than Bart, stops Bart. Albert does not want to admit that he cannot fight his own battles. Bart's father confronts Almanzo for interfering with his son. Bart's father also threatens Miss Wilder that if she cannot control his son and the older boys in class, he will have her fired. When Bart puts a tack on Albert's seat, Miss Wilder orders Bart to stand in the corner. He knocks her chair over and talks back to her. Out of frustration and fear, she dismisses class. When the father takes his son's side, Bart's bullying gets even bolder. He comes to Miss Wilder's house and mocks her. In class, Miss Wilder fires back at Bart and the students laugh at him. Albert makes a papier mache mask and tricks Bart into thinking he is a werewolf. As Bart runs out of the barn, the small boy trips him. Bart promises to behave and apologize until he figures out the werewolf was a hoax. Fearing Miss Wilder will get fired, Laura gets everyone in the school to take on the bully, which is the same tactic used in "The Bully Boys." Miss Beadle was likewise threatened with termination in "Troublemaker" if she could not control the older boys. In the end, Bart apologizes and Miss Wilder stays on as teacher.

"The Election" features two bigger boys, Joel and Kenny, who tease Elmer and push him down. Elmer defends their behavior to Laura even though they call him the "dumbest kid in Walnut Grove." Elmer thinks of the boys as his friends even though they treat him badly. As a joke, the boys nominate Elmer for school president. Elmer's father confronts Elmer about how Joel and Kenny mistreat him, tripping him and tearing his pants. Elmer defends the boys saying they did not mean any harm. Elmer's parents are concerned and want to protect Elmer from the other kids. Later, the boys force Elmer up on a stump to make him give a campaign speech. Most of the other kids laugh, but Miss Beadle stops them. Elmer's father again confronts Elmer about thinking those boys are his friends when they make Elmer eat worms. Elmer begs his father not to talk to the other parents. When Elmer tells Joel and Kenny that he wants to back out of the election, they trick him into getting into pig pen. They push him into the mud, messing up the new shirt that his mother made for him for election day. When Elmer gets to school, he finally stands up for himself. He admits his nomination was a joke and tells the class it is not right for big kids to pick on little kids or make fun of people. Mary withdraws her nomination so the race is down to a tie between Elmer and Nellie. Willie, Nellie's brother, is the tie breaker. Willie votes for Elmer because he says Nellie is mean and threatened him.

Much like *Little House on the Prairie*, *Anne of Green Gables* includes both bullies and mean girls in the storylines. The boys tease Anne on her first day of school. Gilbert pulls her hair and calls her "Carrots." Viewers of the series and readers of the books find out that Gilbert teases her only because he likes her. Further into the school year, Anne insists that she and Diana walk through a line of bullies on their way to school instead of walking around them and chance being late. The bullies throw pinecones at them. Diana screams and runs away. Anne chases the leader Charlie through the woods and gets in trouble for trespassing. The teacher punishes Anne but not Charlie and the other bullies.

Little House on the Prairie also featured an episode on adult bullying. Brothers Sam and George bully the townspeople in "The Bully Boys." They rack up a large bill at the Olesons' store. When Mr. Oleson tells them he cannot extend their credit further, one of the men starts breaking items in the store. The Olesons back down and let the men take what they want. The men also bought lumber on credit. They turned around and sold the order to a third party and kept the money instead of paying back the lumber yard. The brothers also bought beef and hay on credit from the locals, never intending to pay them. The reverend encourages the church members to meet the problem with "turning the other cheek." The brothers tell the minister lies about their sick mother. The reverend feels sympathy for them and the bullying begins to escalate. The brothers stop Caroline on her way to the Olesons' market to sell eggs. They grab her basket, spilling the eggs. They touch her face and rip her skirt, but she manages to get away. Charles goes after the brothers for revenge. Mr. Edwards finds an unconscious Charles in the back of his wagon after a fight. The reverend disapproves of Charles's behavior. He asks Caroline if she misinterpreted the brothers' actions. Convinced the brothers had evil intentions, the reverend finally stands up to the bullies. He grabs one of them and yanks his arm behind his back. Mr. Edwards grabs the other one. The townsmen run the brothers out of town.

The following Westerns were included because the term "bully" or "bullies" was present in the programs' synopses. Dialogue in the shows also identified them specifically as "bullies." Television programs with adult bullies set in a specific era have a much different take on the type of bullying and the remedies to stop the behavior or the perpetrator. The laws of the old West appear very lax by today's standards. Dueling etiquette and revenge standards were different on these television programs. *The Rifleman* and *Gunsmoke* often used duels to solve their issues. A culture of violence and lawlessness and gun access accelerated the bullying. Law officials were much more likely to allow bullied victims to handle to problem themselves.

The lead character of *The Rifleman*, Lucas McCain, is a gunman turned homesteader in a small town in the western territories. McCain is a single father who is trying to raise his son with values such as justice and tolerance. The bullying found in several episodes of the show are generally disputes between townies and outsiders or foreigners. The disputes often results in a fight or duel. In the first season of *The Rifleman*, "The Money Gun," a ruthless loan shark and bully, Jackford, starts slapping around Asa, his bookkeeper. When Lucas steps in, Jackford hits him. The marshal shoots his gun in the air and orders Jackford out of town. Asa threatens that Jackford will not be around much longer. Instead of filing a complaint with the marshal, Asa hires a bounty hunter and gun-for-hire named King to goad Jackford into a duel. If Jackford draws first, King is within the law to kill him. When the marshal asks the town to help out Jackford, they all turn on him, thinking that a dead Jackford is a good thing because he is a bully. Jackford comes to town and calls out King. When they get to the spot of the duel, Jackford does not draw but beats King and breaks his shooting hand. The marshal, Lucas, and Jackford walk away. Asa is upset he did not get his money's worth so he kills an unarmed King. The marshal tells him he will hang for murder.

The next three episodes of *The Rifleman* deal with the bullying of a foreigner by locals. In "Duel of Honor," a visitor from Italy, Count Alfredo or "Freddie," is passing through town. The locals drinking outside the bar look and whisper because of the stranger's frilly shirt. One of the men, Groder, approaches Freddie. Lucas steps in as he is filling in for the absent marshal. Lucas warns Freddie about some of the men in the saloon who are not used to "strangers." Lucas explains that Groder gets drunk, beats people up, wrecks bars, and picks fights for the pleasure of killing. Lucas stands by as Groder takes one of Freddie's Italian lira and carelessly rips it in half. Groder offers to buy Freddie a drink. When Freddie refuses, Groder threatens to forcibly pour it down Freddie's throat if he does not drink it. Freddie slaps him with his glove, challenging him to a duel. Groder fires early and misses. He begs Freddie not to shoot him. Freddie tells him the holder of the gun gets a free shot at anytime. He gives the gun to Lucas who can use it at his discretion. Groder runs away and the bystanders laugh.

In "The Queue," a Chinese man, Mr. Wang, and his son come into town. Their wagon accidently scares the horse of another boy, Noah, throwing Noah to the ground. Noah's father, Vince, threatens to hit Mr. Wang until Lucas steps in to save the day. Vince schemes with another man to ruin the Wangs' laundry business. Vince and one of his cronies shoot at the wagon to chase off the Wangs. The marshal only warns Vince and no arrests are made. Lucas talks the Wangs into staying to open a laundry in town. Noah is a bully just like his father. Noah calls the Chinese boy a "girl" because of his braid. Mark, Lucas's son, jumps in to help and they start to fight. When Mr. Wang comes into the saloon, Vince and his cronies start to hassle him. Lucas steps in, holding is his rifle in the air. That night, the men come to the Wangs' campsite. They throw all their laundry in the fire and cut off Mr. Wang's braid. Mr. Wang has had enough and beats Vince using karate. In the next scene, Vince and Noah are leaving town by judge's orders as the Wangs settle in to their new town.

Two seasons later, Lucas has to deal with another set of bullies in "The Sixteenth Cousin." A Japanese nobleman, Hikaru, and his man servant, Soto, stop in town for a brief visit to learn about other cultures. Two troublemakers on the street call the Japanese men "monkeys." One of them trips Soto. Lucas orders the bully to pick up the suitcase that Soto dropped. Again, the marshal only warns the bullies. At dinner that night, they stop Soto as he goes to get some sake. Hikaru and Soto have lost honor and now must fight the bullies. Lucas warns them that the men are armed. The marshal tells the men to leave town, but the men refuse. Hikaru and Soto change into traditional Samurai war outfits. Hikaru informs Lucas that for the sake of honor, someone must die. Lucas negotiates their ability to regain honor by fighting the bullies using hand-to-hand combat. Hikaru and Soto repeatedly flip the bullies using martial arts techniques until the bullies give up and leave them alone.

Like *The Rifleman*, *Gunsmoke* also addresses bullying in the Wild West. In "The Killer," the bully Crego shoots a man in cold blood and calmly goes back to sleep. Marshall Matt Dillion knows Crego is the murderer but he does not have enough evidence to arrest him. Crego causes trouble in Dodge by challenging a young man, Jesse, to a duel. Seeing it is an unfair fight, Matt breaks it up. He laments that Crego is the kind of man who picks on people who do not stand a chance against him. Crego shoots another man in the hand, the knees, and then the belly. Crego gets away with murder yet again. Later on the street, Crego manhandles the saloon owner, Miss Kitty. This time Matt challenges Crego to a duel. Even the town doctor says that man has "no right to be alive." Matt and Chester come just in time to see Crego killing Jesse in a duel. Matt approaches Crego in the saloon and tells him he is "not fit to live." Matt tells Crego he is going to wait for him in the street to kill him. Crego raises his gun to shoot Matt in the back. Chester warns Matt and Matt turns and shoots Crego. Chester consoles Matt that he had to do it. This was a rare instance when Matt went outside the law and took matters into his own hands.

In the opening scene of "Cheap Labor," Matt stands in the cemetery lamenting that a man who makes a slave of a woman deserves to be in the cemetery. Matt witnesses a man named Stancil bullying his sister, Flora. Flora asks Matt not interfere because Stancil will just take it out on her. A local cowboy, Fos Capper, helps Flora load her wagon outside the general store. Stancil sees them together and knocks out Fos. Undeterred, Fos starts to court Flora. When Stancil catches them together again, he orders two of his cronies to fight Fos. When Flora arrives with bruises on her face, Fos borrows Matt's gun and points it at the bullies. Stancil, deserted by his cronies, flees.

The town bully, Cloud Marsh, takes corn from a vendor but refuses to pay in the episode "The Laughing Gas Show." He pushes the vendor down the stairs when asked for the money. Cloud volunteers to take the gas at a laughing gas show. One man in the audience shouts, "Do us a favor, put that big bully down forever." Once Cloud is under the influence of the gas, he gets upset and begins to cry. Cloud yells at everyone for not liking him and his brothers. The audience mocks and jeers him. They call him "Cry Baby Cloud." When some men tease him in the salon after the show, he pulls a gun but Marshal Matt Dillon stops him. Cloud and his brothers come back to beat up the man who runs the laughing gas show, Earl Stafford. They put him in a coma. Stafford's wife refuses to sign a complaint against the brothers. Her husband is an ex-gunman who changed his identity after he got out of prison and does not want people to know who he is since he has reformed. The Marsh brothers hassle an old man in the saloon and force liquor down the old man's throat. Matt stops the men but no arrests are made. Cloud is arrested for breaking the laughing gas equipment. A lawyer gets Cloud out of jail saying Cloud was not responsible for his acts while under the influence of the laughing gas. In retaliation, the Marsh brothers hold the wife down and force her to breathe the gas. They throw her back and forth, forcing her to dance with them. Earl comes out with a gun and shoots Cloud. Matt takes the blame for killing Cloud so the wife will never know it was her husband who had killed again. There appears to be no repercussions for the brothers' role in the attack. In the next scene, Matt, Doc, and Chester drink coffee and laugh in the office, apparently unaffected by the killing.

In "Tail to the Wind," Burt, a bully, offers a local farmer, Pezzy, and his wife, Cora, a third of what their farm is worth. Burt promises them they will be unhappy if they turn down his offer. The neighboring farmer, Ed, had been killed earlier. Cora accuses Burt of murdering Ed after Burt bought Ed's farm. Cora threatens Burt and his son that if they try anything, she will fight like an animal in contrast to her husband's passiveness. Burt just laughs at her. In an effort to force them to sell, Burt shoots up Pezzy's place and burns down his chicken coop. Pezzy does not report the incident because he does not want any trouble. He lies to the marshal, Matt, about the incident when questioned. Matt offers to put Burt in jail if Pezzy will agree to sign a complaint but Pezzy refuses. Later, as Pezzy and Cora drive away from the store, the wheel comes off their wagon. Burt had tampered with it; however, the townspeople are afraid of Burt so no one will admit to witnessing it. Matt calls Burt "scum" and "yellow" and tells him to "crawl in a hole." Burt and his son come back to shoot up Pezzy's again. This time Pezzy comes into town the next day with their bodies. He tells Matt he found them dead after they ran into a clothesline he just happened to put up the day before. Matt tells Doc to never underestimate a mild man. Doc says "the hanging" was long overdue.

In "The Blacksmith," a bully, Tolman, targets a German immigrant, Emil. Tolman disputes Emil's blacksmith work. He warns Emil that he is going to tell everyone not to come to Emil's shop. Emil tells Marshal Matt Dillon that Tolman started the dispute with him because he refused to sell Tolman his property. In the saloon, Dillon hears a group of men talk about the "foreigners" and how they should tar and feather them and run them out of town. Matt warns them to stay away from Emil. When one of the men laughs, Matt knocks him down. The bullies threaten to return. The men crash Emil's wedding reception. When Tolman forcibly tries to dance with Emil's new bride, Emil carries him out and dumps him in the horse tank. The crowd laughs. Later that night one of Tolman's men lures Emil away from the house with a lie about stranded travelers. While he is away, Tolman starts Emil's house on fire. Emil tells Matt he will handle it himself. He assures the marshal there will be no killing so Matt leaves it up to him. Emil takes on all three men in a fistfight. When Emil knocks them all unconscious, Matt tells the crowd to take away the men and "pile them up somewhere." Matt tells Emil that Emil has the whole town on his side. The culture at this time approved of personal vengeance and men taking care of business on their own.

The single Western movie that came up in the search for "bullies" was *The Man Who Shot Liberty Valence*. The film begins with a stagecoach robbery. During the robbery, Rance Stoddard, a lawyer just arriving to town, tries to stop Valence from taking a widow's heirloom brooch. Valence rips pages from Rance's law book and whips Rance until Valence's cohorts pull him off his victim. Even after the beating, Rance refuses to carry a gun. He announces that he wants to put Valence in jail, not kill him. The cowardly sheriff claims he cannot do anything because the crime happened outside of town. Because Valence stole all of Rance's money, he is forced to wait tables in town. Valence comes into the restaurant but Tom Doniphon, a local rancher, steps in and confronts Valence. Rance is upset with Tom for fighting his battles. Valence and the boys once again terrorize the town by wrecking the newspaper office. Valence whips the editor until his boys stop him. Rance relents and lets Tom give him shooting lessons. Valence calls Rance out for a duel. Rance thinks he shoots Valence in self-defense; however, Tom actually fires the fatal bullet. The reason why Liberty Valence is considered a bully in addition to a murderer is that he is excessive in his beatings. Twice his own men had to physically stop Valence from beating his victims to death. Also when Valence comes into the restaurant, he trips Rance, forcing him to drop a tray of food. The violent culture of the times and the weak sheriff contribute to Valence's feeling of invincibility. Valence is not held accountable for his actions. He bullies because he can.

Conclusion

Bullying portrayals were found in various subgenres of television dramas. The largest contrast in programming was between representations in the teen dramas and the procedural crime shows. Teen dramas appeared to address issues of bullying in a more comprehensive way than either movies or situation comedies. Television serials, which are less restricted by time, featured well-thought-out bullying scenarios as well as school-shooting storylines. Television dramas, particularly teen dramas, are practically the sole venue for addressing LGBT bullying issues. From lighter (e.g., *Glee*) to darker dramas (e.g., *Queer as Folk*), issues of gay bashing, particularly of teenage boys, were thoughtfully developed and more closely mirror real life than other genres or mediums. Bullying of lesbians was less severe and was more quickly resolved, usually in an episode or two.

Crime shows did little to address reasons why the bullying happened, how to solve it, or how to prevent it. Producers mainly used bullying as a motivation or rationale for a murder. These shows sensationalized the issue, perhaps scaring parents, rather than widening viewers' understanding. A search of show synopses for "bully" or "bullies" produced a significant number of hits for Westerns, particularly *Gunsmoke* and *The Rifleman*. Each episode had a moral lesson about how to treat others, especially if the victims were different or unable to stand up for themselves. The Westerns included in this analysis were not only set in the past but originally aired in the 1950s and 1960s. The 1970s series *Little House on the Prairie*, a historical family drama set in a similar time as the Westerns, had a similar sentiment about bullying in each episode.

6

Television Mean Girls

For decades, mean-girl behavior was the realm of adult women on daytime and later nighttime soap operas. It was not until the 1990s that dramas focusing on teens gained popularity (e.g., *Beverly Hills 90210*). While bullies occasionally make appearances on teen dramas, storylines are specifically constructed to feature mean girls, paying special attention to the queen bees who shun and torment the less popular girls on the show. Many of the teen dramas air on traditional broadcast networks (e.g., *One Tree Hill*, *Gossip Girl*); however, cable channels such as ABC Family (e.g., *The Secret Life of the American Teenager*, *Pretty Little Liars*) and TeenNick (e.g., *Degrassi: The Next Generation*) have become the primary venue for shows targeted to teen audiences. Shows targeted to tween and early teen audiences are almost exclusively sitcom types of shows found on Nickelodeon and Disney Channel. Subgenres of the teen dramas include competition (e.g., *Make It or Break It*), supernatural (e.g., *Buffy the Vampire Slayer*), and semi-scripted programs (e.g., *Laguna Beach*). I also included historic portrayals (e.g., *Little House on the Prairie*) and examples of adult mean girls (e.g., *Desperate Housewives*) for comparison.

Teen Dramas

Beverly Hills 90210, which premiered in 1990, is often credited for spawning the teen drama series. In the pilot episode, twins Brenda and Brandon arrive at West Beverly High School from Minnesota. Kelly, one of the popular girls, asks Brenda to be her lab partner in order to avoid partnering with a heavyset, unpopular girl. Kelly dismisses her own mean behavior as part of the social structure of the school. The series generally ignores or excludes any unpopular, unattractive girls in the school. The only exception is the character Andrea, who gives a fake address in order to attend the wealthy school. Andrea comes from a less desirable neighborhood. She complains about being discriminated against; however, she soon becomes part of the popular kids' clique. The true mean girl does not appear until the fifth season when the show introduces the character Valerie. Valerie is played by Tiffani-Amber Thiessen, who, by sharp contrast, played the sweet, loveable Kelly on *Saved by the Bell*. After Valerie's father committed suicide, her mother sends her to live with the Walshs in Beverly Hills. Valerie is sweet to the Walshs' faces but lies and disparages them behind their backs. She leads Steve on while sleeping with Brenda's ex-boyfriend Dylan on the side. When she gets caught with Dylan, Valerie lies and claims he was drunk and attacked her. Valerie drives a wedge between Brandon, who defends Valerie, and Kelly, who sees through her nice façade. Valerie continues to cause trouble and steal boyfriends. Eventually, she becomes friendly with the group, although they do not trust her.

Eight years after *Beverly Hills 90210* went off the air, the sequel *90210* debuted. This time a family from Kansas relocates to Beverly Hills. Unfortunately, Annie does not receive the warm welcome that Brenda did in the original series. One of the teachers has Naomi, the school's mean girl, show Annie around. Naomi rolls her eyes, obviously annoyed. Naomi's friend Adriana, an actress and a singer, joins them. When Annie tells Adriana that she is helping with the scenery for the school play because she got to school too late to try out for a part, Adriana tells Annie in a condescending tone that scenery seems like the place for Annie. When a less popular girl, Silver, sees a sticker for the band she likes on Annie's folder, she starts a conversation with Annie. Naomi whisks Annie away from Silver, telling Annie she is "saving" her. Naomi and Silver were best friends until they had a falling out. Naomi brings Annie into her social circle. To get back at Annie for ditching her, Silver posts a video mocking Annie's Kansas upbringing and calls her a "backstabbing bitch" on her blog. The boys at school then start to call Annie "farm girl" and moo at her. Annie later explains that she did not mean to hurt Silver's feelings by leaving with Naomi, and the two make up. When Naomi is struggling to finish her book report, Annie offers to email her a copy of her old book report to use as a guide. When Annie gets upset at Naomi for copying her paper word for word, Naomi bribes her, giving Annie a very expensive dress to wear to Naomi's party. When Naomi gets caught for plagiarism, she calls Annie a "bitch" and "disinvites" her to her party. Silver posts a mean video about Naomi's boyfriend Ethan cheating on Naomi.

In the second season, Annie gets drunk and takes her top off for a boy. He takes a picture of her and brags to his friends. Naomi thinks it was Annie whom she caught having sex with her boyfriend, Liam; however, it was actually Naomi's sister. Naomi corners Annie in the bathroom and tells Annie she has no idea how hellish she is going to make Annie's life. Naomi does not believe Annie when she denies it was her. Even though she has doubts it was Annie who slept with Liam, Naomi sends out the topless picture of Annie via text message. Annie is shunned at school. Someone writes "slut" on her locker. When Naomi lies about being sexually harassed by a teacher, the school shuns her, except for Annie, who understands because of her own experience. By season 3, Naomi has changed into a relative good girl although she can still be rather rude. For example, she sarcastically disparages Annie's mother because of her Kansas roots.

The premise of *The O.C.* is a kindhearted lawyer, Sandy Cohen, takes in a troubled teenage boy, Ryan. The Cohens live in a swanky neighborhood in Orange County, California. Summer is the resident mean girl on the show. She is mostly mean to the boys, particularly Ryan because he comes from the "wrong" neighborhood. At a party, Summer mocks Ryan's friend Donny when he flirts with her. She asks him, "Aren't you, like, the bus boy?" Summer's best friend Marissa's mother is an even bigger mean girl. Marissa's mother, Julie, grew up outside of the right neighborhoods, married up, and now desperately wants to fit in with the high-society women of Orange County. When Sandy overhears Julie and another woman put down Ryan, he reminds Julie that she herself comes from Riverside, another less affluent community. Julie refuses to give up her lifestyle status even after her husband, Jimmy, loses everything in a shady business deal. After rumors get out about Jimmy's financial scheme, the women in the community discuss how to exclude Julie from social activities. Kirsten, Sandy's wife, stands up for Julie. Kirsten calls the women out about putting Julie down while they have their own substance-abuse problems and cheating husbands to worry about. (Note: *The O.C.* was the inspiration for the *Real Housewives* reality series.)

On *One Tree Hill*, Brooke initially fulfills the role of the teen-drama mean girl. She is rather judgmental and narcissistic but far from the crazy mean girl portrayed on others programs. Brooke has absent parents who give her money but not love and attention. She nicknames a less popular girl, Haley, "Tutor Girl." When a drunken Brooke finds a note that Haley has written to a boy she likes, Nathan, Brooke broadcasts the contents of the note to the rest of the party. Haley gets angry because she thinks Nathan showed the note to Brooke. The next day, Brooke feels bad that she damaged Nathan and Haley's relationship. She apologizes and sets them up on a date. By the seventh episode in the series, Brooke and Haley are on relatively friendly terms. In season three, Brooke meets her match in the mean girl department. Rachel arrives in town and tries out for cheerleading. Rachel befriends the other cheerleaders and starts to move in on Brooke's boyfriend, Lucas. Brooke and Rachel get into a cat fight at the big pep rally when Brooke tries to get Rachel kicked off the cheerleading squad. Brooke and Rachel eventually become friends until Rachel becomes addicted to drugs and steals money from Brooke.

Popular is a series created by Ryan Murphy, who also created *Glee*. Both shows explore cliques and high-school-status battles. The premise of the series is that two arch rivals, Sam and Brooke, become stepsisters when their parents meet and, not long after, elope. Brooke is the pretty blonde cheerleader with the perfect boyfriend. Brooke is insecure and anorexic. She "has it all" but still wonders, "Isn't this the part where I'm supposed to be happy?" Sam, who is just as attractive as Brooke, is brunette and less popular. Although Brooke is set up as the head cheerleader mean girl, Sam is also a mean girl. Sam calls the popular kids "fashion victims" and is particularly critical of Brooke. Brooke and Sam call each other "fake" and "phony" and accuse each other of having low self-esteem. When Sam interviews Brooke for her journalism class, Brooke tells Sam it bothers her that Sam is trying to stereotype her. She tells Sam that the "popularity thing" just happened. Brooke tells her boyfriend Josh that she is tired of living the big lie of being popular; however, she is not able to let it go. When Josh tells Brooke he tried out for the high school musical, she laments that they will never make homecoming court if he is a "drama geek."

Sam friend, Carmen, invites the cheerleaders to her slumber party. She thinks perserverance will get her into the popular group. Only after Nicole, the meanest character on the show, sees Carmen's hunky brother does she let the cheerleaders attend. Nicole later nominates Carmen for homecoming queen as a joke. Sam writes a negative editorial about the cheerleading budget to get back at Brooke and Nicole for not choosing Carmen for the cheerleading squad. Later, Brooke admits to Carmen that she did not make the squad because of her weight. Mary Cheery is another rich, obnoxious character on the *Popular*. She is accepted into the popular group because of her family's money and connections.

The ABC Family shows *The Lying Game* and *Pretty Little Liars* feature very attractive, economically well-off girls. The mean element is secondary to the more elaborate plots of mysteries. The premise of *The Lying Game* is that twins Sutton and Emma, who were separated at birth, are reunited. In order to find the identity of their birth mother, Sutton has Emma assume Sutton's identity. Sutton was raised by wealthy parents, while Emma was placed in an abusive foster home. Similar to the women in the television series *The O.C.*, Sutton's friend Char's mother is obsessed with Char's popularity and success.

Sutton's sister, Laurel, tells Emma she has seen what the Sutton's clique does to others kids, making their lives miserable. The premise of the show *Pretty Little Liars* is that Alison, the mean girl, is found murdered. Her four remaining friends flash back to Alison's bad behavior. At the school cafeteria, a peppy girl named Mona with pigtails and glasses approaches the girls' table. Alison tells them, "If you ignore it, it will go away." Mona looks humiliated and walks away with her tray. After school, Mona calls out after Alison and Aria. The girls call her a "dork" and run to get away from her, laughing. Mona stops and turns back defeated. When an awkward boy, Lucas, accidently spills coffee on Alison in the hallway, Alison tells him he was an accident to his parents. She calls him "Hermie" and gossips to her friends that he was born a hermaphrodite, having with both male and female genitalia. Alison is also snippy and judgmental with her friends, dictating what they should wear to a Halloween party and commenting on how big Hanna's posterior is. Alison claims she "made" all of them. Alison tells one of the girls, Spencer, that Spencer does not exist without her.

Lizzie, one of the characters on ABC Family's *Lincoln Heights*, stands up to mean girls in the hallway who are making fun of her outfit. She says to them, "Your whole 'mean girls' act is so '90s." Lizzie makes a new friend at school, Sylvia. The popular girls trick Lizzie into sending Sylvia a text pretending to be Sylvia's ex-boyfriend. Silvia approaches her ex-boyfriend in the hallway at school, thinking he sent her a text telling her that he missed her. He tells Sylvia in front of everyone that she should go back on her on "meds" and that she was really boring in bed. The popular girls steal a semi-naked picture Sylvia had sent her ex-boyfriend and distribute it throughout the school. The popular girls warn Lizzie that if she stays friends with Sylvia, they are going to make her life "a living hell." Lizzie uses her connections with an even more popular girl to put down the mean girls.

Gossip Girl is a teen drama series on the CW. The title character, Gossip Girl, whispers in a voiceover, "Who am I? That's one secret I'll never tell." Gossip Girl terrorizes students at an exclusive private school on the Upper East Side of Manhattan using text messages containing rumors and incriminating photos. She has spies all over town. Blair is the queen bee at the Constance Billard School for Girls. Blair has an absent, judgmental mother. When her best friend, Serena, comes back from a failed year at a boarding school, Blair becomes defensive over her position as queen bee. Gossip Girl in a voiceover states, "Spotted on the steps of the Met, an S and B power struggle. There's nothing Gossip Girl likes more than a good cat fight and this could be a classic." Throughout the series, Serena and Blair are on a continuous breakup and makeup cycle.

Jenny, new to Constance Billard, is desperate to be part of the social order. She is ashamed that she lives in Brooklyn instead of Manhattan. She is excited to be invited to Blair's sleepover only to find out it was a trap. During a game of "truth or dare," Blair makes Jenny steal a jacket from Blair's mother's store. The girls leave her as the alarm goes off and the door locks. In retaliation of Blair's meanness, Jenny tells Blair's boyfriend, Nate, that Blair lost her virginity to Chuck. After the word gets out via Gossip Girl, the crowd shuns Blair. They call her a "selfish bitch" and a "hypocrite." One of her former minions tells her to "consider yourself dethroned, Queen Bee." The girls throw yogurt on Blair's head as she enters school. Blair warns Jenny that if she walks away from her too, she will ruin her. Jenny walks away and sits with the other girls. Jenny takes over as queen bee and orders a new, awkward girl to handle her mundane tasks such as returning books to the library and fetching coffee. Jenny hesitates about abusing her power but the girls convince Jenny that she should not have to do such things for herself. The minions tell her that Blair has trained her well. When the group finally invites Blair out, they leave her waiting at the restaurant by herself. When Jenny gets caught stealing a dress from one of the girl's mothers' closets, the group abandons her and follow Blair once again.

Rather than a traditional bully, the character Chuck is set up as a mean boy. He is condescending and treats women as sex toys. He nearly rapes Serena and later Jenny. When Chuck targets Jenny, Gossip Girl states, "Looks like Little J might end up with a new boy and a ticket to the inner circle or will C end up with another victim." After Dan saves Jenny from Chuck, Dan flirts with Serena about a second date, dismissing the seriousness of the attack. Chuck goes after Dan and calls him "trash." Dan tells Chuck that they do not need to engage class warfare.

Gossip Girl is the classic example of how familial money allows teens to have access to parties and clubs and have power over others, even adults. Their youth mixed with their independence plays out a fantasy since they do not have to work or pretend to work. They also can manipulate the college system where the rich get richer by going to the right schools with the right connections. The show highlights not only the educational advantages of the rich, but the opportunities for internships and mentoring. There are epic clashes between Dan and Chuck in terms of class and Blair and Jenny in terms of social status.

The series *Gilmore Girls* tells the story of a mother and a daughter. Lorelei, who became a single mother at 16, is exploring her life now that her daughter, Rory, is old enough to have her own life. Rory is adjusting to a fancy private school Chilton where socioeconomic status is an issue. Although Rory's grandparents are extremely wealthy and socially connected, Lorelei has chosen to make it on her own, working as a manager at an inn in a small town.

On Rory's first day of school, Paris and her cronies, Madeline and Louise, steal Rory's academic file. Paris announces to Rory that the school and the school newspaper are her domain, that she is top of the class, and that Rory will never catch up to her. As Rory fights with the lock on her locker, she accidently bumps into Paris who drops and breaks her school project. The teacher requires Rory to help Paris fix her project. Paris objects to the help. Rory sends Paris a note apologizing again, but Paris crumbles up the note without reading it. Paris warns her to stay away or she will make school "a living hell" for her. When Rory gets a D on her first paper, Paris heckles her, saying that McDonald's is taking applications. She tells Rory, "Not everyone can be smart. Someone has to answer the phones." Paris spreads rumors when she witnesses Lorelai kissing one of the teachers at Chilton. Paris later apologizes to Rory. She explains that she just wanted everyone to stop talking about her parents' ugly divorce. Paris's mother is very critical of Paris. Paris was raised by a series of nannies and housekeepers. When Lorelai gives Rory, Paris, Madeline, and Louise her tickets to a concert, Madeline and Louise run off to a party with some older boys they just met. When Lorelai finds them, she reads them the riot act. Paris tells Rory that it was the best night of her life. By episode 13 of the first season, Paris and Rory develop a friendship although Paris is still unpleasant at times.

In the third season, Paris, now student body president, gets some competition in the mean department from Francie, the senior class president. When Francie stands and proposes to raise the hemline of the school's uniform skirts, Paris disparages the idea for being trivial. While walking down the hall at school, one of Francie's cronies grabs Rory and pulls her into the girls' room. In a stern voice, Francie tells Rory that she has the power to make Paris's life a living hell. She wants Rory to tell Paris to "play ball" or she will make Paris ineffectual. After Rory stands up to Francie, Francie warns Rory that if she tells Paris they talked, Paris will think they colluded. In the next episode, Francie tells Rory she wants a truce. Rory thinks it seems sudden but she shakes hands with Francie. The next day, Francie approaches Paris with pictures of her and Rory shaking hands. Francie claims Rory was trying to turn Francie against Paris. Paris takes out her aggression out on Rory in their fencing class for meeting with Francie behind Paris's back. Paris says she cannot believe she thought Rory was her best friend. With everyone mad at her, Rory she sits alone at lunch and gets a paper airplane with "Leper" thrown at her. She puts on her headphones and calmly reads a book. Paris and Rory eventually make up.

The show *Freaks and Geeks* is set in the '80s in a suburb of Detroit, Michigan. The combination of the past and the Midwest gives the show a nostalgic, realistic feel. While some of the cast members were much older than the characters they played, James Francis Daley who played Sam, the lead geek and target of most of the bullying, was 14 years old during the run of the show. His sister Lindsay, a straight-laced mathlete decides to explore the darker side of life. She starts to hang out with the pot-smoking "freaks." Lindsay tells her old friends to go away and that she does not want to compete in the mathlete competition this year. Kim, the mean girl in the freak group, is resistant to Lindsay being around. She calls her a "brain" and says she is just a rich kid. She tries to scare Lindsay away by dumping Lindsay's purse in the hallway. Overtime, Kim appears to tolerate Lindsay since the boys in the group seem to like her. In episode four, "Kim Kelly is My Friend," Kim comes to Lindsay for support when she catches her boyfriend cheating on her. When Kim invites Lindsay over to her house, Lindsay discovers how awful Kim's home life is and understands why Kim is as mean as she is.

Huge was a short-lived ABC Family series about kids at fat camp. The main character, Wil, is an angry, overweight teen whose parents force her to go to camp. Wil channels her anger toward Amber, a slightly overweight, pretty blonde girl. *Huge* demonstrates a reverse discrimination where the heavy kids, instead of being picked on, pick on Amber out of jealousy. They assume because Amber is attractive by conventional standards that she is a mean girl. When Wil asks the boys if they will change the television channel, they refuse. However, when Amber asks, they give her the remote. Wil steals Amber's shorts from the wash and shrinks them in the dryer so that Amber thinks she is gaining weight. During the obstacle course, Amber's shorts split. She runs away humiliated. Eventually Wil and Amber call a truce.

Degrassi's resident mean girl is Holly J. Holly J. is the young sister of Heather Sinclair. Heather was described as the queen bee during her time at Degrassi High School. For years, the running joke on the show was that Heather was never seen on camera. She and her mean antics were only referenced, never shown. After Heather supposedly graduates, Holly J. takes her place. Holly J. is very competitive and feuds with two other girls on the spirit squad. She spreads rumors that Manny, a Latina, is racist when she overhears her joking about breaking up with her Black boyfriend. She puts down another girl, Mia, for being a teen mother. She is even mean to her best friend, Anya. When Anya becomes friendly with Mia, Holly J. retaliates by announcing to the class that Anya is dyslexic. When Anya asks Holly J. why she is mean to her, Holly J. replies, "Because you let me." In the episode "Ladies Night," Anya is in charge of a charity event where the participants fast for twenty-four hours. When Anya finds out that Holly J. is trying to break up Anya and her boyfriend, Sav, Anya secretly records Holly J. eating a cookie. She broadcasts it to the school monitors. Out of revenge, Holly J. brings pizzas to the hungry group, ruining the charity event. When Holly J. is mean to another student, Alli, Alli retaliates by creating an "I Hate Holly J." website. Holly J. becomes a victim of cyberbullying when other students write hateful, threatening messages on the site.

The Secret Life of the American Teenager features a promiscuous mean girl, Adrian. Because her mother is absent and she does not know who her father is until later in the series, she gets validation through male attention. In the pilot, Adrian flirts with the new guidance counselor, propositions Grace's boyfriend Jack, and negotiates to have sex with Ricky on their third date. Adrian is also snarky to Amy, the mother of Ricky's baby, because she is jealous of Ricky and Amy's connection. Adrian eventually seduces Jack, who is frustrated because of Grace's vow to stay a virgin until marriage. Adrian denies trying to steal anyone's boyfriend even though she has sex with Ricky when he is dating Grace. Adrian and Grace eventually engage in a hair-pulling fight. All that being said, Adrian is not the standard mean girl; she is lonely and is mostly acting out to get attention. Her mother is absent and her father was not in her life until her teens. Ricky holds her to a double standard. Although he sleeps with her and several other girls on the show, he tells her she has no class. Even though Adrian keeps pushing her away, Grace forgives Adrian and they become friends. Although she never completely loses the snarky attitude, Adrian becomes a likeable character.

The premise of *Jane by Design* is that Jane, a high school student, lands a prestigious assistant's job with a top clothing designer. The designer, however, does not know that Jane is only in high school. Jane must lead a double life, hiding the truth from coworkers, her brother, and school friends. Jane appears ill equipped to deal with a mean older coworker, India. At the same time, Jane must deal with high school mean girls who call her a "weirdo." During one of India's presentation, Jane's boss asks Jane for her opinion. The boss puts her in an awkward position, further pitting them against each other. When Jane needs help on an assignment, one of her coworkers, Carter, agrees to help but backs out when India gives him a menacing look. He is unwilling to cross India. Another male coworker advises Jane to surrender to India. He explains the industry etiquette about "not hanging each other out to dry." He suggests Jane apologize to India. In a later episode, Jane accuses India of leaking secrets to the competition. India is unjustly fired since it is another coworker who is the leak.

COMPETITION-THEMED DRAMAS

Much like the mean-girl movies that feature competitions of cheerleading and musicals, television dramas have cheerleading (e.g., *Hellcats*), musical (e.g., *Glee*), gymnastic (e.g., *Make It or Break It*), and sorority (e.g., *Greek*) venues to exploit relational aggression between girls competing for a spot at the top. The mean girl's goal is to eliminate her rivals by any means necessary. Wealth and class are often factors in these programs. Mean-girl targets in *Hellcats*, *Make It or Break It*, and *Private* are "scholarship girls," while the mean girls have wealthy, influential fathers. In the case of Alice in *Hellcats* and Lauren in *Make It or Break It*, they eventually become friends with their targets.

Private, a series of young adult novels by Kate Brian, was a series developed for webcast. The headmaster forces a group of popular, wealthy girls to accept a "scholarship" student, Reed, into their dormitory, the Billings house. One girl nicknames Reed "Trailer Park." The girls make Reed scrub the bathroom with a toothbrush and steal an exam as a test of her loyalty to the group. Her reward is that they take her a party. The girls, whom Reed starts to think of as friends, turn out to be not just mean but evil. When one of the girls, Taylor, begins to panic, the girls call her parents who have her committed to a mental institution. Before she is taken away, Taylor leaves Reed a message not to trust the Billings girls. Ariana, the leader of the mean girls, actually kills a boy out of jealousy and frames his brother.

In the series *Hellcats*, Alice, an injured cheerleader feels threatened by a newcomer, Marti, who might permanently take her spot on the cheerleading squad. Alice's father is a rich senator while Marti is poor and needs the cheer scholarship in order to stay in school. Alice steals Marti's towel while she is in the shower. In order to sabotage Marti's performance, Alice invites Marti's mother to their competition. Alice has heard that Marti got nervous and did poorly when her mother came to her gymnastic meets in the past. In later episodes, Alice begins to date Jake, the quarterback on the school's football team. She appears to mellow and become friends with Marti. One of the storylines includes naked pictures of Alice being distributed after her boyfriend Jake's phone was stolen.

In the opening of the ABC Family series *Greek*, Frannie, the president of the sorority, emphasizes the stereotypical, superficial traits of sorority rushes such whether or not the pledges are wearing the most current fashion. The sisters joke about going to "the retirement center" and "spreading cheer," which is really code for meeting at the bar. Frannie holds the future sorority's presidency over Casey's head. Casey is assigned to recruit a powerful senator's daughter, Rebecca. Rebecca is rather ruthless and uses her connections to get the best room in the sorority house, Casey's. Casey's brother catches Casey's boyfriend, Evan, cheating with Rebecca. Frannie pressures Casey to keep having sex with Evan so their sorority will not risk losing his fraternity connection. When Casey becomes sorority president, Frannie gets angry and tries starting a rival sorority. In the end, Frannie is disgraced. When Casey helps Rebecca when Rebecca is close to being expelled, she becomes nicer to Casey.

Make It or Break It is an ABC Family series about an elite group of gymnasts. In true teen drama fashion, Emily, a "scholarship" student who was discovered on a school playground, is the new girl trying out for a spot on the top squad. The boys think Emily is "hot" while the girls make fun of her outfits since she comes from a working class family. Lauren, the most stuck up of the girls, plans to "ice" Emily out of the group. One of the gymnasts, Kaylie, apologizes to Emily for Lauren's behavior. Payson, the top gymnast, is also nice to Emily; however, none of the girls seems to dare stand up to Lauren. In order to sabotage Emily's tryout, Lauren alters Emily's vault measurement. Emily hits the horse and is knocked unconscious. She recovers and revaults, taking third place from Lauren. In order to get into the critical top three, Lauren tells the coach that Kaylie is seeing a boy, which is against the rules. Emily lies for Kaylie and gives her an alibi. Because Lauren's dad, Steve, is a bully, it is not difficult to see how Lauren turned into a mean girl. He hires a private detective to follow Emily in order to find information that may lead to her elimination from the competition. He blackmails the coach into going to another gym, taking Lauren and leaving Kaylie, Emily, and Payson without a coach. Lauren has sex with Kaylie's boyfriend. Realizing she has gone too far, she immediately regrets it and begins to be less mean. Tensions arise between the girls when their new gymnastics coach has the girls write out their resentments on paper. The girls think he is going to burn them so they are honest in their answers. Instead, the coach reads them aloud. In girl culture, it is difficult to be honest without coming across as catty or conceited. Payson reminds them that they were not going to be those girls who stab each other in the back but now they are those girls. Despite the hurt feelings, the girls manage to make-up and all engage in a group hug. Lauren continues to do snotty things but by episode four, she is no longer the really mean girl.

SUPERNATURAL THEMED DRAMAS

Shows that feature supernatural powers often allow victims to retaliate against their abusers. Viewers can fantasize about avenging their own mean girl with superhuman tricks. In *Buffy the Vampire Slayer*, mean girl Cordelia appears very friendly to Buffy on her first day at a new school. She tells Buffy to be sure to know who the "losers" are. Buffy is rather apathetic to the social structure of the school. At lunch, Buffy joins an unpopular girl, Willow, who is sitting by herself. Cordelia comes by and tells Buffy, "I don't mean to disrupt your downward mobility." The next day in school, Cordelia tells everyone that Buffy is "weird" and a "psycho looney." Another girl spreads rumors about Buffy and why she left her old school. Although Willow clearly fears Cordelia and the popular girls, she stands up for Buffy and tricks Cordelia into deleting her computer work. Later, when the vampires attack, Buffy saves Cordelia and the rest of the popular kids. They are grateful; however, because no one can know Buffy's identity as a vampire slayer, she has to erase their memories. Cordelia goes back to being a mean girl.

One of the characters describes Faye as "the resident bad girl" in the pilot episode of the CW series *The Secret Circle*. The show, like many others that target a teen audience, is based on witchcraft and the supernatural. The inclusion of the supernatural is perhaps a way that teens can fantasize about getting revenge on bullies and maintain a fair social order. A group of six teens are joined by their family bloodlines of witches. If they can bind all six together, their powers will grow exponentially. Cassie, a new girl in town, is the sixth. After the death of her mother, she comes to live with her grandmother in the town with the other witches. The gender makeup of the group, four girls and two boys, adds the element of competition for the males' attention. When Cassie gets to her new school, she is befriended immediately by Sally, a popular cheerleader, and, Diana, one of the witches who wants Cassie to join the circle. Cassie is a very strong independent character. She cares little about being included in social circles. Diana and Faye engage in a power struggle over Cassie. Faye wants the power all to herself and does not want share it with the other five. To test Cassie, Faye locks her in her car and sets the car on fire. She wants Cassie to use her powers to stop the fire. One of the boys rescues Cassie. Cassie pushes back against Faye even though Faye is bigger and appears to have more powers. In chemistry class, Faye makes Cassie's glass beaker shatter. In turn, Cassie makes Faye's beaker catch fire. Later, Faye starts a storm, which gets out of control, and Cassie has to help her stop it. In the second episode, Faye gets angry with Sally and pushes her. Because her powers are now magnified, Sally ends up crashing through a guardrail and falls over the pier. She hits her head on the rocks. Faye's mother uses a special crystal to bring Sally back to life. Although Faye is not punished, she is remorseful. Once Cassie joins the group, Faye is no longer as mean.

SEMI-SCRIPTED DRAMAS

These so-called "reality shows" somehow pass as "reality" although they are staged and heavily scripted. The series are cast with attractive females who will be catty on screen.

The three shows are spinoffs of each other; therefore, some characters overlap. Perhaps the most damaging effect of the shows is the pretense that these are "reality" shows. Young viewers may tend to identify with the characters and believe that the behavior is normal. *Laguna Beach* is based a group of teens who live in an exclusive neighborhood of Southern California. Lauren's family is so wealthy that she is going to have a closet dedicated solely to shoes and purses in their new house. The series is one big lesson on relational aggression. Few if any girls in the cast do not meet the definition of a "mean girl." There is a noticeable absence of parents to monitor the girls' behavior. Lauren and Kristin, both blonde and pretty, are pitted against one another mostly because they like the same boy, Stephen. In the first episode, Lauren and her friends are deciding who to invite to their black and white party. When they get to Kristin's name, Lauren coughs. The others chime in with comments such as "drama!" Kristin tells her boyfriend, Stephen, that she will not go to a friend's cookout if Lauren is there. Kristin is portrayed as a wild child at spring break in Cabo, Kristin gets drunk and does a pole dance. Stephen calls her a "slut" several times to his friends. Kristin makes a catty remark about Lauren wanting to go to fashion school and calls her a "suckup little brat." Kristin also gossips about Lauren being a princess. Girl drama ensues as two other girls in their clique, Christina and Morgan, discuss how they did not invite Lauren and Lo to Christina's birthday party even though they were invited to Lauren and Lo's birthday parties. Lauren and Lo then discuss how Christina and Morgan have been acting "retarded" lately and call them "two-faced." When the girls show up at the same manicurist, Lo compliments Christina on her birthday earrings and then makes a rude comment under her breath. Lo calls Morgan a "whore" because they have the same pattern of dress for prom. *Laguna Beach* seems to have been set up for the expressed purpose of highlighting jealousy and petty rivalries.

The Hills does not appear to have girls who are as mean as *Laguna Beach* but they are significantly less intelligent. Heidi is a spoiled girl who takes little responsibility for her actions. Lauren gets an incredibly competitive internship with *Teen Vogue*, for which she is unqualified and has a terrible interview. Although Lauren disobeys strict instructions not to, she lets Heidi and her friends into an exclusive event. Even when her friends cause a scene, Lauren is not fired. The show is incredibly unrealistic and perpetuates the attitude that young people can do what they want and still get their "trophy" for showing up. In the episode "Rumor Has It," the pettiness is incredible not only between the females but the males. Kristin is harping on about how everyone is talking behind her back about her partying behavior and spreading rumors. Spencer, a drama queen, calls his sister Stephanie a "crazy bitch" and mocks her when he makes her cry. He often tries to cover himself with crystals in an effort to calm down. Later, Kristin and Stephanie have a fight in a restaurant about which one is causing more drama.

The City is a spinoff of the spinoff, *The Hill*. *The City* highlights the work and social life of Whitney, Lauren's former coworker on *The Hills*. Whitney, while looking a bit more Midwest than LA, has little trouble adapting to her new job and lifestyle. A voiceover in the first episode introduces the viewers to the different cliques, making it very clear that it is almost impossible to break into the "uptown" crowd unless one is born into it. *The City* casts Olivia, another rich and unqualified employee, as a mean girl. While she does not have much influence in the fashion industry, she appears to carry some clout in the social scene. Roxy is another mean girl who is introduced later in the series. She proclaims during an interview that she does not get along with other girls and that people think she is "bitchy." Roxy is very condescending to Whitney, both behind her back and to her face.

She bullies Whitney into having people over to her apartment, putting her in danger of being evicted. It is quite amazing these characters get high-end jobs working for *Teen Vogue*, *Elle Magazine*, etc. It sends the message that relational aggression has its advantages.

Historic-Themed Mean Girls

Historical-based dramas also include mean girls, demonstrating that relational aggression is nothing new. Two strong female characters, Laura Ingalls and Anne Shirley, are the most well known to young readers. Their stories have been adapted from book series to the small screen, *Little House on the Prairie* and *Anne of Green Gables*. Laura and Anne are very likeable, with big hearts that unfortunately may make them vulnerable to mean people. They often use creative ways to solve problems and cope with mean girls.

Josie is the pretty blonde mean girl in the books and miniseries *Anne of Green Gables*. Josie is jealous of Anne because Josie has her sights on a boy, Gilbert, who likes Anne. Josie does mean things like ask Anne how to spell "freckles," knowing that Anne is self conscious about her freckles. Anne's best friend Diana sticks up for Anne and asks Josie how to spell "ugly." It is rather impressive that Anne's meek friend, Diana, talks back to Josie. On a dare from Josie, Anne walks along the roof of a house. When Anne falls, Gilbert walks past Josie, giving her a disapproving look. Years later, Anne runs into Josie at college. Josie brags that her father is so rich, he can afford to send her back to school if Josie does not pass her exams. Two other classmates ignore Josie's snide remarks and affectionately join arms with Anne and they skip off, leaving Josie to follow by herself.

The *Little House on the Prairie* books and subsequent television series are based on the real life of Laura Ingalls Wilder. The series recounts the struggles and fiscal uncertainty of the Ingalls in contrast to the town's wealthy store owners, the Olesons. Mrs. Oleson came from a large city and is dismayed at having to live in a small farming town. Her frustrations are unleashed on the working people whom she sees as dirty and inferior. Mrs. Oleson passes her air of superiority onto her children, Nellie and Willie. Nellie sees her peers, especially the Ingalls girls, as inferior. She controls the playground and dictates who gets to play and who has to stand and watch. She often uses her parents' store and her access to unlimited candy as a bride to get other children to play with her. The flashback to a "simpler" time demonstrates the timeless nature of the mean girl. It demonstrates the ingrained desire of humans to have power over others.

In the second episode of the series, "Country Girls," Mary and Laura attend their first day at a new school. The other kids stop playing and stare as they walk up to the schoolhouse. One little girl tells her brother to be nice to the girls or she will tell their mother. Nellie takes one look at them and disparagingly murmurs, "Country girls." The teacher, Miss Beadle, has the class welcome them. She corrects the class when their welcome is less than enthusiastic. When the girls confess they do not have a slate, Nellie repeats, "Country girls" in an equally disparaging tone. Miss Beadle pauses but generally ignores Nellie. The class, led by Nellie, laughs when Laura does not understand the concept of an erasable chalkboard.

This time Miss Beadle scolds Nellie for being mean. Laura tells her parents that Nellie made her mad and she wanted to "smack" her. Laura's father Charles corrects Laura and tells her there is no name calling, teasing, or fighting allowed in their family. When the girls visit the Olesons' store, Nellie brags that everything in the store is hers. Nellie reads an essay in class, bragging about how much things cost in their house. Mary says she could never be that mean; however, Laura says she could if Pa would let her. When Laura stands up to Nellie, Nellie keeps pushing her down. Laura pushes back. Charles tells her it was okay but not to do it again. Laura says she will not have to because Nellie is scared of her now. Laura's mother Caroline is likewise frustrated with Mrs. Oleson's superior attitude and mean treatment of farm families. Charles offers to talk to Mr. Oleson, but Caroline declines.

There are a couple of episodes where Laura befriends children with disabilities. In "The Music Box," Laura makes friends with Anna, a girl who stutters. Nellie forms a special club whose members get to play in her room and see her nice things. Nellie announces that Anna cannot be in the club and then mocks her stuttering in front of all the other girls. When Laura refuses to join without Anna, Nellie gives in and invites Anna to her house. Laura covets Nellie's music boxes and, in a moment of weakness, takes one home, intending to bring it back later. She hides it in the barn. Nellie gives Laura a gumdrop and invites her to sit with them at lunch. Because Nellie still refuses to let Anna in the club, Laura refuses to join. When Mr. Oleson hears Nellie teasing Anna, he tells her to go upstairs and "get the strap." It appears at least her father is willing to discipline her for mean behavior. When Nellie catches Laura with the music box, Laura begs her not to tell. Nellie blackmails Laura into joining the club. She forces Laura to play with her and to leave Anna out. Nellie's brother Willie starts to blackmail her as well. Charles and Mary are very critical of Laura's behavior toward Anna. Charles tells Laura she has to tell Nellie she cannot be in the club unless Anna is allowed. Forced to accept Anna, Nellie plots to embarrass Anna by making her read a tongue twister. Nellie badgers her to read it faster and faster until Anna cries. Laura lectures all the other girls about laughing and leaves. Anna is angry at Laura for betraying her but forgives her when Laura tells her she is going to help her not stutter. When Laura confesses to Mr. Oleson about the music box, he forgives Laura and again takes the strap to Nellie for blackmailing Laura. Laura and Anna pour water over Willie's head to get back at him for blackmailing Laura as well.

In "Town Party-Country Party," Laura does not want to pick Olga for the relay race at recess because Olga walks with a limp. Olga quietly goes back into the school house. At Nellie's birthday party, Laura twists her ankle and must sit on the steps with Olga. Olga's father is concerned that the other kids are making fun of Olga and calling her names. He thinks she should have stayed home from the party. Later Charles makes Olga a special shoe so she can run. At first Olga's father is upset with Charles for meddling, but is proud when he sees Olga running and playing with the other girls. To be mean, Nellie suggests they take off their shoes and go wading in the pond.

When Mary gets glasses in the episode "Four Eyes," not only does Nellie and Willie make fun of her but her other classmates call her "Four Eyes." Miss Beadle tries to stop them by putting on her own glasses. The girls pass a note to Mary with "four eyes" on it. Nellie tells Mary she will never get married like Miss Beadle because of the glasses. Laura keeps standing up for Mary but Mary cries and hides the glasses, pretending to lose them. A handsome young gentleman comes to town with flowers for Miss Beadle. Mary catches them kissing, proving there is hope for her in the future. Mary retrieves her glasses so she can catch up with her schoolwork and win the history award. When she confesses to Charles that she lied about losing her glasses, he agrees words do hurt.

Adult Mean Girls

Ugly Betty, Desperate Housewives, and *GCB* are hour-long comedic shows that feature mean girls. Because they are an hour long, these shows take more time in character development than the standard situation comedy that relies on a formula of jokes and gags at a rather rapid pace. Mean plots appear to take longer to develop and execute than simply bullying. Relational aggression often requires a more sophisticated plot where the victim is uncertain whether or not they are really experiencing the phenomenon.

In the pilot of *Desperate Housewives*, Edie is described as the "most predatory divorcee in a five-block radius." Her male conquests range from workmen to a minister. She is referred to as "an enemy" and a "slut" by the other housewives. Susan and Edie become rivals as they compete to win the attention of a new neighbor, Mike. Susan accidentally burns down Edie's house. Susan then discovers her ex-husband, Karl, cheated on her with Edie during their marriage. To annoy Susan, Karl and Edie start dating. Susan in turn sleeps with Karl while he is engaged to Edie. Edie gets back at Susan by burning down her house. In subsequent seasons, Edie takes advantage of Mike's retrograde amnesia and gets him to believe Susan never loved him then sleeps with him. Edie later develops feelings for Gabrielle's ex-husband, Carlos. Edie gets Carlos evicted so he will have to move in with her. When Carlos tells Edie that he does not love her, she fakes a pregnancy. When he leaves her, Edie fakes a suicide attempt. She also blackmails him and tells the IRS about his offshore accounts. In later seasons, Edie tries blackmailing Bree but fails. The housewives then gang up and drive Edie out of Wisteria Lane. In season five, Edie returns a changed woman. Edie and Susan make up; however, Edie hits an electricity pole and is shocked to death. Even after all her tricks and husband stealing attempts, Edie is a bit of a sympathetic character. She is unlucky in love and suffers an untimely death.

The premise of *Ugly Betty* is that Betty is hired because she is unattractive; therefore the boss's son, Daniel, will not be tempted to sleep with her. The cliques from high school appear to have grown up and moved into the workplace. Betty has a tough time finding a place to sit in the lunch room, reminiscent of the school cafeteria. One of the other assistants, Marc, and the receptionist, Amanda, are particularly mean to Betty. Marc tells Betty he likes her poncho and then makes a gagging gesture behind her back. Someone steals Betty's stuffed bunny off of her desk. She gets an emailed picture of the bunny in a noose. She finds another picture with its hands and feet duct-taped. In the last picture, the bunny is in the toilet. Betty stands up to the crowd and asks who thinks the pictures are funny. They all raise their hands. Betty proclaims, "You can take my bunny but you can't take my spirit." Amanda makes a crack that Betty should work some overtime to be able to afford "Invis-a-line" to replace her prominent braces. When Betty bumps into a man, spilling his drink, Marc and Amanda are ready with their camera phones to capture the debacle. Mark says, "More classic moments for Betty's wall of shame." When Amanda packs up Betty's desk along with her bunny, Betty finally stands up to Amanda. By season four, Betty's looks are beginning to change. She grows out her bangs and gets new glasses. She eventually gets her braces off. Even though they still tease her, Betty becomes friends with Marc and Amanda. Mark and Amanda act very childish in their meanness toward Betty. Even when they become friends, they still tease her. There are also some tender moments as their friendships grow.

In *GCB*, which was originally short for "Good Christian Bitches" but was changed to "Good Christian Belles," after protests from religious groups, the roles have been reversed when the high school mean girl moves back to her hometown where her former victims are now mean women. Amanda explains that she was spoiled as a child and no one set limits for her. Amanda's mother plans a welcome home tea for Amanda, but the Belles get all the guests to cancel. Carlene criticizes Amanda for working at a Hooters-type restaurant, the only job she could find. Amanda stands up in church and says she is thankful to Carlene and her husband, whose corporate conglomerate owns the restaurant. When Amanda designs a new brand of jeans, Cricket starts a protest behind Amanda's back that the jeans are inappropriate. The second episode, "Hell Hath No Fury," focuses on the women's daughters. Now the daughters of Amanda's victims are the mean girls. The girls comment that Amanda's daughter, Laura, is unattractively smart and actually eats at lunch. Amanda warns Laura about falling for a trick by the mean girls, a trick that Amanda herself created in high school. In high school, Amanda classified the other girls as "foxes" or "javelina" (i.e., skunk pig). Amanda is horrified when she finds a "javelina" sticker on the back of Laura's jacket. Two of the mean girls, Alexandra and McKenzie, ask Laura to the pep rally. The scene cuts just as some girls are going to dump something on Laura's head. The girls surprisingly make Laura a fox and shower her with confetti. The mean mothers decide it is better if the girls befriend Laura so they can keep an eye on her. Amanda tells Laura she does not want Laura to be in a group of snobby and cruel girls. Laura says she is not like Amanda and just wants to survive a new school. When Laura gets home, Amanda apologizes and tells her she is proud.

Nighttime soap operas have portrayed some classic mean girls. Character Alexis Carrington from *Dynasty* paved the way for current mean girls. Alexis is a combination of bully and mean girl, using her sexuality, money, and position to get what she wants. Daytime soap operas were sustained because of the mean female characters. The demise of the daytime soap is perhaps because of the hyper-mean women on reality shows such as *The Real Housewives* of wherever.

Amanda from *Melrose Place* is a classic mean girl. The producers brought in her character late into the first season. Amanda is Allison's boss at the advertising agency. Amanda is also dating Allison's roommate Billy. At first it appears Allison is being hypersensitive and paranoid about Amanda's actions. Eventually their boss tells Allison that Amanda is tough and has driven out other partners. After several fights, Billy tells Amanda she is too judgmental and they break up. When Allison tries to get her old job back at the ad agency, Amanda puts her back at her receptionist's job. Amanda buys the apartment building at Melrose Place so she can control the tenants. Amanda sends a tenant Jo on a photo shoot so she can have Jake, Jo's boyfriend, to herself. A Netflix summary of the show describes the cast as "backstabbing beauties, lying lotharios and scheming sexpots" (n.d.).

With the success of *90210*, an updated version of *Beverly Hills 90210*, the producers of *Melrose Place* created *Melrose Place 2.0*. In the pilot episode, Sydney resurrects her role as resident bad girl. In the original version, Sydney seduces her sister's estranged husband, Michael, and later blackmails him. In the *2.0* series, she is blackmailing her ex-lover, who happens to be Michael's son. Eight minutes into the pilot she is found stabbed to death in the complex's pool. There are a variety of suspects since Sydney made lots of enemies. There are some flashes of mean girls throughout the short-lived series. Ella, the pretty blonde publicist, could be a little cutthroat. Riley fears Ella is trying to take away her boyfriend, Jonah. Ella is ambitious professionally but it seems she is friendly with the other females, except for trying to steal Jonah. The Ashley Simpson character Violet turns out to be Sydney's daughter. Violet threatens Sydney; however, her character gets cut before she can make good on her threat. Also from the original series, the character Jane returns to blackmail Ella into getting one of her fashion designs on the Hollywood red carpet.

Conclusion

Nighttime soap operas may never have existed if it were not for the mean girl. Her antics appear to drive the storyline. The mean girl has shifted more recently from the adult version (e.g., Alexis Carrington from *Dynasty*) to the teen version (e.g., Blair Waldorf from *Gossip Girl*). The adult mean girls appear to have been relegated to hour-long comedies. Most of the current adult dramas center around doctors, lawyers, or crime solving, leaving little room for the traditional mean woman and her antics. The mean women in *Desperate Housewives*, for example, are comical characters rather than dark figures. The rise in teen mean-girl dramas can also be attributed to the popularity of cable networks such as ABC Family and TeenNick that cater to a tween and teen audience.

Venues such as competition appear to create opportunities for mean-girl behavior (e.g., *Hellcats* and *Greek*). Social status is inherent in rich-teen shows such as *Gossip Girl* and *90210*, which also fosters relational aggression. Generally, the mean girl does not stay the mean girl over time. She often transforms from mean girl to nice girl (and sometimes back to mean girl), not because of some anti-mean-girl strategy or intervention but to keep the storyline interesting. Much like mean-girl movies, mean-girl television's main focus is not to educate but to entertain.

7

Television Sitcoms

A primary venue for portraying bullying is the television situation comedy. This phenomenon may be surprising considering humor has the potential of trivializing and making light of serious issues. On the other hand, Mueller (1981) found that sitcoms have historically had a moral component. Many programs have addressed social issues such as teen pregnancy, shoplifting, divorce, and drug and alcohol abuse. Bullying is now one of those pressing social issues.

The target audience appears to be a significant factor in the occurrence and treatment of bullying and mean girl behavior in situation comedies. No other genre of television programming targeted to adolescents comes close to the number of shows in the sitcoms format. The Disney Channel (targeting 9- to 14-year-olds) and Nickelodeon's (targeting 6- to 17-year-olds) lineups are dominated by sitcoms. In 2009, 13 out of the top 20 spots airing on cable television were adolescent and kid sitcoms (Zap2it, 2009). (For analysis of bullying in children's programming, see Chapter 11.) This focus on bullying and sitcoms is particularly relevant in light of Robinson, Callister, and Jankoski's (2008) findings that children's sitcoms provide a rich source of images which viewers scrutinize and identify.

In this section, I explored factors such as gender and race. Although there are significantly fewer portrayals of female bullies throughout media, situation comedies included a fair number of female bullies. The largest number of African American bullies and victims was also represented in sitcoms.

Mean Girls

The first set of sitcoms discussed contains incidents of relational aggression rather than physical bullying. There are few examples of mean girls, perhaps because relational aggression takes longer to develop than bullying. Mean girls are most likely found in film comedies or television teen dramas. In sitcoms with reoccurring mean girls, (e.g., *Awkward*, *Suburgatory*), the relational aggression runs peripherally through many episodes rather than dominating a single episode.

In the *Full House* episode "Is It True about Stephanie," a new boy, Jamie, asks out Stephanie. Gia, a mean girl at school, is jealous because she likes Jamie. Gia is very cute and looks like she is used to getting what she wants. She demands Stephanie call off her date. When she refuses, Gia tells Stephanie, "It's your funeral." Gia starts a rumor that the only reason Jamie is going out with Stephanie is that she paid him $20. Jamie cancels the date after the kids tease him. To get revenge, Stephanie posts Gia's less than stellar report card for everyone to see. When she sees that Gia is deeply hurt by her prank, Stephanie feels bad and apologizes. They make up at the end; however, it is evident that Gia has not learned her lesson. Shortly thereafter, Gia is rude to their server. The server threatens to spit in Gia's drink.

London is the spoiled rich girl in the Disney Channel series *Suite Life on Deck*. In the episode "Mean Chicks," London tells Bailey a paper bag over her head would compliment her complexion more than the outfit she was wearing. London asks her if she ever shaves her knuckles. Bailey bets London a million dollars that London cannot go a week without insulting her. In order to stop insulting others, Mr. Blanket, the guidance counselor, treats London with aversion therapy. He has her wear a tickle jacket so she gets tickled if she insults someone. London surprisingly goes a week without insulting Bailey and wins the bet. Because Bailey cannot afford to pay the million dollars, London gives her one dollar per insult. When London finishes insulting Bailey, including jabs at how hideous and ugly Baily is, London is exhausted. Bailey sympathetically tells London that it looks like it was harder on London than it was on her. They hug and London tells Bailey she is a true friend for caring. The show also highlights London's insults of adults. At one point, she is looking for her teacher Miss Tutwiller so she can insult Miss Tutwiller's "hideous headband." She tells Mr. Blanket his breath smells, he is knock-kneed, and his hair looks like "a sleeping gopher." The adults are generally imbeciles and do nothing to discipline the children. The children's parents are absent as well.

In *Wizards of Waverly Place*, "Alex's Choice" centers on the mean girls, Gigi and her two cronies. When one of the mean girls suggests they go and make fun of a boy, Eddie, until he cries, the other girls giggle. In the episode, Gigi invites Alex and Harper to a fancy tea. Alex does not understand why Gigi is being nice because she and Gigi do not like each other. When Alex reminds Gigi that Gigi has terrorized her since they were in kindergarten, Gigi explains that that was when they were young and foolish. Alex reminds her it was just yesterday. It turns out the tea is actually a "who can bring the biggest loser" competition. Alex tries to warn Harper but Harper does not want to believe it. Harper still wants to go to the tea and be accepted by the popular girls. Alex casts a truth spell and the mean girls come clean about the loser competition. Alex tells Harper she will always protect her. Gigi's cronies then turn on Gigi. One girl pushes a cake in Gigi's face and the other pours punch on her head. Harper then puts the "loser crown" on Gigi's head.

In the first episode of the series from *A.N.T. Farm*, "TransplANTed," Chyna, an 11-year-old singing protégé, begins the gifted program at her local high school. A.N.T. stands for "advanced natural talent." Her adviser is an incompetent adult who pulls strange items out of his afro. Lexi, the popular high school cheerleader, comes into class and pushes Chyna out of her chair. Lexi feels threatened by Chyna because Lexi normally gets the lead in the school musicals. The teacher casually acknowledges Lexi's bad behavior but does not punish her. Later, Chyna and two other A.N.T. kids crash Lexi's party. They clumsily crash into the sound system, ruining the party. Lexi calls them "freaks" and threatens to "make their lives miserable."

Tyler Perry's *House of Payne*'s "Dodging Bullies" and *Bent*'s "HD" appear to be the only sitcom episodes to seriously address cyberbullying. Perry also addresses inappropriate and insulting teasing as a form of bullying. In "Dodging Bullies," middle schoolers

Jasmine and her friend giggle about insulting jokes on their friend Katie's posts about their friend Amanda being poor. Jasmine's mother scolds the girls for laughing and not considering Amanda's feelings. The mother insists Jasmine call Amanda to make sure she is okay with the emails. Amanda tells Jasmine that she hates the school because of the teasing. Amanda has gone to the principal but the school said there is nothing they can do unless Amanda is being threatened. Knowing the jokes hurt Amanda's feelings, Jasmine feels bad. Jasmine's parents arrange a talk between Jasmine, Katie, and Amanda. Katie gets defensive at first. Jasmine's father defines Katie's actions as cyberbullying. Katie tells them she was getting bullied three years before. Katie apologizes and all three girls hug.

Frankie's aunt and grandfather catch Frankie skipping school in *Bent*'s "HD." She tells them she skipped because a girl in her class, Nicole, is bullying her because Frankie's father is in prison for insider trading. Nicole is posting fake pictures on Facebook, specifically one of Frankie in an orange jumpsuit. Frankie's aunt gives her some options on how to get even with Nicole; however, Frankie's mother, Alex, advises her to take the high road. Some kids come by and spray paint "jail bird" on Frankie's lawn. Frankie tells her mother those kids have been posting negative comments and texting her "jail bird." Alex leaves her own birthday party to confront Nicole and her parents. However, before Alex can get to the front door of Nicole's house, the grandfather, aunt, and guests of Alex's birthday party begin to egg the house. They chant "jail bird" until Alex relents and also throws eggs. When the front porch light comes on, they all run away. Frankie and her aunt send Nicole a picture of her house covered in eggs with "suck it" written as the caption.

Girl Bully: Major Character

Regular girl characters who take on the role of bullies are primarily found in sitcoms targeted to an adult audience rather than the adolescent-focused programs. In almost all of these shows, the characters play supportive roles to the adult characters (i.e., they play a peripheral role in most of the episodes). In a vast majority of the cases, the bullying is a onetime occurrence and is resolved within the episode.

In the opening scene of *Everybody Loves Raymond*'s "Bully on the Bus," Ray and Debra think that their daughter, Ally, is being bullied by a boy on the bus. Debra thinks Ray is overreacting. She states, "That's what kids do." As a protective father, Ray rides the bus with Ally to see which boy is responsible. The bus driver informs Ray that Ally is the bully. The boy was just defending his sister, whom Ally has been picking on. Evidently the little girl, Judy, has thick glasses so Ally calls her "an owl" and hoots at her. The bus driver is aware of it but seemingly does nothing to stop it. Ally is upset that the other kids are making fun of her because Ray rode with her on the bus. She devises a plan to make up a new song about Judy so that the other kids will laugh at the other little girl instead. Ray tries to reason with her that getting picked on does not feel good. The parents are very careful to tell her she is not bad but what she did was bad. She agrees to be nice. In general the show is an awful model of family life. Ray accuses Debra of being pushy and mean, and she is where Ally gets the bullying behavior. Debra calls Ray a "wuss." They proceed to yell at each other. Ray calls her "stupid." Ray's father is another awful character. Ray reminds his father, Frank, that Frank did not care when Ray and his brother, Robert, were getting bullied when they were young. Frank would yell at them, "Stop crying. People are looking at us." Frank is proud that Ally is the bully.

Lauren is sent home from school for bullying in *Still Standing*'s "Still Bullying." She and her friends were pretending another girl, Kathy, was invisible. Lauren's excuse is that Kathy is a "big baby" and they were only fooling around. Lauren's mother, Judy, grounds Lauren from the school dance. The father, on the other hand, disagrees and thinks Lauren's behavior was not that bad. Judy tells her daughter the story of when she was in school and she was bullied. In actuality, Judy was the bully who called another girl names. The dad lets Lauren go to the school dance after all.

The Bernie Mac Show is another series where the father is loud and abusive. He inherits his nieces and nephew when his sister gets caught with drugs. In "Five Stages of Bryana," the younger niece, Bryana, knocks a bowl of popcorn out of her brother's hands. She lies and gets the brother in trouble. Bryana steals her sister's watch and pressures a little girl in her class to buy it. When the little girl does not have the money, Bryana raises her voice, brushes the little girl aside, and starts going through the girl's cubby looking for more money. When Bernie grounds Bryana, she becomes a tyrant. Bernie's wife suggests they get her therapy. Normally, Bernie spoils Bryana and calls her "Baby Girl," but he finally sticks to her punishment.

In the pilot episode of *I Hate My Teenage Daughter*, MacKenzie and Sophie get into trouble, locking a boy in wheelchair the bathroom for two hours. Sophie claims the boy they bullied, Gerard, is the meanest kid in school and does not like black people. She tells her mother that Gerard called MacKenzie, who is mixed race, names and made her cry. She also claims MacKenzie made her promise not to tell because Nikki might go down to the school and embarrass the girls. Annie believes her daughter and allows Sophie to go to the dance. When the mothers see Gerard at the dance, they discover that he is also black, the mothers decide to punish the girls by dancing in front of the girls' classmates.

Boy Bully: Major Character

Many of the regular male adolescent cast members who are portrayed as bullies start as bully victims and become bullies within the context of a single episode. In most cases, the boys get a taste of what it is like to win a fight or dominate another kid, and they like it. The parents have a difficult time reprogramming the boy from bully back into a nonaggressive state. The episode "The Main Event" of *The Bernie Mac Show* begins with Jordan getting bullied by both boys and girls at school and his little sister at home. His uncle Bernie, ashamed of Jordan's passive nature, teaches him to fight back. Once Jordan gets a taste of fighting and winning, he becomes the bully. Jordan begins to push other kids around and take their food. Jordan claims he is just acting like Bernie. Bernie must examine his own aggressive behavior. Jordan brags that he gets whatever he wants now. When Bernie gets Jordan to promise not to be a bully at school, he continues to bully his sisters and his aunt at home. Bernie acknowledges he created a monster, but he wonders how he can stop it without using a belt. Jordan finally stops when he knocks down a girl. As he is helping her up, she hits him.

Kyle does not want to go to school because of a bully in *According to Jim*'s "The Punch." When his parents do not believe Kyle's excuse that his stomach hurts, he tells them about the bully, Murph. Jim tells his wife, Cheryl, that he is taking over Kyle's parenting because his thinks she is babying Kyle. Jim teaches Kyle how to punch. When Kyle gets to school, he runs straight for Murph, holding out his first. After Jim and the teacher stop Kyle from hitting Murph, he breaks free and hits Murph again in the stomach. Kyle gets suspended from school. Jim goes back to try to get Murph to confess that Murph started the altercation. Murph explains he picks on Kyle because Kyle called timeout during a game of dodgeball one day. Jim agrees with Murph that players cannot call timeout during dodgeball. Jim then explains to Murph that is Kyle's mother's fault for babying Kyle. Sympathetic to Jim's position, Murph agrees to take the blame.

In *King of the Hill*, "Bobby Goes Nuts," Bobby is invited next door to the girls' slumber party. A group of bullies crashes the party. When Bobby tries to stop them, Chane punches Bobby in the chest. At school the next day, Chane pushes Bobby to the ground and makes Bobby eat dirt. When Bobby goes to sign up for boxing class, he discovers that the classes are full except for a women's self-defense course. Bobby and the women are taught to kick the attacker in the groin as a form of self defense. The next time he is attacked, Bobby kicks Chane in the groin. Bobby quickly goes from defending himself to becoming a bully. The other bullies in school fear him. Bobby does not understand why he should not kick others in the groin when it works. Even when Bobby's father, Hank, tries to teach Bobby to box, Bobby gets frustrated and kicks Hank in the groin. When Bobby refuses to surrender his video game to his mother, Peggy, she physically wrestles him and takes it from him. Since she has no testicles, she is not affected when Bobby kicks her in the groin. At the end of the episode Bobby tells his father it is worse to get a woman to fight your battles than hitting below the belt.

In *My Three Sons*, "The Bully," a boy, Ralph, pushes Chip out of line in school. Chip comes back and wrestles the boy. The teacher breaks up the fight and scolds Chip. The other kids taunt Chip to get to the end of the line. At dinner that night, Chip's brother, Robbie, tells their father, Steven, that a kid has been picking on Chip. Chip calls Robbie a "squealer." Steven tells Chip that "if it's going to hurt anyway, why not get in a few punches.... You don't have to win the fight, Chip. All you have to do is hurt him." For the next three days, Chip comes home with bruises and a black eye. When Steven comes to pick him up at school, he witnesses Chip bullying Ralph. Chip admits to the principal that he was the bully because he was angry that he kept losing fights to Ralph. The principal chuckles. She recommends the boys talk it out. Soon the boys run off together to find rocks.

In *The Munsters'* "Herman's Peace Offensive," Jack, a stereotypical Irish boy with freckles, threatens to give Eddie a fat lip. When Eddie comes home the next day with a black eye, his father, Herman, reevaluates his previous advice to Eddie not to fight back. Herman proceeds to teach Eddie how to box. Eddie goes back to school and punches Jack. Eddie punches two other boys as well. The principal calls Eddie's mother and tells her that Eddie has been threatening to beat up the entire fifth grade class. Herman walks Eddie to school to show him he does not have to be a bully to get respect. Herman is so intimidating no one dares mess with Eddie.

Ritchie's private school is having an assembly about bullying in *The New Adventures of Old Christine*'s "Old Christine Meets Young Frankenstein." Christine is outraged when she hears that someone at school is bullying others. She is all for "zero-tolerance," expulsion, and filing criminal charges until she learns it is Ritchie, her son, who is the bully. Ritchie has been bullying kids and taking another boy's lunch money. Then she meekly tells the principal, "You got to let kids be kids." When she asks Ritchie, he admits he is quite proud that he is able to bully another student, especially another boy. Christine is concerned because she used to bully a girl in junior high. Ritchie does not understand why he has to apologize to his target if she does not. Christine attempts to make amends with her victim, but it goes terribly wrong (see the adult bullying section). Ritchie's bullying is never really resolved. It is assumed that he no longer bullies although there appeared to be no real punishment or understanding by Ritchie that bullying is wrong.

In *Home Improvement*'s "What About Bob?" Randy gets into trouble for bullying a kid, Curtis, at school. Randy and his friends filled Curtis' shoes with Cheez Whiz. Randy's excuse was that Curtis is annoying and a "total geek." Randy's mother, Jill, invites Curtis over so that Randy can apologize. Curtis comes over wearing a goofy hat and wipes his nose with the back of his glove. As Curtis talks to his mother on the phone, Jill overhears him insulting her and her home. It is clear that Jill understands why Randy bullied Curtis. She restrains herself from doing the same. The next time Curtis comes over and rings the doorbell, Jill and Randy turn out the lights and hide. In a different episode, "Flying Sauces," Randy and Brad repeatedly bully their younger brother, Mark, with little or no reprimand from their parents. The brothers call Mark a "dork" and a "dufus." After Jill insists Randy and Brad take Mark to the park with them, the older boys leave without him so Mark has to play by himself. Later Randy and Brad try to trick Mark into think they are a family of aliens. Tim and Jill devise a plan to torment the older boys to make them see how it feels to be bullied. Tim and Jill scare Brad and Randy with lights, music, and scary alien costumes. Although they celebrate scaring the boys, Jill does not think the boys learned anything. It is not difficult to see why Brad and Randy are bullies. When Tim tells Randy and Brad bullying is wrong, Randy brings up how Tim mistreated his little brother when they were growing up. Tim also mistreats his coworker and friend, Al. Jill calls her sons "obnoxious little pigs" but appears to do little to discipline them.

In another sibling bullying episode, *The Wonder Years*, "Hiroshima, Mon Frere," Kevin gets fed up with his brother Wayne's bullying and name calling. Wayne teases Kevin by holding Kevin's hamster out the school bus window and later holds the hamster over the garbage disposal. When Kevin tries to tell his father about Wayne's behavior, the father says he does not want to hear Kevin's complaints. When Wayne accidentally kills the hamster by sucking it up the vacuum cleaner, Kevin loses his temper and tells Wayne that he has no friends, nobody likes him, and that he is "pathetic." An image of a nuclear bomb goes off on the screen. After a few days, Wayne apologizes. As Wayne and Kevin walk home together, they wrestle in the grass with Wayne playfully punching Kevin. The voiceover of Kevin as adult laments things between them will never be the same since Kevin now knows how to hurt Wayne.

Saved by the Bell is perhaps the only sitcom targeted to an adolescent audience that features regular characters as bullies. The lack of attention by critics to the show's bullying is rather astounding. The episode "Model Students" was one of the few examples included in the analysis that was not identified in the synopsis as "bullying." As discussed previously, the main characters in the show are incredibly mean to the character Screech, who is supposedly their friend. In the episode "Model Students," the lead characters are brazen about their bullying. The episode begins as two extremely nerdy characters are stocking items in the school store. When one of the nerds looks at Kelly, who is attractive and popular, she cringes and moves away from him in disgust. The nerd slinks away with his head down in shame. Zach, the handsome, popular lead character, breaks the fourth wall and says to the audience, "Welcome to the school store, otherwise known as 'Nerds Are Us.'" Zach easily convinces the principal to take control of the store away from the nerds and let Zach run it. When the nerds protest, Slater, another popular boy, scares them away by growling at them. The nerds are stereotypically hyper-nerdy, with thick-rimmed glasses, bowties, and old-fashioned hairstyles. The distinction is exaggerated so perhaps the audience can feel okay about identifying with the pretty, popular kids and joining in on making fun of the nerdy kids.

Two of the few isolated cases where the bully becomes the victim are episodes of *Yes, Dear*. In "Dominic's Buddy," Kim and Greg's nephew, Dominic, is bullying a nerdy kid named Ronnie, calling him names and mildly poking him. Dominic's parents promise Ronnie's father that it will not happen again. Dominic's defense is that Ronnie is weird and all the kids do it. Dominic's father, Jimmy, insists on a play date between Dominic and Ronnie. The boys become friends. Dominic is now starting to get picked on by other boys for being friends with Ronnie. Jimmy tells Dominic and Ronnie not to run away but to stand and fight back. Ronnie's dad is concerned about them fighting. When Jimmy criticizes his brother-in-law Greg for raising his son Sammy to be a wimp, Greg punches him. Greg feels good that he finally fought back after a lifetime of being bullied. In "Baby Fight Club," Greg and Jimmy try to get Sammy to stop bullying by putting him in the victim position. Kim and Greg notice aggressive behavior in their toddler son. When a parent who is new to the playground brings a little girl to play, Sammy steals her toy and tries to choke her. Kim and Greg read through a stack of parenting books. Jimmy devises a plan to set up Sammy with a bigger kid so Sammy can learn how it feels to get hit. The boy is bigger and keeps getting kicked out of his play group. A couple of Greg's friends come to watch the boys fight and place bets on the winner. The boys are wrestling on the ground when Kim comes home and stops them. Back at the playground, Sammy is playing nicely with other children. Evidently Sammy has been "cured" of his bullying.

Another plot device used in sitcoms with regular cast members is what I call the "mistaken bully." Through some slapstick comedy moves, the regular character accidently hits or trips the bully. If it happens more than once, the regular kid is deemed a bully by the peer group. For example, as Ned is gesturing in *Ned's Declassified*'s "New Grade," Loomer walks into Ned's fist. As Loomer goes to hit Ned, he slips and falls. When Ned uses his backpack to swat a bug, Loomer gets hit yet again. The other kids assume Ned hit Loomer on purpose and name Ned as the bully. Loomer, who now fears Ned, no longer bullies. The school social order is in disarray without Loomer as the lead bully. In order to restore balance, Ned's friend Moze hits Ned and makes it look like Loomer did it. Order is restored and Ned gets attention from the popular girls.

In a similar scenario, Bart slips and accidently kicks Nelson, giving him a bloody nose in *The Simpsons*' "Lisa Simpson, This Isn't Your Life." As Bart gestures, he hits Nelson again. Everyone cheers and calls Bart the new bully. The principal even gives Bart the "School Bully" parking spot. Yet again, Nelson accidently trips and stumbles into a locker. Bart gives Nelson his self-confidence back by telling Nelson that he is a good "puncher."

Glenn Martin, DDS is stop motion sitcom on the Adult Swim Network. In the episode "Camp," Glenn's son, Connor, does not want to go to his dad's old camp. The son is excited when he finds out his parents are staying at the camp because he thinks they will protect him from bullies. However, Glenn informs Connor they will not be there as his parents but as counselors. When Connor goes to lunch, his geeky bunk mate calls him over to his table. One of the camp bullies calls Connor "fresh meat." When the bully pushes Connor's lunch tray, Connor accidently hits the bully with the tray, knocking him down. Connor then becomes the tough guy of the camp. Back at the cabin, the other campers wait on Connor in fear that Connor will beat them up next. Another bully, Bronx, challenges Connor to pull down another boy's pants during the talent show. Instead of pulling down the boy's pants, Connor joins the boy in singing a song. Bronx gets mad and pulls down Connor's pants instead. As Connor is falling, he accidently pulls down Bronx's pants. All three boys are shown playing together afterward, bonded by the fact they were all pantsless on stage.

Kevin, a chubby kid, is deemed the most obnoxious kid in the school in *Malcolm in the Middle's* "Shame." Kevin nicknames Malcolm "Stinky" and repeats everything Malcolm says. When Kevin spits on Malcolm, Malcolm attacks Kevin with his fists. Malcolm feels guilty when Kevin turns out to be a seven-year-old. Malcolm's parents laugh at him when he tells them what he did. A family member of Kevin's threatens Hal, Malcolm's father, so Hall beats him up first. Kevin's brother, although he looks older, is only 15. In the end, Malcolm's mother tells Malcolm that it is good he has a conscious.

Girl Bully: Minor Character

The next groupings of sitcoms feature girls who appear in isolated episodes of the program and are portrayed as the bullies. Portrayals vary by sex of the victim and the reason for the bullying. Portrayals of girl as bully and girl as victim strongly leaned toward cable-network, adolescent-target-audience programming.

GIRL VICTIMS

Hannah Montana's "School Bully" introduces a new girl at Miley's school as a bully. Her nickname is "the Cracker" because she can crack walnuts with her hands. Miley tries to give her the benefit of the doubt and goes over to talk to her, only to become a target for the bully. The Cracker roughs up Miley and her friend Lily and ties their hair together. Miley refuses to tell the principal because she does not want to be considered a "snitch." She asks her body guard Roxy, to show her some martial arts moves to protect herself. Back in school, Miley confronts the Cracker with moves that look like something from *The Karate Kid.* Scary, horror movie music plays in the background for comic effect as the Cracker stares down Miley. Roxy, disguised as an even scarier bully, comes to the school to help Miley. Knowing that Roxy's protection is only a temporary solution, Miley devises a plan to get the principal in the cafeteria to witness the bullying however, Lily, is late getting the principal there. There is a teacher in the cafeteria but she is no help as she wipes her coke-bottle glasses and is oblivious to all around her. When the principal arrives and sees that the bully has put Miley in the salad bar, he threatens the bully with expulsion if there are any more incidents.

In *iCarly's* "iMake Sam Girlier: Bully Bash," Carly throws a birthday party for her friend, Sam. In the toasts, friends recall how Sam has caused them emotional and physical pain, broken a boy's thumb when he asked her to a junior high dance, and filled another girl's bra with pudding and put it in the freezer at a slumber party. When a boy that Sam likes calls her "one bad dude," she decides to stop bullying and become more girly. The next day at school, as Sam clears out her "throwing eggs" from her locker, she witnesses a large girl bully named Jocelyn holding a boy upside down in the school hallway. Carly wants Sam to help him. A teacher comes by and tells Jocelyn to let the boy down. When Jocelyn yells, "You irritate me," at the teacher, he does nothing to punish her. Sam tells

Carly she feels bad because of the things people said about her fighting, pranks, and vicious behavior. Carly tells her she is "loveable" and "vicious." A few days later, the bully comes down the hall yelling at kids and knocking them down. When Sam stands up to her, Jocelyn knocks Sam's books out of her hand and pushes Sam into the lockers. Sam asks Carly permission to not be girly. Sam tells Jocelyn, "Nice girls don't fight," and walks away. Later Jocelyn comes in the local pizza place and dumps French fries down Sam's top. Carly stands up to Jocelyn, but Jocelyn pushes Carly to the ground while the bystanders do nothing. Carly gives Sam permission to "rip her head off." Sam makes Jocelyn tap out and pushes Jocelyn out the door. The boy whom Sam changed for tells Sam that he likes her the way she is.

Nanny Agatha has thick eyebrows, a snaggle tooth, a big mole, and sternly pulled back hair in *Jessie*'s "World Wide Web of Lies." Agatha is using another nanny as a foot rest. Agatha informs Jessie that from 1 to 4 o'clock it is her park. The other nannies are cowering in fear of Agatha. Agatha orders Jessie and Zuri, her charge, out of the park. The other nannies literally turn their backs on Jesse. One of the nannies, Fiona warns Jessie about Agatha's Internet site "Toddler Tattler" where she uploads pictures that make the other nannies look bad. Agatha posts pictures that make it look like Jessie is spanking Zuri instead of brushing the sand off her shirt, pulling Zuir's hair instead of trying to get out gum out, and napping instead of playing hide-and-go-seek. Jessie goes to great lengths to hide the site from Zuri's mother. Jessie and Zuri go back to the park and try to rally the other nannies to stick together and stand up to Agatha but they refuse. Believing Jesse over Agatha, Zuri's mother threatens to out Agatha to her twitter-like followers if Agatha does not take down her site. Agatha is finally dethroned.

Phil, in *Phil of the Future*, "Double Trouble," discovers his sister, Pim, is being picked on at school by Jerry, a much larger girl who wears her hat backwards. Phil advises Pim to her to stand up for herself. When Jerry confronts her, Pim acts crazy and starts barking at Jerry. Jerry runs away.

The school bully, Bianca, in *That's so Raven* and her two cronies, Muffy and Loca, are featured in the episode "Getting out of Dodge." They giggle about having given another student a wedgie. The bullies announce that everyone is going to play dodgeball in gym class. When Raven asks if they can play a nice game of jacks, the bullies throw jacks at her. During the dodgeball game, Raven accidently hits Bianca in the head, knocking her unconscious. When Bianca comes to, she hugs Raven and tells her she does not want to be a bully anymore. The other two bullies are lost and looking for a new leader. They pick Raven. When Raven tells them she does not want to see them doing anything bad, they take it literally and do bad things when Raven is not looking. For example, they steal a science book when Raven forgets hers, threaten a boy Raven likes because he has not asked her out yet, and steal a scone for her. To reinstate Bianca as the head bully, Raven shows Bianca pictures of when Bianca bullied another student with a lizard and performed a hostile makeover on a friend. Order is restored when Raven once again accidently hits Bianca in the head. The school nurse rewards the bullies with hall passes since they send her lots of business. The coach is also is incompetent and falls for their ploys to get him to leave the gym so they can bully other students.

In *The Simpsons*' "Bye Bye Nerdie," the students in Lisa's class make fun of the new girl, Francine, because of her red hair and her shoes, which they say look Canadian. When Lisa introduces herself, Francine gives her a black eye. Marge suggests Lisa try to find a mutual interest. This time, Francine steals Lisa's Malibu Stacy doll, bites its head off, and shoves Lisa in a locker. After Francine gives Lisa Indian rope burns on her arm, Lisa tries to hire the regular school bullies to be her bodyguards. The bullies have a victim Ralph hanging from his feet from the bleachers and are throwing tomatoes at him. Lisa is determined to crack the "bully code." She finds that Francine is only picking on the smart kids, leaving kids like her brother Bart alone. Lisa presents her discovery that bullying is a chemical reaction to "smart kid smell" to a group of scientists. When Lisa sprays herself with salad dressing, thus disguising her smart smell, Francine stops attacking her. Francine goes through the crowd of scientists beating them up. Francine's parents smile and laugh, saying that she will eventually wear herself out.

Ashley is being threatened by another girl, Paula, who is stealing her lunch money in *The Fresh Prince of Bel-Air's* "The Mother of All Battles." Will, Ashley's cousin who was raised in a rough neighborhood in Philly, offers to help by teaching Ashley how to defend herself. Will and Carlton, Ashley's brother, show up at the high-class private school. Carlton tries to reason with Paula, but she punches, slaps and knees him in the groin. Will offers to pay Paula to leave Ashley alone. When Ashley's parents find out she has been skipping school because she is afraid of the bully, they invite Paula's parents over to settle the issue in what they call "a civilized manner." The parents get into a shouting match, insulting each others' daughters. Meanwhile, the girls make up in the kitchen. Ashley's father later apologizes to his daughter for being a bad role model.

BOY VICTIMS

A boy who is getting bullied by a girl is almost always the object of ridicule by family and friends even if he suffers physical abuse such as a black eye or split lip. While he has few options to fight back, he is expected to not let a girl have power over him. Dee Dee comes home with his shirt ripped after getting beat up by "Big Lou" in *My Brother and Me's* "The Big Bully." Alfie, Dee Dee's older brother, suggests Dee Dee should run away next time. Dee Dee asks Alfie to teach him how to box. Alfie's friend teaches him how to bluff his way out of a fight. They teach him a mean look and a tough walk. The next day, Dee Dee comes home all muddy via Big Lou. The boys do not tell their parents. Alfie goes with Dee Dee to the schoolyard. Big Lou is actually a slim girl. Seeing Alfie, Big Lou calls her older sisters, who happen to be the cute girls with whom Alfie is smitten. The sisters, who are bigger than Alfie, corner him. Both boys come home muddy, victims of the girl bullies.

Malik tries to make up excuses for not going to school in "The Bully and the Beast" episode of *Tyler Perry's House of Payne*. At first he refuses to tell his family that he is being bullied. Malik's Uncle Curtis goes with Malik to see the principal. When Curtis finds out the bully is a girl, he harasses Malik for letting a girl take his lunch money. Curtis and the bully's foster mother butt heads. The foster mother apologizes when she finds out about the stolen lunch money. The principal requires Malik and the bully to tutor each other. The kids appear to be getting along as they study at the Paynes' house. In another example of poor adult role models, the foster mother tells Curtis' wife that she has a recipe for sweet potato pie that would "take care" of Curtis.

In *New Girl's* "Bully," a chubby boy named Nathaniel asks his teacher, Jess, if he can eat his lunch in the classroom. He tells her that the kids play a game called "coin slot" where they try to put coins in his "butt crack." She addresses the class about bullying in a song "Sad Sparrow: Imagine a World without Bullies." A few of her students record the performance on their cell phones, edit the footage, and post a spoof of it on the Internet. In the new version, the sparrow poops on the teacher's head. Jess finds out it was a girl named Brianna who posted the video. When Jess confronts her, Brianna is rather insulting to her teacher. At the school science fair, Jess tells Brianna's mother that Brianna is "difficult," which outrages the mother. It is not difficult to see where Brianna gets her bullying tendencies. The principal is incredibly supportive of Jess and welcomes her to teaching. Jess makes Brianna sing a song with her in class as punishment for bullying.

Rory from *8 Simple Rules* comes to the nurse's office with a bloody nose in the episode "Secrets." He refuses to name the bully. He finally confesses to his cousin, C.J., that the bully is a girl. C.J. teases him about being beat up by a girl.

In some cross-sex bullying portrayals, the girl is bullying the boy because she likes him. Even characters as young as 9-year-old Hilga in *Hey Arnold* (see chapter 11) bully out of "love." The episode of *Good Luck Charlie* entitled "Boys Meet Girls" begins with Gabe coming home from school with a black eye. The next day he gets a bloody lip. His older sister, Teddy, tells him that if he does not hit back, she will take care of the bully herself. Teddy visits Gabe at school and finds out his bully is a girl. Jo is small, mouthy, and of average intelligence. When Teddy discovers that Jo secretly likes Gabe, she invites Jo to their house and tries to teach Jo not to hit. As Jo and Gabe play a violent video game, Jo goes crazy when she thinks Gabe cheated. The next day in school, Jo approaches Gabe and demands his backpack. Since Teddy is too old to take on Jo physically, Gabe sics his 1-year-old sister, Charlie, on her. Charlie is dressed in a little karate outfit. The audience sees Charlie's tiny foot coming at a frightened Jo.

In *The Steve Harvey Show*'s "Bully Call," Romeo cannot figure out why girls keep turning him down for a date to the school dance. He discovers that a tough girl, Coretta, wants to go with him, therefore she is threatening the other girls if they say yes. Coretta is known for stealing lunches and pulling out hair weaves of other girls. Mr. Hightower, Romeo's teacher, makes fun of Romeo and his friend because they are "scared of a little girl." The water glass on Mr. Harvey's desk shakes as Coretta walks down the hall. Romeo finally admits to Coretta that he does not want to go to the dance with her. At first she is calm, but then she tells Romeo that he hurt her feelings and threatens to break his jaw if he does not unbreak her heart by 3 o'clock. Mr. Hightower warns Romeo that he has to take a stand or run the rest of his life. Mr. Hightower sits Coretta down and scolds her, telling her no one wants to go to the dance with her when she is threatening everyone. When Coretta starts to cry, Romeo scolds Mr. Hightower for upsetting her. She tells Romeo that if he goes to the dance with her, everyone would treat her differently. Romeo agrees to take her to the dance. Soon after, Coretta reverts back to her old ways and begins to bully Romeo once again.

Courtney, a girl slightly larger than Jimmy, calls Jimmy names and rips his shirt in *Grounded for Life*'s "All Apologies." Courtney also bullies Jimmy's sister Lily's boyfriend, Brad. She knocks his book down, takes his wallet, and grabs his nipple. Lily's father makes fun of Brad for getting bullied by a girl. Lily warns Courtney not to mess with her brother. There is a flashback to Lily bullying Brad years earlier. She realizes Courtney likes Jimmy. Jimmy gets up the nerve to confront Courtney and knocks her books out of her hand. They tumble to the ground after Jimmy jumps on her back. Courtney pins him down and they kiss.

In *Like Family*'s "Bobby's Bully," Bobby tells his older friend Keith about being bullied at school but makes Keith promise not to tell his parents. He is afraid if the kids at school find out he snitched, they will give him wedgies. Keith tells Bobby that bullies are cowards and he just needs to stand up for himself. The bully has evidently been stealing from Bobby and threatening him. Keith goes to Bobby's school to intervene; however, the bully is a girl named Emily. Keith watches as she takes Bobby's shoes and pushes him against the fence. Even though Emily is bigger than Bobby, Bobby is still ashamed that is he getting picked on by a girl. Keith calls Emily's mother and they come over to Bobby's house. Bobby's father is surprised the bully is a girl and makes a disparaging comment. Emily admits she bullies Bobby because she thinks he is cute. Bobby and Emily leave the room holding hands.

Step by Step's "Bully for Mark" features a stereotypical nerdy kid with big glasses and suspenders. Max, a new kid at school, threatens Mark, saying, "Do my homework or get your face bashed in." When Mark's mother goes to call the teacher, Mark's stepfather, Frank, says if she does, Mark will look like a sissy. Frank digs out his old boxing gloves for Mark. Mark's stepsister Al teaches Mark some tricky fighting moves to defend himself. When Max comes to the house, the family is surprised that Max is a girl. Max pretends to cry when she is confronted about bullying, claiming she secretly likes Mark. As soon as Mark's parents leave the room, she reverts back to a bully, calling him a "geek," pushing him down, and threatening to stick him in his locker. Al intervenes and threatens to punch Max. Later, Mark stands up to Max. Not noticing that Al is in the background, he thinks he made Max back down on his own. This episode is one example of a girl bully using the excuse that she likes the boy to get away with bullying.

The Dick van Dyke Show is the sole example of a girl bully in an older sitcom included in this "girl as bully" section of the analysis. (Note: Lumpy Rutheford's sister did give Beaver a black eye in *Leave it Beaver*; however, the episode did not focus on an ongoing bullying relationship between the two.) In the episode "Girls Will Be Boys," Laura is concerned that her son, Richie, has been fighting when he comes home with bruises. At first, Richie lies about the bruises but finally confesses it is a girl that has been beating him up. The studio audience roars with laughter when he says it is a girl. Rob and Laura contemplate if Richie is lying about the bully. Laura says getting beat up by a girl makes Richie a "sissy." Therefore, Richie would not likely lie about that. Richie confesses that he is scared to go to school so Laura calls the bully Pricilla's parents. When Rob goes to their house, Pricilla's father is initially quite thrilled that his daughter was able to beat up a boy. Pricilla is very girly and polite. Pricilla denies beating up Richie and declares that she loves him. Next, Laura goes over to talk to Pricilla's mother. The mothers argue when the mother accuses Richie of lying about the bullying. Laura witnesses Pricilla's mother, who herself is a bully, hitting her husband. Richie is excited when Rob tells him that Richie has permission to hit Pricilla back. Laura and Rob are nervous that Richie might lose the fight. Richie tells his parents that instead of hitting her, he kissed her. Pricilla had been threatening to hit him if he did not kiss her. Afterwards, Pricilla tells Richie that he kisses "dopey." When Pricilla tells the boys in her class that Richie kissed her, they called Richie a "sissy" so Richie beats them up, restoring his masculinity.

Boy Bully: Minor Character

In the majority of cases of bullying in sitcoms, the bully and the victim are both male. Rarely is the bully male and the victim female. Strict standards of masculinity dictate boys do not bully girls as boys are not to be bullied by girls as discussed earlier. At younger ages, girls are often similar in height and weight to their male peers. Older male charac-ters bullying females may cross the line into domestic violence. After puberty, male aggres-sion can also be seen as sexual aggression, which is not tolerated, particularly in traditional situations comedies.

Girl Victims

Generally in cases of cross-sex bullying where the bully is male and the victim is female, the parties involved are young, elementary school age or younger. The one excep-tion to the age rule is in an episode of *Clarissa Explains it All*. The bully turns his aggres-sion on 15-year-old Clarissa when she steps in to defend her brother against the bully. He breaks her portable tape player and challenges her to a fight. When Clarissa shows up for the fight, the bully begins to sing her a love song.

In *Back to You*'s "Gracie's Bully," 10-year-old Gracie does not want to ride the bus because there is boy, Xander, who pulls her hair and calls her names. Chuck, her father, instructs Gracie to pull his hair. Gracie's mother, Kelly, advises Gracie to handle the sit-uation in a mature manner and schedule a conflict resolution session at school. The class comes in the news room, where Chuck and Kelly co-host, for a field trip. Chuck and Kelly witness Xander pulling Gracie's hair. Chuck is ready to physically go after Xander until Kelly stops him. However, when Xander trips Gracie, Kelly pushes Xander against the wall and threatens to "rip his head off." Kelly celebrates her victory until Xander's mother is informed. Xander's mother is furious and comes down to the studio to confront Kelly. Before the parents can resolve their differences, Gracie comes in and tells them Xander apologized and told her he likes her.

Axel refuses move from the slide that Zuri wants to use in *Jessie*'s "World Wide Web of Lies." Axel and Zuri are both approximately 8 years old. He tells Jessie, Zuri's nanny, to "shut her pie hole." When Jessie goes to talk to his nanny, Agatha, Agatha sternly tells her that Axel does not share while they have control of the playground. Since Axel is a germaphobe, Jessie tells Zuri that if he picks on her again Zuri is to tell him that her pink eye feels contagious. When Axel pushes Zuri to the ground, Zuri sneezes on him in retal-iation. Zuri's mother saves the day and chases Axel and his nanny out of the park.

In *The Simpsons*'s "Eeny Teeny Maya Moe," Homer discovers a playground just out-side Moe's bar. He leaves his daughter Maggie there and watches from a window while he drinks. He fails to notice a group of baby bullies in the playground. The bully leader wears only a diaper and spiked wrist bands. Later Marge, Maggie's mother, notices that Maggie has become withdrawn and fearful. Because Homer is not helpful, Marge puts a nanny cam on Maggie's bow. Later, Marge watches in horror as the bullies terrorize Mag-gie. Marge then sees Homer coming to Maggie's rescue. The baby bully, however, is get-ting the best of Homer until Maggie takes the bully out herself.

In *Bewitched*'s "Tabitha's First Day of School," Tabitha encounters a bully, Charlton. Charlton steals the bullfrog from their first grade class's aquarium and puts it in Tabitha's desk, getting her in trouble with the teacher. Then he pulls Tabitha's hair. When Tabitha screams, the teacher blames Tabitha for the disruption. When Charlton pulls Tabitha's hair again, Tabitha's mother, Samantha, who is watching from the doorway, casts a spell on Charlton giving him a shock. After school, Charlton grabs Tabitha's arm and scolds her for getting him in trouble. Tabitha uses her magic to turn him into bullfrog. It takes a few tries but Samantha gets Tabitha to turn him back into a boy. Charlton tells his mother he was a bullfrog. Samantha explains that children who do not get enough love and understanding can turn into bullfrogs or bullies. The rather gruff mother turns over a new leaf and takes Charlton to get ice cream.

ADULT VICTIMS

I found a few instances in which the bully is a kid and an adult is the victim. Similar to the quandary a boy experiences when being bullied by a girl, an adult is equally as pitiful and helpless to defend himself or herself. In all three examples, the adult male is a regular character and the bully only appears once in the series. In *iCarly*, "iTwins," Carly's brother Spencer is rather incompetent and not significantly different maturity-wise than the bully, Chuck, who is less than half Spencer's age. Because Spencer is unable to stop the bullying himself, he asks Carly to help. At first Carly does not believe Spencer that Chuck is a bully until Spencer shows her hidden camera footage of Chuck physically beating on Spencer. To stop the bully, Carly, who is tutoring Chuck, feeds Chuck misinformation so he will fail his exam. As a consequence of failing the exam, Chuck's father informs Spencer and Carly that he is sending his son away to an academic summer camp. Although Chuck gets his comeuppance, it is unclear whether or not he will stop bullying. It appears he has not learned his lesson. At the same time, Chuck's father continues to be unaware of his son's bullying behavior, and therefore will likely do nothing to help change his son's mistreatment of others.

King of the Hill's "Hank's Bully" is another case of a child bullying an adult. Unlike Spencer in *iCarly*, Hank is quite intelligent. The new neighbors' son Caleb teases Hank, repeatedly calling him "dusty old bones, full of green dust." When Caleb knocks the beer out of Hank's hand, Hank's friends tell Hank that he is being bullied. He is stuck in a position of not being able to stop Caleb, the bully. Hank tries talking to Caleb's parents but they defend their son's behavior. They make excuses saying, "It's because he likes you," and, "He's just teasing you." When Hank keeps Caleb's bike until Caleb apologizes for riding on and damaging Hank's lawn, Caleb's parents call the police. Hank is forced to return the bike with no apology. The police harass Hank for picking on a kid. Hank enlists his son Bobby's help, not to bully Caleb, but to do to Caleb's parents what Caleb is doing to Hank. Caleb's parents eventually understand and finally discipline their son.

The FX show *Louie* is an unusual comedy in that it does not follow the standard sitcom formula. The show has a darker, more dramatic feel with no laugh track. It is based on the real life of Louis C.K. who plays a version of himself. In "Bully," the title character Louie is on a date in a coffee shop. A group of six young thugs in letter jackets come into the shop and are very disruptive. When Louie asks them to please keep it down, one of the boys, Sean, shows Louie his hand with which he previously beat up another kid. Sean brags that he left the kid bleeding. Sean continues to threaten to "beat the shit" out of Louie and makes Louie ask, "Please do not kick my ass." After the boys finally leave, Louie's date starts acting weird. He explains that he is a grown man with two kids. She tells him she would be angry if he fought, but that it was a turnoff. She explains, "You see a guy totally debase himself just to be safe, that's a turnoff. My chemistry is telling me you are a loser." Outside the dinner, Louie sees the bullies and follows Sean home to Staten Island. Louie knocks on the door and asks to speak to the boy's parents. When he tells them that Sean threatened to beat him up, the father slaps Sean and grabs him around the neck. Louie scolds the father for hitting the kid. The mother starts yelling at Louie, calls him a "faggot," and starts slapping him. The father comes outside and tells Louie that corporal punishment is what he knows since he was hit by his father. Louie and the man sit on the stairs and smoke.

BOY VICTIMS

In the vast majority of sitcoms, portrayals of bullying follows the traditional boy as bully and boy as victim. There are a few reoccurring bullies (see Chapter 1 for analysis); however, the bully almost always makes a one-time appearance. The first selections of adult targeted shows come from the early days of television in the 1950s.

In *Father Knows Best*'s "Bud, the Boxer," Bud's little sister tells their parents that Bud wants to stay home from school because there is a bully outside their house. Bud tells his parents they got in argument and pushed each other, and the bully wanted to fight. The dad tells Bud never start a fight but never run away either. He insists that this is something every boy must go through. The mother wants to call the boy's mother or the principal. The father arranges for the boys to go into a ring and box with gloves. When Bud gets knocked down and loses the match, he reports that the other guys were laughing at him. The dad then pushes him into boxing lessons. Bud knocks the bully down the next time. The crowd cheers for Bud.

In *Leave it to Beaver*, "Lumpy Rutherford," Lumpy bullies Wally and Beaver on their way home from school. He knocks Wally's books down and pulls Beaver's hat down over his face. As he waves his fist in front of Wally's face, Mr. Rutherford calls out to him and Wally and Beaver make their escape. Wally and Beaver's father, Ward, offers to help, but Wally declines because their peers will think there is something wrong with them if he does. Wally and Beaver are counting on Lumpy getting tired of picking on them. Ward recounts how he got revenge on his childhood bully by putting out barrel hoops on his lawn to trip up the bully. June, the mother, scolds Ward for telling that story. The boys imitate their father's prank and put hoops on the Rutherford's driveway. However, Mr. Rutherford gets caught in the hoops instead of Lumpy. When Mr. Rutherford finds out Lumpy has been bullying, he intends to talk to Lumpy. Wally and Beaver do not get reprimanded for the barrel hoops. Later, Lumpy because one of Wally's friends.

In *Dennis the Menace*'s "The Bully," Dennis tells his parents, Henry and Alice, about the school bully, Gifford, who picks on all the kids and is now picking on Dennis. Dennis tells them that if the bully hits him, he is going to clobber Gifford back. Henry tells Dennis it is okay to "clobber" the bully if it is in self-defense. Alice scolds Henry for encouraging Dennis to fight. Alice asks Dennis if he has tried to make friends with the bully. When Dennis tries to make friends with the bully, Dennis comes home with a black eye. Alice then apologizes for giving him the wrong advice. Henry insists there are certain problems children must work out for themselves. Mr. Wilson gives Dennis boxing lessons. Dennis ends up knocking Mr. Wilson out. The next day, Dennis hits the bully, sending him home crying. The father of the bully comes over to the Mitchell house to fight Henry until he finds out that it is his son who is the bully.

In *The Andy Griffith Show*'s "Opie and the Bully," Sheldon, the neighborhood bully, makes Opie pay a nickel to get by his street or Sheldon will give him "a knuckle sandwich." Sheldon also threatens to "pulverize" Opie, "knock his block off," "give him the ol' one two," and then jump on him if Opie tells on him. Opie gives Sheldon the nickel but sticks his tongue out at Sheldon as he is walking away. When Andy, Opie's father, finds out about the bully, he tells Opie a story about when he got bullied as a little boy. Andy tells Opie that he was ashamed because he was scared of the bully. Andy kept feeling lower and lower until he went back and got hit in the nose by the bully. Andy then laughed at the bully and started hitting back. The next day, Opie comes back to the sherrif's office with a black eye and a torn shirt after having stood up to the bully. Andy, Barney, and Opie laugh and celebrate Opie's black eye.

Two of the episodes in this section feature lead female characters. In *The Donna Reed Show*, "Weekend Trip," Donna's son Jeff is late coming home from school. He explains to this mother that a bully was beating up a little kid, Eddie, and the group of them had to break it up. He recounted how he dazzled the bully with his footwork. Eddie tells his mother he is sick. Because Eddie is one of Donna's husband's patients, Donna's family cannot go away on vacation until Eddie is feeling better. Donna does some detective work and figures out that the boy is faking sick because he is afraid of having to go to school and face the bully. When Eddie hears that the bully moved away, he is immediately well.

In *The Patty Duke Show*, "Big Sister Is Watching," Patty is furious when a bully, Jerry, starts pushing around her brother, Ross. However, Patty develops a crush on Jerry's older brother, Alan, so she keeps making excuses for the bully. Patty's friend, Richard, teaches Ross how to box and use karate. When Alan gives Richard a black eye, Patty defends Richard. She goes over to Alan's house and comes home with a black eye herself, although it is not clear who gave her the black eye. She announces to her friends and family, "That's a rotten family." Everyone laughs as she puts a raw chicken on her eye.

Happy Days, although airing in the 1970s-80s, is set in the 1950s. In "Richie Fights Back," Ralph is playing pinball when the bullies, Frankie and Rocko, come in and push Ralph out of the way. The two bullies take Richie's parking place at Arnold's and crush his Thermos. To really insult Richie, the bullies force Richie to make pinball-machine-bell sounds as they play. When Richie asks to stop, they grab Richie's shirt and threaten to "rearrange his freckles." Fonzie enters and the bullies run away. Richie is upset that Fonzie has to fight Richie's battles for him. Richie's father tries unsuccessfully to teach Richie how to fight so Richie signs up for jujitsu classes. Joanie, Richie's younger sister who is also taking jujitsu, flips Richie. Embarrassed by losing to his sister, Richie asks Fonzie for advice. Fonzie tries to teach him to use intimidation. When that does not work, Richie acts crazy and scares off the bullies.

The 1980s begins a more modern era of comedy. In a 1983 episode of *Silver Spoons*, "Twelve Angry Kids," Ricky tells his father, Edward, that he got into a fight at school because a boy, whose nickname is "Ox," insulted Ricky's father. Ricky recounts how the boys shoved each other back and forth. When Ox's pants accidently fell down, Ricky put them in the sewer drain. Edward tells Ricky there are other ways of settling differences than fighting. When Ricky tells Edward the boy called Edward a "balloon head," Edward changes his tone and tells Ricky that he hopes Ricky "knocked his block off." Ricky shrugs it off and refers to the incident as "typical kid stuff." When Ox and his father come to the house, Edward offers to buy Ox a new pair of pants. Ox's dad threatens to sue Edward for $50,000. When Edward refuses to pay, Ox's father takes Edward to court. Ox's father has his son fake whiplash and come into the courtroom in a wheelchair being pushed by a nun. The jury of kids is sympathetic to Ox until Ricky gives an impassioned speech about what a great person his father is. When Ox is caught lying about his injuries, the jury rallies around Ricky.

In *The Cosby Show* episode "Mr. Quiet," Theo brings in a little Hispanic boy, Enrique, from the playground and tells the director of the youth center two boys were bullying Enrique. Enrique has a scratch on his arm. The adults advise Enrique next time to stare down the bullies or run away. Enrique's mother comes down to the center and explained that the boy's father had been killed years before and the man who shot him recently got out of prison upsetting the boy. The episode ends with no resolution.

In *Alf*, "Hit Me with Your Best Shot," Brian comes home with a black eye and a torn shirt. Brian's mother tells Brian to ignore the bully, Bobby. Brian fears he will be called a "snitch" if his mother calls Bobby's mother. Alf, the alien who lives with the family, gives Brian karate lessons. Brian's father, Willie, tells Alf not to teach Brian to fight. Willie recounts how he was bullied as a boy. Willie tells Brian to "turn the other cheek"; however, the next day Brian comes home with more bruises. Alf calls Bobby's father, Mr. Duncan, pretending to be Willie. Mr. Duncan comes to the house and defends his son, claiming it is good for boys to fight. When Mr. Duncan calls Willie "four eyes," Willie retaliates by calling Mr. Duncan "shortie" and asks him to leave. When Mr. Duncan pokes Willie, Willie grabs his arm and pushes him out the door. The neighbors come over to tell Willie that he is the hero of the neighborhood. When Mr. Duncan returns and pokes Willie, Brian's mother throws him out. Brian's sister comes home and announces that Bobby is scared and will not be picking on Brian anymore.

In *Home Improvement*'s "Karate or Not, Here I Come," Brad and Randy refuse to let their little brother, Mark, play football with them. They call Mark a "geek" and a "chicken." Their parents, Tim and Jill, agree that Mark should find a way to improve his confidence. Tim suggests karate, Jill gymnastics. Mark chooses karate. Mark's karate partner turns out to be a bully who slaps Mark on the head when the instructor is not looking. When Jill points out the bullying to the boy's mother, she calls Mark a "weenie" and "stick boy." Jill lightly slaps the mom so she can see what it feels like to get hit. When Tim comes to Jill's aid, the bully's mother hits Tim with her purse. Brad and Randy tease their father for getting hit by a woman and Mark for having his mom fight his battles. Even after Jill yells at Brad and Randy, the boys continue to tease their father. Tim laments about his youth and his use of humor to avoid bullying. Tim tries to discourage Mark from retaliating against bullies. Tim wants Mark to learn to use karate for good. When the bully's father shows up at karate class and threatens Tim, the karate teacher moves Mark to a different class.

In *8 Simple Rules*, "School Nurse," Rory does not want to go to school because the bully warned Rory that if he shows up, the bully will "punch his lights out." Rory's grandfather advises him not to worry, that getting knocked out is like going to sleep. When Rory's mother gets a job at the school nurse, Rory is thrilled that his mother will be able to protect him from the bully. Knowing his mother is nearby, Rory taunts the bully. The bully turns his attention to Rory's adult cousin, C.J. When the bully chases C.J. home, Rory's grandfather threatens the bully he will "ring his bell" if he comes back. The bully leaves, fearful of the elderly but tough grandfather.

In *Grounded for Life*'s "I Right the Wrongs," Brad's girlfriend, Lily, is keeping her relationship with Brad secret because he is a member of the science and math clubs and is thinking about running for school government. Lily's father, Sean, tries to teach Brad not to be such a nerd. Brad tells Sean he was beat up by Scott and Scott's brother in elementary school. The brothers made Brad take naked pictures of himself in junior high. More recently, Brad gave Scott money to buy him beer. Scott never returned either with the beer or the money. Sean tells Brad if he does not stand up to Scott now, he will get bullied all his life. When Brad fails to get the money, Sean grabs Scott's jacket lapels, pushes him against a building, and demands either the money or the beer. When Scott goes in to buy the beer, he is arrested for using a fake ID. The kids at school blame Brad for Scott getting kicked off the basketball team right before the big game. Some of the boys hit Brad with basketballs in the hallway at school. To distract the kids from hitting Brad with basketballs, Lily shouts that Brad is her boyfriend.

In *Grounded for Life*'s "Jimmy Was Kung-Fu Fighting," as Jimmy is running away from Kyle, the school bully, he runs into the tetherball pole. Jimmy's dad, Sean, insists that Jimmy's older sister, Lily, walk Jimmy to school to protect him. Lily stands up to the bully and puts him upside down in a trash can. Not only does Lily make things worse for Jimmy, her friends tease her for beating up an 11-year-old boy. Jimmy's uncle shows Jimmy some moves from a Fung Fu movie. The next time Kyle knocks the books out of Jimmy's hands, Jimmy has a fantasy of flying through the air a la *Crouching Tiger, Hidden Dragon* and taking out all the bullies. In reality, Jimmy hit Kyle on the back of the head with his lunch tray.

Four brothers in the neighborhood are vandalizing people's mailboxes and stealing items from yards in *The Middle*'s "The Neighbor." Their mother, Rita, is very scary as well. Even their dog is terrorizing everyone in the neighborhood. Sue confronts two of the bullies at school. One of the boys knocks her books out of her hands and challenges her to a fight. Sue and her friend dance to the song "Everybody was Kung Fu Fighting." The boys push the girls down and steal their boom box. Sue's mother, Frankie, sees that Rita is not able to pay for all the food she picked out at the grocery story. Frankie brings over some food to Rita and her family. When Rita fails to thank her, Frankie confronts her. The rest of the neighbors come over to watch the argument but are scared to speak up. The neighbors finally all stand up to Rita and reclaim their stolen goods. The episode ends with the bully boys waiting as their mother plots revenge.

In *Man Up!*, "High Road Is the Guy Road," Will tells his friends that his son Nathan got picked on at school. The bully said Nathan looked like an iguana, pushed him down, and put his backpack in the trashcan. One of Will's friends, who is also Nathan's uncle, asks Nathan if he got picked on because of his glasses or funny haircut, as though it was Nathan's fault. The uncle and friend confront the bully. Unfazed, the bully says if the uncle hits a kid, the uncle will go to jail. Later, Nathan tells his father that the bully apologized. It appears the mothers talked. The adults, however, are still feuding (see the adult section on bullies).

The next section of sitcom bullying episodes features animated series that are targeted to an adult audience. Bullying in this category also includes the bullying of a child by an adult. In *The Family Guy*, "The Kiss Seen 'Round the World," one-year-old Stewie teaches the neighborhood bully a lesson when the bully steals Stewie's new tricycle. The bully calls Stewie a "stupid baby." Stewie surmises that the bully acts out because of some deep-seated inner pain. Stewie thinks about joining a gym to get buff to beat up the bully but is turned off by the gym's sales pitch. Stewie then uses a homemade device to trap the bully in a net. Stewie ties the bully up in his basement, slaps him, and threatens the bully with a weapon-like gadget made of sharp objects. There is no resolution, only that Stewie's mother finds the stolen tricycle.

In *King of the Hill*'s "Gone with the Windstorm," Bobby tries to fight back against a bully, Jimmy, who constantly scares Bobby at school. Jimmy jumps out of a locker, barks at Bobby, and runs away. Hank, Bobby's father, goes over some boxing moves with Bobby, but after seeing Bobby's ineptness, suggests Bobby try ignoring the bully. When Jimmy scares Bobby again, causing Bobby to pee his pants, Hank takes charge and goes to see Jimmy's father. Jimmy's father appears helpless because his son scares him, too. Bobby and Hank give Jimmy a taste of his own medicine and hide under Jimmy's bed and closet and scare Jimmy when he comes in the room. Jimmy agrees not to scare Bobby anymore.

In the "Four Wave Intersection" episode of *King of the Hill,* a group of bullies excludes Bobby and his friends from rides at the water park. They pick up Bobby and "help" him over the edge of a big slide. Later they send Bobby down the water ride naked. The kids get Boomhauer, a former surfing great who is now middle-aged, to outsurf the bullies, but he fails miserably. When Boomhauer comes back for another try, he knocks their leader, Bode, into the water. The kids in the water park cheer and jump into the water. Having been humiliated, Bode is shown on a bus leaving town.

In the MTV series *Good Vibes* Mondo, an overweight boy from New Jersey, moves to Los Angeles with his single mother. On the first day at his new school, Mondo gets a wedgie from a large black character wearing a wife beater t-shirt and bandana. Mondo develops a crush on a girl whose boyfriend, Turk, threatens him to stay away from her. Turk spray-paints Mondo's new surfboard to make it look like a penis and later breaks it in half. When Mondo runs into Turk on a wave, Turk threatens to kill him. The girlfriend interferes, saving Mondo from a beating. Turk bans Mondo from surfing at the beach unless Mondo can surf a dangerous beach littered with sharp rocks. Mondo attempts to surf the beach but gets knocked unconscious. When he comes to, everyone is in awe of Mondo's bravery. Turk agrees and allows Mondo to surf again.

One character who is difficult to label is the title character of the short-lived animated sitcom *Allen Gregory.* The pilot episode introduces Allen Gregory as a rich, entitled boy who has been homeschooled and is now going to school. He bullies teachers and other students but is bullied by some of the other students. A boy named Patrick with red hair and freckles tries to be nice to him since he is the new kid. Allen Gregory treats Patrick poorly, calling him by the wrong name. Allen Gregory is pretentious in that he eats sushi and drinks Pino at lunch. Joel, the class president and most popular kid in school, throws his burger in Allen Gregory's face. Although he tries to intimidate and boss around the principal, she scares Allen Gregory and he poos in his pants. The other kids tease him for crying and smelling. Patrick tries to comfort him and tells him that it gets easier. When Allen Gregory refuses to go back to school because of the humiliation, the superintendent pleads with Allen Gregory's father to get him back to school. One dad, Richard, is rich and dominant who bullies the younger, better looking other dad, Jeremy. Jeremy explains to Allen Gregory that he is straight with a wife and kids and is being bullied into being gay by Richard. Allen Gregory's adopted sister, whom the dads ignore, wants Allen Gregory to go back to school so he can get picked on. When he comes back to school, the superintendant tells the student body that he was the one who "crapped" his pants that day.

In "Interracial McAdams," Allen Gregory makes a play for higher social status and a place at Joel's lunch table. Joel pours chocolate milk down Allen Gregory's pants when he tries to sit with them. When Joel gets sick, Allen Gregory manipulates his way into bringing Joel his homework. During Joel's absence, Allen Gregory starts sitting at the lunch table. The gang, especially Bernique, Joel's girlfriend, starts to like Allen Gregory. Joel finds out that Bernique wants to break up with him. Allen Gregory laments that he imagined he and Joel ruling together. When Joel comes back, the gang refuses to make room for him at the table. He starts to tear up. In order to save Joel's status, Allen Gregory sacrifices his own. He disparages the gang, giving them back to Joel. Joel stands up for his friends. He once again pours chocolate milk in Allen Gregory's pants. Patrick offers to still be his friend. Allen Gregory demands Patrick's pants.

In *The Cleveland Show*'s "Yemen Party," a bully named Rodney King is torturing a boy by pushing him violently on the merry-go-round. Rallo, strapped to the front of a very large Cleveland Jr., arrives to superhero-type music. The children on the playground cheer. Cleveland Jr. picks up Rodney and hangs him on a pole by the back of his shirt. Rallo taunts Rodney with insults. The playground is once again a happy place with butterflies, sunshine, and happy music playing. The children erect a monument in Rallo and Cleveland Jr.'s honor. Rodney comes back strapped in a baby carrier to his very large brother, who steps on the monument. The earth shakes as he walks. All four boys square off, kicking and punching. The big brother hits Cleveland Jr. in the testicles. Cleveland Jr. returns the favor. The two big boys collide, causing a nuclear-type explosion. As the big boys lie defeated on the ground, Rallo and Rodney introduce themselves and become friends. *The Cleveland Show* is one, if not the only, animation show that features a minority cast.

Bart is tired of getting beat up by Nelson in *The Simpsons*, "Bart the General." Homer, Bart's father, teaches Bart how to fight dirty. When Bart gets beat up yet again, he goes to his grandfather for advice. Grandpa takes Bart to an army surplus store where the owner, Herman, teaches Bart the "art of war." Bart and his friend Milhouse gather all of Nelson's victims together. The group plots to take Nelson by surprise. They bomb Nelson and his gang with water balloons. When Nelson's cronies flee, the army of victims takes Nelson prisoner. They force Nelson to sign a peace treaty. Nelson will remain a figurehead of menace of the neighborhood but will refrain from bullying.

The Brak Show is a parody of traditional family sitcoms. Brak is a cat-like alien. Zorak, a 7-foot green mantis, is Brak's friend and neighborhood bully. In "Bully," Zorak sets up a "beatings" booth. He collects lunch money from a line of creatures waiting their turn to get beaten. Each time a creature steps into the booth, sounds of punches and screams can be heard from behind the closed door. Zoraks explains that the creatures line up so that he does not have to go looking for them. He reasons, "Everybody wins...except for them." A new kid in town, Butch, takes over Zorak's beating business. Zorak moves into Brak's room. Brak's father advises Brak to convince Zorak to stand up to the bully or Brak will never get his room back. In order to motivate Zorak to fight back, Brak tells Zorak that Butch is about the best bully they have ever had. Zorak is outraged when he finds out that Butch is allowing rescheduling of beatings and offering special discounts. Zorak worries that Butch is ruining his business. After Butch beats up Zorak a second time, Zorak goes back to Brak's house and orders Brak's mother to make him dinner. Infuriated, Brak's mother demands that Butch give the beating booth back to Zorak. After Brak's mother beats up Butch, she declines the position of the new bully, restoring the title to Zorak. She then kicks Zorak out of her house.

KID VICTIMS

Kid victims of adult bullies appear to only be represented in animated programming for adult audiences. The programs *South Park*, *Family Guy*, and *American Dad* are quite controversial in general; it is not surprising they would be represented in this category.

In *South Park*'s "Butterballs," Butters is being bullied by his grandmother. She comes to school and traps Butters in the boys' room. She is about the make him put the urinal mint in his mouth when one of the teachers interrupts. She threatens Butters that if he "narcs again," he is dead. At dinner that night, Grandma stabs Butters in the leg with a fork under the table. Then she picks her nose and puts it in his mashed potatoes when the parents are not looking. Butters gets revenge by promising to visit her hospital bed as she lay dying and show her he is still alive and happy.

In the animated series *American Dad* episode "Bully for Steve," Stan, a CIA agent, bullies his son, Steve, in the hope Stan can toughen up Steve. In the opening scene, Steve comes downstairs wearing an overly large, bright yellow shirt. Stan jokes that a homosexual giant called and wants his shirt back. He tells his son to go upstairs, find his "nads," and ask the guy at the store for the right size. Stan spies on Steve and sees that the crossing guard has to hold Steve's hand while crossing the street. When a bigger kid takes the last piece of pizza from Steve at lunch, Steve calls his dad crying, saying he is sick and wants to come home. Stan tells Steve about a bully when he was young. Stan credits the bully for making him the man he is today. Stan dresses up like a young bully, complete with slicked-back hair and a leather jacket. Stan gets Steve on the ground and demands his lunch money. Next, Stan trips Steve's bike, throwing him off. Then Stan steals the bike. When Steve comes home all scuffed up, his mother, Francine, asks if Steve has tried reasoning with the bully. She suggests that perhaps the bully just needs a friend. Later, Stan throws hot coffee on Steve when Steve tries to reason with Stan. When Francine realizes it is her husband who is bullying their son, she slams her car into Stan's car. When Steve comes home with his underwear pulled up to his chest, Francine trains Steve to fight. After the first lesson, she gets frustrated and tells him he is "terrible." Steve tries to disguise himself as an old lady but Stan is on to him. Steve finally agrees to meet Stan at the playground. Steve pays Stan's childhood bully to come back the playground and beat up Stan. The bully blackens Stan's eyes and bloodies his nose. Stan finally gives in to Steve and agrees to leave him alone.

In *The Family Guy*'s "The Tan Aquatic with Steve Zissou," when his son, Chris, gets bullied, Peter beats up the 13-year-old bully. When Peter is forced to apologize to the bully, Peter and the bully bond over how bullying makes them feel cool. Peter starts to bully. Peter knocks a pan of hot grease out of his wife's hand and makes her hit herself over and over. Peter saying that there are two kinds of people, bullies and nerds, and he is a bully. He bullies his friends and his children. Peter realizes the person he should be bullying is the bully who panted him in high school. Even though his bully now suffers from MS and walks with crutches, Peter takes a swing at him. Chris steps in and beats up his father. Peter promises not to bully anymore.

ADOLESCENT LEAD: BROADCAST

Although airing on primetime broadcast television, the following sitcoms focus on a lead adolescent character rather than the adults. In *Growing Pains*, "Fast Times at Dewey High," Ben fakes being sick because he does not want to go to his first day of school. Ben discovers Louis, the school bully, flunked and will be returning to Ben's elementary school. Last year Louis told Ben he was "dead meat" when Ben did not let Louis cheat off of him. When Ben asks to be transferred to a different school, his father tells Ben that he was also bullied when he was Ben's age. He tells Ben to stand up to the bully; however, if the bully hits him, Ben should run. When Ben finally meets up with Louis, Louis runs away, seeing that Ben grew over the summer and is now physically bigger than Louis.

In *The Wonder Years*'s "Fate," kids scurry to get away as the bully, Eddie, walks down the school hall. Eddie, who is wearing the standard bully leather jacket, is followed by a couple of cronies. Eddie takes over a small boy's locker, throwing its contents on the floor. Kevin stands up to Eddie when he catches Eddie going through his friend Winnie's locker. Eddie grabs Kevin's shirt and pushes him against the locker. A teacher comes by and asks what is going on. Kevin tells him they are "just talking." The teacher makes Eddie apologize, which appears to only make matters worse. The teacher lets them go but tells the boys that he will be watching them. When Eddie comes into class and grabs Kevin and threatens him, Kevin dumps his art paste on Eddie's hand. Eddie corners Kevin in the boys' room and punches Kevin in the face. Kevin's mother is upset when Kevin comes home with a bruise on his face. Kevin's father appears unconcerned with the boys' fight. When Kevin sees Eddie teasing Winnie, Kevin tries to hit Eddie. Kevin misses and gets knocked to the ground. Kevin smiles as Winnie comes to comfort him.

In another episode of *The Wonder Years*, "Ninth Grade Man," Tony, a "serial senior," threatens to take Kevin's thumb and bend it back to his elbow if Kevin does not give up his locker. When the new girl kisses Kevin and thanks him for being nice to her, Kevin gets the confidence to stand up to Tony to get his locker back. In the next scene, Kevin is walking down the street with a wrapped thumb and a smile of his face, happy that he stood up to the bully.

In *Boy Meets World*, "Back 2 School," Cory is getting ready to start a new school. Cory's older brother, Eric, refuses to protect Cory at school. Therefore, Cory plans to befriend a popular senior in order to escape bullying for the year. When Cory and his friend, Shawn, get to the school, they see freshman walking by in their underwear after the seniors took their clothes. Cory assumes those boys must have done something to deserve the prank. Just when Cory is feeling safe, a large boy picks him up and slams him against the lockers. Shawn gets intimidated and puts himself in a locker. Harley, the leader of the bullies, gets caught picking on Cory. Harley threatens to kill Cory after school because he claims Cory got him detention. Cory tries to reason with Harley, telling Harley that he would rather be dead than be known as the coward of the school. Eric comes to Cory's rescue. Just as Harley is threatening the brothers, a teacher comes by and apparently sends the bully away. There is no immediate resolution. Harley returns in several episodes (see the reoccurring bullying section of chapter 1).

In the pilot episode of *Malcolm in the Middle*, Malcolm runs into a bully, Dave Spath, on his way to school. Dave is offering a smaller boy a choice: beg for mercy on his belly, lick the bottom of Dave's shoes, or take a beating. Malcolm advises his little brother to roll into a ball if Dave ever catches him. Later, when Malcolm does well on his art project, Dave pours paint on Malcolm's desk. Malcolm is placed in a gifted program at school, making him even more of a target for bullies. When Dave throws food at Malcolm, Malcolm stands up to Dave and throws pudding on him. As Dave goes to hit Malcolm, Malcolm ducks and Dave accidently hits Stevie, a boy in a wheelchair. Although Dave barely hit Stevie, Stevie makes his wheelchair tip over, making it look like Dave pushed him over. The crowd turns on Dave since he hit a "cripple." Dave cries.

In another episode, "The Bully," Malcolm's brother Reese loses a wrestling match to a girl. Malcolm's friends fear Reese becoming even meaner and more vicious. They recall the past when Reese beat them up, gave them wedgies, stole their lunch, made them eat grass, and made them do his homework. They recommend not wearing underwear to avoid wedgies and bring decoy lunches. On the contrary, Reese confesses that he is sick and tired of picking on little kids. With Reese no longer the school bully, chaos ensues as other boys rush to take his place. Malcolm gets pushed down, hit in the stomach, and has his head put in the garbage. When Reese sees one of the new bullies picking on Stevie, who is in a wheelchair, Reese makes his triumphant return as the school bully.

A similar episode of the dominant bully losing and then regaining his status is *Everybody Hates Chris*'s "Everybody Hates Caruso." An Asian student, Yao, beats Caruso in a fight. When one of Chris's friends offers Yao his lunch money, Yao declines it, saying that he is not there to take over as the school bully. Rather, Yao explains that he was tired of getting picked on so he took karate. With Caruso out of the picture and Yao declining the bullying position, other boys begin bullying. The social order of the school is disrupted. Caruso suddenly starts being nice to Chris. With the hierarchy in chaos, Chris and his friends plot to get Caruso back into power. They offer to help Yao pass his math class in exchange for throwing a fight. Caruso wins the next fight and order is restored.

Adolescent Lead: Cable

Shows targeted at tweens and young teens on cable networks such as Nickelodeon and the Disney Channel have numerous episodes that addressing bullying. The biggest difference between these shows and the network shows that feature adolescent characters is that the following shows include fewer adults. Those adults who do appear are generally inept and unhelpful. The bullying in these shows is sillier, slapstick humor.

In *Salute Your Shorts*, "Brownies for Thud Mackie," Thud, a large boy, threatens Michael when Michael accidently sits on Thud's brownies. Thud gives Michael a week to replace them. Michael accidently throws up on Thud, making Thud even angrier. Michael decides to leave camp when he cannot get replacement brownies. Thud tries to get to Michael as Ug, the incompetent counselor, is driving Michael to the airport in the camp van. Even when Thud bangs on the van's windows, Ug does nothing. Michael decides not to run. Fellow campers tell Michael they will all take on Thud. One by one, the kids get scared and walk away. Michael stands up to Thud alone. Thud hits Michael in the eye. As Michael lies on the ground, the other kids joke. Ug once again does nothing.

Eddie is a typical bully in *100 Deeds for Eddie McDowd*, wearing a bandana and a spike bracelet. Even the teachers are scared of him. Eddie has a reputation as the biggest bully in the Southwest. In the pilot episode entitled "Tagged," Eddie steals one kid's breakfast and puts another kid in a trashcan and sends it rolling down the hill. A new student, Justin, accidently runs into Eddie and makes Eddie spill his milk. Eddie pours white paint on Justin and runs him up the flagpole. When Eddie's reckless behavior almost kills a dog, a devil-like character changes Eddie into a dog and tells him he has to perform good deeds to change back. Justin is the only person who can talk to Eddie as the dog. Eddie convinces Justin to rescue him from the pound. When the new bullies, who have taken over when Eddie disappeared, pick on Justin, Eddie bites them.

In *Big Time Rush*'s "Green Time Rush," everyone is vying to be Logan's partner for the class competition. The bully grabs Logan and claims him as his partner. The bully carries Logan away over his shoulder. The inept teacher acts as though everything is normal. Logan suggests they meet to work on the project somewhere public (i.e., with witnesses). The bully cracks a walnut on his forehead and orders Logan to get to work. Logan approaches the bully wearing hockey equipment. The next day the bully has rebuilt the model for their project. Logan tells the bully that he is not stupid and that the model is amazing. He tells the bully that making other people do his homework only hurts the bully. As they work on their project, they become friendly. The bully learns that it is okay to ask for extra time for his school work and appears to stop bullying.

Louis is a typical victim with curly hair and wearing a loud shirt in *Even Stevens*'s "Hutch Boy." The bully, Lloyd, picks up Louis' sandwich, licks it, and puts it back. Louis tries to reason with Lloyd after Lloyd steals his shelf in shop class. Lloyd traps Louis in the hutch he is building. Louis' geeky friend, Tom, comes to the rescue. Tom, who is secretly a black belt, uses his karate skills to break boards and scare Lloyd away. When the kids on the bus call Louis "hutch boy," Louis asks Tom to teach him karate. Louis challenges Lloyd to a fight the next day. Louis' friends hook him up to a wire so it makes him look like he can do martial arts flips. He gets Lloyd to promise not to bully anymore until the wire malfunctions and Lloyd realizes it is all fake. Instead of being upset with Louis, Lloyd starts to like Louis because they are both into mechanics.

In *Flash Forward*'s "Skate Bait," Tucker and Miles are hapless as they try to skateboard. The bully, Scott, knocks Tucker over and tells the two to leave the park or Scott and his four cronies will beat them up. Tucker and Miles have had previous run-ins with Scott. They enlist a bigger, more popular skateboarder, Gooch, to help them with their bullying problem. They negotiate a skate-off to see who gets claim to the park. Scott engineers a plot to injure Gooch so he cannot compete. Tucker makes the course so difficult that Scott crashes and is also injured. It is assumed that bully will stop. In another episode of *Flash Forward*, "Dog Day After Lunch," Horace, Tucker's little brother, is hiding in his locker from his bully, Garth. Garth's older cousin, Jack, encourages Garth to be a bully. Jack tells him it is part of their family legacy. Jack has been bullying Tucker for years. Garth is only an intimidator and confesses to Jack that he cannot really hit Horace. When Tucker and his friends see Garth pinning Horace to the ground, Tucker pushes Garth off. Jack accuses Tucker of taking unfair advantage of a smaller boy and challenges him to a double fight, Horace versus Garth and Tucker versus Jack. Bystanders gather at the site of the fight and chant, "Fight, fight!" Garth shows up alone and runs away when the bigger kids threaten to beat him up. The gang goes looking for Jack at his house to see why he never showed up. Jack's mother is very sweet. She gives the kids treats and shows them photos of Jack when he was a baby. When Jack wakes up from a nap, he comes out with a blanket. The kids tease Jack at school the next day. It appears Jack will not bother them again.

A gang of boys calls Danny names during a basketball game in *Hang Time*'s "Fighting Words." Danny tells the ring leader, Tony, "Why don't you shut your ugly face, stupid?" Tony comes to Danny's school after the game and threats to fight Danny. At first Danny hides from Tony. Tony delivers a pair of crutches to Danny in order to intimidate him. Danny takes karate lessons. When Tony comes back to Danny's school, Danny's friends hold Tony back but Danny tells them to let him go. Danny uses his karate skills to kick and flip Tony. Even though Danny is winning the fight, he stops himself from becoming the bully and refuses to continue. Tony runs away.

In *Lizzie McGuire*'s "Lizzie Strikes Out," Matt and Lanny create an extravagant plan how to stop the bully, Heywood Biggs, from picking on them. They flash back to the time Heywood used the boys as footballs and put their clothes up the flagpole. Matt and Lanny, who are rather small, decide to work out and take protein supplements. Next, they try to camouflage themselves so Heywood will not see them. They then plot to somehow get Heywood to step in sticky stuff at which point Matt and Lanny will encase Heywood in clear wrap. While Matt and Lanny are thinking up elaborate plots, Heywood accidently rides his skateboard into a tire swing and is put into traction.

The title character in *Mr. Young* is actually a 14-year-old genius who is hired to teach at his own high school. In the pilot, Slab the bully steals Mr. Young's master key and wreaks havoc throughout the school. Slab is a large boy dressed in black who supposedly has been in high school for seven years. The episode "Mr. Witness" opens with Slab using Derby as a human bowling ball and other students dressed as the pins. When Principal Tater sees the carnage in the hallway, he tries to get the students to talk. He finally gets Derby to admit that it was Slab that used him as a human bowling ball by promising Derby that Slab will be expelled. The principal admits that Slab has been terrorizing the school for years. The other kids hold up victory signs and chant Derby's name as the security guards take Slab away. Suddenly the halls are a happy place again until Slab comes back. Slab tells the principal he has a good lawyer who got the expulsion reduced to a one-day suspension. The principal finds Derby hiding in a trashcan. Later Derby comes back disguised as an exchange student, Simon, who looks remarkably like Harry Potter. Slab pressures the principal to put him in touch with Derby. In a panic, the principal tells Slab that Derby has moved to Atlantis. Slab continues to terrify the kids in the cafeteria as he steals their lunches. Not only is there no adult supervision, the principal is hiding in the trash can. When Simon, who is actually Derby, laughs at Slab, Slab decides he does not need to bully Derby. His goal is to make Simon's life miserable. Derby safely comes back to school as himself, having fooled Slab.

In the opening of the series *Ned's Declassified School Survival Guide*, Ned states in a voiceover, "In a middle school full of bullies and insane teachers..." In "Guide to: Cheaters and Bullies," a group of three boys appears to terrorize Ned's school. One small boy, whose nickname is "Coconut Head," is walking around with his clothes on backward and his hair messed after his encounter with the bullies. The leader of the bullies, Loomer, wears black and a thick silver chain, and has spiky hair. Ned's tips to avoid a bully: "Teachers create a bully-free zone; know where the bully is and don't be there; run to the main office." When that strategy does not appear to be working, Ned and his friend, Cookie, devise all sorts of crazy contraptions and traps to counter the bullies' attack. When Ned acts crazy, Loomer gets spooked and agrees to mediation.

Parker and his friend, Mikey, band together against a bully, Larry Kubiac, in the pilot episode of *Parker Lewis Can't Lose*. Larry is a big guy and gets very upset when others interfere with his lunch. He is shown eating a whole turkey leg. Rumors circulate he killed a nun when she misplaced his lunch. When Mikey mistakenly sits on Larry's lunch, Parker takes the blame. Larry picks up Parker by the neck and lifts him up. Larry grunts rather than speaks. Mikey comes to the rescue but both Mikey and Parker end up running away from Larry. Larry catches them and just when he is about to hit Parker and Mikey, Larry's little brother enters the room. Larry becomes a very sweet person around his brother. He threatens that if the two of them ever tell anyone he has a nice side, they will not live. In later episodes, Larry becomes friends with Parker.

In *Phil of the Future's* "Double Trouble," a boy is seen rolling down the hall in a trashcan, which is apparently the bully Myron's way of "escorting" the boy down the hall. Phil witnesses Myron coming out of one of the bathroom stalls with a smaller boy who is wrapped head to toe in toilet paper. When Myron demands Phil's lunch, Phil licks his sandwich first before giving it to Myron. Myron demands a fight and schedules it in his palm planner. Phil's mother advises Phil to try talking and finding a kinder side of Myron. Phil tricks Myron's sister, Jerry, into telling him Myron's weakness, which is rabbits. Instead of fighting, Phil distracts Myron with a rabbit. Now in a calm state, Myron refers to his anger problem and his therapist. Two episodes later, Phil and Myron are friends.

In *Saved by the Bell: The New Class*'s "Squash It," the bully, Kirk, gives Megan some unwanted attention. Bobby tries to defend Megan but Kirk pulls Bobby's shirt over his head. In the next scene, Kirk is shown pouring food on Bobby. Screech, the principal's assistant, sees the aftermath and instead of disciplining Kirk, tries to teach Bobby karate. Later, Kirk squirts mustard on Bobby and threatens to "tear him to bits." Bobby dismisses his friends who start to intervene. Bobby uses his new moves and gets Kirk to the floor. Bobby raises his hand to hit Kirk, but stops and states that fighting is stupid. The inept principal finally shows up at the end and warns them about fighting.

In *The Suite Life of Zack and Cody*'s "The First Day of High School," the school bully, Vance, catches Zack with his arm around Vance's girlfriend, Amber. He puts Zack in the trash can. Mia, a friend of Zach's, calls the bully out, kicks him in the shin, and pushes him into the lockers. Mia and Zach get in trouble with the principal. Later, Vance bullies Cody and his friend, Bob. The principal catches Cody just as Cody jumps on Vance's back. This time Cody gets in trouble. The episode is another example of an inept principal. Vance's girlfriend breaks up with Vance when she realizes what a jerk he is. Vance apologies to Mia and asks her out, telling her he likes the way she stood up to him. In another episode of *The Suite Life of Zack and Cody*, "Neither a Borrower Nor a Speller Bee," Zack borrows money for video games from a junior loan shark, Maynard. When Zach does not have the money when payment is due, Maynard warns him to pay up, "or else." Zach interprets the threat as Maynard will beat him up. Maynard offers to forgive Zach's debt if he can convince his brother Cody to lose the spelling bee and let Maynard win. Zach discovers that he misinterpreted Maynard's threat; Maynard was only going to tell Zach's mother about borrowing the money. Zack calls Maynard the worst bully ever for threatening to tell his mom. Maynard wonders why Zach assumed he was violent.

In *Zeke and Luther*'s "Plunk Hunting," the two bullies are brothers known as "the Plunks." The Plunks like to hold kids down and give them bad haircuts. The Plunks steal Zeke and Luther's grandmother's wig. Luther politely asks the Plunks if they have seen his nana's wig. The bullies tear the sleeves off of Luther's shirt and shave off his eyebrows. Zeke and a couple of his friends go to get the wig back. They chase the Plunks on skateboards. The bullies throw bolts down and end up injuring Luther. When Zeke pulls the bolt out of Luther's behind, Luther screams. The screams scare the Plunks and they not only give back nana's wig back but restyle it for her.

Vince is the kind of guy that makes the girls swoon in the series *Zoey 101*. One of his teachers even hugs him for getting the school to the football playoffs. In "The Great Vince Blake," Chase discovers that Vince and some of the football players cheated on an exam so they could be eligible to play in the big playoff game. Four large football players threaten Chase with bodily harm if he tells. After Chase turns in the players, nearly the entire football team shows up to beats up Chase and three of his friends. In the last scene of the episode, the girls are patching up and comforting Chase and the boys after their beating. There appears to be no resolution within this episode. In subsequent episodes it is revealed that Vince was expelled. In "Vince Is Back," Vince is reinstated after a year suspension. The principal has explained that Vince successfully completed anger counseling. The boys whom Vince beat up are not convinced Vince has changed. They devise crazy schemes to get revenge on Vince. For example, they give Vince a cappuccino with an explosive device in it that fails to explode. When they rig a bucket of goop to fall on Vince's head, Vince voluntarily stands under the bucket so he and the boys can be even.

A group of six bullies approach Brady and Boomer in *Park of Kings*, "Beach Bully Bingo." Hibachi, their leader, bans Brady and Boomer from the beach. The bullies rip off Brady and Boomer's swim trunks when the boys talk back. The boys are forced to make it back to the house naked, covering themselves with a surfboard. The boys reminisce about their old school and having their clothes stapled together by the football team on picture day. They return to the beach to stand up to the bullies. Hibachi pulls them to the ground. Sounds of punching can be heard. In the next shot, Brady and Boomer are being carried back to the castle. The boys' next strategy is to make the bullies laugh. It works for awhile until they go too far with the joking. Brady challenges Hibachi to a surf-off. The boys take surfing lessons and win the surf-off when Hibachi is caught cheating. Hibachi runs off the beach.

Original programs on MTV such as *Awkward*, *The Hard Times of R.J. Berger*, and *The Inbetweeners* are targeted to older teens and contain significantly more mature content. In the opening of the pilot episode of MTV's *The Hard Times of R.J. Berger*, R.J. describes himself in a voiceover as "scrawny and weird looking, awkward and pale." He confesses that he has more pairs of glasses than he has friends. R.J. is wearing a neck brace in a picture of his little league team. In the lunchroom, R.J. sits with his loud, overweight friend, Miles, who is obsessed with being popular. R.J. fantasizes about a popular girl, Jenny. When a geeky girl, Lily, approaches them, Miles comments on her mustache and calls her "a dog." She appears not to be fazed but keeps flirting with R.J. R.J. is the water-boy for the basketball team. The star player, Max, who is also Jenny's boyfriend, wipes his hand on his armpit and puts his fingers under R.J.'s nose and says, "That's what a man smells like, bitch." When all but four players on the team get ejected, the coach, who is also a bully, is forced to put R.J. in the game. Seconds after losing the game, R.J.'s over-sized uniform pants and jockstrap fall to the floor. Evidently where R.J. fails in social graces, he makes up for in "masculinity." The episode shows that even though Miles is an out-cast, he is mean to a girl who is even lower on the social scale.

MTV's *The Inbetweeners* is a comedy about a boy, Will, who transfers from a private school to a public school. The vice principal introduces Will as having to leave his last school because of bullying, which Will claims was not true. The vice principal reasons that Will has a face someone would want to punch. Will's mother also thinks Will was bullied at his old school. When the jocks come into the bathroom, Will's new friends flinch and get out of the jocks' way. During lunch, one boy gets an erection from talking to a pretty girl. His friend forces him to stand up to show everyone. There is a group of kids who are less cool than Will and his friends who eat standing up nicknamed the "wall eaters." Will gets caught skipping school and uses bullying as an excuse. The vice principal announces over the school intercom that Will's mother has threatened a lawsuit if anyone bullies Will. The episode not only spoofs bullying, it downplays the boy embarrassing his friend by exposing his friend's erection.

MINORITY CASTS

The following sitcoms feature a minority-dominated cast, or at least a black lead character. Most shows appear to be careful not to bring attention to interracial issues in their casting. While there are portrayals of white bullies with minority victims, I found only one case of a minority bully with a white victim (*Are We There Yet?*).

In *Good Times*, "The Lunch Ripoff," after leaving his apartment, Michael hides his lunch and milk money. Eddie, the bully, catches Michael in the elevator, grabs his finger, and steals his lunch. Eddie threatens to break Michael's teeth if he tells. When Michael's parents, James and Florida, find out, James threatens to kill the bully. He tells Michael to hit the bully, while Florida advises him not to fight. When Michael comes home the next day, he has invited Eddie to stay the weekend so he can help Eddie pass the sixth grade. Eddie's parents are not around and his teacher picks on him. When he acts up at the Evans' house, James takes off his belt and takes Eddie into the bedroom. The moral is that spanking equals caring. Even after the whipping, Eddie decides to stay.

"The Gooch" first appears in *Diff'rent Strokes'* "The Fight." When the Gooch threatens Arnold, Mr. Drummond advises Arnold to talk it out with the Gooch. Arnold's brother, Willis, gives Arnold boxing lessons. In Harlem, where the boys come from, it is manly to fight. When he comes back from the fight, Arnold has a black eye. Willis is proud that Arnold stood up to the Gooch; however, Mr. Drummond scolds Arnold for fighting. Mr. Drumond tells Willis there is only room for one father. As Willis is preparing to run away from home, Arnold threatens to beat up Willis if he tries to leave. Willis stays. In the next season of the show, the Gooch soaks Arnold's lunch bag in the water fountain and buries Arnold's shoes in the dirt in "Return of the Gooch." Arnold stood up to the Gooch the year before but now the Gooch has evidently grown even bigger. Mr. Drummond signs Arnold up for karate classes. While practicing, Willis takes a dive to make Arnold think he knocked him out. A confident Arnold then challenges Gooch to a fight. Even after Willis confesses he faked it, Arnold insists on going through with the fight to save face. The Gooch fails to show up. Willis explains that he took Gooch to see Arnold's karate teacher, who demonstrated what he has taught Arnold.

In *The Steve Harvey Show*'s "Don't Quit Your Day Job," Bullethead comes to Coach Cedric for help on how to handle DeAndre, the school bully who had been teasing Bullethead. Cedric asks Bullethead if he tried reasoning with DeAndre. Bullethead says he has tried everything. Cedric and Mr. Hightower teach Bullethead how to walk with confidence and put on a "crazy look." The next day when Bullethead gets teased by DeAndre, Bullethead starts to tease back. Cedric breaks the confrontation up. He tells Bullhead that the way he taunted DeAndre was mean and vicious and he has never been prouder.

In *City Guys*, "Bully Bully," El-Train goes to get his friend's basketball from Jerome, the bully who took it. When Jerome takes a swing at El-Train and misses, El-Train hits Jerome a couple of times. The rest of the kids in the schoolyard chant El-Train's name. Word gets out that El-Train beat the toughest guy in the neighborhood. Three of Jerome's henchmen come to the school wanting to hang out with El-Train. El-Train turns "all gansta." Jerome and his older brother, Curtis, come looking for El-Train. The principal catches them and warns El-Train that El-Train will get suspended if he fights. El-Train, having been a bully in the past, tells the principal that bullying is a lot easier than studying and getting good grades. When Curtis and Jerome come to fight, El-Train hears the principal's voice in his head. He stops the fight and starts to walk away. Curtis hits El-Train in the stomach but El-Train still refuses to fight. He apologizes to his friends for acting stupid. This episode is one of the few times a competent adult or school official made a difference.

In *Tyler Perry's House of Payne*'s "Worth Fighting For," as Malik's dream girl, Tori, is leaving his house, Vince, a tough boy in a letter jacket, comes in announcing he is Tori's boyfriend. Tori tells Malik that she and Vince have only been out a couple of times. When Vince snaps his fingers and grabs Tori's arm, Malik steps in to defend her. Tori steps in between them. Vince threatens Malik with a fight. Tori informs Malik that Vince is the captain of the boxing team. Even though Malik's aunt thinks it is a bad idea, Malik's Uncle Curtis and father give Malik boxing lessons. The men set up a boxing ring in the backyard. His father pushes a reluctant Malik into the ring with Vince. Curtis whispers to Malik to hit Vince in the throat. The crowd is chanting, "Vincent, Vincent." Even Curtis has a bet on Vince to win. When Malik raises his hands to give up, Malik accidently knocks out Vince. Tori tells Malik that he is brave, kisses him, and asks him out on a date. In *Tyler Perry's Meet the Browns* "Meet the Bully" episode, two boys named Joquim and Kim are fighting when Mr. Brown and his wife, Cora, come out to stop them. Kim is disrespectful to Cora and tells Mr. Brown to "shut up." Mr. Brown has to hold Cora back from going after the boy. Kim comes back later with his father. Words are exchanged and Kim's father and Mr. Brown arrange a fight. Kim's father wants to teach Kim that violence is not the way to solve problems so he proposes the two men just pretend to fight. Mr. Brown is supposed to hit him softly and Kim's father will take a dive. When Mr. Brown hits too hard, the dad gets angry and wants to fight for real. The dad pushes Cora aside when she tries to intervene. Mr. Brown pushes the dad off the mat, winning the fight. The dad goes home crying. In the end, the boys make up. A popular theme appears to be setting up a sanctioned boxing match to resolve conflict in bullying situation (e.g., *Father Knows Best, Family Matters*).

Additional episodes of Tyler Perry shows take a more sober, serious look at the effects of bullying. It appears Perry is the only television executive who addresses weapons and attempted suicide. Malik tells his family that he is being picked on at school in "The Big Bang Theory" episode of *Tyler Perry's House of Payne*. He waited to say something because he thought that the bullying would stop. He explains how the bully pushed him down the stairs and everyone laughed. His younger sister also laughed because he "screamed like a girl." Malik's father, C.J., asks why Malik did not fight back. When his aunt Ella suggests they report the bully to the principal, Malik says he is afraid everyone will think he is a punk if he tells. Later, Malik finds his uncle's gun in the closet. Shortly thereafter, the gun accidently goes off. Malik explained that he was going to take it to school to scare the bully. The adults warn him that the bully might bring a bigger gun. Malik's father tells Malik that he is going to school the next day and talk to the principal and the bully's parents. Ella chastises Curtis for having an accessible gun in the house.

Tyler Perry's Meet the Browns, "Meet the Troublemaker," goes a step further in addressing severe effects of bullying. Geoffrey, an overweight boy who is new in school, is a target of the bully, Andrew. Andrew is not only mean to Geoffrey but tries to bully the teacher as well. The teacher, Cora bullies right back. She repeatedly scolds the bully but he continues to disrespect her. Although she raises her voice and physically stands over Andrew's desk, she seems rather powerless to do anything and the bullying behavior continues. Geoffrey comes to class the next day with a black eye. After enduring more harassing comments, Geoffrey pulls a gun out of his backpack and points it at Andrew. The teacher admits that she did not realize the situation was that bad. Cora showed the usual ineffectiveness of adults since she had to have seen Geoffrey's black eye. Cora finally talks Geoffrey into giving her the gun. She scolds Andrew about how he has pushed Geoffrey over the edge. When Cora asks Andrew if he has "peed himself," the bully runs out of the room humiliated. The episode ends with the Cora and Geoffrey waiting for the police.

In *Tyler Perry's House of Payne*, "Do the Fight Thing," DeShawn, a foster child who is living with the Ella and Curtis Payne, is playing a video game he claims was given to him by a classmate, Tommy. Tommy's father comes over to the Paynes' house and accuses DeShawn of stealing the video game. Tommy comes in with a black eye. Tommy tells them that DeShawn threatened to beat up Tommy's friends if he told. Ella makes DeShawn apologize. Tommy's father threatens to call the police if it happens again. As they are leaving, DeShawn whispers to Tommy, "It's not over." Tommy's father comes back later. He lunges at DeShawn and angrily shouts that Tommy tried to kill himself by taking pills. Fearful he will get sent back to the group home, DeShawn joins the anti-bullying group at school. When Tommy and his father return to the Paynes' house, DeShawn explains he bullied Tommy because Tommy has everything, such as nice clothes and video games. DeShawn tells them he has no friends. DeShawn looks and sounds truly sorry. Curtis sends mixed signals about punishing DeShawn and excusing the behavior. Curtis gives DeShawn boxing gloves and tells DeShawn he has to have control. Ella comes back and scolds them both for fighting. Curtis claims he is rechanneling DeShawn's anger. At the end of the episode, the actor who plays DeShawn delivers a public service message about how bullying is unacceptable and cannot be ignored.

The next grouping of shows has mixed-race casts. *Are We There Yet* is perhaps the lone example of a black bully with a white victim. In the episode "The Fall of Troy," Kevin, who is also black, stands up for his white friend, Troy, against a black bully. The bully then turns his attentions to Kevin (see "Boy Bystanders" for description). The remaining examples in this section are white bullies with black victims. The *Everybody Hates Chris* series, based on the life of Chris Rock, includes a white bully. Chris's mom is rather overbearing and could be considered a bully; "she had a hundred recipes for whooping ass." In the pilot, Chris is being bused to a better, "whiter" school. As for Joey Caruso, the school bully, adult Chris in a voiceover states, "I couldn't beat him, but maybe I could out-black him." Chris makes friends with another one of the bully's victims. As Chris puts it, "Mutual ass-kicking seems to bring people together." The bully steals Chris' lunch money and bus pass and challenges him to a fight after school. A police offer walks by the fight and keeps on going. Chris narrates that he did not tell his dad about the fight because his dad went to school during the civil rights era. After "hoses, tanks, and dog bites," Chris laments that Joey Caruso did not compare.

In *Everybody Hates Chris*, "Everybody Hates Sausage," the principal tells Chris and Caruso that he does not want any trouble, even though he witnesses Caruso stuffing Chris into a locker. Caruso throws batteries at Chris. Chris throws one back, misses, and breaks the school window. The voiceover of adult Chris states, "Bully are kind of like dogs. They don't chase you unless you run." Chris comes up with a plan. He gets Caruso's attention and runs past the principal's office. When the bully and his friends catch up with Chris and begin to throw batteries at him, the principal finally catches them in the act. The boys are shown getting detention.

Jett is a teen television star who goes back to his hometown to attend high school in *The Famous Jett Jackson*. The show has a mixed-race cast. In the episode "Something to Prove," Jett describes to his friend how it feels good to be powerful on television. A white bully, Robert, bumps into Jett and starts taunting Jett about wearing makeup. Robert jokes about how Jett's father, the town's sheriff, hangs out at the donut shop. There is a rumor that Robert got expelled from his old school for tying the principal to the top of the flag-pole. The teacher scolds Jett instead of the bully when Jett stands up for himself. Jett's dad tells Jett that he arrested Robert for fighting and perhaps Robert is retaliating against Jett for being sent to reform school. Later, Robert slaps Jett lightly on the face and calls Jett and his father "punks." When Jett goes after Robert, Jett's father stops Jett and tells him not to fight. Robert threatens Jett that if Jett does not show up to fight, Robert will go after Jett's friend, J.B. When Jett's father catches the boys fighting, Jett lies and tells his father that he and Robert were just stage fighting. Jett saves Robert from going back to reform school. Because Jett gave him a break, Robert vows to reform. The episode sends a mixed message, that the bully is reformed but only after Jeff tells his father a lie.

A white bully, George, trash-talks Junior at school in *My Wife and Kids* "Snapping and Sniffing." Junior's parents invite the bully's parents over so they can get ammunition on the bully so Junior can use it to taunt back. When Junior talks back, George pushes him down. Junior's sister steps in and punches George in the nose. Junior is mad at his sister for making him look bad. George and his father come back to the house. Junior's father gets into a trash-talking match with George's father. Eventually it looks like the fathers will come to blows before Junior stops his father. The fathers admit that they are behaving foolishly and sending their sons the wrong message. They shake hands.

Girl Bystanders

Problems arise when a girl, usually an older sister (mothers and other adult females were excluded in this analysis), intervenes when a boy gets bullied. I found a number of shows where a girl stood up for a boy who was being bullied. There was a distinct difference in the reaction to the intervention depending on whether the bully was male or female. A girl intervening on behalf of a male victim with a female bully appeared innocuous. On the other hand, problems arose when the girl intervened with a male bully. The following episodes are examples of girl intervention with boy bullies. There were no examples of a girl intervening with a girl victim.

Dustin, Zoey's little brother in *Zoey 101*, is a small boy who is taking eighth grade math as a sixth grader. When Dustin corrects the bully's math problem in front of the teacher and the rest of the class in the episode "Defending Dustin," the bully threatens Dustin and forces him to do the bully's homework. When Zoey confronts the bully in front of a group of boys, the boys only laugh at her. Dustin runs away humiliated that his sister is fighting his battles. To punish Dustin for his sister's interference, the bully adds his laundry to Dustin's duties. Dustin stands up to the bully and the bully backs down. The other sixth graders are impressed, unaware that the school janitor posed as "The Dean of Discipline" and threatened the bully. Dustin and Zoey make up at the end of the episode.

In *Romeo!* "Minimum Cool," Romeo and his geeky friend Louis get picked on by a bully, a bigger white boy wearing a shirt with the sleeves cut off and a chain on his pants nicknamed "Booker." Booker pins Romeo to the bulletin board and puts Louis in the tro-phy case after giving him a wedgie. When Booker challenges Romeo to a fight after school, the boys hide in a locker and a trash can. Just as Booker catches the boys, Romeo's older sister, Jodi, threatens Booker. Booker retreats. Romeo is upset at Jodi for interfering. Romeo looks for a way to restore his masculinity. Booker makes Romeo a deal that Booker will let the kids at school think Romeo beat him up if Romeo sets up Booker on a date with Jodi.

The series *Clarissa Explains It All* features Clarissa, a cute popular girl and her younger brother, Ferguson, a redheaded, brainy nerd. When the bully, Clifford, begins stealing from Ferguson in "The Bully," Ferguson asks Clarissa to help. Clifford is big, wears a leather jacket with a denim vest, and does not talk but he has a lacky who talks for him. When Clarissa stands up to Clifford, he takes her portable tape player and stomps on it. He then threatens to fight her instead. Clarissa starts to lift weights and practice boxing in preparation of the fight. When Ferguson comes home with ripped clothes, Ferguson's father calls Clifford's parents. Clifford's mother defends Clifford and accuses Ferguson and Clarissa of bullying Clifford. As the fight is about to begin, Clifford breaks into a love song to Clarissa. He is later seen standing outside her window holding flowers. This is the one example where a boy bullies a girl because he likes her. Generally it is girls who bully the boys they like in sitcoms.

When Corey, Raven's younger brother, and his friend, Larry, get to their new school in *That's so Raven*'s "Juicier Consequences," they witness a bully, the Juicer, stealing lunches. The Juicer grabs the boys by the back of the shirts and eats Corey's lunch. In a sarcastic tone, he informs them they are going to have a great three years. The next day when the Juicer confronts him, Corey tells the bully that if he stands up to the bully, the bully will respect him forever. The bully recognizes the line from a Kung Fu Cats' episode and continues to go after Corey, telling him he is about to "get juiced." Corey proposes a plan where they can team up to resell the lunches that Juicer steals but does not eat. Corey projects a large profit margin. The Juicer calls Corey a genius. In the meantime, Raven has disguised herself as a lunch lady to keep an eye on Corey. She and Larry are disappointed that Corey has teamed up with the Juicer. Eventually all the kids in the cafeteria get angry with Corey for selling them out. When Corey stands up to the bully, the kids slowly get up and stand behind Corey. They cheer when the bully agrees to sell their lunches back to them at half price. The Juicer is stereotypically dumb, saying the seventh grade has been the best four years of his life.

In *Lizzie McGuire*'s "Sibling Bonds," Lizzie's brother, Matt, sees the school bully at the arcade. Matt flashes back with a montage of stills where the bully is giving Matt noogies and pulling Matt's shirt over his head. Instead of showing compassion, Lizzie confronts Matt about being annoying and making himself a target for bullies. The bully trips Matt, taking Lizzie down with him. Lizzie yells at the bully and calls him a "punk." The bully runs from Lizzie in fear. Matt thanks her. She tells Matt that no one gets to beat him up except for her. When a cute boy asks Lizzie to go get something to eat, she turns him down to chase her brother's bully yet again.

When Sam comes home from school in *Diff'rent Strokes*' "Carmilla Meets the Gooch," he shows Arnold, his new stepbrother, his lunch box, which has been destroyed by the Gooch. The Gooch is Arnold's bully who was featured in two previous episodes. Sam told the Gooch that Arnold would take care of the Gooch the next day. Arnold's adopted father, Mr. Drummond, offers to tell Sam that Arnold is not allowed to fight. He recommends Arnold try to reason with the Gooch. Arnold and Sam decide to bribe the Gooch; however, Arnold comes home covered in the items with which he tried to bride the Gooch. Sam says he will just have to get used to getting beat up. Arnold warns their parents that if they go to the principal, Sam will suffer. Arnold asks Carmilla, an Italian exchange student who moves in next door to the Drummonds, to help. She turns out to be a large African Italian girl who orders Arnold around. At first she refuses because she claims she is a "young lady." When Arnold promises Carmilla a date with Willis, she quickly responds,

"The Gooch is dead meat!" When Carmilla gets to the playground to meet the Gooch, a pile of destroyed lunch boxes is thrown from the bushes. She is seen going after Gooch in a Judo stance. In the next scene, Carmilla comes back victorious and gets her date with Arnold's borther, Willis.

Vicky, a robot who looks like a 10-year-old girl, lives with a family with a son, Jamie, in *Small Wonder*. In the episode "The Bully," Jamie's club is deciding on a president when a bully steps in and declares himself president. When Jamie stands up to him, the bully threatens to punch Jamie so Jamie backs down. The bully, Ernie, is tall and is wearing a jean vest with his shirt sleeves rolled up and spiky hair. Ernie demands a dollar-a-week protection money from the boys for "a chance to stay alive." Jamie's father tells Jamie he has to stand up to the bully and try to talk it over while Jamie's mother tells Jamie to walk away. When the mother leaves the room, the father shows Jamie how to punch. Jamie comes home the next day with a black eye. Jamie decides to have Vicky, who is freakishly strong, teach Ernie a lesson. She lifts Ernie off the ground. She shows Ernie how she can punch and puts a hole through the garage door. Ernie gives the money back and runs off. The boys cheer Vicky.

Family Ties' "Designated Hitter" is the only episode where a girl, Jennifer, stands up to her boyfriend's bully. At school, the bully, Rick, takes Adam's lunch. Rick pushes Adam down into a chair and takes his hat, with which he and the other boys play keep away. The principal comes to the lunch room just as Jennifer steps in and punches Rick in the stomach. Jennifer gets into trouble for fighting. Jennifer's parents ask her why she did not call a teacher when Adam was getting bullied. She told them there were no teachers around. Jennifer's parents, although disapproving of violence, are secretly proud of her. Adam breaks up with Jennifer because he does not want his classmates to think a girl had to defend him. Later, Adam tries to warn Rick that if Rick beats him up, Rick will get expelled and put in jail. Rick's cronies convince Rick to leave Adam alone. Adam eventually thanks Jennifer for sticking up for him. She tells him that she likes him because he is not a tough guy.

The school is doing experimental classes so Laurie has to take self-defense and auto shop, while Keith her brother takes home economics in *The Partridge Family* is "This Male Chauvinist Piggy Went to Market." The kids at school tease Keith when Laurie wins a bet by changing a tire better than Keith can bake a cake. Keith tries to reason with the bully, Goose, who is teasing Keith. When Goose goes to hit Keith, Laurie flips the bully instead. Keith is upset at Laurie for fighting his battles. When Goose approaches Keith backstage at their concert, Keith's mother stands up to Goose. Keith asks her to step aside so he can handle the situation. Keith tells Goose that he is not going to fight on principle. Goose starts to take a swing at him but backs down. He compliments Keith on his bravery.

Boy Bystanders

Cindy comes home crying from elementary school in *The Brady Bunch*'s "A Fistful of Reasons." She tells her parents that a boy, Buddy, has been teasing her, chanting, "Baby talk, baby talk, it's a wonder you can walk." Her parents, Mike and Carol, advise her to ignore the bully and give her tongue twisters to practice. When Peter stands up for his sister, Cindy, Buddy calls him a "chicken." Although his brother, Greg, insists Peter fight

Buddy, Mike tells Peter to try reasoning with Buddy. Peter comes home the next day with a black eye. Mike tries reason with Buddy's father, who defends his son, saying, "Kids are kids." Carol tries talking with Buddy's mother, who is so intimidated by her husband, she refuses to get involved. Mike and Alice, the housekeeper, teach Peter how to box. When Buddy challenges Peter, Peter punches Buddy in the mouth, causing Buddy to have a lisp. Cindy leads a group of bystanders in mocking Buddy the same way he mocked her. Peter scolds them all for retaliating and being bullies. Later, Buddy comes over to borrow Cindy's tongue twister book. All are friends.

In *Are We There Yet*, "The Fall of Troy," when Troy's friend, Kevin, sticks up for Troy, Jason, the bully, asks Kevin if he is sticking up for his boyfriend. Jason then tries to befriend Kevin. Kevin is torn because of his friendship with Troy. When Jason starts picking on Troy again, Kevin tells Jason he is like a bully from an old '80s movie, "but not the good kind like *Breakfast Club* but *Zapped*." Jason threatens and pushes Kevin. Kevin gives Jason a black eye. Jason and his parents meet with Kevin and his parents. Jason tells his parents that Kevin is the bully. Jason's dad yells at Jason for getting straight Bs instead of straight As. Jason admits he has a hard time making friends; that is why he is a bully. The boys make up.

Family Matters' Steve Urkel is the quintessential bully target. He has a high-pitched, nasally voice, wears large glasses that fall down his nose, buttons his shirt up all the way, and wears suspenders and a pocket protector. In "In a Jam," Urkel is being bullied by a boy nicknamed Bull. Urkel offers his friend, Eddie, $10 to protect him. After Eddie leaves, Bull comes in and threatens Urkel. When Urkel tries standing up to Bull, Bull picks up Urkel and sets him on the counter on a tray of food. Eddie's father, who is a police officer, suggests that if Eddie, who is bigger than the bully, shows up, it might stop the bully from picking on smaller Urkel. Eddie shows up at the diner. Bull takes a swing at Eddie, who ducks. Eddie hits Bull in the midsection. Bull vows to leave Urkel alone.

In "*Requiem for Urkel*," the bully Willie is about to trash Urkel's locker when an elaborate alarm system Urkel has installed goes off. Urkel, tired of the bullying, takes on Willie in the school hallway. The gym teacher, who witnesses the scuffle, puts up a boxing ring in the gym so the boys can fight it out. After seeing Urkel takes some blows, one bystander finally stands up to Willie. One by one the rest of the boys in the gym stand up. Outnumbered, Willie goes running from the gym.

Adult Bullies

Because of the number of adult bullying episodes in sitcoms, it was necessary to include a section on how bullying was portrayed among adults. Much like the criterion of the adult bully in movies, adults were included if their bullying actions were similar to adolescents. There are a variety of scenarios portrayed from current bullying to a childhood bully returning. The most common themes were either past bullies who tried to make amends to a victim or a past victim who sought revenge from a bully.

ADULT BULLIES IN THE PRESENT

Adults who bully in sitcoms are very similar to their adolescent counterparts. The episodes feature sillier, less physical forms of bullying. Many of these episodes, however, quickly escalate into physical violence and fighting, much more quickly than in adolescent portrayals. The bully appears to taunt victims about not fighting back in addition to threatening them physically. Bullying appears more embarrassing than frightening for adult victims, who should be able to defend themselves.

At the same time his son, Eddie, is being bullied at school, Herman is continuously being tricked by practical joker, Clyde Thornton, at work, in *The Munsters*, "Herman's Peace Offensive." Clyde had attached a boxing glove to Herman's locker so that when he opens it, he gets hit in the face with glove. Herman plays a joke on his bully by using a hand buzzer. Herman gleefully shouts, "Now I'm the bully, now I'm the bully." His wife, Lily, tells Herman she will not tolerate violence and then proceeds to hit Herman twice, knocking him over the couch.

In *Gomer Pyle: USMC*'s "Gomer Learns a Bully," the sergeant berates the troops. He compares their performance to a lady's knitting group. When a troublemaker, Phillips, joins the unit, the sergeant decides to let the platoon straighten Phillips out themselves. First, Phillips takes Gomer's bunk. Gomer, being a nice guy, lets him have it. Gomer reasons that Phillips is just shy. Then Phillips tricks Gomer into doing his work. Gomer gets in trouble with the sergeant for not having his own work done. Gomer still insists on not giving up on Phillips. Phillips admits that he is playing Gomer for a sucker. One of his platoon mates encourages Gomer to let Phillips "have it." Gomer tells Phillips he does not want to embarrass him, but tells Phillips the other guys do not like him. Phillips tells Gomer he does not know if Gomer is "dumb" or "chicken." Gomer overhears the sergeant say that Gomer would be doing Phillips a favor if he put Phillips in his place, making Phillips a better recruit. Gomer volunteers to take on Phillips in a training fight. Gomer knocks Phillips down three times in a row. Shortly thereafter, Phillips gets transferred. Sergeant explains to Gomer that one knockdown will not change a bully but if Phillips gets knocked down again and again it may work.

In the episode of *Frasier* titled "Bully for Martin," Frasier confronts his father, Martin, about letting Martin's boss, Rich, bully him. Frasier meets with the head of security to complain. The head of security happens to be the son of Martin's boss. The son defends his father and tells Frasier that perhaps Martin needs to be tougher. Rich makes Martin do some graveyard shifts in retaliation. In the end, Martin and Rich bond over complaints about their sons. In another episode, Frasier is the target of some "mean boys." The morning team at Frasier's radio station pranks Frasier in "Radio Wars." They get Frasier to believe he won an award for psychiatrist of the year. They go so far as to get Frasier to describe his behind for the marble status they were making of him. Martin laughs when he finds out it was a practical joke. When Frasier sees the morning team in the coffee shop, he wants to scold them. Roz his producer warns him that guys like that will prey on weakness. If they see Frasier getting rattled, the bullies will never stop. The team pranks Frasier a second time pretending to be his building's superintendent. They get Frasier to stomp around his bathroom singing. Next, the team pieces together sound bites to make it sound like Frasier and Roz are having sex. In the end, Frasier inadvertently gets the two arguing with each other, forgetting about all about the feud.

Flight of the Conchords was an HBO series that follows the band Flight of the Conchords. The episode "The Tough Brets" is about a group of Australians who make fun of the band members who are from New Zealand, Murray and Jermaine. At first Murray is simply annoyed and uncomfortable with the jabs. When it starts to really get to him, Murray reports the incidents to his supervisor. At first it looks as though his supervisor is going to be sympathetic to Murray; however, he too joins in the ribbing. Things get silly when Murray and Jermaine hold a *West Side Story*-like dance off with Bret, the bully, and his gang. Murray tells the Aussies that they have hurt his feelings. Bret defends himself saying they were just joking. Bret then discloses that sometimes he gets hassled at work. Bret apologizes and tells Murray they did not mean to hurt his feelings. It is an interesting commentary on childish bullying, that when the target tries to address the mean-spirited teasing in an adult manner, it looks like the adult is too sensitive and has no sense of humor. It is as though the adults in the situation are "tattletales" who are incapable of handing a childish situation.

In *Will & Grace*, "Bully Woolley" is the one example of an adult male bully and an adult female victim. Scott Woolley has a plan to destroy Karen's life after she foils his plan to take over her husband's company. He begins by continually calling her and hanging up when she answers. He next pretends to be a potential client for Grace and threatens to not give Grace the job unless she fires Karen. Karen gets revenge by putting cat urine in his champagne that he drinks when he thinks he got her fired. At the end of the episodes, he confesses he is in love with her and was just trying to get her attention.

The following episodes feature fighting or threats of fighting, which in the context of a situation comedy are quite serious. All scenes are between hyper-masculine male bullies and male victims. *Mork and Mindy* was a sitcom that ran from the late 1970s to the early 1980s. The show was a social commentary about an alien who makes astute observations about American culture. In "Mork's Greatest Hit," Mork finds it hard to believe that earthlings still physically fight each other. He states that his culture has long evolved past barbaric traditions. The episode begins with a large man, George, hitting on Mindy at a diner. When Mindy refuses his advances, he manhandles her. No one else in the diner, including Mork, helps her out as she is getting accosted. It appears that Mork does not understand what is happening. When George forces Mindy to dance with him, Mork asks if he can cut in. Instead of rescuing Mindy, he begins to dance with George. When George pushes Mork, Mork pushes back and shouts, "Tag, you're it!" When George tells Mork to "take it back," Mork literally goes backwards. Mork then playfully puts his finger in George's back. Everyone in the diner laughs at George for thinking Mork's finger was a gun. George vows revenge. Mindy later tells Mork that he should have made George stop mistreating her. Mork explains that his planet got rid of violence because it was humiliating. In order to please Mindy, Mork begins to train like Rocky Balboa. Mindy's father tries to teach Mork how to box. When the bully comes into the music shop, Mindy's elderly grandmother chases him out. Mork goes back to the diner to confront the bully. George pours water on Mork's head and grabs Mindy again. This time, Mork takes action. Whenever the bully tries to hit him, Mork goes into a time warp and ducks, leaving George to stumble when he hits nothing but air. A defeated George apologizes to Mindy.

Anthony is already emasculated by working for four powerful women in the sitcom *Designing Women*. In "High Noon in the Laundry Room," he tells the women about a new tenant in his building who is a bully. Some of the females in the building have asked Anthony to take care of the bully for them. Julia, Anthony's boss, advises Anthony to stand up to the bully. Having spent time in prison, Anthony wants to just "lay low." Charlene, the naïve receptionist, tells Anthony how she read that bullies act out because they did not get enough attention from their mothers. After putting it off, Anthony finally tries to reason with the bully. The bully is a very large man with a beard and a jean jacket with the sleeves cut off. The bully just spits. Charlene intervenes with no luck. The bully grabs

Anthony by his shirt and threatens him not to come back into the laundry room. The next night, Anthony confronts the bully again. He tries telling the bully he is in the mob. The bully punches Anthony. The female bystanders attack the bully with the laundry basket. The bully calls Anthony outside. In the next scene, Anthony is sitting at the office with an ice pack on his eye. Suzanne, Julia's sister, suggests Anthony call her next time since she has an arsenal of weapons. Anthony concludes that he feels better that he stood his ground even though he lost the fight.

In *Cheers* in "Cliff's Rocky Moment," Cliff is at the end of the bar rambling on as usual about some trivial facts. Victor, a large man at the other end of the bar, gets annoyed with Cliff and calls him a "boob." Cliff approaches Victor and offers to buy him a beer to smooth things over. Victor refuses the drink because he does not like Cliff. The waitress, Carla tells Cliff that she will be ashamed to know him if Cliff does not stand up for himself. When Victor challenges Cliff to a fight, Cliff goes out and gets a larger, tougher postal carrier, Lewis, to come to the bar. Lewis begins to agree with Victor about Cliff being a "know-it-all." Lewis leaves the bar, embarrassed to be seen with Cliff. Victor threatens to beat up Cliff again. The patrons of the bar laugh in disbelief at Cliff when he informs them that he knows karate. Victor offers to walk away if Cliff admits he is a "coward" and a "liar." After a long silence, Cliff leaves the bar. Everyone looks embarrassed for Cliff. Cliff returns shortly with a board and a brick. He kicks the board in half with his foot and breaks the brick with his head. The patrons apologize to Cliff for not believing him. Cliff admits to Diane that he never actually took a karate class and asks her to take him to the hospital.

In the *Friends* episode "The One with the Bullies," Ross and Chandler get bullied by a couple of guys in the coffee shop who take their seats and steal Chandler's hat. When Ross and Chandler get up enough courage to return to the coffee shop, the bullies call them outside. Before they begin to fight, they all remove their wallets and watches, which get stolen. Ross, Chandler, and the bullies chase the thief. Back at the coffee shop, the four bond over their combined effort in catching and beating up of the thief.

A thug named Shank comes into the pool hall in *The Wayans Bros* episode "I Do." He wins a bet with Shawn by cheating and then intimidating the bystanders into supporting him. Shank demands 20 percent of Shawn's store profits for protection. Shank threatens to burn down the family's business and put them all in the hospital if he refuses. One of Shank's female cohorts gives Pops, Shawn's father, a black eye. When Shank hears that Shawn's brother Marlon "tapped" his sister, Charmaine, he insists that Marlon marry her. Shawn stands up to Shank during the wedding. Charmaine gets angry at her brother for forcing Shawn to marry her and tells everyone Shank still wets the bed. Shank cowers when his sister threatens to tell their mother that he is carrying a knife.

The episode "The Teacher's Lounge" is an example of adult bullying that somewhat parallels the students' bullying in the series *8 Simple Rules*. When C.J. is promoted to a full-time teacher, he is given access to the teachers' lounge. C.J. makes fun of Mr. Edwards for being a male home ec teacher. C.J. then accidently breaks Mr. Edward's favorite coffee mug. The next day, C.J. is shown eating lunch in the hallway. When he does go into the lounge, everyone goes silent. Mr. Edwards humiliates C.J. by making him sit in the corner. Mr. Edwards kicks C.J. out of the lounge when C.J. takes the last muffin. When C.J. gets home, he vows he is never going back. When Katie, C.J.'s cousin, intervenes and confronts Mr. Edwards, he tells her he is a 6{ft}2{in} male home ec teacher named Marion; therefore, he has no choice but to be a bully. She insists he let C.J. in the lounge. The next scene is of C.J. hanging on the flagpole and the video posted on the Internet. The next day, C.J. points out to all the teachers that C.J. is the class clown and Mr. Edwards is the class bully, just like high school. The grandfather surmises that the only way Mr. Edwards will leave C.J. alone is if he finds another victim too scared to fight back. The episode ends with Mr. Edwards picking on Rory, a freshman student and C.J.'s cousin.

Community's "Comparative Religion" is a comical look at a middle-aged bully who knocks cookies out of Abed's hand. Abed compares the incident to the camp movie *Meatballs*. The bully returns and knocks Jeff's Spanish final out of his hands. Jeff challenges him to a fight after school by the bike racks. The bully is wearing a sleeveless sweatshirt and fingerless gloves. Pierce suggests the gang should teach Jeff how to fight, like in *Rocky*. Troy, a black student, tries to teach Jeff how to trash talk. Shirley is upset because the fight is scheduled for the day of her Christmas party. When Jeff glances at his "What Would Shirley Do," bracelet, he decides to not fight. When the bully punches Jeff in the stomach anyway, Shirley tells Jeff to "kick his ass." The bully's friends take their shirts off to expose ripped stomachs as they do martial arts flips. Jeff's friends, men and women, fight back. At Shirley's Christmas party, the gang smiles as they put ice on their scrapes and bruises.

In *My Name is Earl*'s "O Karma, Where Art Thou?" Earl works at a fast food restaurant to make up to a man whose wallet he stole years before. The boss is a tyrant. He makes Earl eat a french fry that he wiped on the dirty counter. A fellow employee confesses to Earl that he had to eat a burger the boss wiped on a toilet seat. Earl finally stands up to the bully boss. Earl's voiceover contemplates taking the high road just as Earl is shown punching the boss. Another employee joins in kicking the boss while he is on the ground, getting retribution of all the bullying she has had to endure. The incident sets off a chain of events that leads to the bully losing his wife and going to prison.

In *Happy Endings*' "You Snooze, You Bruise," David gets bullied at the gym. The bully, Corey, steals David's weight machine and calls David a "bitch" when he asks for it back. David tells the manager, who makes the bully apologize. As soon as the manager is gone, the bully grabs David and threatens him if he ever comes back. David's friends are not supportive. Alex, who used to be a bully herself when she was young, warns him that "snitches get stitches." David decides to stand up to the bully. David tells Corey that is likely that Corey bullies because he got bullied for being gay when he was young. David says they should deal with 10-year-old Corey. Cory punches David in the face. David sees Corey bullying other gym members, calling them names, and knocking the exercise ball from under one man. A crowd gathers outside the gym for the fight. As David is giving a speech about standing up to bullies, a stereotypical, skinny gay man steps in and punches the bully. The puncher tells David he was inspired by David's speech.

ADULT MEAN GIRLS IN THE PRESENT

Christine is the target of the mean moms, Marly and Lindsay, at her son's private school in the series *The New Adventures of Old Christine*. The mean moms look down on Christine because she works. They ask Christine rude questions such as how long ago her ex-husband divorced her. They take great joy in informing Christine that her ex-husband has a new girlfriend. The moms are condescending to Christine but they are also very catty to each other, taking jabs at their fake hair color and plastic surgeries. When one mother brags about her son being ranked in tennis, the other mother chastises her for working it into the conversation in the first sentence. In the episode "Popular," Christine befriends a father, Mike, whose children are new to the school. Christine soon discovers that the mean moms have invited Mike to their weekly coffee group. She warns him not to trust those two. Mike, thinking that Christine is being the petty one, calls her "meanie mom." Christine decides she is going to make more of an effort to be nicer and get more involved in school activities. In an effort to bond with Marly and Lindsay, she tells them they are too thin and too tan. Because the mean moms are so shallow, they take the remarks as compliments. Christine finally gets invited to the coffee group; however, Mike is not invited. Instead of refusing to go because the mothers are being exclusive, Christine quickly turns on Mike and tells him that he is "on his own." When the mean moms are disruptive at the school's concert by answering their cell phones and fighting with each other, Christine and Mike join together in scolding them. Christine smiles as she is "uninvited" to coffee group.

The series *Don't Trust the Bitch in Apartment 23* features the ruthless mean girl, Chloe. In the pilot, Chloe's strategy is to get roommates to give her first and last month's rent. Chloe then drives the roommates out by behaving so badly that the roommate is willing to leave while Chloe keeps the money. June fires back at Chloe's scheme by selling Chloe's furniture to make up for the extra rent money Chloe overcharged her. Chloe is impressed and lets June stay.

BULLIES FROM THE PAST

Many of the sitcoms feature a bully from the past who comes back into one of main character's lives. In *How I Met Your Mother*, when a minister cannot stay to speak at Marshall's father's funeral, the minister asks his son, Trey, to fill in for him. Marshall recounts how Trey terrorized him in back in high school. Marshall's friends cannot believe Trey gave Marshall noogies because Trey is a nearly two feet shorter than Marshall. Marshall explained that Trey made Marshall carry a step ladder with him.

Leonard's childhood bully, Jimmy, comes to town and wants to have a drink in *The Big Bang Theory*'s "The Speckerman Recurrence." Sheldon, Leonard's roommate, asks if Jimmy is the bully who peed in his Hawaiian Punch, gave him a wedgie that damaged his testical, or used his head to open a nut. Leonard admits those were all different bullies. Leonard also notes the bully who made him eat his own arm hair was Jimmy's sister. Leonard's nerdy friends go with him to confront Jimmy. Jimmy, who is now fat and out of shape, gives Leonard a big hug. He congratulates Leonard on a physics medal he recently won. Jimmy reveals the reason he wanted to see Leonard is that he is looking for a partner to develop an idea he has for 3D glasses. Sheldon steps in and tells Jimmy that he is a "terrible person," providing a list of things Jimmy did to Leonard. Jimmy explains he just thought they were having fun. Jimmy saw he and Leonard as a "comedy team" back in high school. Jimmy comes to Leonard's apartment later to apologize for bullying him. Jimmy is drunk so Leonard invites him in to sober up before he drives home. Jimmy admits that now he, Jimmy, is the "loser." The next morning, Jimmy has sobered up and has forgotten that he apologized. He steals Leonard's French toast and calls him Nancy. Leonard stands up to Jimmy and pushes him out of the apartment. In the next scene, Leonard and Sheldon are running down the stairs trying to outrun Jimmy.

There is a distinct subgroup of bullying episodes where the adult who was once bullied now wants revenge. Will is confronted by a childhood bully, Kevin, in *Will and Grace*'s

"Past and Present" episode. Grace remembers that Kevin would dump Will in the cafeteria garbage can if Will did not do Kevin's homework. Kevin changed the name on Will's locker from "Will Truman" to "Will Woman." Kevin, who is employed at the same law firm as Will, reenacts the bullying behavior at work. When the Kevin makes Will write a brief for him, Will sabotages the work. The boss reads the brief aloud, which includes a disclosure that Kevin did not write the brief and has not done his own work since he was 8 years old. Will does a victory dances outside the office window where Kevin, but not the boss, can see him. Kevin leaves the boss's office and runs after Will.

In *Raising Hope*'s 'The Men of New Natesville," Jimmy and Frank flash back to their childhood bully, Tommy. Tommy made Frank bang his own head against the school bus window. Tommy harassed Jimmy because Jimmy has to wear his mother's hand-me-down shirts. Jimmy's father keeps telling Jimmy to stand up for himself. When Jimmy fails to take action, Jimmy's mother threatens Tommy. She smears lipstick on him and makes him walk like he has on high heels. Jimmy and Frank, as adults, decide to get their revenge. When they get to Tommy's house, they discover that Tommy is now "Tammy." Tammy apologies and makes excuses that Tommy was just angry and confused about his gender identity. Frank punches her anyway. Tammy ends up beating them up but not before Jimmy gets in some good punches. Jimmy is just happy he finally fought back.

In *iCarly*'s "iStakeout," the Seattle Police Department uses Carly and Spencer's apartment for surveillance. One of the police officers turns out to be the bully that used to spank Spencer when they were at summer camp. Sadly, the bully has not changed that much since he was a kid. The bully is rather small and obnoxious. Spencer gets revenge for the childhood bullying by tricking the bully into getting handcuffed to the couch. Spencer then spanks the bully with a broom as the bully's son cheers.

Will tells his friends that his son, Nathan, is getting picked on at school in the *Man Up!* episode "High Road Is the Guy Road." The bully's dad, Dennis, bullied Will when they were in junior high. The bully's mother, Sharon, is an important person on the PTA. Nathan's mother, Theresa, needs Sharon's help to save the science club. Sharon was Theresa's mean girl. Sharon spread rumors about less popular girls and made up unflattering nicknames. When it appears Dennis is still a bully, Will decides the best strategy is to just agree every time Dennis says something disparaging. Will's friends plot to get revenge on Dennis by vandalizing his house but get distracted by Dennis's wide-screen television and man cave. Dennis takes video of Will, edits it to make Will look stupid, and posts it on the Internet. At the PTA meeting, Sharon continues to be the mean girl, making fun of other people. Dennis and Will exchange insults at the meeting. Will tells the other parents that in high school Dennis got caught masturbating at a sleepover and reminded them that Dennis fumbled the ball during the big football game. Dennis goes to fight Will but he cannot get the baby carrier off his chest. Dennis is about to fight with the baby still strapped to him when the other fathers intervene and hold him back. When Will and Theresa get home, Will brags to his son that he left Dennis crying in his car.

Although he does not want to admit it, Kyle is afraid to go to his class reunion because of Lester Tate in *Living Single*'s "School's Out Forever." In high school, Lester put marmalade in Kyle's shoes, locked him in a closet, gave him wedgies, and put him on top of the flagpole. Kyle admits he was chunky as a kid and was a target for bullies. At the reunion, Kyle points out to Lester how successful he is and how Lester is a "loser." Kyle then finds out that Lester is out of work and his wife just left him. The members of the class sympathize with Lester. Kyle starts to apologize to Lester in the hallway; however,

Lester tries to steal Kyle's wallet. Kyle traps Lester in a closet, calls the police, and gets his revenge.

In *It's Always Sunny in Philadelphia*'s "High School Reunion," the gang is excited to show off to their classmates. Dee and Charlie reminisce about getting bullied and rejected. Dee's plan is to lure some of the popular kids in and then be mean to them. Dee joins one of the bullies in heckling Mac and Charlie, she says, in order to get invited to the cool kids' table. She will then destroy them. Dennis is trying so desperately to be popular that he strikes out on his own, waiting for his "minions to swarm him." No one does. The popular kids corner Mac and Charlie in the men's room and give them wedgies. The gang starts plotting their revenge on the cool kids. The gang performs a dance routine to show how cool they are. Their classmates are horrified. The bully invites everyone except the gang back to his house for an after party.

I Hate My Teenage Daughter features the one instance in the "revenge" analysis where the bully victim seeking revenge is female. In the pilot episode, the principal at Nikki's daughter's school, who was a mean girl to Nikki when they were teenagers, is still mean to Nikki. When the principal comes over and makes fun of Nikki at the school dance, Nikki's friend Annie stands up for her. The principal claims she was just kidding and asks her where her sense of humor is. Annie says it is hilarious when the principal's husband hits on Annie at school fundraisers. The principal walks away, defeated.

Victim from the Past

Occasionally the regular character on a show will admit to having bullied others when they were young. In the next set of episodes in the analysis, the goal of the regular character is to try to get the bully to make amends with the bully victims years after the fact. In all the episodes, the attempt to make it up to the victim works out badly. The lesson here is perhaps for children not to have bullied in the first place. Efforts to make amends usually result in making things worse. Also it shows the adults have not really changed over time.

Niles and Frasier reminisce about how they got bullied when they were young by a boy named John in the *Frasier* episode "Liar! Liar!" To get back at John for being a bully, Niles and Frasier set off the fire alarm at school and blamed John, who was then expelled. They reasoned that John deserved expulsion because he was a "brute and a meanie." Frasier complains that he had to resort to wearing gym shorts in the shower because of John. Upon hearing his sons' admission, Martin scolds them and tells them that getting John expelled from school was worse than John's bullying. Feeling remorse, Frasier visits John in prison. Frasier figures out that John's getting thrown out of school for fighting was the beginning of John's life of crime. Frasier tries to make it up to John by offering to counsel John and his wife. When Frasier arrives at their home, the wife tries to seduce Frasier. John comes home unexpectedly on parole. To get out of the apartment without John seeing him, Frasier sets off the sprinklers in the apartment.

In *My Name is Earl*'s "Bullies," Earl tries to make amends with an old schoolmate, Wally, who Earl used to torture. At the time, Earl reasoned that since the new kids usually gets bullied, he needed to find someone lower on the totem pole to pick on. He pushed Wally's head down in the dirt, killing a butterfly he was admiring. Years later, when Earl knocks on Wally's door, Earl sees a huge, muscular man. Earl hides his identity from Wally out of fear. When Wally discovers Earl is the one who bullied him as a child, he goes after Earl, intending to do bodily harm. Earl apologies to Wally and tells him he feels bad that he bullied the sensitiveness out of Wally. In the end, Wally becomes a body builder who loves butterflies.

The next set of episodes feature female adult bullies and mean girls attempting to make amends. In *Will and Grace*'s "Alice Doesn't Lisp Here Anymore," Grace sees a death announcement for a former classmate, Alice. She recounts how the other kids, not her, made fun of Alice. As she is telling Will how the kids made fun of Alice, she chuckles and admits she thinks it is funny. She eventually confesses that she was the one who gave Alice the nickname Mrs. Lazy Face. Will and Grace go to the funeral; however, it is actually Alice's grandmother's funeral rather than Alice who has the same name. Grace wants to leave. Will insists she stay, mostly because he wants to flirt with Alice's good-looking brother. Grace apologizes to Alice about giving her that nickname. Alice calls her a "bitch" in the middle of the funeral service. After Grace apologizes further, Alice finally forgives her. That is, until Grace burns her tongue on hot coffee and starts to lisp, making Alice think Grace is making fun of her speech therapy clients.

In *Caroline in the City*'s "Caroline and Joanie and the Stick," Joanie, a former classmate of Caroline's, shows up at Caroline's door. Caroline insists that Joanie stay at her place while Joanie is in New York. Joanie is rather neurotic. She rambles on about how Caroline was the only one who was nice to her in school. Caroline confesses to Joanie that because she was jealous of Joanie's first place win in the fifth grade science fair, Caroline told the other kids Joanie had pinworms. Joanie gets angry and leaves. Caroline tries to make it up to Joanie by getting Joanie's children's really bad children's book published. Shortly into the book reading, the kids in the audience all fall asleep out of boredom. Caroline then confesses to Joanie that her book is not very good and likely will not get published. Joanie is upset that Caroline lied to her. A publisher approaches Joanie to publish the book because it made his son fall asleep quickly. Joanie disparages Caroline, criticizing her for living in such a small apartment and being too attached to her cat. Joanie then tells everyone Caroline has pinworms.

Still Standing is another sitcom that features a loud family. The daughter, Lauren, is sent home from school for bullying another girl in the episode "Still Bullying." Disappointed in Lauren's behavior, the mother, Judy, tells her daughter the story of when she was bullied in school. It turns out, however, that it was Judy who was the bully and called another girl names. At the end of the episode, Judy calls the girl she bullied and apologizes. She finds out that the girl has become more successful than she is. Judy becomes agitated and ends up calling the woman names.

In *The New Adventures of Old Christine*'s "Old Christine Meets Young Frankenstein," Christine finds out her son, Ritchie, has been bullying another boy in school. She is concerned because she used to be a bully in junior high. Ritchie does not understand why he has to apologize to his victim if she does not have to apologize to her victim, Francis. Christine agrees and goes to see Francis. Francis appears quite successful, well dressed and living in a large house. Francis makes fun of Christine for being poor. Christine tells Francis that Francis should thank her for making Francis what she is today. Christine's friend inadvertently threatens Francis and her children. Francis panics but Christine will not let Francis leave until she listens. Christine ties Francis up. Christine blames Francis for making her do it. Francis tells Christine that she was finally over the past bullying when Christine brought it up again. Christine apologizes and lets Francis go.

In *The Big Bang Theory*'s "The Speckerman Recurrence," one of Leonard's bullies from high school comes to visit. This prompts the female characters to reminisce about the mean girls in their high school. Bernadette shares how a mean girl stole her clothes in gym and left her with an Elf costume. Amy tells how the mean girls in her school put Rogaine in her hand lotion, prompting the other kids to call her "gorilla fingers." Penny, the pretty neighbor, claims there was no bullying in her school; kids just pulled pranks. She describes how she and her friends left a girl who got good grades in a cornfield overnight. Bernadette and Amy, rather geeky themselves, disagree. They think the prank was awful. Penny argues that it was funny because everyone laughed. Bernadette and Amy confront Penny for being a bully. Penny feels bad and later calls her old targets to apologize. None of the women are willing to accept Penny's apologies. In order to feel better, Penny donates her old clothes to charity. However, once Penny sees the other clothes that have been donated, she starts to raid the donation bin. She comes back the next day with a laundry basket to get more clothes. Clearly Penny learned little about not being mean and petty.

Parodies

A very popular form of comedy is parody. The following examples are parodies or spoofs of bully portrayals and anti-bullying programs. As in many representations of unconventional themes, all the examples are animated shows targeted to adults.

The series *Moral Orel* is a spoof of the religious claymation show *Davey and Goliath*. In "Turn the Other Cheek," a bully gives Orel a black eye. Orel is elated because he gets an opportunity to turn the other cheek as prescribed in the Bible. By turning the other cheek, the bully gives Orel another black eye. Time and time again, the bully bashes Orel all over his body. Orel even devises a contraption that punches himself. He tells his father he has to be bloody for Jesus. His father explains that the expression "turn the other cheek" has been misused ever since violence "went out of style." He explains that the phrase is only applicable if someone insults you or jokes about your wife. He tells Orel that God does not want Orel to get hurt; therefore, Orel can defend God's righteousness and teach the bullies about the Bible. The dad teaches Orel how to make a fist and describes it as "one hand praying by itself." Orel totally misinterprets his father's advice and beats up the bully when the bully makes a fist in order to give the bully a chance to turn the other cheek and thus be closer to God. Orel starts beating up other kids, cats, and an old man at church whenever he sees something that looks like a fist. For example, when he sees his mother dusting, she is making a fist to hold the duster. Orel takes her down. Orel learns a song with the lyrics: "Turn the other cheek, turn the other cheek, show the world how strong you are by simply acting weak. Inherit all the world someday 'cause you will be the meek. Show them just how meek when you turn the other cheek."

In *South Park*'s "Bass to Mouth," Cartman is spreading gossip on the South Park Elementary site Eavesdropper that a boy, Pete, "crapped" his pants. A year earlier, Cartman had so badly teased a boy who had an accident in his pants that the boy killed himself. The school officials ask Cartman to ignore Pete so he can have a normal life. Cartman replies, "[Pete] was dead the second he crapped his pants." In order to help Pete through the ordeal, Cartman gives Jenny, a popular girl, cupcakes laced with laxative. His plan is to have her have an accident in her pants, thus taking the focus away from Pete. Jenny barely survives her suicide attempt. Cartman talks the school officials into slipping laxative into pizza for the whole school so that everyone will have an accident and no one will be singled out for teasing. When the adults fear they are going to get caught, they literally throw Cartman under the bus to take the focus off of them. Cartman survives and gets revenge by giving the school officials the laxative cupcakes.

South Park takes another opportunity to parody anti-bullying efforts in "Butterballs." "Bully expert" Bucky Bailey's Bully Buckers comes to South Park, bullying his way into leading a school assembly. He mocks the school counselor and calls him "an uninformed backwoods little dork," making the counselor cry. At the assembly, Bucky bullies a bully victim. He calls the students all "chicken" when no one volunteers to be in charge of an anti-bullying video. Stan eventually volunteers. The kids role-play bullying and break into song and dance. Kyle confronts Stan about being a bully about making the video. Bucky makes Stan cry. The president of the movie company that bought Stan's movie makes Bucky cry. Kyle criticizes Stan for using Butters, a victim of bullying, when Butters does not want to be in the film. Kyle asks Stan if he thinks everyone should see the movie, why does he not put it on the Internet for free? Butters and Stan appear on a spoof of *The Dr. Oz show.* Dr. Oz keeps prompting Butters about his bullying experience. Butters finally stands up to Dr. Oz, telling him to stop making him say things on the show. Butters physically attacks Dr. Oz. Jesus bullies the movie producer because of his bad behavior. Stan gets booed by the students since the studio backed out after finding out Butters was a violent psychopath. Dr. Oz is suing as well.

Conclusion

Stereotyped characters are standard for situation comedies, as they are for most media portrayals. Bullies' physical appearance (e.g., leather jacket, bandana) is easily identifiable and little back story is needed for the audience. The victims are also stereotyped, often physically smaller with stereotypical poor posture and glasses. In many ways it appears little has changed over the decades of television history; bullies still force their victims to do their homework and take their lunch money. There was very little variation between the older sitcoms and the more current shows except for the significant amount of father involvement in older shows. The mothers in older shows tended to be more traditional by showing concern for their bullied children but letting their husbands handle the situations.

Differences are evident between portrayals in sitcoms targeted to adults and adolescents. For example, storylines about bullying were more fully developed on programs where adolescents were the lead characters, particularly shows which aired on the Disney Channel or Nickelodeon. Adults were often absent and almost always incompetent; therefore, the adolescent characters were left to deal with the bullying and relational aggression on their own. Ways of dealing with bullies were more slapstick and comical if the program was targeting a younger audience. Programs targeting adult viewers on the broadcast networks often focused on the adults' role in the adolescents' bullying or the adults' experiences when they were bullied as children.

Gender is a significant factor as there are far fewer girl bullies. The female bullies' aggressive style is often expressed through verbal threats rather than physical contact. Aggression also varied by the sex of the victim. It is unlikely female victims of girl bullies will be physically harmed, with the exception of Lisa's black eye in *The Simpsons'* "Bye

Bye Nerdie." Boy victims, on the other hand, suffer black eyes and ripped clothing at the hands of girl bullies. Being bullied by a girl is portrayed as humiliating for boys. Not only are they victimized by the bully, but they are also teased by family and friends. The male victim's masculinity appears to be challenged when a girl intervenes, particularly when the bully is male. In almost all cases, the girl is the male victim's older sister. The two exceptions are *Family Ties*, where it is the bully's girlfriend who stands up for him, and Arnold from *Diff'rent Strokes*, who bribes the girl next door to take care of the male bully. Lily, in *Grounded for Life*, stands up for her brother Jimmy with both a female and male bully in separate episodes. In "Jimmy Was Kung-Fu Fighting," Lily's friends make fun of her for beating up an 11-year-old boy.

Race of the victim and the bully was also noted. White bullies with black victims were present, although rare, while casting a black bully with a white victim appears to be taboo. No reference to race was mentioned with the exception of *Everybody Hates Chris*. Chris' white bully Caruso called Chris racially charged nicknames such as "Kareem" and "Tito." There was one Asian (*King of the Hill*), one Hawaiian (*Pair of Kings*) and no apparent Hispanic portrayals of bullies or victims. There was one Filipino victim in *City Guys* and one white victim in *Are We There Yet?*; however, in both cases, the black bully quickly turned his focus on another black character.

When analyzed more closely, beyond a simple head count of bullies and victims' racial makeup, distinct cultural differences were present. In *Diff'rent Strokes*, *City Guys*, and *Good Times*, fighting and physical solutions were associated with masculinity and urban (read black) culture. In *City Guys*, the lead character Lionel, whose nickname is El-Train, has overcome a rough upbringing and being a bully to do well in school and stay out of trouble. He is tempted to go back to that life in "Bully Bully" but a caring principal helps him stay on the right track. Even when the bully hits him, El-Train still walks away. In the first season of *Diff'rent Strokes*, Arnold and Willis are adjusting to their move from Harlem to Park Avenue. Mr. Drummond adopts Arnold and Willis after their mother, the Drummonds' housekeeper, dies. In "The Fight," Willis and Mr. Drummond have a disagreement about whether or not Arnold should fight The Gooch when he challenges Arnold. Willis insists that in their old neighborhood Arnold would lose face if he did not fight.

The Evans family, from the series *Good Times*, lives in the projects in Chicago. When the bully Eddie acts up after being invited to dinner, James, the father, takes Eddie in the back bedroom and apparently whips him with his belt. After the whipping, Eddie decides to behave and stay. The cultural lesson is that Eddie's family did not care enough to discipline him. In *Tyler Perry's House of Payne*'s "Bully and the Beast," Malik's Uncle Curtis starts to take off his belt when Malik refuses to tell him what is wrong. Malik changes his mind and tells Curtis that a bully has been stealing his lunch money. It is rather ironic that the uncle bullies the kid into admitting he was being bullied at school. Malik's father, C.J., tells Curtis that he and his wife do not believe in whooping their kids. The uncle quotes the Bible. The aunt says Malik's father was whooped and he turned out okay.

The length of this chapter is an indication of the popularity of the bully theme in situation comedies. While a vast majority of the episodes trivialized the bullying by framing it in comedy, other episodes, particularly in the Tyler Perry shows, took a break from the comedy to portray bullying as a serious issue.

8

Glee's Bullies and Mean Girls

Glee is an in-depth look at the power structure within one of the lowest cliques in the social structure of schools, the glee club. This chapter analyzes portrayals of high school cliques and mistreatment of the out-group on the Emmy Award winning show *Glee*. The show includes mild, humorous bullying incidents such as glee club members being hit with slushies (i.e., a play on the 7-Eleven convenience store's Slurpee) in the school's hallways and nerds being tossed into school dumpsters. In contrast, Kurt's storyline illustrates the escalation of bullying of a gay student from being shoved into lockers to unwanted sexual advances and death threats.

The pilot episode establishes the school's social order. The glee club director Will Shuster comes to Sue Sylvester, the Cheerios cheerleading coach, to ask if he can recruit from the Cheerios for the glee club. Sue lectures him on the high school caste system: the jocks and the popular kids are up in the penthouse; the "invisibles" and those who play live action druids are on the bottom floor; the glee kids are sub-basement. When Will approaches the football coach in order to recruit members for the glee club, the coach tells Will that he doubts any players will join considering the players once shaved off a kid's eyebrows for watching an episode of the hospital drama *Grey's Anatomy*. When the team finds out that Finn, the quarterback, tried out for glee club, the players corner Finn and pelt him with paintballs.

The signature bullying move in *Glee* is the slushie in the face. The camera follows a hand holding a slushie as it moves down a school hallway. Peppy acapella music plays in the background as the hand with the cup heads toward the members of the glee club. Each member flinches and shrieks, thinking the slushie is meant for him or her. Eventually the target is selected and "slushied." As part of rejoining the football team after he is kicked out for participating in the glee club, Finn must slushie one of the glee club members. When Finn zeroes in on Kurt, the gay member of the club, Finn hesitates. He says he does not want to slushie anyone but has been threatened that if he does not, the guys on the team will kick "the crap" out of him. Kurt "takes one for the team," taking the slushie from Finn and dumping it on himself. Later, the glee members mistakenly think that winning sectionals will make them popular and immune to slushie attacks. They are wrong. They endure a barrage of slushies once again. The bullies even create a special green-colored slushie to celebrate the holiday season in "A Very Glee Christmas." At the end of the episode "Mash Up," the glee club slushies Mr. Shuester, who has never been slushied before. They all laugh and cheer. It is as if the social outcasts have taken back the slushie.

The comical scenes, while seeming to trivialize the severity of bullying, potentially offer an outlet for viewers who are uncomfortable with realistic portrayals of bullying and are watching *Glee* as an escape. Other viewers perhaps flashback to their own experiences of being low in the social pecking order in school and are relieved to see they are not alone. Media also provides a safe distance from the actual bullying. *Glee*, however, also treats over-exaggerations of bully as humorous. For example, Brittany, as student body president, wants dinosaurs as the prom theme. When the prom committee disagrees with her, she says, "When you insult my dinosaur prom theme, that's bullying and I will not accept it." She fires them all.

The following analysis of the portrayals of bullies and mean girls is organized by character. Quinn and Santana have typical cheerleader mean girl qualities. It is revealed early in the series that Quinn is pregnant. She names her quarterback boyfriend Finn as the father; however, Puck, the rebel, is actually the father. Santana is the fiery Latina cast member who is hyper-sexual and comes out later as a lesbian. While being bully victims themselves, Puck and Finn have done their fair share of bullying in the past. Finn is the clean-cut quarterback of the football team who struggles with his love of music. His character struggles the most with the social structure of the school. Puck is portrayed as the juvenile delinquent with a good heart. Puck's character evolves in the first three seasons from bully to loving father. The main bullies of the show are Sue Sylvester, the cheerleading coach, and David Karofsky, a football player who is confused about his own sexuality. Kurt, a mildly flamboyant gay character, is the primary victim of bullying. The glee club starts with five members: Rachel, Kurt, Mercedes, Arnie, and Tina, all social misfits in the school.

Characters

The producers of *Glee* appear to have taken great care to avoid portraying bullies and mean girls as one-dimensional characters. Almost all characters are both perpetrators and victims during some point of the series. The show reveals the back stories of the characters in an attempt to explain and perhaps soften the bad behavior.

QUINN

Quinn is the head cheerleader and president of the celibacy club. The celibacy club, instead of appearing to come from a place of deep religious faith, is rather a group that is condescending to other, less publicly chaste members of the student body. When Quinn's pregnancy is revealed, she is shunned and falls dramatically in the social hierarchy. When she names Finn as the father of her baby, he too loses his social status. The two are surrounded by the popular jocks, who drench them in slushies. Quinn initially joins the glee club, along with fellow Cheerios Santana and Brittany, to spy for Coach Sue. Sue is hell bent on destroying Will Shuester and the glee club. Quinn and Santana are incredibly disparaging and condescending to the glee club members, especially the other girls. Brittany goes along with the other two, who are battling to be the queen bee. When Rachel, one of the original members of the glee club, posts a video of herself singing on her My Space page, members of the Cheerios cheerleading squad post nasty comments such as, "If I were your parents, I would send you back," "I'm going to scratch out my eyes," and "Please get sterilized."

The third season opens with Quinn separating from the Cheerios and her friends Brittany and Santana. Quinn rebels against her good-girl cheerleader image, dyeing her hair pink and wearing leather and other tough girl attire. She quits glee club and joins the Skanks, who are a gang of tough girls, everything the Cheerios are not. The Skanks harass a girl in the bathroom, performing all the standard bully moves such as giving her a "swirly" (dunking her head in the toilet and flushing) and demanding her lunch money. One of the Skanks warns, "Don't test me. I was a foster kid, which means I'm used to stabbing people." When one of her victims accuses a Skank of being mean, she responds, "That's right. That's what passed for love in my house." The girl makes a run for it. Sue sees the girl run out of the bathroom but ignores the scene. A few episodes later, Quinn begins to realize that she is experiencing the pain of losing her quarterback boyfriend and getting kicked off the cheerleading squad, all the trimmings of the popular mean girl. By the end of the episode, Quinn rethinks her new image because it endangers her relationship with her daughter. After Quinn comes back to the glee club, she resigns herself to getting slushied every day. She is assured that the glee club is there to help clean her up.

SANTANA

Although Santana is very open about her sexual promiscuity, she looks down on Quinn for getting pregnant and takes the opportunity to take Quinn's spot as head cheerleader. After she pressures Finn to have sex for the first time, she uses the information to hurt Rachel, who is in love with Finn and expected them to lose their virginity together. Santana also has sex with Puck, the father of Quinn's baby, and Finn, Quinn's ex-boyfriend, partly out of competition with Quinn. Santana is both mean girl and bully. She is exclusionary and manipulative but also threatens physical harm to those who cross her. Her Latin roots are also used in the development of her fiery personality. Over time, Santana's character becomes more sympathetic. When Santana confesses her love for Brittany, it is the first time that Santana shows vulnerability. Later, Santana's grandmother rejects Santana when Santana tells her grandmother she is a lesbian. She stands up to Karofsky when he is bullying Kurt and blackmails him into apologizing to Kurt and forming an anti-bullying club.

PUCK

In the opening scene of the first episode, Mr. Shuster walks by as the football team is harassing Kurt in the parking lot. After Mr. Shuester passes without saying anything, Puck and a couple other boys in letter jackets pick up Kurt and prepare to toss him into the dumpster. Just when it looks like Finn might try to stop them, he only offers to hold Kurt's jacket. Kurt announces that one day they will all work for him. They rather gently put Kurt in the dumpster as he puts up no resistance. There are other comical scenes of the jocks bullying the nerds. The nerdy kids submissively stand in line, waiting to be tossed into the dumpster. They each walk up to Puck, voluntarily folding their arms over their chests as Puck picked them up to hurl into a dumpster. The dumpster appears to be a relatively clean place. The audience doesn't see the victims covered in disgusting trash.

As a reward for Finn quitting the glee club, Puck gets him a "present": Artie, who is in a wheelchair, trapped in a portable toilet called a "rent-a-loo." Puck announces they are going to flip it over and are saving the first roll for Finn. Finn stands up for Artie and gets him out of the portable toilet. Puck responds, "I can't believe you are helping out this loser." Finn replies, "We are all losers." While Artie seems distressed while stuck in the toilet, he recovers quickly after he is rescued. Puck eventually makes amends with Artie and the two become friends. When Puck later tries to recruit football players to the glee club, he is forced into a portable toilet, which his fellow football players overturn on its side, blocking the door. Puck is rescued 24 hours later.

In one story arc, Puck has his Mohawk shaved off. Because he has lost his hair and thus his power, mimicking the Samson story, the geeky kids in the school take the opportunity to exact revenge. They put Puck in the dumpster. In order to get his ranking back at the school, Puck begins dating Mercedes, one of the glee club members who has gotten cool since she joined the cheering squad. Since Puck's "cool meter is off the charts," geeks once again fear him. Puck exerts his dominance by taking the head geek Jacob's lunch money. Jacob is a rather unlikable character who gossips about and blackmails glee club members with threats of printing their dirty laundry in the school newspaper. Puck directs other jocks to put Jacob and the other geeks into the dumpster. The geeks line up passively and patiently wait their turn to once again get put into the dumpster.

Puck has a dream which he interprets as a message from God that he needs to be with a Jewish girl, so he goes out with Rachel. Rachel flinches as Puck approaches with a slushie. She closes her eyes, resigned that she is going to be hit with it; however, Puck hands her the slushie. He tells her it is grape, her favorite flavor. He knows this because, as he puts it, "The last time I hit you with a slushie it was grape and you licked your lips before you cleaned yourself off." Later, after Puck gets slushied by Karofsky for being in the glee club, he apologizes for ever hitting Rachel with slushies. Puck laments, "No one deserves this feeling. You know what the worst part is? It's not the burning in your eyes or when the slushie drips all the way into your underpants. It's the humiliation."

FINN

Even Finn, the golden boy of the show, has bullied in the past. Kurt reminds Finn that it was Finn and his friends who threw pee balloons at Kurt. Finn apologizes and says that is not who he is. After Karofsky hits Finn with a slushie, he explains that he has been wanting to get back at Finn since the fifth grade when Finn made fun of him for getting pubic hair. In the third season, Finn becomes impatient with Brittany, telling her that she needs to stop believing in Santa and leprechauns and to stop being an "idiot." Brittany calls him out and says that calling her an "idiot" is bullying.

Finn is also the target of bullying. Karofsky and Azimio rough up Finn in the locker room to warn him against getting his picture taken for glee club for the yearbook. They inform Finn that the system is in place to keep order. In another scene, Karofsky and Azimio rip Finn's letter jacket in half. Finn takes a swing at them but misses and hits the locker. Just as Karofsky and Azimio are about to attack Finn, Artie intervenes. Because of a "moral" code not to hit "crippled people," Karofsky and Azimio leave. In the third season, Finn comes to the aid of a new foreign exchange student from Ireland, Roy, who is harassed in the hallway by a group of jocks. One of the jocks knocks Roy's hat off and another tells Roy to go back to Mexico. They push Roy down, breaking his phone. The bullies have Roy pinned against the locker. Finn stands up for him and chases the jocks away with threats of telling Coach Beiste.

OTHER MEAN GIRLS AND BULLIES

Other attempts are made to incorporate mean girls into the cast, but none quite successfully. Rachel is normally the target of bullying. She is a diva who stands out from her peers and is often unlikeable because of her ego. In the episode "Auditions," Rachel becomes jealous of a new student, Sunshine, who threatens to take away Rachel's solos. Rachel pays Karofsky $100 to slushy Sunshine to dissuade her from trying out for the glee club. Instead of giving Sunshine accurate directions to the glee club auditions, Rachel sends Sunshine to a crack house. Lauren joins the glee club in the middle of season two. The Lauren character is a mix of "bad ass," bully, and mean girl. Although she is very large, she has significant confidence. She is a state champion wrestler. A new character Sugar joins the cast in the third season. She has self-diagnosed Aspergers so she claims she can say whatever she wants without any repercussions. Her father is wealthy so she has that spoiled girl "gets what she wants" attitude. When Mr. Shuester tells Sugar she did not make glee club, she calls him "a washed up Broadway wannabe." Later, Sugar's father pays the school to feature Sugar in an alternative high school musical.

While gay students are most likely the victims of bullying, Sebastian is the bully. He breaks the stereotype of a bully. Sebastian, in an attempt to steal Blaine away from Kurt, pulls a prank in which he throws a slushie spiked with rock salt at Kurt. The slushie misses Kurt and hits Blaine in the eye, scratching his cornea. Santana gets Sebastian's confession on tape. Sebastian blackmails Rachel, threatening to post fake pictures of Finn on the Internet if she competes in the show choir regionals competition. Later, Sebastian puts down Karofsky, contributing to Karofsky's depression and eventual suicide attempt.

SUE

The character Sue Sylvester was created from *Glee* producers Murphy, Brennan, and Falchuk's "inner mean girl" (Lynch cited in Itzkoff, 2000). Sue is a notorious bully. Her insults are comical but can be biting as well. She manipulates the system to gain control and power over others. At one point Sue drugs Principal Figgins, gets into bed with him, takes photos, and threatens to send them to his wife. After a run-in with the principal where he shuns her threats of blackmail, she leaves the office, throws a phone book, and pushes a student in the hallway. She bullies the female football coach, Coach Beiste. Sue is particularly abusive to glee club director Will Shuester. To stir up trouble, Sue tells Will's wife, Terri, about his flirtation with Emma, the guidance counselor. Sue trips the school nurse so the nurse falls down the stairs, thus opening up the position for Terri so Terri can spy on Will and Emma. Sue laments about a time when she sold a nice young couple a house and then salted the backyard so nothing could grow there for a hundred years because they tried to get Sue to pay their closing costs. She wins a coin toss with Will by cheating with a double-headed coin.

Sue does not limit her bullying to adults. She holds her cheerleaders hostage with constant threats of expulsion from the squad. She is shown pushing kids into lockers as she storms down the school hallways. When Principal Figgins tells Sue not to pit the students against one another, she vows to pit the students against one another. Sue plots to make the glee club a toxic environment. She divides the kids in glee club along racial lines, sexual preferences, and disabilities.

As the second season begins ("Auditions" episode), Principal Figgins has reallocated money from glee club and the Cheerios to the football program. While Mr. Shuester attempts to set an example for his club, he is not always an innocent bystander. He agrees to help Sue bully the new football coach, Shannon Beiste, into quitting, thus restoring funding to the Cheerios and glee club. Coach Beiste is an easy target as she is a female coaching the boys' football team and her physical appearance is very masculine. Sue tells Coach Beiste that a female football coach "a sin against nature." Sue plays on the fact that Coach Beiste was likely bullied in high school. Sue's treatment is intended to bring back to bad memories to humiliate and devastate Coach Beiste. Sue and Will order 25 pizzas in Beiste's name and have them delivered to the locker room. They fist bump to celebrate their plan. When Coach Beiste comes into the teachers' lounge for lunch, Sue and Will both shun her, not allowing her to sit with them. The bullying then gets out of control. Sue makes Coach Beiste cookies made from dog excrement. Sue then has Brittany accuse Beiste of sexually touching her. Will feels terrible for teaming up with Sue and asks Coach Beiste for forgiveness.

One of Sue's favorite targets of insults is Will's hair and his use of hair products. In "The Power of Madonna" episode, Sue tells Will that she lost her train of thought because of all the margarine in his hair. He stands up for himself and tells her "enough of the hair jokes." He then insults her and asks how the "Florence Henderson look" is working for her. She has a very pained look on her face. As he is walking away, he turns back and suggests she change the setting on her Flo-B. (The Flo-B was a late-night infomercial product that was hooked up to a vacuum cleaner and used to cut hair.) He punctuates the insult with an "Aw, snap!" As Sue heads back to her office, she pushes students into lockers and knocks books out other students' hands.

Sue does exhibit some redeeming qualities. In "A Very Glee Christmas" Sue plays the Grinch and tries to destroy the glee club's Christmas. After seeing the glee club still singing after she has vandalized their Christmas tree and stolen their gifts, she has a change of heart and returns the gifts to homeless children. When Sue is forced to hold tryouts for the Cheerios, Becky, a girl with Down's syndrome, tries out for the squad. There is a feeling of impending doom as Sue has been known to only accept perfection. She is also not known for her politically correct remarks. Before Mr. Shuester can dismiss Becky, Sue surprisingly congratulates Becky for making the squad. Sue explains to Mr. Shuester that much of her bitterness comes from having a "handicapable" sister. She explains that she herself has been bullied all her life because of her sister's Down's Syndrome. She tells Will she has dedicated her life to protecting her sister from a cruel world. Sue is often seen visiting her sister in an assisted living facility. She sweetly cuddles with her sister on the bed and reads to her, expressing her love of her sister both verbally and through physical affection. She treats her sister and Becky with compassion and viciously protects them from outside criticism. Will sees Sue being hard on Becky during practice. He tells her he is not going to let her bully Becky. Sue replies, "Oh, I bully everybody, Will. It's the way I roll." Sue explains that she is not going to treat Becky differently because her disability.

KAROFSKY

David Karofsky's character starts small, with brief scenes of him throwing slushies at the glee club members. Kurt and Tina, dressed in elaborate Lady Gaga costumes and makeup for a glee club number, are shoved into the lockers by Karofsky and Azimio. Kurt sticks up for himself and defends Tina. Karofsky accuses them of dressing funny and then "rubbing it everybody's faces." Azimio threatens them if they continue to dress like "circus freaks" he will use his fist. They call Kurt "homo" and "fancy." Later Finn appears in a long red plastic, Gaga-like dress to defend Kurt against an attack by Karofsky and Azimio. The rest of the glee club members join in to stand up to Karofsky and Azimio. Karofsky and Azimio back down, vowing to bring reinforcements the next time.

In "Never Been Kissed," Karofsky's harassment of Kurt accelerates. He bullies Kurt alone, without Azimio or the other football players. The subtle threats appear to be getting to Kurt. Mr. Shuester witnesses the aftermath of an altercation and brings Kurt into his office. Kurt is reluctant to talk about the incident. The next time Karofsky slams Kurt into a locker, Kurt loses his temper. He follows Karofsky into the locker room to confront him. Karofsky awkwardly kisses Kurt. At first Kurt is shocked but pushes Karofsky off when he tries to kiss him a second time. A distressed Kurt confides the details of the incident to Blaine, another out gay teen from a competing glee club. Blaine comes to the school to help Kurt talk to Karofsky about Karofsky's sexual confusion. The talk only makes Karofsky more defensive. Kurt confesses to Blaine that he had never been kissed before this incident and is devastating that this will always be his first kiss. Karofsky's homophobia turns out to be a sign of his self-loathing because of his own sexual orientation. The situation accelerates to the point where Karofsky threatens to kill Kurt if he tells anyone about the kiss.

Mr. Shuester once again witnesses the aftermath of the threat and takes up the issue with acting principal Sue. Sue reasons that bullying is just a part of high school, a "dry run" for the rest of the students' lives. Sue uses her experience of being bullied her entire life as a lesson that bullying has made her stronger. Kurt shares that it is particularly frightening because he does not know when it is coming. Kurt's reaction appears to change Sue's attitude. She shows empathy, encouraging Kurt to come to her if he is physically harmed and she will immediately expel Karofsky. She apologizes and explains that there is nothing she or the school board can do legally.

The girls in the glee club ask their boyfriends on the football team to stand up for Kurt. A brawl ensues in the locker room when Sam, Mike, and Artie tell Karofsky to stay away from Kurt. Later, Kurt's dad, Burt, witnesses Karofsky giving Kurt a limp wrist. After pressing the issue, Burt gets Kurt to admit that Karofsky has been bullying him and threatened to kill him. Burt goes after Karofsky and pins him against the wall. Karofsky and his father are called into the principal's office. Mr. Karofsky appears to be a gentle, thoughtful man, unlike the expected brute who would produce a bullying son. Mr. Karofsky says he has been concerned that his son has been talking back and his grades are falling. After Sue informs Karofsky that he has been expelled, Mr. Karofsky calmly thanks Sue for her time and leaves. The school board eventually overturns the expulsion. Sue steps down as acting principal out of protest and promises to be "an extra pair of eyes." Kurt's father pulls him out of school and enrolls him in a private school. Kurt states that the only way he will feel safe is in a school with a zero-tolerance bullying policy.

In "Born This Way," Santana catches Karofsky "checking out" Sam as he is bent over getting a drink from the water fountain. Santana blackmails Karofsky to pretend to date her in order for her to win prom queen. Karofsky apologizes to the glee club for throwing slushies on them. He confesses that he is a bully and promises to change. Santana tells the glee club that she is doing it to try to get Kurt to come back to McKinley High. The students form a new group called the "Bully Whips." Figgins deputizes Karofsky and Santana to roam the halls and stop bullying. They stop Azimio from taking a boy's pants. Karosky apologizes to Kurt. When Kurt doubts his sincerity, Karofsky confesses that Santana is blackmailing him. Kurt agrees to come back but insists that Karosky be educated and join a PFLG group (parents, family, and friends of lesbians and gays). Karofsky eventually switches schools.

After seeing Karofsky talk with Kurt on Valentine's Day, one of Karofsky's new teammates tells the rest of the jocks. Karofsky finds that someone has spray painted "fag" on his locker. As he tries to leave the locker room, one of his teammates pushes him into the lockers. There is an approximately three-minute montage of Karofsky looking upset as he sees that his social networking site has been tagged with homophobic remarks. The scene is overlaid with the song "Cough Syrup," sung by Blaine. Karofsky carefully gets out his suit and a belt and tries to hang himself. Mr. Karofsky comes home and catches his son in time. Sebastian feels bad because he ridiculed Karofsky one night at the gay bar. He made fun of Karofsky's weight and told him no gay guy would be attracted to him. Later Karofsky tells Kurt that his mother told him he had a disease. Kurt has Karofsky close his eyes and imagine a happier time in the future, a moment with a loving partner and a son laughing together. David finally smiles and sees hope.

Criticism and Comments

One theme that stands out is *Glee*'s inclusion of homophobia and gay bashing. Originally, creator Ryan Murphy had not planned on including a gay character until Chris Colfer, the actor who is eventually cast to play Kurt, auditioned for the part of Artie (Kuhn, 2009). Colfer, a gay teen, reportedly inspired Murphy and the other producers to include the character of Kurt. *Glee* is full of homophobic comments and jokes about gay stereotypes, as would be expected in a series about a show choir. In the huddle at football practice, some of the players question Finn's decision to join glee club. One player tells Finn, "We are taking heat because you like kissing dudes all of a sudden." Puck calls glee club "homo-explosion," just before joining glee club himself. At one point Kurt tells Sue that her nickname for him, "Lady," is bullying and hurtful. She apologizes and offers him a choice of one of three new nicknames, Gelfling, Porcelain, or "Tickle me Doe Face." He nonchalantly chooses Porcelain, as though any of the choices is not homophobic.

Shrank (2011) argued that *Glee* portrays bullies and bully victims as lacking self-acceptance. Two of the characters who bully, Karafsky and Santana, are both struggling with their own sexuality. When they finally come out, they are portrayed as nicer and more sympathetic characters. Shrank (2011) claims that the strength of *Glee* is that the bullied characters go on to teach the lesson that gay and lesbian students should accept themselves for who they are.

While receiving high praise from many LGBT groups about raising the issues of homosexuality and bullying, the show has drawn its share of critics about how they handled the issue. Peitzman (2010) accused *Glee* of hypocrisy because producers tell their audiences to be tolerant while the show lacks tolerance by portraying Kurt as flamboyant and feminine, often "played out for laughs." Peitzman described Kurt's characters as "another dull, simplistic cliché." Peitzman (2010) criticized the show's mix of farce and seriousness as well. He contrasted the show's making fun of Coach Bieste (i.e., the stereotype of a lesbian gym teacher) while at the same time telling the audience that laughing at her makes them bullies. Twaddle (2012) pointed out discrepancies between the way *Glee* treats gay and lesbian character. She claimed that the show represents "gay as negative" and "lesbian as positive," mirroring the male fantasy of "girl-on-girl action." Twaddle (2012) supported her claim by pointing out that Kurt is bullied and receives death threats when he comes out. Santana, on the other hand, is not only supported and encouraged by her friends but receives positive attention from male students with fantasies of threesomes with Santana and her girlfriend Brittany.

The FOX Network's *Glee* discussion board was filled with both positive and negative reviews of the series. Some viewers, whom I will refer to by their screen names, were mixed about the attention to homophobia and bullying. Waypylant accused FOX of celebrating bullying rather than condemning it. Jan6158 was aggravated with the way Puck's bullying is treated. Separate from the storyline, Keith was excited to see Karofsky as a representation of a gay male that did not fit the "thin, fashionable, feminine gay male model" stereotype. He hopes the *Glee* writers will make Karofsky more loveable. What was perhaps most interesting about the gay bullying storyline of "Never Been Kissed" was the reactions from viewers. Max Adler, the actor who plays Karofsky, commented, "I've gotten so many messages from people all around the world these last couple of days thanking me because either they are Karofsky, they were Karofsky or they know a Karofsky" (cited in Berk, 2010). Discussion board posts after the airing of the episode were mixed, positive and negative. Charm0722 thought the portrayal should have included police involvement. Mary thought that Karofsky needed mental counseling. She also questioned whether or not male-on-male bullying was treated differently than if it would have been a girl who was sexually assaulted. Megan was quite outspoken, posting several comments. She was frustrated with the ending of the episode in which Blaine texts Kurt, "Courage" and presumably makes things all better. She accuses FOX of being cowardly and not addressing the issue further.

Comments which were "pro" Karofsky were interesting as well. One viewer posted that he relates to Karofsky's confusion about his sexuality. He wrote that he understands why Karofsky is so angry. Adam felt pity for Karofsky rather than anger after he found out that Karofsky was secretly gay himself. Note that most of these postings add that they in no way excuse the bullying behavior. Jon begins his post, "Poor Dave and Kurt!" Although he thinks it is a "crummy" situation, he hopes the two become an item later in the series. DW, Mike, Maya, and Jo all agree that they would like to see Kurt and Karofsky as a couple. While Fitzgerald thinks that Karofsky's character is more understandable after the kissing incident, he rejects Karofsky and Kurt as a couple. He would like to see Kurt with someone who is "out and proud." Amanda was critical of Kurt and Blaine confronting Karofsky in the stairwell at school. She would like to see Kurt and Karofsky meet one-on-one to discuss the issue in private.

In 2010, *Glee* joined the American Express "Members Project," an effort to raise awareness about protecting the environment and giving to charities. In a PSA, Sue sarcastically puts down efforts to make the world a better place. She asks, "Why should children be burdened by the tyranny of reading?" She proclaims that artists do not need funding, they need soap. At the end of the PSA, Sue bumps a girl off a bench so she can sit. The tag line reads, "Don't be a Sue. Do something good instead." In another PSA, Puck is about to give Kurt a swirlie (i.e., sticking his head in the toilet and flushing). Kurt stops him and negotiates moving down the hall to use a low-flush toilet instead because it is better for the environment. Puck is concerned with how much time it will take since he is scheduled to throw Artie's wheelchair off the roof in five minutes. Critics argue that the PSA is trivializing the seriousness of bullying, which they find especially offensive since the PSA is for a charitable organization.

One additional note of interest is the age of the actors playing these high school students. The October 2010 issue of *GQ Magazine* caused a controversy when three of the *Glee* cast members appeared on the cover. Twenty-four-year-old Leah Michele (Rachel) and Diana Agron (Quinn) cling to 28-year-old Cory Monteith (Finn) in a provocative pose. Mark Salling, who plays Puck, was 27 in the first full season of *Glee* in 2009. The advanced maturity of the actors may be confusing for young viewers who wonder why they are not that poised and attractive. These adults are playing high school sophomores while audience member are still going through puberty at 15.

Conclusion

The television show *Glee* was singled out for analysis because of its focus on high school social structure and inclusion of gay and lesbian characters. The hour-long serial format allows development of characters and storylines. The show has received both praise and criticism for its handling of bullying and mean girls. The lighthearted comedy is interspersed with heartfelt moments. The show juxtaposes slushies in the face with a suicide attempt. *Glee* also includes "loveable" bullies such as Sue and Puck, which some critics see as confusing and counter-productive to the anti-bullying movement. Supporters, on the other hand, argue that *Glee* is one of the few shows even addressing the issues of bullying.

9

Documentaries and Talk Shows

The films and television programs included in this chapter are nonfiction programs that follow either a documentary or talk-show format. The documentaries and news-style television programs mainly focus on collections of stories, almost exclusively from the perspective of the bullied or mean-girl victim. Programs also include reports on the work of anti-bullying campaigns in schools and communities. The talk-show format in known for delving into social issues; therefore, it is no surprise that bullying and mean-girl behaviors have been a topic of many conversations.

Documentaries

Film and television programs offer a range of informative and exploitative material in a documentary, storytelling format. While some critics argue documentaries have the capacity to exploit the pain and suffering of others in order to entertain, the focus of the majority of the following examples appears to be to educate and promote anti-bullying campaigns in schools and communities.

FILM

The film *Bully* (2011) is a feature-length documentary following the story of five bully victims, two of whom committed suicide. The story of 12-year-old Alex showed actual film footage of the callousness of the bullies on the bus. Even knowing they were being recorded, they hit and cursed at Alex. The students clearly did not understand the severity of their bullying probably because it had gone on so long unchecked. One of the major problems appears to be a lack of understanding what bullying is. Alex was hesitant to call what the boys were doing to him "bullying." He admitted to being so desperate to have friends that he was willing to put up with abuse. Ja'Maya was the one victim who brought a weapon to school to try to scare the bullies and make them stop. She was also very slight in stature and the only minority in the film. A voiceover explains that the charges against her for carrying a gun had been dropped and she was being held in a psych facility waiting to be cleared by her doctors to return home. In the story of the two suicide victims, the sorrow is not only for the bully victims but for the families and friends left behind. Tyler's father, Ty's parents, and Ty's best friend brought the movie theater audience to tears. The innocence of Ty's 11-year-old best friend in describing how he used to be a bully in the second grade but realized he was hurting kids and stopped was striking. The friend explained that he stood up to the bullies who were picking on Ty, but Ty told him not to bother.

Kelby's story was painful not so much because of the bullying from her peers but because of the teachers who humiliated and adults in the community who shunned her and her family. The crowd reaction in the theater was strongest against the school administrators. When a boy was being bullied by another boy, the assistant principal made both boys apologize and shake hands "like adults." She mistakenly treated the incident as a "conflict" rather than a case of bullying. The victim tried to explain to her that the bully physically hit and threatened him. She tells the victim that by not shaking the hand of his tormentor that he is just as bad as the bully. When Alex was getting bullied on the bus, the camera showed the bus driver glancing in her rearview mirror but not acting or saying a word. When one of the boys was brought into the assistant principal's office to discuss the bus incident, he had a coy smile on his face rather than fear of consequences. When Alex's parents met with a school official, she tried telling them that those kids on the bus were "as good as gold." The white police officer discussed his push to charge Ja'-Maya with dozens of felony counts for bringing a gun onto a school bus for protection against her bullies.

Lee Hirsch, director and cinematographer of *Bully*, created a quiet narrative, which was in contrast to what is thought of as the raucousness of bullying. Even the rallies at the end of the film were rather subdued. Hirsch chose to include small gatherings at small venues. The music selections in the background gave it a solemn feel. The choice of location and families added to the sentimentality of the film. Stories from the "heartland" lacked the gritty urban feel of gang violence. The communities, especially in Kelby's case, were heavily religious and therefore the film seemed more poignant when they turned their backs on Kelby's family. Ty's father had a remarkable line in the film, "We are nobody."

Other documentaries include *Bullied* (2010), which featured the story of Jamie Nabozny, a teenage boy who helped bring a federal case to ensure gay and lesbian student have a constitutional right to be free of bullying and harassment. *Rats & Bullies* (2004) detailed the court proceedings of three girls who bullied and threatened 14-year-old Dawn-Marie Wesley, who then hanged herself. *Finding Kind* (2011) was written and produced by Molly Thompson and Lauren Parsekian, who had been victims of mean girls in middle school. Parsekian and Thompson traveled cross-country interviewing a variety of experts, victims, and parents about vicious behavior between girls. In addition to the documentary, they started an anti-mean movement called the Kind Campaign. They travel to schools where they screen the film and following up with discussions.

TELEVISION

Television productions of documentaries vary in focus, ranging from educational (e.g., PBS *Frontline*) to sensationalistic (e.g., Investigation Discovery). Producers include the major broadcast networks CBS, NBC, and ABC, the educational network PBS as well as entertainment-driven cable networks such as E! and MTV.

Not in Our Town: Class Actions is a PBS production that highlights stories about communities standing together to stop hate. Students in a California school district came together to address bullying, adopting the slogan "Not in Our School." In the segment, the high school students talked to both elementary school kids and their teachers about what could be done to create safer schools, such as vowing to not be silent bystanders. Surveys show that a significant number of kids felt safer at school after the program. The PBS series *Frontline* featured an episode entitled "Growing Up Online." Although not primarily focused on cyberbullying, it did relate how the Internet contributed to the suicide of a victim of cyberbullying. The special also featured the story of Ryan Halligan. Several comments on Ryan's social networking site accused Ryan of being gay. A popular girl flirted with him on IM and then humiliated him when she told him it was a joke. The special's narrator referred to the computer as "a new weapon in the arsenal of adolescents." The episode also featured information about schools that are instituting programs that teach "good cyber citizenship" and instruct students what to do if they are being cyberbullied.

In a segment of *Discovery Health: Mean Girls*, mean girl expert and author of *Odd Girl Out* Rachel Simmons discussed how problems arise between girls. She argued that relational aggression happens because girls are not socialized to resolve conflict in direct ways. She talked about the lack of a middle ground for girls, either they are "nice" and passive or "bitches" because they confront the situation. The special included footage of a focus group conducted by Simmons. The girls in the group discussed backstabbing by friends or being dropped by friends for unknown reasons. Some girls expressed that they want to address the issues directly, while others want to avoid conflict at all costs. The girls talked about how easily gossip starts. Another girl interviewed expressed how annoying it is when adults try to give advice because she feels they do not understand. Simmons added the overall goal of her work is to make the world of girls less secretive and more accepting.

The 48 Hours Special: Words Can Kill featured a school in Providence, Rhode Island, that had experienced a dramatic increase in reported bullying cases. The special traced the story of several students. One of the cases highlighted in the special was the story of Johnny. After being bullied in three different schools and called horrible names such as "fag," Johnny began cutting himself. While it looked as though Johnny was making progress with the school's new anti-bulling policies, he took an overdose of cold medicine. Another story featured Jessie, who was so desperate to fit in, she let the girls be mean to her. She sent a naked picture of herself to a boy. Three girls took the photo from her phone and spread it to other students. She started getting harassing text messages. Because the police told her filing charges was not possible since she was 18, Jessie went on a local news program to tell her story. The bullying just got worse. She reported that kids were spitting on her. Jessie eventually committed suicide by hanging herself in her closet. Another mother told the story of her daughter Dara, who was bullied starting at age 6. By the fourth grade, Dara's classmates were telling her they wished she was dead. The Catholic school Dara attended did little to intervene. When Dara switched schools, girls from her old school posted lies about her on Facebook, which her new friends read. The principal of the school talked to the girls but did not discipline them. The mother filed a lawsuit against the school and 11 girls. The special also highlighted steps Dara's new school was taking to solve the problem. For example, the guidance counselor had the bullied students turn their experiences into a play. The kids made boxes for anonymous reporting. Birchwood's efforts seem to be somewhat effective in curbing incidents of bullying.

The *E! Bullying Special* included interviews with bullying witnesses, family members, school administrators, law officials, and bullying experts such as Cheryl Dellasega. The special reported on incidents of bullying, including stories of those who committed suicide because of bullying such as Phoebe Prince and Jared High. The special also featured an incident in one middle school where a student instigated a "Kick a Ginger Day," inspired by an episode of the television show *South Park* where the kids pick on kids with red hair. The incident attracted significant media coverage and three students were arrested. Another story highlighted the bullying of Dylan Theno and the inaction of the administration at his junior high school. When a student called him a "fag," Dylan finally fought back. The school attempted to implement a ban on slurs but the kids in Dylan's class just laughed. In true E! fashion, however, producers also include blurry reenactments and eerie background music.

One method that the networks employ is to set up hidden cameras to assess the reaction of bystanders to bullying. The footage has both informative and entertaining qualities. Viewers can watch scenarios from a safe distance and image how they would react if put in the same position. Viewers may feel a range of emotions from superiority to empathy for the bystanders who fail to act. On the episode *Dateline NBC: My Kid Would Never Bully*, the producers used hidden cameras to find out what kids would do if they witness a bullying situation. Rosalind Wiseman offered her professional opinion during the segment. In the first segment, two actresses bully another female actress as the parents watch the reaction of their daughters on a monitor. The mean girls have the victim put on an unattractive jacket and take a picture of her to post on the Internet. When one girl speaks up, the others join in one by one as the mother cheers them. When the victim is overweight in the next scenario, the bystanders quickly stand up for her. However, when the mean girls target the victim's weight, one of the bystanders laughs along with the mean girls. In the next group, one of the bystanders takes the victim aside and gives her support. Finally one of the girls, Lilly, directly confronts the bullies. Lilly immediately reports the behavior to the producer when the producer enters the room. As a side story, one girl named Veronica is shown getting upset after witnessing the mean behavior of another girl, having experienced mean girls and bullying herself. In a follow-up interview, Veronica reports that she now stands up to her bullies at school.

The same episode of *Dateline* also included a segment with a group of boys and a bully. The actor playing a bully shoves another actor and tells him to "stop acting like a girl." The bystanders look uncomfortable as the bullying continues. Once one boy expresses support for the victim, some of the others do the same. When the bullying behavior is repeated with an adult in the room, the bystanders appear to side with the bullies and the coach. In another scenario, the bystanders use humor to try to diffuse the situation. One of the boys steps in between the bully and the victim when the bully becomes physical. When the producer enters the room, the boys fail to report the bad behavior. One thing to note is that the kids who participated appear to have very supportive parents. Parents who would allow their sons and daughters to participate are likely more confident in their kids' reactions.

The ABC News series *What Would You Do?* also used hidden cameras to expose adult bystanders' actions and reactions in various situations. In "Mean Teen Girls," a group of young actors pick on another girl in a park. What is interesting is that almost all of the males who walked by did nothing to help. It was the female bystanders who stopped and stood up to the mean girls. Some of the women passing by scolded the mean girls and mimicked the way the mean girls were treating the victim, even getting into a verbal sparring match with the mean girls. Some of women choose to comfort the victim instead.

One of the men who walked by the incident explained that because the girls were not getting violent, he did not intervene. Bullying expert Roseland Wiseman commented that bystanders should not have to wait for the confrontation to get physical to do something about it. One woman walked by but came back to help when she saw that another woman was intervening. Wiseman assessed the actions of the women who mimicked the actions and vocal tones of the mean girls. She proposed that the mean behavior brought back memories of the women's youth and perhaps their own experiences as the target of mean girls. In another episode of *What Would You Do* entitled "'Mean Girls' Bully Teen," hidden cameras were placed in a cafe. Three girls sit at a table plotting how they are going to cyberbully another girl. When no one intervenes, the girls push the issue and ask adults to take part in saying negative things such as telling the girl they are targeting that she is "ugly." One male participates, later telling the interviewer he thought the girls were just teasing another friend. One female bystander becomes visibly upset and keeps giving the girls dirty looks as they discuss how they are going to target a girl in their class. The woman, like many other bystanders, finally scolds them when the mean girls ask her to participate.

MTV has produced a number of programs addressing bullying from documentaries to panel discussions to the younger side of its 12- to 34-year-old target audience. The documentaries range from teens who admit to being bullies and mean girls to a victim of bullying in a detention facility to kids discussing bullying at a fat camp.

If You Really Knew Me is an MTV documentary series that looked inside of high schools across the United States. In the episode "Anthony Wayne High School," students joke that the motto of their school is, "If you have something bad to say about someone, say it." The school counselor reports that there is a great deal of bullying in the school. One of the students highlighted is Abby, a self-proclaimed mean girl. She admits when she and her friends do not like someone, they do not tell them directly but instead put it on Facebook. Aaron is a self-proclaimed bully. He explains how he picks on other kids now because he was picked on himself. Aaron confesses that the "tough guy thing" is just an act. Many of the mean girls and bullies interviewed admit they are not comfortable in their own skin. Abby confesses that she never shows her true emotions to others at school. In order to address the bullying situation, school administrators invited a program called Challenge Day to the school. In one group session, the kids were asked to finish the statement, "If you really knew me..." In the session, Emily admits she can be mean sometimes. Her best friend is not speaking to currently after they had a fight. Emily vows things are going to change. Most of the kids are in tears and hug at the end of the session. In another session, students are asked to step forward and cross a line if they have ever been teased or humiliated. A majority of the students do. The moderator asks if the other students who crossed that line did so because of them. Aaron apologizes to a girl for teasing her about her weight. Emily apologizes to her friend, Karlee. Kyle vows to be nicer to the freshmen. The next day some of the sophomores are speaking at a freshmen assembly. Although the short-term effect of Challenge Day looks promising, there is no report of any lasting effect on bullying and mean behavior in the school.

The MTV series *Juvie* followed first-time offenders in a juvenile center in Indiana. LaRico is the new kid in school who is sent to a juvenile detention center for retaliating against a bully. In the center, LaRico fights back when a larger boy pushes him out of his seat. LaRico explains that since he was the smallest kid at the center, he had to do something to exert his dominance otherwise all the boys would make him do "stuff." LaRico was in a new school because all his family's belongings were lost in Katrina and the family was now living with his grandmother in Indiana. No mention was made of LaRico being black in a sea of white faces.

Too Fat for 15: Fighting Back is an MTV documentary series about Wellspring Academy, a camp for overweight and obese teens. In the episode entitled "Sticks and Stones," the kids admit to turning to food after getting bullied for being fat. They talk about the emotional scars left by bullies. They appear more confident and outgoing since they began the camp. Bullying expert Barbara Coloroso speaks to the teens. She has the kids define "bullying" and share their experiences. One boy finally tells his bullying story after years of keeping it to himself. The staff shares their experiences of being bullied as well. The kids were visibly affected by the staff's stories. Coloroso advises the teens not to be passive or aggressive but assertive. The camp also brings in a martial arts expert to teach some basic self-defense and thus, self-confidence.

Some of the documentaries have a storytelling feel about them. For example, the special, *Saved: Temple Grandin* recounts Grandin's life with autism. The special highlighted the cruelty and bullying the other children inflicted on Grandin when she was a child. In retaliation for being called "retarded," Grandin threw a book at a mean girl's head. Grandin was expelled and was sent to a boarding school where the bullying continued. She overcame great odds to earn her Ph.D. and become a well-known writer and speaker. *This American Life*, a successful public radio show, had a short-lived television version. In the episode "No Respect," kids who had been bullied took their experiences and made them into a standup comedy routine in a segment entitled "Thanks, Folks, I'm Here All Eighth Grade." The boys were involved in a two-week-long exercise called "Camp Kids and Comedy." One of the boys tells how he was bullied because others saw him as weak. Another boy confessed he cried every day of fifth grade because he was bullied. Yet another boy talked about how his bully was popular, which made it even worse. That year is when the boy got into comedy.

Much like their fictitious counterparts, the following crime shows often feature extreme results of bullying, such as murder, rather than addressing the bullying itself. The caught-on-camera shows exploit bullying for entertainment rather than education. Producers use special effects to make the crime scenes more dramatic, stage reenactments of events with actors, and overlay dramatic music and an eerie voiceover. *Investigation Discovery*'s "Very Bad Men" recounts a 14-year-old student, Michael Carneal, who opened fire at his school, killing three and injuring five. The show speculated he acted out because he was bullied. The episode aired interviews with some of the witnesses to the shooting and one female victim who is paralyzed after being shot. The witnesses interviewed report that Carneal shot at kids who were nice to him rather than the kids who bullied him.

The episode "The Bully" on the series *Solved*, which also aired on the Investigation Discovery Network, began with the finding of human remains in a sewer. The victim, identified as Tristan Jensen, is a 14-year-old boy who was reported missing. Investigators call the crime one of the most gruesome murders they have ever seen. One of Tristan's classmates is suspected as the killer because he was a loner who had bullied Tristan in school. Police later find evidence to prove that the boy did indeed kill Tristan. These shows appear to be capitalizing on the popularity of the bullying topic rather than providing any insight into or solutions to the problem. They are using bullying footage to titillate the audience rather than educate. Others are produced in more of an informative or educational fashion. There is little quality content other than exploiting a situation for entertainment.

Talk Shows

Bullying is very popular a topic on self-help programs and daytime talk shows. The most prominent coverage of bullying is featured on *The Dr. Phil Show*, which has aired over a dozen episodes on the topic. McGraw is one of the few hosts who interviews the bullies and their parents and has them speak for themselves. When focusing solely on the victim, the shows could subtly imply that bullying is the victim's fault or at least the victim's responsibility to handle. Other "help" shows such as *Dr. Drew's Lifechangers* and the *Dr. Oz* show have also addressed bullying. This section includes both interview shows and panel discussions.

The Dr. Phil Show bullying episodes range from nuisance incidents to high-profile suicides. The host Phil McGraw often discusses the issues with the parents of victims and bullies. On the episode "Anti-Bully Movement," a mother describes how her daughter is receiving messages from cyberbullies such as, "If I was you, I'd kill myself" and "If you are in my class next week, watch out." "Behind the Headlines" featured the father who confronted the bullies on his daughter's bus when the school and the bus driver would not make it stop. His 12-year-old daughter has cerebral palsy. The bullies on the bus would not let her sit down and threw condoms on the bus. The girl came on the show and described how the bullies hit her in the back of her head and yanked her hair. "Bullies Beware" featured the mother of a bully. She describes how her 13-year-old son used to be bullied from the first grade to the sixth grade and but now he is the bully. He put a cigarette out on the back of another student's neck. He also called his teacher a "dirty bitch." The school calls the mother a bully as well. McGraw points out her rude behavior toward his staff. She reportedly told the staff member, "If you don't shut the f* up, I will have your ass." On the episode "Bullying: The Power to Protect Your Child," which is subtitled "Are Adults to Blame for Teen Bullying?" a father admits that his 13-year-old daughter, Sam, is a bully. McGraw explains how the girl even got into an altercation with a woman at her church. When McGraw asks Sam why she bullies, she tells him she was bullied and bullying made her to feel powerful. Sam admits she fears being perceived as a "wimp." McGraw addresses the father's specific role since he has not held his daughter accountable. McGraw offers Sam a chance to go to a wilderness camp for counseling.

Besides the numerous shows that include physical bullying, there are a number of *Dr. Phil Show* episodes addressing relational aggression of girls. "Mini Mean Girls" featured 9-year-old Kayla who punches and steals other kids' lunch money. She uses quite sophisticated mean-girl tactics such as threatening to turn the other girls against her target if the target does not comply. She tells McGraw that she thinks it is "cool" to be mean because the popular kids do it. Kayla is very thoughtful and deliberate about why she bullies. She is very upfront that she is in the wrong crowd. Kayla is being bullied at home by her older sister, Haley. Haley calls Kayla "fat" and "lazy." Later in the episode, six 5th grade girls come on the show to talk calmly about how three of them sometimes feel excluded by the other three. The popular girls appear unaware that they are using passive-aggressive techniques. A self-described adult bully is interviewed in the episode "Taming the Terrorizer." TemicaRoshawn is on caught on tape talking about how she hates the handicapped and how they get special parking. She snaps her fingers at the server, whom she calls "Asian Lady." She tells overweight people to "put down the donut." She justifies her behavior because she is bullying an adult and not a child. McGraw scolds the woman, telling her she should know better and to "grow up." Other episodes addressing adult bullying include "Adult Bullies" (2003), "Bully Husbands" (2008), "Bully Dads" (2007), and "Bully Moms" (2010). The bully dads and moms appear more physically abusive than bullies, however.

On *Dr. Drew's Lifechangers,* Dr. Drew Pinksy gives advice to people in need. In "Bi-Ra," Pinksy hosted a set of bi-racial twins. One of the twins, who has much lighter skin and is able to pass for white, got bullied growing up. His twin, who has much darker skin and is gay, did not. The twins are on the show to help a 9-year-old boy who is currently getting bullied see that life gets better. The boy is particularly bullied because his physical appearance. The boy describes how kids flick his ears because they stick out. At the end of the show, producers offer the boy free plastic surgery to have his ears pinned back because his mother cannot afford the $10,000 surgery. In a similar episode of *Anderson Cooper 360,* Anderson Cooper featured 12-year-old Savannah Robinson, who, after being bullied, created an anti-bullying PSA for YouTube that has received over 250,000 views. Cooper also invites a younger girl who is being bullied on stage. Savannah gives the younger girl advice on how to handle the bullying. The producers of the show give the two girls tickets to go see *Wicked* on Broadway. The producers of *Wicked* have teamed up with anti-bullying groups to help combat the problem.

The "Tyra Banks and Body Bullies" episode of *The Dr. Oz Show* was promoted as "Tyra Banks takes on bullies." Tyra tells her story about being bullied when she was young. She confronts a man in the studio audience about "bullying" his wife about her weight. Tyra also brings an overweight girl on stage whose mother is "bullying" her about her eating habits and lack of exercise. It is not clear from the interviews whether or not the husband or the mother were being bullies or simply being insensitive and inappropriate. Dr. Oz and Tyra talk to a couple of thin girls in the audience about getting teased. The show, however, gives little insight into the problem of bullying and offers little advice on solving the problem.

In 2009, Oprah Winfrey announced that she was beginning a "national conversation" on bullying. In an episode of *Oprah* entitled "The Truth about Bullies," Winfrey hosted the family of bully victim Carl Walker's family, who was featured in an episode of *Extreme Makeover: Home Edition.* Bullying expert Dorothy Espelage joins the discussion. She addresses the homophobic remarks made to Carl by the bullies and how bullying is often a climate problem within schools. Winfrey also interviewed Ryan Halligan's parents. Ryan was featured in the documentary *Bullies* (2011). Another bullying expert, Susan Lipkins, counseled bully victim Chase, giving him advice on how to stand up for himself. On *Oprah's Next Chapter,* Winfrey interviewed Paris Jackson, 14-year-old daughter of Michael Jackson, about being bullied at her private school. Olympic gold medal gymnast Gabby Douglas also reported being bullied or at least felt isolated from the group on *Oprah's Next Chapter.* Winfrey offers advice and resource materials on her website. One example is "Meanies: How to Deal with Kids Who Bully Other Kids" (2009). Winfrey is also a major supporter for Lady Gaga's "Born This Way" campaign. Ellen DeGeneres's show *Ellen* plays a duel role in that it is also an entertainment show and a vehicle for social change. DeGeneres has done shows on bullying, which include both celebrity and non-celebrity victims. She has featured celebrities such as Justin Timberlake, Taylor Swift, and Selena

Gomez on her show talking about their experiences with bullies and mean girls. DeGeneres also includes anti-bullying material on her website.

Talk shows can also exploit bullying for entertainment. The *Steve Wilkos* show is more of a Jerry Springer type show. In fact, he was the director of security for Springer. A former Marine and police officer, he bullies the bullies. Steve Wilkos' "Bullied Out of School" hosted a 16-year-old girl, Tichina, whose best friend, Aabrea, posted a video of her on YouTube calling her a "ho." Aabrea heard rumors that Tichina was talking "trash" about her. Aabrea jumped Tichina in a playground. The girls are African American. Aabrea agrees with Wilkos that the only way she has of resolving differences is through violence. Aabrea's 26-year-old sister comes out and defends her sister and the video because "it's true." She sees it as her sister defending herself. When Tichina and her mother, Jennifer, join them on stage, it becomes a shouting match. Security has to hold Jennifer back from attacking Aebrea. Jennifer trashes the girls' mother. In the end, Aebrea apologizes for beating her up and Aebrea's sister agrees to take down the video. A case on the court show *Judge Judy* was quite similar to *The Steve Wilkos* episode. The plaintiff Jessica tells the judge that Angelica was spreading rumors and saying Jessica was not a good friend. Jessica admitted to calling Angelica "ugly." Jessica tells the judge that she had previously gotten suspended for fighting with another girl over some "drama." Judge Judy went on to scold the father of the bully because three out of four of his children have been involved in criminal cases. All parties in this case were black.

A onetime event, the *AC360 Special Report* "Bullying: It Stops Here," focused on a study by Diane Felmlee and Robert Faris that revealed that bullying is about climbing the social ladder. The researchers found that the higher the students climb in social standing, the more aggressive and victimized the students became. Faris, who appeared on the panel, explains how social-status bullying, or social combat, is more common than chronic bullying. The panel also featured Lee Hirsch, director of the documentary Bully; Dr. Phil McGraw; and Rosaline Wiseman, author of *Queen Bees and Wannabes*. The special also included input from a parental angle from celebrities Kelly Ripa and Jane Lynch, who added very little if anything to the discussion.

There are some lesser-known talk shows that focus on the religious aspect of addressing and preventing bullying. *Kraze* is talk show sponsored by My Christian Films. In the episode "Bullying," the host interviewed the McBride family, whose children describe an experience of getting bullied at a park. The mother tells another story about how the kids were bullied on the school bus. The principal's solution was to make the victims, not the bullies, sit in the front of the bus. The content around the interview was full of Bible verses and songs; however, there was no discussion of God or religion during the McBride family interview. On the other hand, in *Lifestyle Magazine*'s "Bullying," the mother of a bully victim discusses how when the school did not help, the church members got together and assisted the bully victim in enrolling in a new school. The mother attributes the Heavenly Father with putting in a good principal at the new school. *Lifestyle Magazine* is part of Faith for Today Television and focuses on health, family and socially challenging issues.

The panel style of talk show appeared to be an effective format in understanding the victims' experience. The telling of stories live seems more real than prerecorded footage that may have been rehearsed and edited. The live audiences also create raw emotions as the panelists are able to see the faces of other victims as they recount their tormentors.

A panel of young gay and lesbian adults recall being bullied in school in an episode of *MTV News Impact*, "Bullied to Death." The special was part of the Canadian MTV series *1 girl and 5 gays*. The makeup of the panel was similar to that of the *It Gets Better project*. These young adults were able to share their stories of survival and are examples of thriving gay and lesbian individuals. In the special, Jill shares her experience being outed in a small town. David describes how he was threatened with a knife by three boys in school. He explains how he was unwilling to tell the teacher about the incident because he was ashamed that he had let it happen. After the event, David explains that he would look to see if there was a teacher or other adult in the hallway before going out in case the bullies were waiting for him. Shameal recounts how he was jumped by a boy who was supposed to be suspended from school. The bully threatened Shameal with a knife. Shameal confides that he started to think maybe the bullies were right, that he should be dead. When Jonathan got his school project back, someone had marked it with the word "fag." Jonathan reports that he suffered severe anxiety and hid his feelings from his friends. He tells the audience that he understands how paralyzing it is for victims to speak up. One member of the audience asks if there are so many resources for gay and lesbian students, why things are not changing. Jonathan points out that the student would have to come out to be eligible for the resources. A former bully in the audience confesses that she was not educated about or exposed to homosexuals at the time. She and her bully victim are sitting next to each other in the audience and report being friendly now. The panel discusses mixed reaction about creating a segregated classroom for gay students.

The "High School Confidential" episode of the MTV series *1 girl and 5 gays* featured current high school students discussing their daily experiences. The purpose of the show is to provide a safe place to discuss who these boys are and what their lifestyle choices are. Although not the main topic of discussion in this episode, bullying came up several times in the answers given by the panelists. The question, "Describe your best and worst day in high school," elicited the most bullying responses. One boy describes how he fell apart when he was called a "fag" three times in one morning. Another boy expresses his disbelief that some of the freshmen at his school were calling him a "fag." He states that he was confused about why the freshmen would be so inappropriate at a new school, especially an art school. He describes his best day as standing up to those students who called him a "fag." Another boy recounts how he was called names and "faggot" outside of school. The bullies tried punching him but he ran away. He describes his best day was turning that experience into an impact project at school. One of the more muscular boys on the panel shares how got into a fight with a group of bullies who had been calling him "fag." He explains that he did not really care about himself because he is a confident person, but he says it gets frustrating because the kids who have not come out hear these words. He identifies his best day as applying to college to get away from such behavior. Per the question, "I'm not going to miss "blank" once I get out of my teens," there was no mention of bullying. The fact that the panel was made up of current high school students was significant. Generally the It Gets Better campaign features adults whom the current targets of bullying may consider too far removed to understand their experiences.

Conclusion

One goal of many film and television producers is to educate audiences, particularly parents and school officials. However, there is a danger of creating hysteria and overreactions by overinflating the issue. The most severe cases where teens commit suicide as a result of the bullying and relational aggression are often highlighted for dramatic effect. The style and tone may be dark and ominous, with shadowy reenactments and gloomy music in the background. Another goal of the programming, whether producers admit to it or not, is to gain sufficient box-office sales and television ratings.

Documentaries and talk shows are primarily targeted to adults; however, youth-oriented networks such as MTV have made inroads into the format. The panel-discussions format, in particular, allows young people to relate their stories to other young people in their own voice. A theme often addressed on alternative networks such as MTV was the bullying of LGBT teens. Popular syndicated talk shows (e.g., *Dr. Phil*, *Ellen*) often invite younger celebrities to tell their story or endorse anti-bullying campaigns in order to attract younger viewers. The shows also include additional anti-bullying materials and links to other resources on their websites.

10

Television Reality Shows

Of all media genres, reality programming may be among the most likely to promote relational aggression in girls, or at the very least, change their expectations of what it means to be a mean girl. Archibald (Girl Scouts, 2011) argued that reality-show portrayals perpetuate a "mean girl" stereotype and normalizes bad behavior among girls. A vast majority of girls surveyed thought that reality shows promoted bad behavior, specifically pitting girls against each other (Baysinger, 2011). Teenage girls who watch reality TV expect drama, aggression, and bullying in the programming. Even worse, the effect appears to extend to real life. Lieberman (2011) reported that reality-television viewers are more likely than non-viewers to believe that gossiping is normal in relationships between girls. The Girl Scouts Research Institute (2011) conducted a survey over a 1,000 girls between the ages of 11 and 17. In the survey, two thirds of regularly television viewers reported that gossiping is a normal part of a relationship and it is natural for girls to be catty and competitive with one another. Over half of the girls surveyed reported having a hard time trusting other girls. What was perhaps most frightening was that 85% of the girls surveyed thought that "competition" style shows and 79% "real-life" based shows are real.

The structure of reality shows appears to lend itself to relational aggression. Coyne, Robinson, and Nelson (2010) identified the prime ingredient for reality shows in the UK was significant interaction between the cast members with very little plot. Relational aggression was particularly evident among female cast members. Aggression was both indirect (e.g., anonymous rumors) or direct (e.g., threats to end friendships or alliances). The UK programs that Coyne and associates analyzed appear to be very similar to programs in the US, where the lack of plot is likewise significant. With little to do, cast members of these "spectacle" shows spend an inordinate amount of time gossiping, badmouthing, and hashing and rehashing past altercations.

Lipkins (2011) argued that the emphasis on winning and losing in "competition" type shows encourages dominance and aggression. Coyne's team (2010) found that participants in shows with a competition component often used relational aggression to turn their rival contestants against each other. They found no difference use of aggression between the interactive shows, where there was voting involved, and other types of shows. Bullying in both competitive and spectacle shows is rewarded with not only prizes but additional camera time and covers of gossip magazines. Our society, which Lipkins (2011) referred to a "vulture culture," rewards humiliation and the demeaning of others and actually encourages bullying.

Reality shows were broken down into "competitive" and "spectacle." Competition shows were further classified as general (e.g., *America's Next Top Model*), talent (e.g., *American Idol*), and dating (e.g., *The Bachelor*). Makeover business shows (e.g., *Kitchen Nightmares*) were also included in the competitive category because of the similarity of structure even though no prizes were awarded. Spectacle shows include mean women (e.g., *Real Housewives*), weddings (*Bridezilla*), and teen shows (e.g., *My Super Sweet 16*).

Competition

Reality shows, especially those involving competition, cast some of the biggest bullies on television. Many of the casting decisions are made in anticipation of which participants will be the most controversial. Scenarios are staged and footage is edited to maximize conflicts. In addition to the mean contestants, the hosts of these shows often have a bullying reputation (e.g., Donald Trump in *The Apprentice* and Gordon Ramsey in *Hell's Kitchen*). Lipkins (2011) compares some reality-show judges to gladiators who kill their foes to the delight of spectators. Simmons (2011) described the reality show *Survivor* as "a disturbing ritual in cliques of girls" who coldly turn against each other after having formed alliances (p. 87). The competition show brings out the worst in cast members, judges, and even audience members. Viewers can participate in the destruction of a contestant by voting him or her off the show by voting for the competitors.

In the first season of *The Apprentice*, one of the female contestants, Omarosa, became notorious for being a mean girl. Turner (2008) argued that Omarosa and other African American women are featured as backstabbing, ruthless, shallow and materialistic on reality shows. In the beginning of the third episode, the women call a meeting to discuss personal issues, particularly the tension between Omarosa and Heidi. Omarosa quickly becomes defensive and leaves the room. She tells the other women that she did not come there to make friends and accuses the others of being too sensitive. Katrina apparently reaches her breaking point and tells Omarosa that women do not get anywhere being "bitches." Later, Amy suggests losing a challenge so they can get rid of Omarosa. At one point, Omarosa tells Erika to go get her blanket and pacifier and go cry. She appears to push buttons and then complains that she is being treated disrespectfully. In her return to *Celebrity Apprentice* four years later in 2008, she gets in trouble for accusing fellow contestant Piers Morgan of being secretly gay. After one of their conflicts, ex-boxer Lennox Lewis commented, "I've never seen a bad fight like that... I've fought with Tyson." Morgan called her "a piece of low-life trash." In 2010, Omarosa had a feud with *Real Housewives'* Bethany, accusing Bethany's husband of being gay in an interview with Perez Hilton. Omarosa also clashed with talk-show host Wendy Williams on Williams' show in 2008. A few seconds into the interview to plug Omarosa's book, Omarosa tells a confused Williams that she will not be disrespected.

The hosts of the competitive shows often set the tone and even encourage bad behavior among the contestants. The host of *The Apprentice*, Donald Trump, is somewhere between a bully and a mean boy. The contestants file into the boardroom where Trump is scowling at them. He warns them that the next 16 weeks will be "hell." The boardroom is dark and the music is daunting. Although the contestants do not officially work for Trump, he defines the experience as a job interview. He uses the expression "you're fired" to show his power. After he fires them, Trump tells everyone "go ahead" and leave. He rarely if ever wishes them well or good luck in the future.

COOKING

Gavin (2011) described restaurant shows as "taunting and backbiting among the contestants." The judges smirk and ridicule contestants. Gordon Ramsey, host of *Hell's Kitchen*, *Master Chef*, and *Kitchen Nightmares*, often swears and uses scatological references. He noted that one competitor's hamburger looked like a "turd." He continues to badger and berate even after his victim is reduced to tears. To make a point, Ramsey will banish contestants from the kitchen/stage and send them to their room like a parent would do to a small child. He has also made them sit in a "timeout" position. One female contestant was kicked off for not fighting back after he screamed at her. Ramsey tells her to get some dignity. He often tells contestant to "piss off" or "f*ck off" and to "hang their heads in shame." He tells a male contestant, "F off or I'll stick your head in that oven and talk to you through that F'ing gas burner." On an episode of *Master Chef*, Ramsey first makes a female contestant cry with his vicious comments, then he makes fun of her. He states, "If you are going to cry in the tartar sauce at least you are going to season it."

To add to the aggressive environment, the graphics going into the commercial break on *Hell's Kitchen* is an ax being sharpened. At the conclusion of the show, Ramsey stabs the eliminated contestant's chef jacket on a meat hook as their photo goes up in flames. Ramsey's sous chefs, who are there to help the contestants, also swear and scream at the contestants. Because there is no wall between the kitchen and the dining room, the customers appear to look horrified at the outbursts. In one episode, Ramsey scolds the contestants for not getting food out to the children in the dining room, yet the editing shows the children's shocked reaction to Ramsey screaming swear words from the kitchen. Although the reactions could be from other footage, it is edited in such a way as to give the viewing audience the impression that the children could hear the swearing.

Hell's Kitchen not only focuses on the bullying behavior of Chef Ramsey, it highlights cat fights between the contestants, especially the female contestants. Even the voiceover emphasizes the point, "Chef Ramsey will push this group harder than any other, but not as hard as they will push each other." One contestant warns that it is going to "get dirty." In the 2012 season, the women in the cast appear to be snarkier than ever before. They regularly call each other "idiot" and "stupid bitch." A very large contestant, Kimmie, is particularly vile. She fits the stereotype of an obese, angry woman. When one contestant, Robin, tries to regain some civility in the house and asks the women to stop using the "b" word, Kimmie refuses. Thinking that contestants were talking about her, Kimmie attacks the women and calls them "pieces of sh*t" and "lying bitches." In the previews for the next show, the announcer states, "Everyone, and I mean everyone, is at war."

Master Chef is a competition among amateur cooks that follows *Hell's Kitchen* in the primetime timeslot. The audience sees a somewhat kinder, gentler side of Ramsey, although he still tells participants their dishes look like "shit." He said one dish looks like he "got a hold of my granddad and turned his colostomy bag on your plate." Although the tone is much less volatile than *Hell's Kitchen*, *Master Chef* judge Joe Bastianich often gives contestants glaring looks and spits out their food as a hostile gesture. Bastianich tells contestants their food belongs in a garbage basket and tells one woman that her scallops are "a joke."

MODELING

America's Next Top Model portrays the modeling world as a prime environment for the mean girl. The most glaring inconsistency of the show is that for all of Tyra Bank's anti-bullying talk, she rarely addresses the snide comments and the pettiness of the contestants, who call each other "bitch" and "trash." The title of an episode in season four, "The Girl the Lionesses are Hunting," is a clear indication that the competitors are turning on one of their own. Amanda excuses the contestants' bad behavior by saying, "The house has to have a target. That's just mob mentality and human nature in competition." In "Takes to the Streets," Whitney complains in a confessional that Dominique "doesn't stop running her mouth." Dominique accused Whitney of being a racist. In the next episode, "House of Pain," Claire is screaming at Dominique because Dominique did not shut off her alarm.

In an ironic episode, "Estelle," Tyra has the models team up with tween girls to compete to create an anti-bullying video. The models shed many tears as they exchange stories about how they were bullied in the past. This episode began with voiceovers and scenes from previous shows highlighting the petty rivalries between the contestants. One model states that she does not trust Kyle's "skinny ass" and is going to do her best to "knock that bitch off her feet." Kyle tells the camera, "Keep hating, I really don't care." The models criticized and gossiped about their teammates during the anti-bullying competition.

The episode "Diane Von Furstenberg" focuses on the pain the models feel inside about a word or label that was used to bully them in the past. Models discuss that they were teased for being tall, pasty white, lesbian, etc. The hurtful word such as "oreo," "queer," and "stupid" were replaced with more empowering words. For example, instead of "giant," the contestant wore "Amazon." Instead of "oreo," the contestant wore "Nubian queen." Shortly after the contestants experience a moment of soul searching about the pain they feel inside about having someone be mean to them, they turn around and are incredibly mean to each others. The titles of some of these episodes, such as "Highlights and Catfights" make it clear that producers wish to incite infighting so viewers will tune in. The catty spats do not seem to be addressed by the judges, and therefore, it appears that Tyra is tolerant of them.

TALENT

Haxton (2010) argued there is a humiliation factor when judges are able to critique dancers or singers on the competition shows. *American Idol* judge Simon Cowell is often cited as a bully. One reason critics may think Cowell is a bully is his tone and mannerisms. Cowell often watches contestants as he leans back with his arms crossed. At times he has them stop prematurely, potentially putting off contestants who feel they were not given a fair or sufficient chance to be heard. Generally his comments are harshest in the initial auditions. It is evident that producers put a dichotomy of good and awful contestants in front of the judges. In one audition show Cowell tells a contestant she should get a lawyer and sue her voice teacher. When Paula tells another contestant, "You're not ready," Cowell corrects Paula and tells the singer, "You will never be ready." He tells *Idol* wannabes such gems as, "Never in a billion years," and, "That was a complete and utter nightmare." Cowell, however, adds comments such as, "I'm saying that to be kind." In a sense, Cowell appears to believe he is doing contestants a favor, albeit lacking tact, by being honest and telling them not to waste their time on a futile endeavor.

Cowell appears to be less volatile on the talent show *The XFactor* than on *American*

Idol. The difference may be due to the fact that *The XFactor* narrows down choices to mostly viable contestants. In addition, contestants appear weekly in front of a live audience thus Cowell may have more pressure to be kind. Occasionally Cowell will make a remarks such as, "It's like I'm living in a nightmare" and "When you started to sing I wanted to slit my wrists." At times he waits until the contest has left the stage before he makes a negative comments such as, "She's a nut case." Some of Cowell's responses are mixed. He tells one contestant that he is "talented but deluded," but puts him through to the next round anyway. He tells an older woman, "This is going to sound odd but it is meant as a compliment...when I hear you I think of wolves mating in the forest." He can, however, show some compassion. Instead of criticizing the performance of an older couple whose act was really bad, he told the couple they were "adorable" and wished them the "best of luck." As a very successful talent-show producer, he appears to have some sense of who deserves or can handle harsh criticism. Cowell tells a female performer that she "interests" him and he "loves her ambition." He scolds the other judges who disagree.

When the show *America's Got Talent* hired Howard Stern as a judge, many critics thought he would fill the "mean" judge niche. Stern has a reputation of being harsh, even brutal, to guests on his radio show. The opening acts in Stern's first episode were very, very odd acts. It is likely they were chosen on purpose to allow Stern to be funny. Perhaps the most outrageous comment he made that night was when he asked one contestant if anyone ever told him he could sing, perhaps his parents. The contestant shared that his parents were dead. Stern asked if they "died of embarrassment." He commented that a magician/stripper had "man boobs" but noted that he has them, too. He advised one buxom woman to marry a rich guy, implying she had no talent. Stern could also be somewhat compassionate. When a very large woman pole-danced in a bikini, Stern told her she was "a beautiful spirit," "a good soul," and "a good sport" instead of going for the obvious fat joke. At times, it is evident that contestants have comebacks ready for Stern because of his reputation of being mean. When Stern tells a guitarist that his act is even too weird for him, the man quickly responds that Stern's comment might hurt his feelings if he respected Stern's opinion. There were gasps from the audience as Stern told him to "get off my stage." Stern chuckled about how brokenhearted he was that the contestant had no respect for him. After an older man's less than stellar opera performance, Stern called it a "disaster." The man said, "If you didn't like it, I appreciate that. I don't appreciate the rudeness." Stern defended himself by saying it was the truth. It is evident that Stern is a big fan of the show and is happy to be there. His appearance does not appear to be a gimmick where he is there to abuse contestants. He is blunt but is also very caring toward many of the performers.

DATING

Perhaps more than any other competition shows, dating shows portray female contestants in the worst light. In a promo for *The Bachelor*, the voiceover announces, "Let the cat fights begin!" According to Holiday and Rosenberg (2009), promoters use expressions such as "cat fight" and "backstabbing" to increase interest in women-centered media content. The promo for the 2012 season of *The Bachelor* touts, "25 girls just ready to attack!" Sound bites from contestants include, "This is war!" and "I'm going to shave her eyebrows off in the middle of the night." The comments the contestants make about each other on camera include "mean," "nasty," "psycho," "fake," "evil," "two-faced," and "bitch." Holiday and Rosenberg (2009) argue that reality television marginalizes, stereotypes, and oppresses women. The behavior on these shows makes hostility and hateful treatment of others more normal and acceptable in society. Holiday and Rosenberg (2009) pointed to shows like *Age of Love* that pit "cougars" (40-year-old women) against "kittens" (women in their 20s). The strategy of many female contestants on the *Bachelor* is to scheme and lie to make the other contestants look bad and thus get them eliminated.

In season one of *The Bachelor*, women competed for the affection of Alex, a handsome and wealthy bachelor. The show features confessional clips of the contestants commenting on their experience and, more importantly, each other. The show is set up where the bachelor initially goes on group dates with five of the women at a time. Anytime Alex paid attention to one woman over the others or requests "alone" time with one woman, the other contestants viciously attacked her on camera. During the bus ride back from a group date, Melissa worked her way up to the front of the bus and sat on Alex's lap. The others ridiculed her and called her "pushy." Rhonda was also criticized for being too wild. The other contestants labeled her as "aggressive" and claimed she cared only about herself, while they were there of course to find "true love." Rhonda commented that she was not on the show to make friends but to "win." When Rhonda did not get picked during a rose ceremony and was sent home, she had an anxiety attack. In her exit interview, she was very critical of her fellow contestants Trista and Shannon. When Shannon did not get picked as one of the final two contestants, she refused to hug Alex and would barely shake his hand. As she left, she told the camera that he was "weak."

The premise of the reality show *Joe Millionaire* was that the female contestants thought they were competing for a multi-millionaire. It would be revealed at the end that "Joe," Evan Marriott, was a lowly constructor worker. The show cast women as not only as desperate for a husband but as gold diggers. In one challenge, the female contestants were allowed to select a dress from a rack for that evening's dinner. The women pushed and shoved, leaving contestant Zora, who did not participate in the drama, with a dress that did not fit her. Later one contestant snarked, "Poor Zora, she is just a different shape and a different size."

MAKEOVERS

The business makeover shows are generally hosted by individuals with strong personalities who have a tendency toward a no-nonsense approach. Business owners knowingly invite these strong personalities into their businesses and then generally complain and get defensive when the "expert" criticizes their work. The formula of the show is that there is usually an altercation midway during the makeover process. Once the work is completed, however, there is a joyous reunion and a tearful goodbye to the host. The names of the shows are powerful, *Nightmares*, *Takeover*, and *Impossible*. There is something about these shows that lets viewers enjoy business owners getting scolded and their flaws exposed. Swearing is also a staple of these shows by both the host and the participants to add drama. A professional consultant is unlikely to drop the f-bomb dozens of times in the course of a day. These shows often set a standard of "I can be as nasty as I want as long as I am helping others." Even though there are almost exclusively happy endings, the harsh tone of these shows appears to add to the culture of mean and rewards bullying.

Gordon Ramsey brings his "charm" and "mild nature" to the business makeover show

Kitchen Nightmares. When he visits a failing restaurant of an older couple who have sunk their retirement savings into the business, he tells them their food is like "dog shit." When they disagree, he asks them if they are "stupid." He describes another restaurant's food as looking as if it came out of a baby's diaper. Ramsey also tells one owner's daughter that her acrylic fingernails are disgusting. He tells another owner he wants to take the plate and smash it on the owner's head. Ramsey's actions are oftentimes conflicting. For example, to make sure the owner does not bring back the old décor into the restaurant, he burns it along with the menus and dining room chairs in the parking lot. When the owner watches in tears, Ramsey puts his arm around her and tells her it will be fine.

In a similar show, *Restaurant Impossible,* chef Robert Irvine also displays tough love. Irvine gets a little short with this design and construction crew nearly every episode, to perhaps play up the pressure of the deadline. Observing the relationship between his crew and Irvine, it is apparent that any conflict is played up for dramatic effect. Irving can be harsh but generally does not swear. He tells one restaurant owner that she has the worst kitchen he has seen in his career. He warns her that she is going to kill someone and that her restaurant should be shut down. Irving gets impatient with one restaurant owner who refuses to let him have control. Irving stands with his arms crossed threatening to pack up and leave the barbeque restaurant when the owner hides from Irving in his house. On the other hand, Irving can also be compassionate. When the head chef of one of the restaurants gets choked up because he had been demoted, Robert tells the chef he still believes in him. He shakes the chef's hand and comforts him.

Paul Fisher goes into small modeling agencies and fixes them in the show *Remodeled.* He claims he is there to protect the "little guy" from being taken advantage of by the New York agencies. He states, "I know I sound like I'm a hard ass. I'm actually doing this from a place of love." In one agency, he gets so upset at the owner that he throws pictures off the shelf. He states again, "My passion gets the best of me but it's coming from a place of love."

Tabatha Coffey is one of the few, if not the only, females to host a business makeover show. *Tabatha Takes Over* is a balancing act for her because she cannot be too nice nor too pushy. At times Tabatha uses her small frame and Australian accent to get away with saying harsh things. Famous Tabatha lines include: "You're a man. So you may as well stand up like a man and take some responsibility for the f—-ing pigsty that you've created here," "The management in Sweetgrass is absolutely f—-ed," and "I would have sent customers home, but there aren't any in here." After telling an employee to spits out her gum, the employee puts the chewed gum on the counter. Tabatha calls it "f'n disgusting." The show follows the standard transformation from defensiveness to gratitude. In the episode "Avanti," one of the stylists from the salon has come to work an hour late straight from a party. In her confessional, the stylist refers to Tabatha as a "bitch" for criticizing her behavior. She tells Tabatha the next day that she left "bawling her eyes out" and that Tabatha was too hard on her. In the end, the stylist gets her act together and is grateful for the feedback. She now calls Tabatha "fabulous." The owner of the salon states, "Tabatha is pretty cool. I don't care who all says she is a bitch or whatever. She tells it like it is and she is right."

Spectacle

The "spectacle" has no official competition component except for fighting for attention and media exposure. There appears to be no other reason for spectacle shows' existence other than to portray mean women as entertainment. The women and girls on the "spectacle shows" appear to play mean-girl roles, much like professional wrestlers who play bullies (personal communication, Hewitt, 2012). They take on the persona created on the show and carry it over into "real life." They do not break character, sending mean tweets and giving blasphemous interviews to tabloid magazines outside the show. Technology allows them to continue their meanness 24/7. The "mean tweets" and blogs bring the nastiness directly to the audience, seemly bypassing the producers' scrutiny.

The Simple Life is one of the earliest spectacle shows. Pseudo-celebrities such as Paris Hilton are envied for their exclusionary world of clubs and parties. The premise of the reality television series *The Simple Life* was to watch two Hollywood starlets make fun of lower-class people who were kind enough to let them (Hilton and Nicole Richie) live with and work for them. It highlights the privileged who fail to be sensitive to others' feelings in order to get by in the world. Richie and Hilton put ordinary people's livelihood in jeopardy and then simply laugh. The behavior on the show represents a clueless type of mean, which is no less hurtful or insulting to others. Richie and Hilton give up their luxurious life and live with a farm family for a month. The two young women are incredibly disrespectful to the people of the town and their host family. They say things like, "I can't imagine living here. I would die." Nicole asks in a condescending tone if they hang out at Wal-Mart. They appear not to think how their actions will affect others. Nicole at least thanks the family for letting them stay. Paris asks, "Do you get used to the smell?" When they spill a significant amount of milk at the dairy farm, they laugh, not realizing the financial cost to the dairy farmer. When they have to dress up as shakes at a fast food restaurant, they flip off the passing drivers. When they go to the store for some feed, they buy frivolous items and rack up a large bill on the farmer's account. When they get in trouble, Nicole pretends to cry. Behind their backs she calls them "god damn penny pinchers." When Nicole loses her purse at a bar, she throws a fit, breaking things and pouring bleach on the pool table.

In its ninth season, *Bad Girls Club* is a collection of girls in their early twenties whose mission is to "out bad" each other. Coming back from the bar, one of the cast members urinates in the back of the limo into an ice bucket. She then hands the bucket containing the urine to the chauffeur and giggles. One of the young women, Rima, proudly announces that when she goes to a club, the first thing she asks is, "Whose dick do I gotta suck to get in? Cuz I'm not waiting in line." Each episode appears to begin with fight scenes from the previous episode. Buff security men rush in to break up fights, making it apparent that the producers are anticipating, and likely encouraging, physical fights. Another bad girl, Julie, proudly announces that she can "outbitch" everyone else. She brags that all the fights in the house have started because of her. Like many of these shows, there is no host to either intervene in disputes or critique the behavior of the participants. There are few if any consequences to their behavior. In the episode "Girls Gone Ham," Rima's housemates pack all of her thing in plastic bags and put them by the door. They write "dirty slut" and "ratass bitch" on her poster in the entrance of the house. One housemate, Ashley, feels bad and goes to warn Rima, although she fears the whole house will be against for telling. Erika tells Rima to "go get yourself some dental floss and hang yourself, bitch." When Ashley sticks up for Rima, Erika tells her she can "get herself killed," too. Erica and Rima get into a fight in the episode "Pretty Girl Bounced." Afterwards, Julie says Rima "loves getting slapped, it's her favorite thing." Producers kick Erika off the show for taking the fight too far and punching Rima in the face. More troubling is that Rima has left her young son so she could be on the show. The producers are just as culpable for casting a single mother as Rima is for leaving him.

THE "WIVES" SHOWS

There have been six different versions of *The Real Housewives*. The first incarnation, *The Real Housewives of Orange County*, premiered in March 2006. The show was created in response to the fictional television drama *The O.C.* The one thing the two versions have in common is perhaps that one of the most common lines in the show is "that crazy bitch." Bennett's (2010) impression of reality television women is that they are all "desperate, competitive, plastic-surgery-obsessed bimbos...money-grubbing, plastic-surgery-plumped fame whores—a cadre of women who seemingly can't resist a good catfight." Sammons (2011) referrer to the *Real Housewives* as "bullying, backstabbing, high school brat grows up to be Botox Mean Girl." The wives consistently call each other "liars" and "phonies." They accuse each other of accusing each other. There appears to be class issues among the women as well. It appears the producers of the franchise select groups of women for whom the need to work a regular job is not an issue. Jobs would seemingly cut into their gossiping and backstabbing time. They can jet off to vacations and take time to meddle in each others' lives.

In *Real Housewives of New Jersey*'s "In the Name of the Father," a series of fights break out at a christening. In this episode, the men are just as mean and stereotypically petty as the women. The children in attendance are getting visibly upset as the adults are screaming obscenities at one another. When Theresa approaches her brother, Joe, and his wife, Melissa, tempers flare. Theresa's young daughter tries to pull her mother away from the drama. Joe calls his sister "a piece of garbage." Theresa's husband physically goes after Joe, shouting, "I'll f**ng kill every one of you!" as a group of men drag them apart. The scene looks like an episode of *The Sopranos*.

In *The Real Housewives of Atlanta*, the women say nasty things to each other such as, "She appears to be 'ghetto,'" "I am not to be messed with," and "Kim...that's a low down dirty monkey with a wig on." The episode "Catwalks & Cat Fights" features a brawl between NeNe and Kim. NeNe puts her finger in Kim's face. Kim slaps her hand away. NeNe put her hands on Kim's neck so Kim calls the police. After the altercation, the two wives come together to arrange a truce. Before long, they are screaming at each other, "This bitch is stupid" and "Is your wig squeezing your brain too tight, heffer?" Kim keeps calling NeNe a "moose" and jokes about wanting to hit NeNe with her high heel.

The *Real Housewives of NYC* season-six reunion does not go well. One would think that these women would behave better during the reunion show where they have time to reflect on their past actions. Seeing replay clips showing them acting badly does not seem to deter their behavior. They often dig in deeper in defending their bad behavior. The women split into two cliques, the blondes versus the brunettes. They interrupt and shout over each other. Even the host, Andy, tells them they are acting like "beasts." It does not appear to embarrass the women since they continue to do it. A typical conversation sounds like something one would hear on a middle school playground:

> Wife 1: "What about the things you have said about me?"
> Wife 2: "Like what?"
> Wife 1: "I'm not even going to go there."

In "Reserved Travel," the NYC wives put on a fundraiser, ironically for an anti-bullying program. During the event, the usual mean behavior appears. Before the end of the evening, one wife calls another "a thug in a cocktail dress."

Whereas the women on the *Housewives* shows are often passive aggressive, the women in the *Basketball Wives* and *Mob Wives* are more overtly and physically aggressive. On the show *Mob Wives*, Karen, Ramona, and Renee are identified as coming from families where their fathers and/or grandfathers were affiliated with organized crime. Another mob wife, Drita, is seen as an outsider, which is often the source of the conflict. Drita grew up outside the neighborhood. Several times during a *Mob Wives* reunion show, the women stand and physically go after one another. Large male security guards are at the ready to pull the women apart. One of the wives announces that they are going to fight after the show, "no cameras." One of the show's highlights of the past season was a physical altercation during a birthday party between three of the wives, Drita, Ramona, and Karen. In a confessional afterwards, Karen brags that when she beats people up, ambulances come. The host, Joy Behar, asked the women if, since they so quickly lose their tempers, they are afraid that their children will become "rage-a-holics." The women deny it. One of the *Mob Wives* producers, who is the sister of one of the wives, came out on stage for the reunion show. She was just as confrontational and unprofessional as the women on the show.

It is apparently mandatory for the *Wives* shows to include physical fights. Pia and Christina get into a hair-pulling fight in the first episode of *Mob Wives: Chicago*. The altercation begin when Pia "got in the face" of Christina. A friend of Pia's shrugs and says, "Get in my face, get a funeral." The episode or two following a fight are generally spent rehashing the fight. Two other wives, Renee and Nora, get into a physical altercation when Renee is late for Nora's father's memorial service. Supposedly a 40-year friendship dissolved into a girl fight. Only an episode or two earlier, the two proclaimed their undying friendship. Renee, who is reportedly in a fierce custody battle with her daughter's father, starts the public fight in a restaurant in front of the cameras. Once again, large security men are at the ready to break it up.

Shaunie O'Neal, ex-wife of Shaquille O'Neal, is one of the producers of *Basketball Wives*. Generally the "wives" are ex-wives, ex-girlfriends, or "baby mamas" of NBA players and other professional athletes. In season two, a war breaks out between Tami and Kesha. Tami tells Kesha that she does not respect Kesha so that is why she is calling Kesha a "bitch." One entire episode revolves around Tami threatening not to give Kesha's purse back until Kesha apologizes. Kesha looks genuinely scared of Tami. Tami slaps her fist into her other hand and threatens, "Any bitch who doesn't want to get it popping should keep her mother-f'n mouth closed." The other wives sitting at the table listening to Tami have their hands over their mouths in shock. In the era of new technology, the feuds continue off camera as well, with cast members getting into Twitter battles. In one episode, Shaunie consults her pastor about continuing with the show because of the fighting and negativity.

Because of their bad behavior, there has been a backlash to *Basketball Wives*. A petition was circulated by viewers complaining about the bullying and violence on the show. Celebrities such as Star Jones are calling on black women to take a stand against the show (Scott, 2012). Jones described the participants in *Basketball Wives* as "women of color slap[ping] the crap out of each other & run[ning] across tables barefoot." Beyond *Basketball Wives*, Turner (2008) criticized the portrayal of African American women on most reality shows as loud, domineering, and ready to pick a fight. She pointed to the cartoonish character of Omarosa on the first season of *The Apprentice* and the "resident mean black girl" in the casts of the first few seasons of *The Real World*. She argued that young black women are making fools of themselves for fame and attention. *Basketball Wives, Love & Hip Hop*, and *The Real Housewives of Atlanta* present black women as catty and evil and clearly negative examples for young, impressionable women ("Catty, Evil Black Women," 2011). The shows *Basketball Wives* & *Love and Hip Hop* take the two strongest arenas of African American achievement, sports and music, and turn them into a stage for shrill shouting matches. The bad behavior perhaps reinforces racial discrimination by demonstrating these women cannot conduct themselves in a civil manner and therefore could not be trusted to businesses or professions outside of the sports and entertainment industries.

In the very first scene of the first show I analyzed of *Love & Hip Hop*, Chrissy gets up from her seat and blindsides Kimbella. Evidently Chrissy did not like it that Kimbella confesses to Emily that she had slept with Chrissy's man three years earlier. Chrissy is involved with Jimmy, who is business partners and friends with Kimbella's baby daddy. As Chrissy tells Jimmy about the fight the night before, he questioned her actions in a calm, almost indifferent manner. It appears the men are getting into the drama as well as the women in *Love & Hip Hop: Atlanta*. A music producer, Stevie, comes to his "baby mama" Mimi's house to try to get her back after she breaks up with him for cheating on her with Joceline, one of Stevie's clients. Mimi is upset because Stevie got Joceline pregnant. They are very open about Joceline later having an abortion.

The women on *Texas Women* on CMT are as mean as their northern counterparts. CMT at one time was a very upstanding network that bragged about its Christian morals. The women proudly flaunt their "redneck" ways of getting drunk, getting into fights, and backstabbing their friends. The show is based on an ongoing feud between former friends Brooke and Hannah. In "Take the Bull by the Horns," one of Hannah's friends' boyfriends calls Brooke the "c" word. Brooke's husband Jason lunges at the guy. People are trying to hold Jason back but he and Brooke throw punches at the guy. When the police arrive, Brook gets handcuffed and put in the cruiser. As the officer is handcuffing Brooke, she defiantly says, "I'll bet you do that to your wife in bed." Another officer has Jason up against the building with his forearm on his neck. They release Brooke on the condition she and her husband get into a cab and go home. As soon as the police leave, Brooke and Jason get out of the cab and go back in the bar to do more shots. Hung over, Brooke and her husband discuss the incident the next morning. She admits in her confessional that the fight was not her first "knock down drag out."

MOM SHOWS

Abby Lee Miller, the dance coach in the reality series *Dance Moms*, is a very large no-nonsense woman with a gravelly voice. In the episode "No One Likes a Bully," two of the mothers, Cathy and Christi, have a screaming match in front of the girls. This behavior is not unusual and, in fact, appears to be the premise of the show. The mothers are physically getting in each other's faces. Christi calls Cathy a "bitch." They each complain that the other speaks disrespectfully in front of their children. When the mothers are not criticizing each other, they spar with Abby. One mother calls Abby an "evil bitch" behind her back. Abby and Christi accuse each other of being horrible role models. In the episode "No One Likes a Bully," the group dance number that week centers around bullying. Two of the mothers find it ironic that Abby picked the theme since they consider her to be a bully. For example, when Chloe cries, Abby tells her to "suck it up." Abby accuses Peyton of being "cocky" for saying she thought she did better than the other girls on her team. Abby argues, "She shouldn't belittle others. That's my job." She explains that people pay her for her opinion so she can say anything.

Dance Moms: Miami appears to be in competition with the original *Dance Moms* to be more outrageous. The show sets up conflict by bringing in a very talented girl Mia and her mother, Leo, to the studio. The other mothers are extremely jealous, while the children handle the situation much more maturely. The dancers greet Mia with smiles and hugs. One of the girls, Hannah, sees the competition as a challenge, while her mother is throwing a "hissy fit." Hannah asks her mother, "Why am I the one comforting you?" In the same episode, one of the mothers tells Leo to go "f" herself and calls her the "b" word. Leo calls the other mother "jealous" and "insecure." Yet another mother, Bridgette, slaps Leo's hand away from her face as they are verbally fighting. The coaches have to hold the mothers back before a physical fight breaks out. Leo cries, saying she feels bullied. It is remarkably that the children do not act out in these programs with their mothers as role models.

BRIDE SHOWS

Reality wedding shows arguably take a most sacred day and turn it into a mean-fest. The shows *Bridezilla* and *Say Yes to the Dress* demonstrate how creating a culture where brides are princesses contributes to a culture of mean and bullying of others. Movies also use the theme of the bride and bridesmaid to perpetuate the bad behavior of the betrothed. The title of the movie *Bride Wars* pretty much says it all. Getting engaged for some women appears to give them license to mistreat salespeople, wedding planners, family members, grooms, and their supposed best friends. After seeing these brides in action, it is hard to believe the men still want to marry them. It appears that getting attention trumps any lessons in diplomacy, friendship, or the sanctity of marriage.

In one episode of *Bridezillas*, "Alex & Melissa," Melissa threatens everyone around her with her bullying. She calls her own bridesmaids "bitches" and "skanks." Her threats to her mother include, "I'm going to take out that earring and stick it in your eyeball." She talks about punching the cake bakers in the face and making them bleed. She calls her fiancé "retarded," a "cry baby," and an "idiot." The bride LaJune is likewise abusive to her family and friends. She calls her bridesmaids "fat" and "bitches." She admits that she will likely lose 50 percent of her wedding party as friends before the event is over. She calls her grandmother to tell her she will need to sit with the kids because she moves too slowly. LaJune just watches as she makes her bridesmaids go through exercise bootcamp. She screams at them about dieting as she is off snacking. In the episode "Minyon & Jennifer," Minyon calls her bridesmaids "heifers." She throws champagne at the bridesmaids and breaks her glass. She gets into a physical fight with her sister. She shouts that if she does not get what she wants, she is going to make her fiancé's life a living hell. The producers do not just capture the drama but create drama by rewarding the behavior. To make it on the air, the brides amp up their bad behavior.

Brides are also often portrayed as abusive to their bridesmaids and mothers in *Say Yes to the Dress*. When a rather large bridesmaid, Rakia, tries on an unattractive dress, the bride falls over in her chair laughing at Rakia. She calls Rakia the "Jolly Green Giant." In the "Princess Brides" version of *Say Yes to the Dress*, the sales staff says the most commonly heard expression is "I wanna be a princess." The staff labels some of their clients the "Spoiled Princess." On the other hand, bridesmaids can be equally as mean to the bride. In an episode of *Say Yes to the Dress: Bridesmaids Edition* entitled "Maid of Honorzilla," the maid of honor gets into a feud with the matron of honor over who in the bridal party is most important. Jessica, a childhood friend of the bride Megan, proclaims herself "boss of the bridesmaid." Jessica says mean things like she thinks the color of the dresses looks like someone threw up on them. Megan finally stands up for herself and kicks Jessica out of the bridal party and disinvites her to the wedding.

TEEN SHOWS

The reality shows featuring adolescent girls appear to portray females in a slightly less negative light than their adult counterparts. *My Super Sweet 16* should be a cautionary tale for parents who overindulge their children. The teen girls are often portrayed as bullies, treating their parents as emotional hostages, especially in the first season of the show. The daughters capitalize on their fathers' self-confessed need to be loved and desire to be seen as a hero. The girls also use the invitations to their 16th birthday parties as a weapon, strategically plotting who gets an invite and who does not. Invitations signify social status and the mean girls capitalize on that status. The distribution of the invitations is often done in a public place so receiving an invite or not is evident to their peers. In one episode of *My Super Sweet 16*, Jacque plans to invite the popular kids who would not normally talk to her in order to heighten her social status. Natalie wants to have a big party in order to get back at the people who, she claims, are jealous of her. She and her friends laugh about how they are not going to invite "losers" to the party. Natalie states, "We are so mean...I love it." Sierra (daughter of singer Cee Lo) boldly claims, "These people are giving me the attention I deserve." She has the invitation distributers let invitees know that if they do not bring her a gift, they will not get into the party. As Lauren prepares for her party, she refuses to get off her cell phone, making it quite difficult for her hair and makeup people to do their jobs. Lauren is particularly rude to her father. She orders him to find her shoes. After the extravagant party, for which her parents paid dearly, she comments that it was nothing special and she is "over it." The lack of gratitude and appreciation is stunning. Ava admits to blatantly manipulating her divorced parents. She threatens to stop speaking to her father if he does not get her dream car.

There is also this meanness or almost bullying of the parents on MTV's *Teen Moms*. The girls use the threat of not seeing their grandchildren to get what they want from their parents. These programs teach a tremendous disrespect for parents and show rewards for being a brat. In one particular episode, Amber Portwood and the father of her child, Gary, scream obscenities at each other in front of their child. Amber also physically hits Gary and bullies him by threatening to refuse to let him see their daughter. Because of the footage from the show, the police investigate and arrest Portwood for domestic battery (Bonner, 2012). Portwood failed to complete rehab as part of a plea deal, choosing to serve a five-year prison term.

Among the clutter of mean as entertainment media, there are a few shows that portray strategies to stop bullying and relational aggression. On the show *Queen Bees*, seven young women who range from 18 to 20 years of age, think they are competing to become the top diva of the house. Instead, the show is a competition of who among them can change the most. The contestants' family and friends have nominated the contestants because of their mean girl behavior and selfish attitudes. After a series of challenges and many tears shed, each contestant appears to have progressed. Stassi is no longer in denial about being selfish. Michelle's focus is no longer on her and others' appearance, etc. In the end, each of the contestants makes progress toward becoming less mean. The show had a positive message; however, the lack of drama likely caused its low ratings.

In MTV's series *Made*'s "Bully to Beauty," a tomboy, Devon, requested a transformation from a bully to a beauty queen. Devon's friends tell the interviewers that she punches and pinches and they are afraid of her. Although she says she does not steal lunch money or post pictures online, Devon admits to verbally abusing people. She says she does it so people will not "mess" with her now because she was picked on in the past. Her family thinks she is verbally abusive because she is insecure. Devon wishes to be made into a beauty queen, hoping that it will give her self-confidence. Kyle from the MTV crew sets out to transform Devon in four weeks. The students are told if Devon does something to scar them, they should put a Band-Aid on her face. Her victims jump at the chance to get even for past hurt Devon has caused. Kyle delves into Devon's hurt caused by her mother not taking her seriously. In the end Devon gives an anti-bullying talk to a grade school class. Devon is elected Miss Congeniality in the pageant she enters and her friends attest to her change for the better.

Conclusion

In many of the *Housewives*-type shows, the verbal fights have turned physical. Even a scene in *Dance Mom: Miami* almost turns into a physical altercation. Coyne and associates (2010) concluded that displays of aggression by female cast members potentially communicate to viewers that this behavior is normal and an acceptable way to achieve goals. Many of these women are mothers and insist their children are the most important part of their lives; however, they are horrible role models in handling conflict with other women. While conservative political groups are fighting for the "sanctity of marriage," reality shows are exploiting it. Bride shows encourage outrageous behavior and normalize the bridezilla mentality. One would hope that mean girls will eventually outgrow their bad behavior; however, these shows demonstrate incidents where it just gets worse. At least *My Super Sweet 16* participants are teenagers. The adults, one would assume, should know better.

The consistent theme portrayed on reality shows is a lack of empathy or concern for anyone except for one's self. Each participant appears to be more selfish and self-centered than the next. Females, especially, are cast in a horrendous light. Women used to exploit their sexuality to get attention, but now they are just plain mean. Reality shows deliver *Jerry Springer*- and *Cops*-like content with large men in black t-shirts ever at the ready to jump in and tear hysterical women apart. Producers of *Mob Wives* counted Renee saying the f word 407 times in one season. The sentiment expressed in most of these shows is in stark contrast to the cooperative, nurturing ideals our culture has about women. Simmons (2011) argued that girls appear to be caught in a dichotomy of either being nice and taken advantage of or being aggressive and mean. There are few role models in between in media portrayals in general, and almost none in reality shows.

11

Children's Programs

Researchers have long agreed that children are the most susceptible audience to media effects (Singer & Singer, 2000). They often lack the cognitive ability to process media messages and are more likely to imitate behavior they view in the media. This chapter looks at bullying and mean girl portrayals specifically targeted to young children and early adolescents. While there are a few examples from film that focus on the bullying element for younger children, the vast majority of programming comes from television. While movies have generous time allotment, many of the television shows targeted to children are split into two 15-minute segments rather than the one 30-minute episode format found in teen- and adult-targeted programming. The short segments perhaps reflect the shorter attention span of the young viewer. The shorter segments, however, also require the show to introduce, present, and resolve bullying in an even shorter amount of time. (An analysis of children's books portraying bullies and mean girls can be found in Chapter 12.)

Television

The first category of children's programming analyzed includes animated shows, which I broke down even further into human characters (e.g., *Hey Arnold*, *Phineas and Ferb*) and animals or creature-type characters (e.g., *Sponge Bob Square Pants*). There were a fair number of action programs, which I divided up into animated (e.g., *Kick Buttowski: Suburban Daredevil*) and live action (e.g., *The Troop*). Perhaps the most significant category that emerged was fantasy and sci-fi (e.g., *Adventure Time*). I included educational programs (e.g., *Sesame Street*), sketch comedies (e.g., *The Amanda Show*), and religious programs (e.g., *Veggie Tales*) as well.

ANIMATED PROGRAMS: HUMAN CHARACTERS

Two of the earliest representations of animated kids and bullies are *Charlie Brown* and *Fat Albert*. When Charlie Brown gets to camp in *He's a Bully, Charlie Brown,* Joe the bully introduces himself and starts in with the insults and physical jabs. He especially picks on Snoopy, tripping him. Marci complains that Joe has been calling her names as well. Linus gets tricked into losing his marbles to Joe, who has taken most of the other boys' marbles as well. Linus explains to Charlie Brown that he thought Joe was just teaching him how to play. Charlie Brown plots to win Linus' marbles back. Snoopy coaches him on how to shoot. Things look grim when Charlie Brown is down to his last two marbles. Charlie Brown pulls off the victory and even offers Joe his original marbles back. Joe tells him to keep them all.

In *Fat Albert and the Cosby Kids*, "The Bully," Slappy and his sidekick, Fungle, disrupt the boys' baseball game. Slappy replaces the ball with a grapefruit. It explodes all over Bill when he hits it. Slappy calls another boy "string bean." Later Slappy and Fungle play keep away from Russell. Fat Albert is disappointed when he catches Russell holding Slappy down. He mistakenly thinks Slappy is an okay guy and reprimands Russell. Slappy continues to bully and get away with it. He ties a rope to Bill's skateboard; however, the plan backfires and Slappy gets dragged instead. Fat Albert believes Slappy when he says Bill tied the rope to Slappy's arm. Slappy fills a bag with water and drops it off the roof onto Fat Albert. Albert thinks Bill did it. When Fat Albert overhears Slappy admitting to bullying and calling Albert a "tub of lard," he makes Slappy promise not to hassle the kids anymore. Slappy begs for mercy and complains that he is the youngest of 15 kids and just wants attention. Slappy quickly breaks his promise and steals the boys' ball. Russell tickles Slappy until he runs away. At the end of the show, Fat Albert recommends being friends with a bully. He tells bullies to try being nice because nobody likes a bully.

Newer animated comedy series are likely to air on a cable network such as Nickelodeon or the Disney Channel. In the episode of *Doug* entitled "Doug Bags a Neematoad," Doug meets some new friends at the fast food place. He slips and accidently gets ketchup on the bully's shoe. Roger, the bully, is wearing a leather jacket and has a shock of red hair. He sends Doug to capture a neematoad. He tells Doug he will be the most popular kid in town if he can find one. He bullies the kids into going along with him convincing Doug that neematoads exist. Doug agrees to meet at the pond at 7am. Roger calls him "dumb" and the other kids laugh. He makes Doug perform a silly mating call, while the group mocks Doug. Doug finally catches on and feels humiliated. Doug declares he found a neematoad, which is really Doug's dog covered in mud. The dog comes out of the bushes and scares the boys. At the end of the episode, it is Roger who is standing in the middle of the pond in the dark doing a mating call, trying to lure his own neematoad.

While many shows have one resident bully, *Hey Arnold* has a series of different bullying portrayals. In "24 Hours to Live," Arnold accidently hits the bully, Harold, with a line drive while playing baseball. When Harold threatens to fight Arnold, Arnold tells Harold, "I'm crazy and no one should hit crazy." Arnold sings and dances in a crazy manner. Harold asks Arnold to join their club. In another episode, "New Bully on the Block," Arnold and his friends are confronted by two bullies, Ludwig and Wolfgang. One of the bullies takes Arnold's lunch money. They are shown tripping one girl and giving another girl a black eye. Ludwig and Wolfgang fight over the lot, which the 4th graders have cleaned up and claimed for themselves. Although the actual violence was not shown, Arnold has a black eye in the next scene. Arnold and his friends try to trick the bullies into beating each other up by proposing they play a football game to determine who gets the lot. Instead of the bullies playing each other, they decide to coach the 4th graders in a game. Since the bullies are turning into friends, Arnold wants to tie the game so that neither bully loses and gets angry. The plan backfires since now they will dominate the field together. The 4th graders are hung on the goal posts at the end. In the episode "Tutoring Torvald," Torvald is laughed at by the 4th graders when he gets a math question wrong. Even the teacher disparages him by pointing out that he is 13 years old and still in the 4th grade. He is large and wears a cutoff sleeveless shirt with a bandana. He is shown holding up two boys, demanding money he says they owe him. Arnold and his friend, Gerald, do nothing to help. When Arnold goes to tutor Torvald at his house, Torvald's mother answers the door. She seems very nice and brags about how good of a son Torvald is. When Torvald goofs off during their study session, Arnold threatens to leave. Torvald confesses that he does not want to disappoint his mother. Arnold makes him a deal that if he stops beating up his friends, he will help him get another C. They have a deal. Arnold shows Torvald that he already understands math because he can figure out the terms of loan sharking and other ways he bullies. The gang's football lands on the porch of the Stoop Kid in *Hey Arnold!* "Stoop Kid." The Stoop Kid yells at and threatens anyone who comes near his stoop. Arnold figures out that Stoop Kid is afraid to leave his stoop. Soon all the kids are teasing Stoop Kid and laughing at him. When Stoop Kid eventually leaves his stoop, the crowds cheer. Stoop Kid is overjoyed that now he can harass other kids on or off his stoop.

Jacob goes to get the bagels for his family in *Jacob Two Two*'s "Big Bagel Bungle" but is confronted by a pack of bullies on the bus. When Jacob pulls the cord to stop the bus, the head bully stumbles and spills his drink. The bullies chase Jacob but Jacob hides. On the way home, Jacob runs into the bullies again. Since he has been gone so long, Jacob's brother and sister go looking for him. The brother and sister threaten to engage the bullies in a snowball fight unless they leave Jacob alone. Jacob pulls a scarf from the lead bully's nose as a magic trick. The other two bullies laugh so the lead bully starts a snowball fight with his cronies, leaving Jacob and his siblings to go enjoy the bagels.

The show *Phineas and Ferb* has a resident bully, Buford. Buford is significantly larger than the other boys and sports a crew cut. In "Raging Bully," Buford pushes Baljeet, a small Indian boy, off his stool, pushes his books of the table, and drinks his drink. When Phineas accidently drops his ice cream on Buford's lap, Buford picks him up by the front of his shirt and makes a fist. Before he can hit Phineas, one of the girls intervenes. Baljeet also comes to his defense. Just then, heavy weight champion Evander Holyfield comes upon the scene. He arranges for Buford and Phineas to fight behind the mall. The kids remember back to the last kid Buford fought. In a flashback, the boy is shown with a toilet on his head. Holyfield offers to train Phineas. The kids build a stadium outside the mall. As Buford comes out, the announcer shouts, "He's from a broken home. His hobby is breaking bones. Buford the Bully!" Buford and Phineas proceed to thumb wrestle. Phineas loses. Just then ice cream falls on Phineas' head. Buford proclaims that since they both got ice cream on them and were humiliated, they are "even steven" and they shake hands. When Buford threatens Ferb, Ferb casually pinches Buford's neck, knocking him unconscious for a few seconds.

In "Bully Code," Baljeet saves Buford's life when he is choking. Buford then vows to be Baljeet's slave because according to the bully code, "If a nerd saves a bully's life, the bully is the nerd's slave for life." Baljeet is annoyed by all the attention. Phineas and Ferb tell him that having the biggest, toughest kid in school as a bodyguard is a sign of supreme coolness. Buford ends up saving Baljeet's life and goes back to bullying others. Buford continues to bully Baljeet in "Bully Bromance Breakup." He gives Baljeet a wedgie. When Buford picks plastic bags over paper, the environmentalist Baljeet gets upset and refuses to be his nerd. Baljeet is feeling so confident having stood up to Buford, he does all kinds of adventurous things like mountain climbing. A mad scientist is amazed at Buford's bullying. He wants to use Buford to take over the tri-state area. On command, Buford knocks over the other scientists so the mad scientist can get ahead in the coffee line. The mad scientist learns how to intimidate parking cops and waiters. He threatens the dry cleaner with spilling coffee all over the clean lab coat. The mad scientist buys himself and Buford matching bullywear. However, Baljeet starts to miss Buford. He sings a song about getting Buford back as pictures of them together flash across the screen. Baljeet laments that there is a "bully-sized hole" in his heart. Buford sings a similar song about missing Baljeet, a "nerd-sized hole" in his heart. Buford tells the mad scientist, "There's a time when you don't want to bully everyone, just Baljeet." When Buford returns, Baljeet gives him a wedgie. Buford admits he had not realized wedgies were so uncomfortable so he apologizes. Baljeet apologizes for his earlier outburst.

Rugrats is a program about a group of babies who are bossed around and bullied by an older girl, Angelica. "New Kid in Town" begins with Angelica making the babies dig a moat around the jungle gym, which she refers to as "her castle." A new boy, Josh, comes to ask the babies if they want to play with him. The babies tell him that Angelica will not let them. She is bigger and stronger and if they do not do what she says, she will pour sand in their hair. Angelica threatens the babies to get back to digging. The babies stand up to her and go with Josh. At first, Josh is very nice to them. Then he becomes very passive aggressive. He makes the babies push him on the swing. When Tommy wants a turn, Josh explains that that would not be fair since swinging was his idea. Josh takes all their cookies, explaining that because he is bigger, he needs more cookies. The bullying progresses. Josh then raises his fist and his voice and orders them to dig. The babies begin to miss Angelica. Tommy escapes and asks Angelica for help. He explains that Josh is "more mean" than she is. Angelica refuses to help at first. Josh makes the babies lay down while he swings so he can jump over them. Before he can jump, Angelica hits him with water balloons. Angelica pushes Josh down. Josh goes running to his mother crying. The babies hug Angelica. She pushes them down and things go back to normal. The babies agree that Angelica is the "greatest." When Angelica gets ready to move away in the episode "Moving Away," the babies reminisce about when they first met her and Angelica tried to turn them against each other. Angelica overhears the babies say they are going to miss her. She cries and hugs them. She tells them they are her best friends. As soon as she finds out she is not moving, Angelica claims she made it all up goes back to her old mean ways.

There were girl bullies—for example, Angelica from *Rugrats* and Hilga from *Hey Arnold*—but they played minor roles in the episodes. Boy bullies were more prevalent in the freestanding episodes. There was a girl bully in *Rugrats'* "Showdown at Teeter-Totter" named the Junk Food Kid. Tommy and Chucky visit a new playground. At the play bar, the saloon keeper Belinda has a boo boo. She warns them about the "Junk Food Kid." Tommy steps in to defend Belinda from the Kid. She hits Chucky with a popsicle. Then she puts another one down Tommy's diaper. Belinda's mom had to cut off Belinda's hair after the bully put gum in it. The babies do the one thing they can do; start to cry. Tommy has nightmares that night. The next day, he decides to be a "tough omlette." The crowd cheers Tommy as he plans to stand up to the bully. Belinda and Chucky stand by him when everyone else runs away and hides. The bully blows a big bubble. Tommy pops it with a candy cane. The Kid starts to cry as her mother takes her away covered in gum. The crowd cheers Tommy. Later, the bully comes back with short hair eating carrot sticks. She agrees to play nice with the other babies. There is a very cute lesson here about the evils of mixing junk food and kids.

In the animated series *Kid vs. Kat*, the Curly Swirl ice cream cart driver is one of the neighborhood bullies. The word on the street is, "He never met a kid he wouldn't pick on." Coop vows to get back at the bully in "You Scream, I Scream." Coop and his friend, Dennis, set a trap for the bully, but it backfires and the boys end up in the stream. The boys set another trap that backfires again. When the boys stretch a net across the road, the bully is launched into a tree, hanging by his underwear. The bully is humbled and is seen giving rides to the kids on his ice cream cart.

Very few of the programs targeted to children have a female lead character. Even fewer of those programs incorporated bullying. Two examples presented are Canadian productions and both are based on a series of children's books, *Pippi Longstocking* and *Anne of Green Gables*. The third example, *As Told by Ginger*, is one of the only children's programs that addresses mean girls.

Pippi Longstocking is an animated series based on the children's books by Astrid Lindgren. Bengt, the bully in the series, is introduced in "Pippi Enters the Big Race." Bengt is confident he can win the big ski race. Pippi, who is trying to teach her horse how to ski jump, accidently gets into the race. She knocks Bengt down and wins and advances to the Nationals. Bengt growls his revenge. When Bengt tries several times to get Pippi disqualified, the principal of the school picks up Bengt and tosses him into a tuba. Bengt plans to create an avalanche by blowing his trumpet just as Pippi is passing by him. However, Bengt is unable to blow the trumpet because there is a banana inside of it. He yells in frustration, causing an avalanche in which he gets caught rather than Pippi. Pippi wins the race.

In the episode "Pippi Doesn't Go to School," Willie, a small boy who wears glasses, hides from Bengt. Willie tells his friend Tommy that Bengt promised to "get him" when school started. Tommy tells Willie not to worry, that he will protect him. Bengt's cronies surround Willie on the playground and Bengt pushes him to the ground. Tommy stands up to Bengt but he gets pushed down, too. Their friend Anna tries to help by kicking Bengt in the shin. However, it does not stop him. He only yells at Anna. Bengt punches Willie again, knocking off his glasses. Before Bengt can step on them, Pippi interferes. The bully and his cronies tease Pippi about her large feet, funny clothes, and red hair. Bengt reminds her that she tricked him before but now he has his pals with him. Pippi takes on all four bullies and wins. She puts Bengt up a tree so he cannot get down when it is time to go back from recess. Later, Willie is nervous about walking home. Bengt stops Anna and tries to take her backpack. He grabs her wrists. Mr. Nilsson, Pippi's pet monkey, is hiding in Anna's backpack and scares Begnt. He runs off when Pippi shows up. Bengt has not learned his lesson because he appears again in "Pippi Longstocking: Pippi Doesn't Go to School...or Does She?" Tommy warns Willie about wearing his new backpack to school. As predicted, Bengt takes the backpack from Willie and dumps the contents on the ground. Willie has played a trick on Begnt. The package inside the backpack is actually whale blubber from the school field trip up north. Bengt eats the blubber and makes a face. The boys laugh.

Anne of Green Gables is another series of children's books, written by Lucy Maud Montgomery, which was adapted into an animated series. During school lunch in "Bully by the Horns," a new student, Orville, trades his lunch with Felix without Felix's permission. Next, Orville steals Felix's book about airplanes and calls Felix an "egghead." Anne stands up for Felix. She stops Orville temporarily, but he comes back later and takes Felix's airplane. He threatens Felix if he tells. Orville shows off the airplane to his friends. Fearful of Orville, Felix lies to Anne and tells he lent Orville the plane. When he finally tells the truth, Anne starts to go after Orville until Felix tells her that Orville threatened him if he told. Anne advises Felix to try ignoring Orville. Orville picks Felix to be his partner for the science fair. Orville tells Felix since he snitched to Anne, he has to do all the work by himself. The next day, Felix does not want to go to school, claiming he is sick. Anne assures him he has friends to stand beside him. Anne wants to tell the teacher but Felix warns her that the bullying will get worse. When Orville brags to the other kids about what he has done on the school project, Anne calls him a "bully" and pushes him down, accidently breaking Felix's airplane. Diana tells Anne that now she is being a bully. Anne feels bad about being overly mean. Felix finally stands up to Orville and tells him he does not want him as a partner anymore. Orville promises not to bully him. Orville, who is actually good with his hands, makes an adjustment to Felix's plane, making it better. They win the prize for the best project. At the end of the episode, they share cookies on the steps of the school.

As Told by Ginger was really the only representation of mean girls I could find in the sample of children's programming. Perhaps relational aggression is not considered appropriate for young viewers. *As Told by Ginger*, which aired on Nickelodeon, focuses on solving problems and social status as Ginger and her friends navigate junior high. The show also includes storylines of Ginger's younger brother, which give it a younger feel as well.

In "New Girl in Town," the mean girls, Mipsy and Miranda, gossip about a new girl, Laetitia. Laetitia stands out because she dresses Goth and her father is a mortician. Ginger sticks up for Laetitia and invites her over to her house after school. The popular girls make up stories about Luticia's dad embalming a person who was not dead. Ginger suggests Luticia have a party to show she is normal. Although they refuse to come at first, Mipsy and Miranda end up coming because they admire Ginger for taking a stand. Also they confess they do not like to be excluded, even if it is someone less popular. In a second storyline about boys being mean and exclusive, Ginger's younger brother Carl and his friend Hoodsey are rather mean to Brandon. When Brandon gives them invitations to his birthday party, they say they cannot take them because their hands are dirty from art class. After Brandon leaves, they say are relieved that they "dodged that bullet." Hoodsey reasons they should go to Brandon's party because then Brandon will have to come to their birthday parties and bring them presents. When the boys hear about Laetitia's party, they bail on Brandon. Brandon cries when they tell him. It is clear that the trash can is full of his invitations he gave to other kids in his class. Carl and Hoodsey They feel guilty and decide to go to both parties. Brandon cries when they try to leave his party early because he wants his parents think he is popular. Hoodsie feels bad so they take Brandon with them to Laetitia's party.

In the next season's episode "Wicked Games," Mipsy and Miranda are unhappy because now that Ginger has a new boyfriend, she has been ignoring the dirty looks they give her. They convince Dodie, Ginger's friend who is feeling a bit jealous of Ginger's new boyfriend, to join forces with them to break up the happy couple. Dodie and Macie make sure Ginger's boyfriend overhears them discussing rumors about Ginger and another boy. When Dodie starts to feel guilty, Miranda tells her the guilt feeling that comes with stabbing a friend in the back goes away after doing it a couple hundred of times. Courtney, the most popular girl in school, overhears the plan and warns Ginger. After the girls confess to Courtney, Ginger lets them know she was listening the whole time. The episode ends with Dodie leaving a message for Ginger apologizing for her role in the plan. In the next episode, nothing is mentioned so it appears that Ginger has forgiven her.

ANIMATED PROGRAMS: CREATURE/ANIMAL CHARACTERS

Children's programming, much like picture books, features anthropomorphic animals and creatures. *Adventure Time* is a poorly drawn animated series. (Note: the characters are described as a boy and his dog, but the drawing is so vague, the boy looks more like a creature and thus included in this section.) In the episode "Donny," Finn and Jack come upon a town where a big green ogre named Donny is bullying house people. Donny squeezes eggs out of the chickens. He puts one of the houses on his back so the house cannot move his feet. To stop Donny, Finn jumps on Donny's back. After they struggle for awhile, Donny gets tired so they take a break. Finn thinks that although Donny is rough and tumble, he is sensitive inside and bullies because he is treated like an outsider. Finn invites Donny to hang out with them. Donny loses his temper and breaks the video game when he loses. When Donny throws his apple juice on Finn, Finn tells him to quit being "a jerk" and starts to push him. Donny asks, "What did I do? Everybody's getting mad at me for nothin." Finn tells him he must think about how his actions make other people feel. Finn sings the "empathy" song. Donny becomes cultured. Soon after Donny's transformation, a scary pack of wolves attacks the house people. One of the wolves explains that Donny's bully presence was a deterrent. Now that Donny is cultured and no longer bullying, there is an opening for new bullies. The wolf describes it as "the chain of life." Finn tells Donny he must go back to being "jerk" Donny. Donny wants to stay nice. Finn tells Donny that everyone thinks his songs are dumb, trying to get him angry. It works. Donny gets angry and scares off the wolves. The house people hug him. Donny goes back to squeezing eggs out of chickens and announces he loves being a jerk.

Otis gets a message from his old bully saying he is coming back for a visit in *Back at the Barnyard's* "Brave Udders." Otis flashes back to getting beat up every day. The bully made Otis squirt on himself. Otis starts to build a barrier of barbed wire and sand bags. He then tries a disguise. The other animals encourage Otis to fight back. Otis goes online to buy a flame thrower. When that does not work, Otis packs his bags and buys a plane ticket. Krebs, the bully, turns out to be a small duck. His friends laugh at Otis since he is a full grown cow. Two of the animals taunt Krebs. Krebs warns them to cut it out. Krebs turns into a furious ball of energy that beats up all the animals. Otis jumps into the well to hide. Dr. Pig begins to give advice about handling bullies; however, Krebs crashes in and beats up Dr. Pig. Seeing his friends standing up to Krebs, Otis decides he needs to stand up, too. Otis throws Krebs around until Krebs spins him and throws him against the barn. Krebs asks Otis for forgiveness. Krebs claims he has been getting help for his anger issues. The episode is quite violent for children. It is also unlikely a child would understand the concept of anger management therapy.

Keeping with the cow theme, the old school bully in the animated series *Cow and Chicken* leaves town in the episode entitled "School Bully." A new bully moves in and grabs Cow and Chicken by the throats. He hoists them up the flagpole. A bigger bully comes along and cuts down the flag pole. He threatens the old bully and takes his locker. Cow and Chicken are rather sentimental about the old bully, Butch, saying he has been their bully since kindergarten. They reason that at least with the old bully they know what to expect. They reminisce about how original he was. Butch used to send them down a hill in a dumpster. They laugh hysterically. After the new bully comes and beats them up, they agree that it is "just not the same." The new bully jams a banana down Butch's throat when old bully confronts him. The gang goes to help Butch with no success. Chicken stabs the new bully with a pin, which deflates him. Then he stabs Butch with the pin and deflates him, too. Then he does it to his teacher and other friends and finally himself. They all become miniatures of themselves. A wimpy kid then declares himself the school bully. The moral of the story is similar to other comedies that define bullies as a sentimental part of life. The other lesson is that one better be careful about wanting the old bully gone because the next one could be worse.

In the much more sedate program *Babar*, Alexander is a little elephant who wants to be like everyone else. Since he is small, the other kids tease him. Babar, his father, tells him about his first day at human school as an elephant from the jungle in "School Days." Babar sees Francois, a small boy, not wearing his glasses because he is being teased by the school bullies, brothers Marcel and Maurice. When the teacher makes Francois put on his glasses, Marcel shakes his fist at him. Babar becomes the hit of the class because of the things he can do with his trunk. Maurice grabs Babar's trunk and will not let go. Marcel calls him a "nose hose," tugs on his ears, and pushes him down. The bullies pressure the other kids to laugh. Babar is upset that everyone laughed at him. The other kids lament how they are all victims of the bullies so they hide their differences. They tell Babar that if he tells the teacher, he will be in double trouble. The teacher appears competent but somehow does not notice the bullying. Babar refuses to give in to the bullies even when the bullies push him into a waste basket. That evening Babar tells his guardian that he does not want to go to school anymore. After some coaxing, he tells her that he is getting bullied because he is different. She tells him everyone is different and it will just take time. Babar comes up with a plan. He puts on a fake beard to hide his trunk. Unfortunately, Babar is allergic to the beard material. All his other disguises do not work. Every day the bullies tie his trunk in a knot. Babar stands up to bullies on fencing day at school. The other kids join in to help Babar defeat the bullies. After hearing the story of how his father handled the bullies, Alexander declares he will not get teased again and starts swinging around a pool stick. His parents lament that Alexander has not gotten the right message. The mother is going to try a different approach.

In *Fanboy & Chum Chum*'s "The Incredible Chulk," Chum Chum turns into a chulk like his ancestors. He becomes big and orange. He and Fanboy run into Boog, who is bopping the store owner on the head when the owner does not bow to him. Fanboy slaps Boog around then waits for Chulk to back him up. Chulk shrinks back to Chum Chum when he gets scared. Without Chum Chum's protection, Fanboy gets beat up. Fanboy tries to figure out how to change Chum Chum into a chulk again. They discover that Chum Chum turns into a chulk when he laughs. In a fit of laughter Chum Chum swings his fists, inadvertently bopping Boog. It stops Boog for the moment, but it looks pretty likely Boog will continue bullying in the future.

Fish Hooks has a reoccurring bully, Jocktopus. In the episode "Milo Gets a Ninja," Jackopus is bullying the other fish. He has one of his tentacles around Albert's neck, shaking him back and forth. Milo steps in to help but Jocktopus kicks him across the room. Milo asks a ninja to help him to establish justice in the school. The ninja makes Jocktopus cry and they put him in lockup. It works so well that Milo sics the ninja on his teacher for announcing a pop quiz. Power hungry, Milo puts everyone in fishbowls for potential violations. He ends up trapping Albert, whom he tried to save in the first place. Milo is shocked when his friends tell him he has become a bigger bully than Jocktopus. Jocktopus agrees he has never been that bad. Milo sees that he is wrong and gets rid of the ninja. The friends laugh and are glad things are back to normal until they see Jocktopus bullying Albert once again. In the episode "Happy Birthfish, Jocktopus," Jockopus invites the gang to his birthday party, or rather he demands they come. He threatens to pound them if they do not attend. The guests have to bring him presents. He yells at one kid for bringing him money and puts him in a box that reads "to be punched later." The gang is scared because they also brought him money. With no time to think, Milo and Bea offer Oscar as Joctopus' present. Jocktopus brings Oscar into his special room inside his school locker. Milo and Bea come to rescue Oscar with plane tickets and fake passports. Oscar puts Jocktopus on the clobber list causing Jocktopus to hit himself. He gets angry, relieves Oscar from his duties, and tells him to get out of his life.

In an episode of *Scaredy Squirrel* entitled "Way of the Fishlips," Rex, the bully, is a hugely muscular dog with an Austrian, Arnold Schwarzenegger-like accent. Squirrel is trash-talking about Rex when Rex comes back and hears. When Rex is holding Squirrel by his throat, Sally pokes Rex sending him flying. Rex threatens to hurt Squirrel the next time he sees him without his "girlfriend." In repeated scenes, Sally scares Rex away each time he picks on Squirrel. In one scene, Rex hides in the toilet to get to Squirrel. Sally flushes him. Sally has an accident and is no longer able to defend Squirrel. Sally has Squirrel learn Fish-foo (a version of Kung Foo). The old grand master puts him through exercises like the Karate Kid. Squirrel is able to beat Rex. It turns out that the grand master was actually old Uncle Carl and not a Kung Foo expert. Squirrel did not seem to mind having a girl protect him from the bully.

In *Sponge Bob Square Pants'* 'The Bully," the teacher introduces a new student, Flatts the Flounder, to the rest of the class. Flatts tells everyone that he likes to "kick peoples' butts." Flatts even bullies his own father. The hapless teacher laughs it off. After Flatts threatens Sponge Bob, Sponge Bob makes out his will. Flatts tries to run over Sponge Bob with a truck. Even when Flatts gets into an accident and Sponge Bob saves his life, he continues to bully Sponge Bob. When he finally catches up to Sponge Bob, he starts to punch him. Because Sponge Bob is a sponge, he does not feel any of the blows. Flatts continues to hit him until he is exhausted.

Older cartoons, particularly Looney Tunes and Hanna Barbera productions, were tailored for a duel audience, adults as well as children. The bullies and the victims are mostly adults as well. In the first example, *Looney Tunes All Stars'* "Alpine Antics," the big bully is lurking behind a tree smoking a cigar. Beans is getting ready for a ski race. The bully comes out and breaks Beans' skis. Beans makes a pair of skis out of the sled and reenters the competition. The bully is surprised to see Beans at the starting line. The bully pulls Beans' hat over his eyes and puts a rocket on Beans' skis, sending Beans backwards into a building. Next the bully puts a rope across the path so other skiers fall into the snow bank. The plan backfires and Beans is able to use the rope to tie up the bully. Beans wins the race.

Tom and Jerry Tales' episode "Beach Bully Bingo" also has a rather adult theme. Two bullies, one cat and one dog, intrude on Tom and Jerry's beach experience. The bullies throw Tom and Jerry into a trash can. The bullies get competitive and turn on each other. Tom whispers in the cat bully's ear and Jerry into the dog bully's ear. They put up a ring and duke it out. In the end, an octopus strangles them both as Tom and Jerry enjoy themselves on the beach with an attractive female cat and female mouse.

Inglis (2011) suggested using the story of *Rudolph the Red Nosed Reindeer* as a teaching moment for children about bullies and being true to their uniqueness. Santa and Donner are insensitive to Rudolph's red nose (although I am not sure it should be considered bullying as Inglis, 2011). Many of the residents of the North Pole are initially intolerant of "different." The head elf raises his voice to Herbie, who wants to be a dentist. He tells Herbie that Herbie cannot take a break and threatens to fire him if he does not finish his job in the allotted time. Over at the reindeer games, Fireball invites Rudolph to play with him. Clarice tells Rudolph he talks funny but she does not mind. Everyone is impressed when Rudolph can fly; however, when his nose cover falls off, everyone laughs and calls him names. Santa scolds Donner for hiding his son's nose. The coach leads the group in excluding Rudolf from the reindeer games. Clarice, who can see past Rudolph's nose, stands by him. Clarice's father, who is not as open-minded as his daughter, forbids her from seeing Rudolph. When Herbie and Rudolph return as heroes, everyone has second thoughts about misfits. The lesson is that the adults are the ones who teach bullying and meanness. The show first aired in 1964 in the midst of the Civil Rights Movement.

ANIMATED ACTION

In the animated action series *Jackie Chan Adventures*, Maynard, a big bully, grabs his smaller victim and shakes free his lunch money. Jade tells Maynard to stop. He calls her a "shrimp" so she gives him a wedgie. Although his mother told him to never hit girls, he tells her is he going to make an exception. She kicks him, knocking him out. It is Jade, not the bully, who gets in trouble with the principal. Jackie is called into the principal's office. Jackie reminds Jade that martial arts are only for discipline. He tells her to watch her temper. Later, Maynard confronts Jade in the hall. She runs, not wanting to fight and disobey Jackie. The bully does not want to fight but wants Jade to teach him some martial arts moves. When Jade gets in a disagreement over a ball with another boy, it is the bully who stops them and tells them not to fight.

In the animated series *Kick Buttowski: Suburban Daredevil*, the title character Kick is bullied by his older brother Brad. Brad has spiked hair and dark coloring around his eyes to make him look more menacing. In the episode "Drop Kick," Brad is out of control. He stabs Kick's hand with a fork when he tries to eat, throws him in the trash can, and trips him on his skateboard. There appears to be no adult supervision. When he attempts to take wrestling lessons, the teacher refuses to let him in the school because Kick is a younger brother. However, there is an annex where the teacher's younger brother, a washed-up wrestler nicknamed Paper Cut, agrees to train Kick. Kick breaks the fourth wall and talks directly to the audience, telling them to "get ready for the training montage." The episode becomes a spoof of the Karate Kid film genre. Kick helps Paper Cut fight his older brother. It turns out Brad has been training with Paper Cut's older brother in the main gym. Kick uses his skateboard and beats Brad. Paper Cut gains confidence and beats his older brother, too. In the second season of the show, Brad appears to still be bullying Kick. In "Luigi Vendetta," Brad has ripped Kick's clothes off and given him a wedgie so hard that it ripped off his underwear. He kicks Kick across the mall. He hangs Kick upside down on a clothesline and contemplates how he is going to hit him next. Kick goes to Luigi for help. Luigi is a little, mafia-looking guy. Brad calls Luigi a "shrimp." Luigi breaks into song about how big brothers should be role models. Brad just laughs. Luigi does not stop singing until Brad gets so annoyed that he gives up. Brad promises to be the best older brother.

ANIMATED SCI-FI AND FANTASY

Many of the animated shows have an element of science fiction or fantasy. For example, the main character has magic powers or robots to help deal with the bullies. In *Chalk-*

Zone, "Disappearing Act," Reggie, the bully, becomes angry when Rudy plays a practical joke using his magic chalk and ruins Reggie's magic trick. The teacher, who has been grading papers wearing headphones, finally pays attention and sends Reggie to the principal's office. The principal does not look surprised to see Reggie. She pulls out his file, which is a huge stack of papers. She calls Reggie's father in to the office. When Rudy discovers that he got Reggie into trouble, he feels bad that he humiliated him. He explains that he just wanted to teach Reggie a lesson not to be mean. He admits he is just as big of a bully as Reggie. Rudy fixes the magic trick and lets Reggie save face. At first Reggie's father is angry that he has been called in to the principal's office; however, his mood changes when the kids in the class tell him what a good magician Reggie is. His dad tells Reggie he is proud of him. Reggie is now nice and asks Rudy to be his assistant in future magic shows.

The title character of *Danny Phantom* has special powers. He is able to change into a phantom and time travel. In "Splitting Images," a ghost trashes Danny's locker so Danny has to take locker 724. Rumor has it the owner of the locker, Poindexter, was severely bullied when he was in school and now haunts it. The jocks in letter jackets throw Danny into the locker. Danny changes into a phantom and makes the lead bully walk into the lockers. Later, when Danny sees the bullies playing keep away with a tuba player and AV equipment guy, bad things begins happening to the bullies. It is Poindexter getting revenge on the bullies. For example, Poindexter makes a jock spill his tray on a female bully. One of the jocks throws food at Danny. Danny gets revenge by giving the jock a wedgie and putting frogs in his pants. Thinking that Danny is the bully, Poindexter confronts Danny. Danny laments how he used his powers for evil and became the bully himself. At the end of the episode, Danny gets a new locker, and the jocks go back to bullying him.

The bully in *My Life as a Teenage Robot*'s "Attack of the 5½ Foot Geek" holds Sheldon upside down in shop class and steals his batteries. The shop teacher appears oblivious when the bully and his friends play keep away with Sheldon. A robot named Jenny saves Sheldon from the bullies. Usually boys are quite sensitive about getting saved by a girl; however, Sheldon becomes smitten with Jenny and follows her around like a puppy. The kids tease her for having a new "pet." They all chant, "Jenny's got a boyfriend." The teacher, who did nothing about the previous bullying, asks the class to please wait until after school to ridicule Jenny about her new boyfriend.

In *The Adventures of Jimmy Neutron*'s "Safety First," Jimmy has his lunch stolen by a bully named Terry. Terry has a unibrow, gap between his teeth, and an exposed butt crack. Jimmy tells his friends that he needs the extra energy from the lunch for when Terry puts him in the dumpster. The girls tell Jimmy he has to tell a teacher or his parents. Jimmy says he will tell eventually but hopes Terry will get tired of bullying him. Pushed to the edge when Terry puts glue in his backpack and plays bongos with his stomach, Jimmy creates an anti-bully device, a spaceship that spins and kicks Terry. The kids cheer Jimmy as he walks down the hallway. When a classmate congratulates Jimmy with a friendly punch on the arm, the spaceship douses the boy with itching powder. The spaceship goes after Jimmy's teacher when the teacher corrects Jimmy. Soon all the kids are fearful of Jimmy and the spaceship. Jimmy realizes he has become the bully.

In "Kung Timmy," an episode of *The Fairly OddParents*, Francis, the reoccurring bully, holds Timmy upside down, making his lunch money fall out of his pockets. When Tootie stands up for him, Francis teases Timmy about letting a girl fight his battles. Timmy's father comes along and demands the bully let go of Timmy and return the lunch money. In the next scene, the father is flying through the air. The bully eventually evicts the entire family from their house, taking the deed. The father tries teaching Timmy Kung Fu from the book *Stupid Dad's Guide to Teaching his Weak and Defenseless Son Kung Fu.* The first rule listed in the book is to use Kung Fu for self-defense and not vengeance. Timmy disregards the rule and wants to beat up the bully. Timmy wishes for Kung Fu powers and takes out an entire class of Billy Blank's Tao-Bo students. He comes back to his house to confront the bully, but fails. His powers will not let him fight because he is not following the self-defense-only rule. When Francis grabs Tootie by the neck, Timmy fights to defend her. The family gets their house and car back. The father is shown bossing Francis around as he is washing the graffiti off the house from a wheelchair.

In *The Grim Adventures of Billy and Mandy's* "Billy and the Bully," a boy runs by Billy with his underwear over his head. Billy also gets a wedgie from the bully. Billy goes to the Grim Reaper for advice and asks the Reaper to intervene. The Reaper creates a fire to scare the bully but the bully ends up scaring the Reaper instead. When the bully is caught stealing milk from a baby, Mandy stands up to the bully. The bully backs down. Billy scolds Mandy for being mean. The bully cries and tells them all he wants is to be loved. Billy gives him a handkerchief and offers to be friends, which they do in the end. It is unusual for a female to be accused of being the aggressive party in this genre.

In *The Replacements'* "The Insecurity Guard; Quiet Riot," Buzz, the bully, steps on Todd's new shoes. Todd is pretty average, red hair and freckles, but his friends are very nerdy. For example, one kid has buck teeth, glasses, and big ears. Just then a bigger bully, Donny, comes along and scares off Buzz. Donny puts Todd in a trash can, kicks it out the building, and steals Todd's new shoes. The school security guard is inept and does nothing to help. Todd's father is incompetent so he asks his mother for help. However, she is very odd as well. Todd's sister invites Donny over so he and Todd can work out their differences. Behind closed doors there are sounds of a beating. Todd emerges with scratches and bruises on his face. A robot takes over as security guard and beats up Donny. Unknowingly, Todd takes over the role of bully with the robot's help. When the robot goes after Todd's sister, Todd stands up to the robot. Once the robot is destroyed, Buzz takes his place as bully again and social order is restored.

"BULLIES," as in the *Codename Kids Next Door* stands for "big ugly lunks like intimidating entrapped scaredycats." The episode "Operation BULLIES," begins with a boy named Jerry who has created "Bully Island" where he has collected bullies and put them in cages. He uses electric shocks to keep the bullies in line. His goal is to see what makes them tick so he can create a new strain of bully to give victims a chance. He set up dummies, which the bullies hit with spit wads. If there is a break in the system, Jerry has a device that projects a hologram of the middle school's principal to scare them. Numbuh 4 and Numbuh 2 are called to the island to rescue Jerry's sister; however, it is a trick. Jerry wants revenge on Numbuh 4 for a previous wedgie Numbuh 4 gave him in first grade. The wedgie was so bad, the doctors were unable to remove his underwear. Jerry has to endure a permanent wedgie. Numbuh 4 gets attacked by one of the bullies, Wedgy-saurus. To stop Wedgy-saurus, Numbuh 2 offers to do his homework. The bullies eventually get loose and go after Jerry. Numbuh 4 and Numbuh 2 escape from the island, leaving Jerry with the bullies.

In *Jumanji: Animated,* "Masked Identity," Peter and his sister enter a magic world of fantasy. In between adventures, the bully, Rock, and his cronies ask Peter if he wants to play football. To play, they tell Peter he must get their ball out of a tree. Peter falls in a mud puddle and the other kids laugh. When Peter asks which team he is on, the bullies push him back into the mud puddle and tell him that no team wants him. Later, Rock again tells Peter he can play if he gets their ball. Peter says, "No way," now that he has gained courage from his adventures in Jumanji. When the bullies chase Peter, Peter steps aside, causing the bullies to fall into the mud puddle.

In *Yu-Gi-Oh! Zexal*'s "Go With the Flow," Yuma's friend Brunk loses his deck of role-playing cards to the school bully, Shark. Brunk explains to Yuma that he had to play Shark because Shark called him a "big chicken." Yuma challenges Shark to a game in order to win Brunk's cards back. Shark grabs Yuma's necklace with a key his parents gave him. Shark drops the key, smashes it with his heel, and kicks it off the stairs. Yuma is angry and declares that the feud is no longer about the deck of cards. Shark needs to be taught a lesson about treating other people with respect. The two-part episode contains a significant amount of fighting, although it is mostly between the role-playing characters. Yuma is victorious in the end. He gets his key and Brunk's cards back.

Pokemon: Black & White is a similar animated series featuring a role-playing card game. Glen, the bully in "Rival Destinies: Battling the Bully," challenges Mick, a small boy with glasses, to a battle. Glen threatens to drag Mick to the game if Mick does not show up. Glen wears a tank top and a bandana on his head. His sidekick Shawn is smaller and wears a vest and tie. Glen bosses Shawn around. Mick asks the gang if he can borrow Pikachu, a character from the game, to battle the bullies. The gang agrees and trains Mick. After Mick wins, Glen comes at him with his fists up and says, "Hey punk, I don't remember telling you you can beat me." Shawn stops Glen from hitting Mick. Shawn tells Glen he does not want to hang around him anymore. Glen apologizes in the end and makes up with Mick and Shawn. The lesson is to battle "fair and square." The episode is very similar to *Yu-Gi-Oh! Zexal*. The regular kid challenges the bully to a game. They use their brains to outwit the bully.

Dino Squad features a parallel world where five teenagers have to fend off bullies in civilian life and protect the planet in their roles as superhero dinosaurs. In the episode "Bully 4 U," the bully, McFinn, has an eyebrow piercing and wears a hoodie. He pushes Buzz into the lockers and asks him if he brought "cookies from his mommy." He tells Buzz that he looks stupid and that makes him mad. McFinn and his cronies call Buzz "freak boy." Buzz fantasizes about going "dino" on him; however, he knows he cannot reveal his powers. When the bully jokes about Buzz in class, all the other students laugh except for Fiona, who stands up for Buzz. Roger, another boy in Dino Squad, had teased Buzz in the past but now stopped. Roger presents Buzz with the dilemma of whether or not to use force to combat a bully. Fiona is proud of Buzz for having self-control. The squad tries to teach Buzz to be more confident, to have a more confident stance, and make eye contact. Fiona gives him a lecture on the cycle of violence when dealing with bullies. The squad suggests Buzz tell the principal or his parents. Buzz tells them that when he tries to avoid McFinn, McFinn follows him. Buzz finally stands up to McFinn. McFinn's cronies taunt McFinn about Buzz talking back. They shout, "Don't take that from him." When Buzz's pet snake crawls on McFinn, McFinn screams. His cronies walk away and call McFinn a "coward." Buzz assures McFinn that his snake will not hurt him. McFinn pets the snake, declaring it "cool." Buzz tells him he should never judge things or people by the way they look. McFinn realizes what it must feel like when he teased Buzz and has a change of heart. The principal comes in and sets up a meeting between Buzz, his parents, McFinn, and his parents. Buzz says he would like that very much. This show goes further than the other shows with its lessons. It does not simply use the bullying as a subplot. The characters are more intense and less cartoonish than most live-actor shows even though it is animated. Buzz appears more upset by the bullying than other victims. The principal also gets more involved and follows through with a meeting between the parents, even though it appears the boys have resolved their differences.

LIVE-ACTOR SCI-FI AND FANTASY

There is a subgenre of action programs for kids that feature live actors which includes *Power Rangers: Dino Thunder*. A bully, Derek, kicks a ball that knocks the laptop out of Ethan's hands in the episode "Bully for Ethan." Derek calls Ethan a "geek" when he tries to talk to him about his laptop. He tells Ethan it is his field and he can kick the ball wherever he wants. He goes to hit Ethan but the other players on the field hold him back. Derek later trips Ethan in class. The teacher gives Derek detention. Ethan refuses to use his Dino-power to fight Derek. He tells the other power rangers there are other ways to deal with bullies. Ethan makes Derek a proposition: if he can improve Derek's soccer game, they do not have to fight. Ethan shows Derek a computer graphic of what his kicking form looks like and what it should look like. When the adjustment works and improves Derek's game; Derek apologizes to Ethan for the bullying. Derek confesses that he did not think a brain like Ethan would want to talk to him.

Tattooed Teenage Alien Fighters From Beverly Hills, a clear knockoff of the *Power Rangers*, dealt with bullying in the episode "Bully for You." The bully, Dwight, demands Swinton give him his physics class notes. Swinton refuses because it is against school policy. Initially Swinton pushes back until he realizes he is in danger of revealing his super powers. He retreats to his nerdy self. Laurie, the artist of the fighters, asks Gordon, the jock, if they should do something to intervene. Gordon fears it will attract too much attention. Swinton later loses his confidence and his power to fight as his alter ego Apollo. The other three fighters must help Swinton get his confidence back. First, Drew fakes not being able to work the espresso machine. When Swinton tries to help, he breaks it. Laurie then tries to set him up with a girl by promising her to babysit her little brother if she says yes to a date. Swinton gets so flustered while asking her out she refuses. He tells his fellow fighters to accept that he is a "loser." The kids then plot to get Apollo's confidence back by having Gordon pretend he is the creature, Culebra, and allow Apollo to defeat him. When the real Culebra shows up, Apollo is able to defeat him. The next time he sees Dwight, Swinton feels he has powers from Apollo. When Swinton refuses to give Dwight the notes, Dwight hits Swinton but hurts his own hand.

The Troop is a collection of four high school students who are part of a secret global society. Felix has glasses and is described as the nerd of the school. One of the reoccurring bullies is Alejandro, who is larger than his victims and appears simple minded. The episode "Unpleasantville" begins with Alejandro hitting Felix in the head with a cell phone. The bully demands $5 or he will give Felix an atomic swirly. When Felix tries to stand up to him, Alejandro grabs Felix's finger and squeezes it. Finally, Hayley, another troop member, comes and stands up to the bully. A swarm of flies comes and attacks the bully turning him into a zombie and making him and the other bullies nice. Alejandro hands Felix all the money he has taken from him since the third grade. He hugs Felix and apologizes for bullying. After the troop destroys the monster who is responsible for the swarm, things go back to normal. Bullies are once again harassing victims in the hallways, holding one kid upside down and shaking him.

In the next season's episode, "The Monster Within," Alejandro challenges Felix to a fight. A creature goes after a fly that has landed on Alejandro. The creature accidently knocks Alejandro out just as Felix takes a swing. Felix, having gotten credit of winning the fight, is invited to sit at the cool kids' lunch table. When Felix sees another boy in a headlock, he stands up to the bully. The bully runs away. Even though Felix finds out he did not knock out the bully, he still has the confidence to stand up to yet another bully who is giving a boy a wedgie. In another storyline in "The Monster Within," a new girl in a leather jacket causes havoc in the lunchroom. She yells at the lunch lady and knocks over food trays when they run out of burgers. She takes one of the muffins without paying. She gets into a food fight with one of the troop members, Hayley. As they are both serving detention, she calls Hayley "princess" and mocks her. When Hayley stands up to her, they become friends. They commiserate about being strong, smart, and beautiful girls. When the cheerleaders invite Hayley to a party, Hayley stands up for the new girl who was excluded. The new girl is actually the creature that knocked out Alejandro in the earlier episode. Hayley, in her troup persona, fights the creature. She eventually lets the girl get away, realizing that it is difficult to be stuck in two worlds, part human and part creature. When Hayley sees the girl back in school, they share a knowing nod.

In "No More Master Nice Guy," a bullied kid named Gus discovers that he has powers. Gus takes over Alejandro's extortion ring. He becomes the bully of the school and the troop's nemesis. Gus gets upset when Hayley spurns his advances. When he discovers that Hayley is part of the troop, he threatens to destroy them. They fight and the troop wins. After the fight, Gus's powers appear to be gone and his memory erased. The plot follows the fantasy of the bullied becoming the bully.

One of the sci-fi action series is based on *The Haunting Hour* novels by R.L. Stine. In "Stormin' Norman," Norman uses his command over bugs to retaliate against a bully. The bully hits Norman, a nerdy kid, with a rubber band during science class while a video on bugs plays. Some of the other boys laugh. The bully threatens to squash Norman like a bug if he does not stop turning around. The teacher does nothing to address the bullying problem. Norman retaliates by making fun of the bully's grades, while the boys in the class laugh again. The teacher tells everyone they should be like Norman, who is excited about the bug project. The class groans. In the next scene, three boys are dunking Norman's head in the toilet because they claim he was "sucking up" to the teacher and being a general pest. Norman shouts after them that they cannot push him around. When the bullies come back, Norman recants and tells them they can push him around. The bully steals Norman's bug journal and mocks him in front of all the kids. No one helps Norman as the bully rips the pages of the journal. Later, Norman catches a praying mantis that appears to be the leader of the bugs. All the bugs now follow Norman's command. When the bully gives Norman a wedgie in the school hallway, Norman unleashes countless bugs on the bully. The bully cries for help. Norman demands the bully give himself a wedgie. As Norman walks down the hall, all the kids stand back in fear. Norman, thinking he is invincible, starts crushing the bugs. The praying mantis does not look happy. That night, bugs start to congregate outside Norman's bedroom window. When Norman starts to bully the praying mantis, the bugs attack Norman. The moral of the story is to not abuse power, especially when the perpetrator has been the victim.

In another episode of R.L. Stine's *The Haunting Hour* entitled "The Dead Body," Will is walking down the hall and accidently bumps into a bully. Will tries to apologize, but the bully whacks him on the head. The other boys laugh. Will sees a mysterious older boy, Jake, in a leather jacket is standing outside the school. On Will's walk home, one of the bullies scares Will with a mask. The next day as Will is asking a girl to a dance, bullies throw water on Will's crotch. Jake appears again and tells Will that the bullies will not stop until someone makes them. Jake tells him he will take care of the bullies if Will promises to do something for him later. They make a deal. On a field trip, the bullies once again pick on Will. The boys find a dead body. The bully makes Will touch the body. The body is really Jake. The bullies run scared. While Will is willing to put the bully matter to rest, Jake is not finished. Travis, one of the bullies, is dragged off screaming by an invisible spirit. Later, the janitor tells Will that Jake died in 1961, thirty-nine years earlier. The janitor explains that some jocks were picking on Jake. When Jake played a trick on them, it just made them angrier. To get back at Jake, the jocks threw firecrackers at the spring dance. The school caught on fire and Jake was killed. Jake reminds Will he still owes him a favor. Will finds himself back in 1961. The jocks lock Jake in the equipment locker. Will gets the lock off but gets caught in the fire. Will wakes up to find his is back in the present. He goes to the dance but his date cannot see him. She is with Jake, as he has taken over Will's body. The moral of this episode is to be careful about how far victims will go to retaliate against their persecutors. Both stories are cautionary tales of going too far to get rid of bullies. They start out as fantasies about the weaker victim getting back at their bullies through supernatural means.

EDUCATIONAL PROGRAMS

Educational programs, specifically those airing on PBS, balance the educational component with entertainment. Binky, the bully in the animated series *Arthur*, steals lunches from students in the school cafeteria. In the episode "Bully for Binky," Arthur recalls to his friend that Binky has always been the biggest bully in school, even in preschool. Binky would do things like steal all the crayons and not share. Binky once stood in front of Arthur to block his view during a parade. Binky is larger than all the other characters because he was held back a grade. Arthur calls for an "anti-Binky plan." One idea the victims have is to feed Binky until he gets so full he cannot chase them. Binky continues to bully until a new girl, Sue Ellen, who is taking taekwondo, stands up to him. She calls Binky a "clumsy oaf." He retaliates and calls her a "pipsqueak." Sue Ellen challenges Binky to a fight, but he keeps not showing up. Arthur and his friend are happy that Binky is getting a taste of his own medicine. Binky confides in them that he has never fought anyone before because they have always run away. He argues that bullying is the one thing he is good at. Since he does not want to fight her, Binky plans to humiliate Sue Ellen in a music recital. When Sue Ellen turns out to be a better musician than Binky, he gets jealous and leaves the hall. Arthur explains to Binky that being the best is not the most important thing. Binky is afraid kids will laugh at him if he does not beat them. Binky returns to the stage and plays a duet with Sue Ellen. The next day Binky is back to his old ways of stealing lunches. Sue Ellen arrives and deters him, still ready to fight. Arthur deems her the anti-Binky weapon. It is unusual in an educational program for the bully not to learn a lesson. It appears the only thing stopping him from bullying is fear of a girl.

At the park, a bully takes Bali's ball in the episode of *Bali* titled "You're Mean." The bully is a rhino with a sleeveless shirt and skullcap or do-rag. Bali lies to his grandmother, telling her he lost his ball. Bali wants his grandmother to come and watch as he plays. He runs into the bully again. This time the bully will not let Bali use the slide. Bali lies again and tells the bully he does not like the slide. Bali also sees the bully bullying other kids. Bali goes straight to his room when he gets home. Instead of going back to the park, he wants to stay in bed where he feels safe. He fantasizes about a super hero, Robobear, coming to the rescue. Robobear tells the kids they are all going to stop the bully together. When the kids should put on earmuffs and ignore the bully, the bully starts to shrink. The next time Bali and his friend run into the bully, Bali gets up the courage to stand up to him. The kids ignore the bully and continue to play on the slide. Bali tells the bully if he was nicer they could play together. The bully has a change of heart and becomes their friend. The lesson is that sometimes bullies just needs a friend and they are being mean to get attention.

In the episode "The Bully and the Bunny" of the PBS series *Maya & Miguel*, a new boy, Jimmy, moves in across the street. Jimmy is a little rough but Maya has a soft spot for him. Jimmy overhears one of the boys make fun of his size. Jimmy gets upset when he loses a video game and breaks the game out of frustration. The group labels him a "bully" against Maya's judgment. There are rumors that Jimmy got kicked out of his last school for bullying. Jimmy is quite grumpy because he thinks the other kids are making fun of him. Even Maya eventually admits he must be a bully. When Maya sees Jimmy being gentle with a bunny, she changes her mind. Jimmy confesses to the other kids that because he is big, strong, and shy, people assume he is a bully. The story is a case of self-fulfilling prophecy. Because Jimmy is large, other kids assume he is a bully and treat him poorly. Because he is treated poorly, Jimmy acts out.

"The Good Birds' Club" segment of *Sesame Street* teaches children how to recognize and combat bullying and relational aggression. The segment begins with two little birds who are excited that Big Bird wants to join their club. However, the bully bird wants to exclude Big Bird. He arbitrarily picks a reason to exclude Big Bird. The bully tells Big Bird that his feet are too big. Even though Elmo and Abby tell him his feet are just the right size, Big Bird wants to make his feet smaller because he wants to be part of the Good Birds' Club. He asks Abby, who is a fairy, to cast a spell to make his feet smaller. Big Bird returns to the club with his new small feet. The bully bird still refuses to let him in. This time, the excuse is that the rest of him is still big. The two other birds reluctantly agree. The bully calls him "Big Goofball" and "Big Foot." Big Bird now begs Abby to make him smaller. He goes back again. Now the bully bird says he cannot be in the club because he has yellow feathers. Abby turns him blue. When they reject Big Bird again, Abby and Elmo tell a grownup. The grownup tells Big Bird that he is being bullied. The grownup suggests they make their own club that includes everyone and accepts each member just the way they are. Big Bird, Abby, and Elmo create the "Happy to Be Me" club. Big Bird has Abby change him back to big and yellow. The two birds want to join because in the new club no one gets yelled at or made fun of like they did in the old club. Big Bird accepts them into the club. The bully threatens to throw the birds out of the Good Birds' Club forever. The bully gets frustrated and flies away, saying he does not need any of them.

Sesame Street has aired other bullying segments. In "Bully at a Baseball Game," a bully puts his foot on the ball and will not give it back when the baseball is hit out into the field. One player imagines different strategies to get the ball back, such as threatening the bully with his slingshot, bribing the bully with an ice cream cone, and using his dog. He chooses the dog option. The dog growls and scares away the bully. The boy retrieves the ball and gets the player out and is a hero. The message is one of finding a bigger bully to scare away the original bully. In another segment, one of the monsters takes the ball and will not give it back to the other monsters who were playing with it. One of the other monsters calls him a bully. Not knowing what a bully is, the other monsters sing a song to explain. In the song, the monsters tell the first monster that if he is going to be a bully, they cannot be friends. The first monster sings he will share with the other monsters and not be bully. They all play together in the end.

Ernie and Bert learn a lesson about bullies. While on the beach, a bully in a leather jacket walks by and knocks over Bert's sand castle. Ernie scolds the bully. The bully grabs the towel around Ernie's neck and introduces himself as "Tough Eddie" because he is tough. The bully shows his fist to Ernie and says, "If your friend is angry because I knocked over his sand castle, tell him I got 'something' for him." Ernie wakes up Bert from his nap. When Ernie tells Bert the story, Bert gets nervous and hides, thinking that "something" is going to be a violent act. The "something" Eddie has for Bert is an ice cream cone. Instead of beating up Bert as he and Ernie feared, Eddie apologizes for knocking over the sand castle. The lesson is not to bully but also not to judge people by their appearance.

RELIGIOUS PROGRAMS

I found two examples of religious programming that addressed bullying. An episode of *Veggie Tales: Minnesota Cuke* teaches kids how to deal with bullies from a Christian perspective. When the neighborhood bully, Gordon, comes to the playground, he asks Junior what Junior is doing on "his" playground. Gordon claims that no one is allowed to play on his playground unless he says so. Junior fantasizes about being big and strong so he could fight the bully. Then he dreams that they are in outer space and he zaps Gordon, thus saving the universe. Junior tells his dad about Gordon. His dad tells him about when he was bullied as a child. The dad hid and tried to ignore the bully but it did not work. Finally, he faced up to the bully. The dad admitted he got "pounded" but told his son he was never picked on again because the bully knew he was not afraid of him. The dad tells Junior that God gives them a spirit of courage and, therefore, Junior should stand up for himself. If that does not work, he advises Junior to turn the other cheek. When Junior gets to the playground, Gordon knocks him down again. Junior stands up and tells Gordon that it does not matter how many times he beats him, he is going to keep coming back. Junior then invites Gordon to play with them. Gordon refuses the invitation and says he will enjoy beating Junior up every day. When the other veggies back up Junior, Gordon says the playground is lame and goes home to play video games.

The children's program *Davey and Goliath* is produced by the Evangelical Lutheran Church. In the episode "Bully Up a Tree," Davey stops a boy who is about to shoot his dog, Goliath, with a slingshot. The boys exchange punches. The bully runs away when he sees Davey's grandfather. Davey says he sure wishes he could get even with the bully. His grandfather tells him it is easy to hate but hard to love those who are mean. He asks Davey what he thinks God would want him to do. He tells Davey those who hurt us the most need our love the most. Later, Davey and his friend Tom run into the bully at the fishing hole. The bully pushes Tom into the water. The bully corners a wild pig and shoots at him. The pig gets mad and chases the bully up a tree. When the bully's foot gets stuck, Davey's first impulse is to leave him there. Davey remembers back to what his grandfather said. Goliath chases away the pig and Davey helps the bully get his foot unstuck. The bully confesses to Davey that other kids usually run away from him. He introduces himself as Jerry. Jerry tells Goliath that they are friends now. Jerry also apologizes to Tom.

Jerry goes fishing with them. Davey tells his grandfather that Jerry really isn't a bully; he just didn't have anyone to play with.

SKETCH COMEDIES

You Can't Do That on Television was a 1980s sketch comedy show targeted to early teens that aired on Nickelodeon. Each episode revolved around a different theme. In the episode on bullying, one of the male performers claims he does not get bullied because he studied the martial arts for two years. Another boy says he did, too; however, the first boy teases him that playing the piccolo in the school band does not count as martial arts. In the opening skit, a man dressed as a South American dictator orders a firing squad to shoot a prisoner. Another boy, Alistair, comes and bullies the dictator. When the firing squad misses, Alistair bullies the firing squad. In another skit, Kevin returns to the locker room with a black eye. He jokes that he has been studying martial arts but it did not help because the bully was not holding a piece of wood. When Kevin is late coming outside to meet the bully for a fight, the bully sadly laments that it is always the bully that has to stand outside waiting in the pouring rain. Alistair says he is bullied in real life yet still likes getting to play a bully on the show. When the cast members interview real kids on the street, two boys laugh at how fun it is to bully others. Another bully declares that when he bosses others around they do what he tells them. It is a very odd episode with a rather pro-bullying message.

The Amanda Show was another Nickelodeon sketch comedy show. In a 1999 episode, Amanda and another female cast member dress up like stereotypical boy bullies, Jack and Jake, with a jean jacket, a leather jacket, and bandanas. They attempt to bully their classmates and teachers; however, in a comical twist, none of their bullying works. Instead, Jack and Jake get bullied by their targets. First of all, a couple of girls stuff them in lockers after the bullies try flirting with them. When they demand a nerdy boy, Marvin, give them his lunch money, Marvin thumps them on their heads. Then the bullies try to tag the school hallway with graffiti, but it turns out their spray paint is the same color as the walls. As a finale, they try to bully a baby in a carriage but the baby urinates in their faces. The star Amanda Bynes is a very cute, thin girl. She is not glamorous and often plays more of a tomboy than a fashion princess. She is very relatable to young girls.

Mad About is a production of the National Theater for Children. The skit "Bully for You" is about reverse bullying. The nerdy guy, Perry, is overly stereotypical with taped glasses, a speech impediment, a shirt buttoned up all the way, and a pocket protector. At first it looks as though the Perry is scared of a cheerleader and two jocks as they walk down the hall toward his locker. He fumbles with his books. He suddenly gains confidence and begins to bully the cool kids. He pushes the books out of the cheerleaders' hands. He pressures them to give him their lunch money. Perry even bullies the teacher and the security guard who try to stop him. He talks with her other nerd friends in the library, who are also overly stereotyped. The girl is wearing glasses and a neck brace. One boy has Spock ears and a Star Trek shirt. Another boy is gender ambiguous and Goth. They are concerned about Perry being too hard on the athletes. The girl tells Perry not to call them "jocks" as she takes a whiff off her inhaler. They ask Perry to imagine what if the roles were reversed and the athletes were the popular ones. He snorts with laughter. Perry promises to take it easy on the athletes. Near the end of the skit, an athlete hacks into Perry's computer and interrupts his role-playing game. Perry throws a fit as the athlete smiles with revenge. It is perhaps a fantasy that gives hope to the nerds that one day they may be in a position to be the bully. The intended lesson appears to be that no one should bully.

INSTRUCTIONAL VIDEOS

The video version of *Bullies Are a Pain in the Brain* is based on the book by Trevor Romain. In the instructional video, Trevor talks to his cartoon creations as they go through a day of junior high. Trevor coaches the kids and points out educational moments. Jack wants to stay home from school. He hides his money in his shoe after Henry, the bully, has pushed him into garbage cans and smashed cafeteria food in his face. He is embarrassed to tell his friend Skye. Skye is surprised how small Henry, the bully, is. Skye remembers back to when she was mean to a girl when she was younger. She called the girl names and got all the other kids to ignore her. She denies being a bully because she never hit the girl. The other kids on the bus laugh when Henry mocks Jack, takes his lunch money, and slaps him around. There appears to be no teachers around. Ignoring the bully appears to make things worse. Jack tries teasing Henry back with no success. Henry defaces Jack's campaign posters and tags his locker. Fighting back does not work either. Even when Henry knocks him out and sends Jack to the nurse's office, no one intervenes. When Jack stands up to Henry and tells Henry that he could not care less about what he thinks, the kids on the playground clap. When Jack makes jokes at Henry's expense, the crowd laughs and Henry runs off. Trevor advises Jack to be the bigger person and go talk to Henry. Henry confesses he was only bullying to try to make friends. Jack gives a lecture about bullying to the student body at the end.

Movies

Surprisingly, very few children's movies meet the definition of adolescent bullies and mean girls. The exceptions were *A Little Princess*, *The Bratz Babyz: The Movie*, *The Ant Bully*, and *Toy Story*. Movies such as *Matilda* and *Annie* had mean characters; however, they were grown women. It is interesting to note that although Disney animation movies are targeted kids, a significant percentage of them do not include children in major roles. Many of the animated Disney-type movies have adult villains rather than child bullies. The only three adolescent bullies that stood out were Mullet Boy in the *Ant Bully*, Sid in *Toy Story*, and Alvin in *Paranorman*.

Bratz Babyz: TheMovie features twin sisters Nina and Norah. Nina is very bossy to her twin sister Norah. When Norah accidently brings their puppy to the mall, the puppy gets away. A bully gets a hold of the puppy. He tries to sell it back to the girls for $50. They must win a Karoke contest to win the $50 to pay the bully. The bully is big kid with spiky hair and spaces between his teeth. Half the Babyz want to stand up to the bully. The other half do not think they should. The bully steals an ice cream cone from another little boy. One of the Babyzs' male friends is lowered down to try to steal the puppy back. The bully takes the boy and flings him into the bushes. The bully also takes the change that fell out of the boy's pocket. The bully then steals some girls' nachos. When one of the twins steals the puppy back, the bully goes after her but is stopped by security at the movie theater. The girls win the karaoke contest. Just as Norah is handing the money over to the bully, Nina stops her and tells her not to give in to the bully. She gives the bully a piece of her mind instead. She stops him physically. The rest of the kids join her. The bully starts to sweat. When the puppy gets nervous and urinates on the bully, the bully drops her. The kids surround the bully and he begs to be let go. He runs off crying.

In the movie *Matilda*, the title character comes from an abusive family. Matilda's mother and father refuse to let her go to school. They punish her for being smart. She figures out how to punish her parents. She puts peroxide in father's hair tonic and "super super" glue in his hat. When her mother tries to get the hat off him, they fall onto the dessert cart and other restaurant tables. When forced to watch television, Matilda concentrates and makes it explode. When she finally is allowed to go to school, there is a military-style principal. The principal is so mean she throws a boy out the window for eating candy in class. She swings a little girl around by her braids and propels her out into the garden. The little girl makes a soft landing and the children cheer. The principal calls Matilda a "piss worm" and a "low life." Slowly, Matilda develops her powers to make things move. Matilda makes a newt fall on the principal. The children all gang up on the principal and throw items from their lunch boxes at her, driving her out of the school forever. Matilda's parents sign adoption papers as they flee the country. Her teacher, Miss Honey, adopts Matilda and they live happily ever after.

The girls in the orphanage are rough and tumble in the movie *Annie*. They fight each other and threaten to knock out each others' teeth. However, they have a common enemy in Miss Hannigan. The girls join together to save Annie from the evil Miss Hannigan.

In *A Little Princess*, Sara must start a new school when her father is called to war. She watches as a mean girl, Lavinia, dips a chubby girl's hair in ink. Lavinia is looking at Sara the whole time. The girls spread rumors about Sara before she gets to breakfast. Sara talks to the little black girl Becky who is serving them. Becky is told she is not allowed to talk to the other little girls because she is a servant and has dark skin. Sara starts to tell a little girl a story, and soon other girls join to listen. She seems to make friends easily, which makes Lavinia jealous. When Sara's father goes missing and her funds dry up, Sara is forced to move to the attic and become a servant in the school. Lavinia gets Sara's old room. As Sara makes a fire for her, Lavinia tells her she smells. Sara puts a curse on Lavinia and warns her not to brush her hair too much. Later the Lavinia finds extra strands in her brush and faints. Sara's father comes back to get Sara. As she leaves the school, even Lavinia hugs her. Lavinia starts to be nice to the other girls as well.

The movie *The Ant Bully* begins with Lucas getting a wedgie from the bully, Mullet Boy. Mullet boy pulls so hard he rips Lucas' underwear. All the other kids walk off with the bully laughing. In frustration, Lucas shoots his water gun into an ant hill. He mimics the bully saying, "What are you going to do about it? I'm big and you're small." He stomps around until his mother calls him inside. His mother asks what is wrong. He is dirty from the bullying but tells her he was just playing with his friends. A wizard ant shrinks Lucas as a punishment for nearly destroying their ant hill. To get back to full size, Lucas must help save the ants. When Lucas is restored to full size, he finds a new inner strength. The bully comes back and threatens to "dog pile" Lucas. This time Lucas stands up to the bully. Mullet Boy calls his gang a bunch of "losers." When he yells "dog pile," all the little kids chase the bully. The bully runs away calling for his "mommy." One of the little boys invites all the kids, including Lucas, to come play at this house. One interesting note: the movie ends differently than the book. In the book, Lucas is left with a shrunken bully rather than the bully getting away intact.

In the original *Toy Story*, the toys witness a neighborhood boy, Sid, torture his toys for fun. He looks like a stereotypical bully with bad teeth and wearing a black shirt embossed with a skull. Sid takes his sister's doll and performs an operation on it, squeezing it in a vise. He takes the doll's head off and replaces it with another toy's head. When Sid gets a rocket in the mail, he duct tapes the Buzz Lightyear action figure to the rocket. Rain delays the launch. Sid is shocked when he finds out Woody, a cowboy toy, can speak. Woody lectures Sid about being mean to toys. Sid's deformed toys come to life and rise up in protest. Sid runs screaming into the house. He vows never to abuse another toy.

The main character in *Paranorman*, Norman, gets pushed down in the school hallway. Someone has written "Freak" on his locker. Norman has the ability to speak to dead people and must save his town from zombies. Alvin, the bully, is a nuisance, getting in Norman's way as he tries to stop the zombies. When the zombies come out, Alvin hides behind Norman. In the end, Norman becomes the town hero. Alvin tries to impress some girls, telling them that he and Norman are good friends.

The villains in the other animated children's movies are almost always adults. For example, Jafar in *Aladdin*, Gaston in *Beauty and the Beast*, and Scar in *The Lion King* are adults and far too evil to just be bullies. Lotso in *Toy Story 3* is a bully although his voice is that of an adult. In *Chicken Little*, the town laughs at Chicken Little's misfortunes, but again it does not rise to the definition of bullying. In *Cars*, Chick Hicks is rather obnoxious but not quite a bully.

Conclusion

The animated television series *As Told by Ginger* and the movie *A Little Princess* were two of the few portrayals that dealt with relational aggression in children's programming. Bjorkqvist, Lagerspetz, and Kaukianen (1992) found that relational aggression can begin as soon as children have the verbal and social skills to manipulate other children. These skills can be acquired as early as preschool. However, bullying had a much stronger presence in television and movies targeted to younger children. Mean girl portrayals are more prevalent in teen dramas.

A majority of the bullying portrayals targeted to children are animated, resembling children's picture books where illustrations range from children to animals to fantasy creatures. A popular theme in bullying portrayals for younger children is the fight-back fantasy. Fighting-back options include having special powers, which were represented by both animation and live actors. These storylines were similar to superhero comic book characters in that often they could not fight back against the bully for fear their powers would expose their undercover identities. Several of the animated shows had a reoccurring bullying character whose role appears to be accepted by the other characters as inevitable and normal. Outcomes generally mirror that of programs targeted to older viewers. Except for the educational programs, there was little difference in the level of violent portrayals compared to programming for older adolescents. Programs that aired on public television, mainly PBS, tended to have a stronger moral and education message incorporated into the portrayal. Even though all examples included in this chapter were intended for a young audience, little time was dedicated to the dangers of bullying and relational aggression. Entertainment appeared to be the main focus of media producers.

12

Children's Literature

While much of this book's analysis focuses on electronic media, print appears to still be a viable channel for bullying and mean-girl portrayals. A survey done by the Association of American Publishers reported strong revenue growth of books between January 2011 and January 2012 (Sporkin, 2012). The numbers were particularly strong in children's and young adult's book sales. Books are a way to regulate pacing and when adults read to children, they can monitor the reactions and decide if the material is appropriate. According to Gill (cited in Alexander, 2008), "Sharing stories of bullying situations with successful resolutions can provide children with good information. Reading with children creates a safe connection between caretakers and children." The following analysis includes books that range in target audiences from children as young as age 3 to young adult readers. Books are also organized by theme and anti-bullying strategies.

Picture Books

The first set of picture books in this analysis stand out because of the emphasis on teasing and mean behavior rather than what is thought of as traditional or physical bullying. The next set of categories that emerged incorporated solutions or strategies to handle the bully or bullies. The themes included standing up to the bully, becoming the bully's friend, tricking or reasoning with the bully, using super powers or some fantasy to quell the bullying, including a teacher, adult or bystander, and the bully getting bullied. Picture books even touched on themes of racism and bigotry.

MEAN BEHAVIOR AND TEASING

A number of books feature mean behavior and teasing rather than traditional bullying. Unlike many television and movie portrayals, both girls and boys were represented. Many of the books celebrate children's unique qualities and encourage them to embrace their differences that often make them targets.

Sassy stands out because she is tall and thin in Allen's (2003) *Dancing in the Wings*. The other girls in Sassy's dance class make fun of her for the way she looks. Sassy tries teasing back with no success. In the end, her height gives her advantage and she is chosen above the other dancers. Sassy is fortunate in that she has a very loving and supportive mother and uncle. Her brother and his friends, unfortunately, are especially mean to her. In this book, something that makes someone different can be an advantage rather than a target of bullying.

Stand Tall Molly Lou Mellon (Lovell, 2010) is a similar story of being happy with who you are. When Molly Lou starts a new school, Ronald makes fun of her for being short, buck-toothed, and clumsy. Remembering the encouragement she received from her grandmother, Molly Lou uses her lack of height, bucked teeth, and clumsiness to show Ronald that his teasing does not affect her. In the end, Ronald gives up teasing her and they become friends.

The two next books are about how boys handle unwanted teasing and negative messages. The boys in Cosby's (1997) book *The Meanest Things to Say* create a game where the goal is to say the meanest things. The "game," however, creates a hostile atmosphere rather than a playful one. One of the boys' fathers teaches him that an effective way of responding is to confuse the bully rather than add to the meanness. After one boy silences the bully, his next strategy is to help the bully save face. The boys also learn to tease each other in a friendly rather than mean way. The preface to the book discusses the ineffectual methods of fighting back and ignoring the situation.

The narrator in *Enemy Pie* (Munson, 2000) gets angry when another boy, Jeremy, laughs at him when he strikes out during a baseball game. Jeremy then invites the narrator's best friend, but not the narrator, to his trampoline party. The narrator's father tricks the narrator into being nice to Jeremy as a way to throw the bully off guard. The boy thinks his father is helping him get rid of Jeremy. As the boys get to know each other better, they become friends, which was the father's intention all along.

In Martin's (1997) book *Little Chicken Chicken*, the other chickens laughed at Little Chicken Chicken's eccentric games and ideas. She is teased by everyone from the largest rooster to the littlest chicks who blow dandelion fluff at her. After the thunder scares everyone in the barnyard, Little Chicken Chicken helps them to not be afraid by distracting them with her games and tricks. In the end, everyone joins Little Chicken Chicken in "jumping, shouting, and flapping across the garden."

RACISM AND BIGOTRY

Themes of three of the picture books analyzed stood out as addressing prejudice in the form of racism or homophobia. These themes could be considered "adult" themes; however, the authors and illustrators were very careful to make the stories and pictures age appropriate. In Aubrey's (2008) book *The Rainbow Club*, a group of four friends decides one day to all dress in green and only be nice to others in green. The children wearing other colors feel excluded. The children in green start to be mean to the non-green wearers. Finally, Ella stands up against the meanness. The friends change the Green Club to the Rainbow Club that includes everyone. The book is an illustration of prejudice without targeting an actual ethnic or racial group.

Araboolies of Liberty Street (Swope, 2001) is also a story about prejudice and how bystanders can combat bullies. Whenever there is fun in the neighborhood, Mr. Pinches threatens to call in the army on his bullhorn. The children are ordered to stay inside in the summer. The Araboolies move in next door bringing generations of people and odd animals (e.g, elephants, walruses, sloths, etc.). The Araboolies do not seem to care when the Pincheses threaten them because they cannot speak English and do not understand the Pincheses. The Araboolies decorate their house with crazy colors. When Mr. Pinches calls the army, the children who live on the street get together and decorate all the houses in crazy colors. Thousands of soldiers come with guns, bombs, and helicopters. Their instructions are to get rid of the house that was "different." The soldiers drag away the Pincheses because now it is the Pincheses' house that is different. The book was a very interesting take on racism and intolerance. The author and illustrator did not identify a specific minority group (although "Arab" is in part of the name). It was the children in the neighborhood who had the courage to stand up to the bullies and the army.

Howe's (1996) *Pinky and Rex and the Bully* is about a second grader named Billy whose nickname is "Pinky" because pink is his favorite color. A group of bullies make fun of Pinky for liking pink and playing with girls. They knock a soccer ball out of his hands. One third grader, Kevin, pushes Pinky off his bike. Pinky feels so bad he changes his name back to "Billy" and gives all his stuffed animals to his sister. When an old woman catches Kevin picking on Pinky, she chases Kevin away. She tells Pinky a story about how when she was young, she let the bullies win by not standing up to them. Pinky finally stands up to one of the bully by poking him in the chest and telling him that he is not a "sissy." The bully is so shocked, he presumably stops bullying Pinky. This book contains one of the only times the bullies call their male target a "girl" and a "sissy." It is a precursor to homophobic terms found in older bullying.

STANDING UP TO THE BULLY

One lesson that children are taught in picture books is that standing up to a bully will show the bully the victim is not afraid. In Cuyler's (2009) book *Bullies Never Win*, Brenda tells Jessica that her legs look like toothpicks. If Jessica succeeds at something, Brenda will say Jessica either cheated or got lucky. Brenda will not let Jessica sit with her and her friends at lunch. Their teacher had told the class to ignore bullies, but Jessica feels like Brenda is always "in her face." Some other kids tell Jessica that she should stand up to Brenda. When Jessica's father asks what was wrong, Jessica says, "Nothing." Jessica asks her mother if she can stay home from school because she feels sick. Her mother tells her to tell her teacher about the bullying. Brenda calls Jessica a "tattletale." Jessica finally stands up to Brenda and says, "Toothpicks may be thin, but bullies never win." Brenda blushes. Jessica tells her family that she thinks Brenda will not pick on her anymore, and if she does, Jessica knows what to do. In this and other stories the victim stands up to the bully and handles the situation on her own. Brenda is not only bullying but is using relational aggression tactics such as exclusion to hurt Jessica.

The title character in *Sneaky Weasel* (Shaw, 2008) is described as mean, nasty, measly, and rich. When no one comes to his party, he asks them why. They tell him it is because of his past behavior. The weasel feels bad, apologizes, and sends out new invitations. They all come to his party this time and they live happily ever after. It is pretty unrealistic that the bully is going to care, but nice for young children to think so. It is also interesting that the author described Weasel as rich, implying perhaps that money buys power over others.

In Mayer and Mayer's (1999) *Just a Bully*, the bully does all the traditional bullying things such as stealing, name-calling, tripping, etc. Little Critter tells the teacher, but it just makes it worse. Little Critter stays home from school even though he says his mother knows he really is not sick. When the bully picks on Little Critter's sister, he fights the bully. The teacher breaks it up and gives both of them a good scolding. On the bus, the little sister pushes the bully and he stops his bullying. The book teaches the lesson of fighting back. It is also an example of a teacher misunderstanding the cause of the situation and punishing both the victim and the bully.

The other dogs circle around Fabio to see his new brother in Johnson's (2005) book *My Sister Gracie*. They laugh at him and tease him when they see he got a sister instead. Gracie is overweight and old. The other dogs call her "Fatso" and make her cry. Fabio, who initially wanted to get rid of her, now stands up for his sister. The lesson is a familiar one where it is okay to pick on siblings but others better not pick on them.

The title character in Lonczak's (2006) *Mookey the Monkey Gets Over Being Teased* does not care that he was born without hair until the first day of school. The other animals call him names and point and giggle. Mookey buys a fur suit at a costume shop. Next he tries gluing fur clippings to his body and drinking a potion that is supposed to make him grow hair but nothing works. The owl tells Mookey he cannot change his outside but can change what he does when he gets bullied. One friend tells him to joke. Another friend suggests he breathe and walk away. His parents tell him that kids tease so they can feel better about themselves or because they "feel uncomfortable when someone is different." A combination of the various strategies seems to work. Mookey is even proud of being hairless. The fact that the teasing did not stop completely gives the story a more realistic ending.

BEFRIENDING THE BULLY

In many picture books and stories for very young children, victims of bullying are advised to be nice to the bully because he or she may not have any friends. Attempts to befriend a bully have mixed results in the picture book world.

In *The Recess Queen* (O'Neill, 2002), "Mean" Jean pushes, smooshes, hammers, and slammers kids on the playground. A tiny new girl named Katie Sue defies Jean. Jean grabs Katie Sue by the collar, but Katie Sue gets away and continues to defy Jean. When Katie Sue asks Jean to play with her, Jean joins Katie Sue and becomes nice. The book not only suggests trying to be friends with bullies but highlights the defiance of a physically smaller child who stands up to a bully.

Peter moves into a new neighborhood in DeBode and Broere's (2011) book *Leave Me Alone!* He is soon confronted by Jack, a boy with spiky hair who is not very friendly to his classmates. Jack grabs Peter's stuffed tiger and stomps on it. Jack laughs at Peter when Peter does not know the answer to a teacher's question. When Jack punches Peter, many of their classmates start picking on Peter, too. Peter dreams that he is a tiger and chases Jack. In the dream, Jack wets his pants. When Peter wakes up, he realizes he has wet the bed. Peter tells his mother and teacher about Jack. The bullying stops at school, but Jack still picks on Peter after school. Peter's mother makes Peter invite Jack to his party. Peter goes to Jack's house when Jack has the chicken pox. Jack's mother is surprised to see Peter and tells him that no one ever comes to play with Jack. Jack also has a plastic sheet on his bed. Peter thinks Jack must wet the bed, too. The boys bond over stamps and stuffed animals. The book offers several solutions and reasons why someone might bully. It is the only book to address bed wetting, which may be a sign of bullying or distress.

In *Chester Raccoon and the Big Bad Bully* (Penn, 2008), the raccoons do not want to go to school because of a bully. The mother raccoon walks them to school and tells them to be brave. The bully pops the raccoons' ball and squashes their fingers. Even the teacher cannot get the bully to behave. The mother raccoon tells the story of a stone that was rough until everyone pitched in and worked together to smooth the edges. When the animals approach the bully, the bully is scared, thinking they wanted revenge. Instead, the animals ask him to play. The bully becomes their friend and never bullies again. It is unusual that a teacher is described as being unable to control a bully. Normally in children's book, teachers are shown to be competent unlike situation comedies. This book is one of many stories that suggest befriending a bully. Perhaps at a young age, bullies are still malleable enough for it to be effective.

Henry and the Bully (Carlson, 2010) is one of the few books that features a girl bullying a boy. A new second grader, Sam, kicks Henry's ball over the fence at recess and calls Henry "Shrimp." A bunch of second graders laugh. Henry, a first grader, tells his teacher. The bully waits until the teacher is not looking to bully the first graders again. Because of the bullying, Henry's stomach starts to hurt and he gets his spelling words wrong. Henry tells his mother he is sick but she fails to pick up on the fact that bullying is the cause. Henry sees Sam, which is actually short for Samantha, trying on a dress at the store. Sam threatens Henry if he tells anyone at school. He tells her she looks nice. At the next soccer game, Sam winked at Henry. The teacher, seeing the change in Sam's behavior, says, "Glad I could help." The story points out the cluelessness of adults. It also informs teachers and parents that bullies often get good at bullying when adults are not around.

Mim, Gym, and June (Roche, 2003) is an example of teamwork to achieve a common goal bringing together a bully and a victim. At the beginning of the story, June calls Mim names and tells her to "prepare to die!" The second graders make up a song: "Mim's the first-est, June's the worst-est." This song just makes June angrier. Mim's mother suggests Mim try to make friends with June. Mim brings June a cupcake, which June stomps on. When June and Mim are paired up in an obstacle course competition, the two work together. Because Mim is small and can easily get through parts of course, they win. In the last illustration of the book, June and Mim have their arms around each other. It is peculiar that there are no teachers intervening in the playground, lunch room, or gym as June bullies the other students.

TRICKING OR REASONING WITH THE BULLY

In the following set of books, the victims use tricks or reason to stop the bullying. The title character in *Big Bad Bunny* (Durant, 2003) is looking for money. When the animals do not have any, Big Bad Bunny takes their nuts, milk, and corn. When Big Bad Bunny gets to the bank and demands money, the Wise Old Bunny cleverly stacks the money bags all around Big Bad Bunny until he cannot move. The Wise Old Bunny makes the Big Bad Bunny promise not to take any more money. The Big Bad Bunny gives back all the things he took and turns into the Very Good Bunny. Although the solution was quite simplistic, it showed that sometimes outsmarting the bully is a successful plan.

Bootsie Barker in *Bootsie Barker Bites* (Bottner, 1992) not only bites but kicks and is a "deliciously mean" bully. The narrator's mother tells her that she must learn to get along with other children, even Bootsie. The little girl invents a new game that scares off Bootsie, using the same threats as Bootsie had used on her. Bootsie gets her comeuppance in the end; however, it appears the little girl uses bullying techniques, which is unusual in children's books since parents and teachers do not want to encourage such behavior. The illustrations show very physical forms of bullying (e.g., hair pulling, arm twisting).

Hassett and Hassett's (2002) book *The Three Silly Girls Grubb* is a play on old folk story, the Three Billy Goats Gruff. On the way to school, Ugly-Boy Bobby threatens to stuff toads in the littlest sister's sneakers if she does not give him her donuts. He gnashes his teeth at the middle sister and threatens to tangle bats in her hair if she does not give him her donuts. He shakes his fists at the extra-large sister. The extra-large sister says she will not give him her donuts until she plants "a dozen mushy kisses on his nose." Ugly-Boy Bobby runs away and never missed school again. Now he is called just Robert. The book is an interesting play on gender and the fear of a girl's kiss as more powerful than a physical threat.

The jungle animals in *Jungle Bullies* (Kroll, 2010) are shown bullying the next smaller animal in the jungle. When bullying trickles down to the baby monkey, his mother tells him he has to stand up to the bullies. The monkeys devise a plan to get the animals to cooperate. They write a poem, "Don't you tell me what to do...share it with me as a friend, don't be mean to me again." Each animal up the hierarchy chain complies. In the end, Hippo and Elephant are having fun in the water together. The moral of the story: "Bullies aren't ever fair, it's a lot more fun to share!"

FANTASY SOLUTIONS

The next category of picture books incorporates some kind of fantasy or special powers that the victim can use to combat the bullies or mean girls. Only two picture books in the sample fit in this category. Many more portrayals of fantasies are found in television programming (see chapter 11). *Don't Be a Bully, Billy: A Cautionary Tale* (Cox, 2004) is a book about a boy named Billy who punches, snatches, pulls, and scratches. He kicks, shakes, chases, and picks on. He ignores the other children when they tell him to stop. When Billy picks on a new boy, the boy introduces him to his brother, who is an alien. Billy runs away and the other children cheer.

Sid, the neighborhood bully in *The Ant Bully* (Nickle, 1999), is especially mean to Lucas, a boy who wears funny glasses. Sid steals Lucas' hat and sprays him with a water hose. In frustration, Lucas transfers his anger and bullies some ants in his lawn by putting water down their hill. The ants shrink Lucas down to ant size and put him on trial. The queen finds Lucas guilty of bullying and sentences him to work with the worker ants. When Lucas sacrifices himself to help his ant friends, the queen restores his size. When Lucas wakes up from his adventure, he is frightened by Sid. However, the ants shrink Sid. The story ends with an illustration of Sid on Lucas's finger. It is unclear what Lucas will do with Sid. He may retaliate or he may show compassion as the ants did with Lucas. In the movie version of *The Ant Bully*, the other kids in the neighborhood stand up with Lucas against the bully.

BYSTANDER OR ADULT INTERVENTION

In the next set of stories, a bystander or adult makes a significant difference in resolving the bullying situation. Many anti-bullying campaign messages instruct children to tell an adult; however, in many media portrayals, telling an adult only makes matters worse either because the adult is incompetent or ill-equipped to handle bullying situations or the bully or mean girl becomes more covert in their aggression.

In *Lucy and the Bully* (Alexander, 2008), Lucy is bullied by a classmate named Tommy.

After Tommy breaks Lucy's model for which she won a prize, he warns her not to tell anyone "or else!" The following days, Lucy brings home a ripped storybook, a crumpled painting, and broken pencils. At first Lucy refuses to tell her mother why she is sad. Finally she tells her mother about Tommy's bullying. Lucy's mother calls the teacher. Lucy cannot sleep that night and does want to go to school. The next day, Tommy is very quiet and looks sad. Lucy tells him she liked his art project. He apologizes to Lucy. Tommy and Lucy laugh and go out to play. It was not clear what Tommy was told or if he was punished, just that he did not want to go to school and was quiet and sad. It appears a bit unrealistic that Tommy would be so forgiving of Lucy for getting him in trouble. She followed up with something nice by complimenting Tommy.

A little girl and her dragon friend go out to play in Pendziwol and Gourbault's (2007) book *The Tale of Sir Dragon: Dealing with Bullies for Kids*. A bully and his friends tell the dragon that he cannot play with them because he is too tall and they take his stuffed animal. A little girl yells at them but the bullies just laugh. The little girl and the dragon tell the king and queen (assume that means her parents) about the bullies. The king and little girl sit down with the bullies. The king instructs the bullies not to pick on the dragon. The bullies let the dragon play and return his stuffed animal. When the group discovers a kitten stuck in a tree, the dragon is the only one tall enough to reach it. They all cheer. The group creates a Dragon's Decree: "I will use my words and actions to help, not hurt. If ever I or someone else is bullied, I will get help. I will not encourage a bully. I will learn to accept others for who they are and treat them with kindness."

Everyone at school giggles at the title character's name in *Chrysanthemum* (1991). The classroom teacher ignores the teasing. Chrysanthemum's parents are supportive, hug her, and tell her she is special; however, they offer no help or advice how to handle the girls at school. The music teacher, whom the children adore, defends Chrysanthemum and tells them all she was also named after a flower. The girls change their attitudes toward unusual names and want to be Chrysanthemum's friends. The story demonstrates the impact of a strong adult role model.

Katie Couric's book *The Brand New Kid* (2001) begins with kids at Ellie's school bullying a new student named Lazlo. Lazlo's mother is upset that her son is being picked on. When Ellie sees Lazlo's mother crying, she takes action and asks Lazlo to play. Having just one kid stand up for the victim leads the other kids accept him as well. The book is written from the perspective of the bystander and shows how powerful just one person standing up against bullying can be.

Leave Me Alone: A Tale of What Happens When You Stand Up to a Bully (Gray, 2011) is about a group of animals who wants to help a little boy who looks sad. The boy tells the animals to leave him alone. A giant, whom the author describes as "full of nasty words," descends upon them. All the animals shout at the giant to leave the boy alone. The giant frowns and walks away and never bothers them again. The book illustrates the power of the bystander, even when it appears the bully victim does not want help.

Bateman's (2004) *The Bully Blockers Club* also addresses bystanders as solutions to bullying. Lotty, a raccoon, begins a new school year. Grant Grizzly tells Lotty that she smells. Lotty tries to ignore it when Grant kicks her chair, calls her "stupid," and whispers nasty things about her. Lotty goes to the nurse's office complaining her stomach hurts. Lotty gets a series of suggestion from her family. When Lotty tries to be nice, Grant tells her he is allergic to "ugly." When Lotty tries laughing, Grant knocks the books off her desk. Finally the teacher intervenes. She tells Grant and Lotty that it is a school rule that people should feel safe. The teacher tells Lotty that she and other adults will "keep an eye out" for trouble. Grant makes sure no adult is around before he steals her dessert and calls her "fat." When Lotty tells him to leave her alone, Grant just laughs. The next day Lotty forms a club of all of Grant's victims. The next week, the school has a discussion about bullying. Afterwards, Lotty tells everyone about the club. Grant begins to behave and Lotty is happy again. In the illustrations, the chalkboard had tips for bullying: "ignore them," "walk away," "tell them to stop," and "tell a grownup." "Fight back" was written and crossed off, noting that it is an ineffective strategy.

BULLIES GETTING BULLIED

The books included in this section demonstrate how the bullies can get bullied. The hope would be that bullies would learn a lesson about how it feels to be on the other side. One would also hope that victims of bullies would have empathy for other victims and not bully themselves.

In Caseley's (2001) book *Bully*, Jack steps on Mickey's hand on the jungle gym, steals his cookie, and breaks his pencil. The other kids tell Mickey that he should tell a teacher; however, Mickey is afraid because Jack is bigger than he is. Mickey's father tells him bullies are cowards and he should use his brave words and tell him to stop. Mickey's mother figures out it must be Jack's new baby sister that is upsetting Jack. She suggests Mickey be nice to Jack. Mickey tries giving Jack cookies, but that does not seem to work. When Jack gets braces, the other kids tease him and call him "Track Mouth." When Jack gets embarrassed, Mickey is nice to him and makes Jack laugh. The story ends with an illustration of Jack and Mickey is walking down the hall with their arms around each other. This story includes problem solving. Jack was just acting like a bully because he was jealous of the attention given to his little sister. It is also a lesson about being nice to a bully and standing up for a bully getting bullied.

The title character in Henkes' (1997) *Chester's Way* has unusual ways of doing things. Lilly, a new girl in the neighborhood, also has her ways of doing things. When Lilly asks Chester and his friend, Wilson, if she can play with them, they say they are too busy. When she calls on the phone, they disguise their voices and say they are not at home. Chester and Wilson cross the street and hide from Lilly when they see her coming. When some older boys yell "personal remarks" at Chester and Wilson, Lilly, wearing a fierce looking cat costume, frightens the older boys away with her fangs and squirt gun. After being saved by Lilly, Chester and Wilson include her. The book ends with "and then Victor moved into the neighborhood..." It is not clear whether or not the three of them will include Victor. This is a different kind of story than the others where the main characters are guilty of social exclusion. Wilson and Chester experience what it is like to be the target of bullying. One would hope Chester and Wilson learned a lesson and will not exclude Victor.

Irving regularly teases Violet in class in Best's (2001) book *Shrinking Violet* for being shy. When the teacher assigns parts for the school play, Violet is chosen as the narrator. When Irving misses his lines in the play, Violet covers for him so Irving does not get teased. She gains great confidence from this experience. Irving thanks Violet in the end and they appear to become friends. The book illustrates self-confidence as a way to reduce teasing and bullying.

In *The New Dog* (Hazen, 1997), a very pampered dog named Tootsie gets a new dog walker. The older dogs pick on Tootsie. Tootsie waits to be picked up and carried over mud puddles. Danny, the dog walker, tells Tootsie not to whine when Tootsie gets a pebble stuck in his paw. The dogs tease Tootsie when Danny is not looking. One of the dogs smacks Tootsie's paw, sending him into the gutter. When the other dogs push Tootsie into the fountain, Danny scolds Tootsie. Tootsie breaks free and bites a mean-looking man. The man turns out to be a robber. Tootsie is a hero. The old dogs now accept Tootsie. The next day, a new dog named Tiny Timmy joins the group. Tootsie steps in front of the other dogs who are going to pick on Timmy. The lesson here is that the victim of bullying did not then turn to victimize a smaller character. Many times, when given the chance, past victims will take the opportunity to bully someone else. This story highlights the empathy a former victim has toward future victims.

Hooway for Wodney Wat (Lester, 1999) is a story about rodents who make fun of the way Rodney pronounces words with Rs in them. The illustration shows the bullies circling around Rodney, laughing at him. The teasing makes Rodney shy. He does not speak up in class, eats alone at lunchtime, and hides in his jacket during recess. A very large rodent named Camilla joins the class, announcing herself as the biggest, meanest, and smartest. She bumps the other rodents, steps on their tails, and tramples them on her way out to recess. Rodney leads the games at recess and orders the students "weed the sign," "wap your paws around your head," play "wing awound the wosey," and "wake the leaves." Not understanding that Rodney has a speech impediment, Camilla takes his directions literally. She pulls weeds, whaps her head, and tries to wake up the leaves. The other rodents laugh at Camilla. When Rodney tells everyone to "go west," the rodents lie down in a pile. Camilla, however, heads west and is gone forever. The other rodents never teased Rodney again. This story is a lesson about bullies getting bullied and changing their attitudes and behaviors.

MISCELLANEOUS

There were two books that I liked that were difficult to categorize. The first was *Don't Laugh at Me* (Seskin & Shamblin, 2002). The illustrations for the book range from children with glasses and braces to an older homeless person and a boy in a wheelchair. The copy is very touching as the characters ask readers "Don't laugh at me. Don't call me names. Don't get your pleasure from my pain." There is a sentimental message, "In God's eyes we're all the same. Someday we will all have perfect wings." This text is the same as lyrics to a popular country song of the same name. Another book with a positive theme was *Martha Walks the Dog* (Meddaugh, 2003). This book is a cute story about a mean dog, Bob. Bob is apparently mean because his owner constantly calls him "bad dog." Even Martha calls him names such as "thug," mangy mongrel," and "big baboon." When Bob is called a "good dog," he changes into a good dog. This story is a tale of self-fulfilling prophecies. It may be a better lesson for parents reading the book to their children than for children about using negative labels.

The following books fit into my "not crazy about" category. In comparison to the other picture books on the market, they lacked strong morals and clear resolution. The title character of *Petit, the Monster* (Isol, 2010) can be nice when he wants to, but he can be mean to girls and pigeons. Petit is confused about why he has these conflicting feelings. He also receives different consequences to his actions. He realizes that his mother can be "good" because she is understanding, but "bad" when she sends him to bed without dessert. He figures it runs in the family. This story takes the perspective of the bully, but a not very enlightening one. The book starts strong with an important theme, but does not appear to solve Petit's tendency to be mean.

In Ezra Jack Keats' (1998) book *Goggles!*, Peter and his friend find a pair of goggles and must protect them from the neighborhood bullies. The bullies, represented by a shadowy illustration, demand the goggles. However, Peter refuses and puts up his fists. The bullies knock Peter to the ground. The younger boys run away with the goggles and hide from the bullies. In some ways, the book teaches a rather dangerous message. The small boys confront bigger boys who are threatening them with physical violence. There is no resolution to the bullying problem, just a temporary reprieve.

Bear, a Lion, and an Elephant find a golden crown in the forest in *The Mightiest* (Kasza, 2003). The beast who can scare a vulnerable victim the most gets the crown that distinguishes him or her as the "mightiest." Each of the beasts takes turns scaring a little old lady. The little old lady's son happens to be a giant, who then scares all of the beasts. The old woman warns the giant that he is not to pick on smaller victims. He promises and therefore, she is proclaimed the mightiest. She refused the crown saying, "The mightiest didn't need the crown after all." The book ends with a quiet forest; however, the author warns, "But not for long..." The moral is that power should not be abused and that crowns and titles are unimportant. The secondary messages, however, is that competition for superiority is a given and will continue regardless of the lesson learned by a few characters in the book.

Patrick and the Big Bully (Hayes, 2001) features a boy named Patrick who is being bullied by Big Bear. Patrick's mother tells him to remember that he is a "dragon." Patrick practices roaring. Big Bear stops Patrick, calls him "Stripey-Pants," and demands a cookie. Patrick refuses and runs away. When Patrick remembers his mother telling him he is a dragon, he roars loudly and scares Big Bear away. When Patrick's parents ask if Patrick met any big kids, Patrick said no, "just a big Muddy-Pants." While Patrick has learned to stand up for himself, it looks as though he has learned to name-call.

When Pete enters his new classroom in *The Juice Box Bully* (Sornson & Dismony, 2010), he is on the defensive. Having been bullied in his past school, Pete starts to tease kids before they can pick on him. The students in the class have taken a vow not to bully and to stand up for each other. When Pete squirts his juice box on Ruby, she loses her temper, telling him he is mean and that he will not have any friends at that school. Ralph stands up for Pete. Ruby comes back later to apologize, stating that she made a promise not to make other students feel bad. Pete, seeing that the class will stand with him, apologizes to Ruby and takes the pledge not to bully. Rather than have the teacher preach about the rules of the classroom, the students continually reiterate the climate of the class. The book is rather Pollyannaish and simplistic, however. It is a "turn the other cheek" type of book. No one tells the teacher that Pete has misbehaved. The children appear quite young to be making such a promise. The pledge seems to ignore the fact that bullying has complexities and can be physically dangerous.

INSTRUCTIONAL BOOKS

The next section includes instructional books targeted to slightly older readers. The themes are more sophisticated and the solutions more thoughtful. The illustrations in the books also look more like real boys and girls rather than characters or animals.

Nobody Knew What to Do: A Story about Bullying (McCain, 2001) begins with the passage, "Nobody likes to think about it, even though we know it is not okay to hurt a person with words, or things, or with the way we behave" (p. 1). When kids are picking on a boy named Ray, the narrator tells the reader that the teachers were busy and did not see it. The narrator, not knowing what to do, closes his eyes and covers his ears and hopes the mean words would fade away. He and the rest of the kids bunch together at recess for protection, except for Ray. A boy is holding Ray's arm behind his back. The bullies threaten the bystanders so no one helps Ray. One boy yanks at Ray's book while another boy shakes his fist at Ray. The bullies cheer the next day when Ray does not come to school. The bullies discuss what they will do to Ray when he does come back. The narrator finally tells a teacher. When Ray comes back, the narrator invites Ray to play with them at recess. The bullies are caught in the act by the teacher and the principal and their parents are called. The book ends with the passage, "Nobody bullied that day. We won't let it happen. Together we know what to do and say to make sure bullying is NEVER okay. We worked together to make it end." On the last page, there is a note about bully prevention. The author informs parents that children are no longer advised to "fight back."

The narrator of *Say Something* (Moss, 2008) tells the story of a boy who is getting picked on. The boy looks sad and hardly ever says hello to anyone. The narrator feels sorry for him and comments that she does not pick on him. Another student gets teased, called names, and pushed in the halls. The narrator comments that she is not involved in the bullying; she just walks down the other side of the hall. A girl sits alone on the bus and gets things thrown at her and called names. The narrator comments that she does not laugh with the other kids. One day the narrator's friends are absent and she has to sit alone at lunch. Kids start joking about her and laugh when she starts to cry. When she tells her brother she is mad at the kids who were sitting at the next table, he asked, "Why? They didn't do anything." The next day the narrator sits next to the girl who is sitting alone. She is able to empathize with others now that she too has been a victim. This story is a very poignant look at the inaction of bystanders contributing to the problem of bullying.

Ludwig's books emphasize that bully targets can be anybody. The message resonates that the target did not ask for or deserve the abuse. Ludwig also does an excellent job of bridging the developmental gap between picture books and young adult readings. *Trouble Talk* (Ludwig, 2008) is a story about a new girl in school named Bailey. Bailey appears nice at first; however, she begins to gossip, spread rumors, and say hurtful things about the other girls. Maya, one of the girls Bailey has gossiped about, confides in her school counselor, Ms. Bloom. Ms. Bloom helps Maya deal with mean girls and helps Bailey realize the harm she is doing. Although Bailey writes apologies to the girls whom she has harmed, the girls do not trust her right away. The book is a very realistic story with excellent examples of what might appear to be harmless acts. The book begins with a foreword that defines "trouble talk" as negative talk about others that is damaging. The author explains that in adolescent culture, girls especially bond over this kind of talk and sharing secrets. She explains that the need for power and status among peers is a motivator for cutting other kids down. In *Just Kidding*, Ludwig (2006) tells the story of a boy named D.J. who is the victim of some negative teasing. Vince jokes to the other boys that whoever loses has to have D.J. on their team. D.J. is upset and goes home early. Vince has also makes fun of D.J.'s clothes and pokes him on the bus. Whenever D.J. complains, Vince keeps saying that he is just kidding. D.J.'s father teaches D.J. a game of responding to the teasing. That particular strategy does not seem to work with Vince so D.J. and his father speak with a teacher. The teacher sends Vince to the school counselor to help him learn how to be a better friend. The teacher also explains to D.J. the difference between tattling and reporting and helps him deal with putdowns. D.J. starts to hang out with boys who have fun without making fun of each other.

In *My Secret Bully* (Ludwig, 2005), the narrator Monica talks about her friend Katie who is really nice to her at times. Other times, Monica sees Katie whispering and laughing with other girls. Katie dictates with whom Monica can play. Monica's mother suggests Monica talk to Katie about it. When Monica tries to talk to Katie, Katie accuses Monica of being too sensitive. Things get worse and because Katie has told them not to, so no one will play with Monica. When Monica complains of stomachaches, her mother listens and helps Monica by role-play how to deal with Katie. The next day, Monica confronts Katie in front of the other girls. Monica makes new friends and stops having stomachaches. The book addresses the nuances that are difficult to maneuver. As children's relationships and interactions become more complex, the books guiding them need to reflect that sophistication and not shy away from the topics because it may cause distress or confusion.

Confessions of a Former Bully (Ludwig, 2012) follows the story of Katie, who was caught bullying others kids in her class. (I assume this is the same Katie from *My Secret Bully*.) Katie is not simply punished for her bad behavior but is required to talk with the guidance counselor and figure out ways to make up for the damage she has caused. The bulk of this book is Katie's journal, which reveals secret motivations behind her actions. Katie initially has trouble distinguishing her actions of laughing at other kids' mistakes and excluding others from physical bullying. Ludwig introduced the concept of the tool belt, emphasizing that every tool doesn't work in every situation. She also distinguishes which tools are appropriate for little kids and which are appropriate for bigger kids. Ludwig shows that bullying is a learned behavior that is developed over a long period of time and that a onetime punishment will rarely remedy the situation. The book includes small sections on cyberbullying. It distinguishes between "tattling" and "reporting." The cover and graphics of the book looks like a young person's handwriting, which may make it more accessible to young girls.

Chapter Books and Young Adult Fiction

The lead characters in the chapter books in this analysis range from second grade through high school. Stories span from lighthearted to heartbreaking. Perhaps two of my favorite books were older publications: *The Hundred Dresses* (Estes, 1944) and *The Bully of Barkham Street* (Stolz, 1963). The authors took their time in developing the story and presented a complexity to the characters and their motivations.

Martin, the main character in Stolz's (1963) book *The Bully of Barkham Street*, is disrespectful to adults and a bully to the other boys in his class. Martin appears to have trouble making friends and often strikes out before they can reject him. The boys often make fun of him because of his weight. He is bigger than the boys in his class and uses his size advantage to try to intimidate them. Martin gets frustrated when he feels his parents are favoring his sister. He has a horrible day at school, sassing back at the teacher, tripping a student, and picking a fight. Punishing him for his behavior appears to make it worse. Slowly, Martin starts taking responsibility for his actions. He is not getting much recognition for the changes but finds that he is feeling better inside. It is a relief to him to not be fighting all the time. When Martin has a setback, his father acknowledges Martin's effort and is empathetic to how hard it is to live down the reputation as a bully. By the end of the story, Martin is gradually losing weight and getting along better with his family and classmates. The book was sophisticated in its message. It is perhaps the most insightful into the motivation of a bully of all the books surveyed. The conversations Martin has with his sister and adults in his life were well thought out. The pacing was also realistic, in that Martin did not just one day change his behavior and his reputation.

The Hundred Dresses (Estes, 1944) is written from the perspective of a girl named Maddie. Maddie is friends with a popular girl named Peggy. The girls in Maddie's class admire Peggy and the many new dresses that she wears to school. On the other hand, the girls look down on Wanda, a poor girl of Polish background who wears the same blue dress to school every day. When Peggy condescendingly asks Wanda how many dresses she has, Wanda insists she has a hundred dresses in her closet. The girls all snicker, except for Maddie. Maddie has doubts about going along with the group yet she does not saying anything to defend Wanda. The teacher appears not to help Wanda either. One day, the girls find one hundred drawings of dresses lining their classroom. Wanda wins the class contest for best drawing; however, she does not get to pick up the prize because her father has moved her and her brother to another town because of the teasing the children have had to endure. Maddie and Peggy try to remedy the situation and write her an apology letter, hoping the post office will forward it to her new address. It is a very touching story. Perhaps as bad as Peggy's behavior was, Maddie, as the bystander, was equally bad because she did nothing to stop Peggy when she knew Peggy was hurting Wanda's feelings. The hope is that Peggy and Maddie learned a lesson.

Thaddeus, or Thud, as he likes to be called, has always been a problem child in *Three Rotten Eggs* (Maguire, 2002). Thud's mother has all but given up on him and shuffles him from school to school as he gets into trouble in each one. A kind teacher, Miss Earth, tries to discuss Thud's behavior with his mother but she refuses to get involved. She tells Miss Earth that she has already tried military and boarding schools. She does not say what he did exactly but tells that he has been expelled and charges were brought against him. She fears Thud is just a "bad seed." She leaves a blank check to cover any future damage he causes to the school. Later, Miss Earth tries to talk with her again. The mother tells her to come back when he has wounded another child or caused an unreasonable amount of damage. On the first day of school, Thud is irreverent to Miss Earth and lies about his father. It comes out later that his father is in prison for tax evasion and grand larceny. Thud performs rude gestures and makes up unflattering nicknames for the other students like "Maggot" and "Slim." He warns the class that he is good at "providing blood." The other children appear to tolerate his behavior because they want him to join one of their two clubs in order to gain a majority and thus power in the class. He asks his classmates for help, arguing, "Cause I'm the new kid in town, fragile and unsure of myself. A kind gesture might make me feel welcome and help me change my nasty ways... Also, I can beat you up, easy" (p. 57). It is clear that Thud understands his actions and has been to counseling. He is clearly smart enough to know how to manipulate others. When Thud and two of his classmates find three eggs, they hide them until they hatch. For the first time, Thud actually loves something. The author describes him as no longer having a heart "like a time bomb." Thud teams up with his classmates to have his mother, a famous singer, put on a concert for charity.

Joshua T. Bates In Trouble Again is part of a series by Shreve (2000). In this installment, Joshua is promoted to the fourth grade after being held back. He wants to impress his classmates on the first day so he wears his father's shirt and puts mousse in his hair. The boys in the fourth grade are very hierarchical. One boy ranks his best friends, telling Joshua he is his fourth best friend. The popular boys select who is "in" and who is not. They pick who gets to play soccer and exclude anyone they consider to be "nerds." Joshua seems to be on the edge between popular and unpopular. When Joshua finally stands up to the mean boys, the less popular boys cheer him. The social shunning seems to be as hurtful as if not more so than physical bullying. Joshua cannot sleep at night worrying about his social status.

The two main characters in McNamee's (2001) book *Nothing Wrong with a Three-Legged Dog* are fourth graders Lynda, whom the kids call "Zebra" because she is mixed race, and Keath, whom the kids call "Whitey" because he is the only white student in the school. Keath witnesses the school bully, Toothpick, being bullied by his older brother. Toothpick hits Keath and threatens him not to tell. Keath's father tells Keath about the bully, Dan, who picked on his Chinese friend Freddie. Freddie was heavy so Dan would call him "Chunk" instead of "Chink." Freddie coped by pretending Dan was invisible. Keath's father told Keath it worked because all Dan really wanted was the attention. Later Keath gets ambushed in the school hallway. Toothpick hits him between the shoulders. Lynda and another boy stand up for Keath and tell Toothpick to leave him alone. When Toothpick insults Leftovers, the three-legged dog that Keath has grown to love, Keath loses his temper. Toothpick slips and hits his nose on Keath's elbow. All the kids think Keath hit him. Toothpick gets suspended for starting the fight. Toothpick appears to stop bullying because he is fearful he will be expelled if he gets in trouble again. The story is a metaphor of how kids can feel like outcasts, like the three-legged dog. Keath and Lynda's nicknames are offensive; however, there is very little about race in the story.

The novel *Blubber* by Blume (1986) is narrated by a fifth grader, Jill, who is complicit in the teasing of a girl named Linda, although at times she takes more of an initiator role. Jill tells her mother that Linda does not stand up for herself so she deserves being picked on. She writes, "Blubber lives here" in chalk outside Linda's house. Her mother forewarns Jill that one day Jill could be in Linda's place. When the kids pull a prank on Linda, the teacher makes everyone but Linda stay after school, which makes matters worse. To get revenge on Linda, Jill's friends developed a list of things to do to Linda, for example, "hold your nose when she walks by," "trip her," and "push/shove/pinch." Jill blames Linda for not being able to laugh it off. The mean girls make Linda show her underpants to the boys. When they force her to eat a piece of chocolate they told her had an ant in it, Linda throws up. They lock Linda in the supply closet. When she threatened to scream, one girl tells her, "You do and you're dead." Jill finally stands up to Wendy, the ring leader, on Linda's behalf. When Jill returns to school, she finds that Wendy has befriended Linda and now Jill is the outcast. The mean girls trip Jill and hold their noses when she walks by. Jill finally makes the other girls question whether or not Wendy is their friend. They stop bullying Jill, but there is no clear resolution or big lesson learned. Jill still lets Linda eat by herself and Wendy finds a new best friend.

Voigt's novel *Bad Girls* (1996) features two girls, Mikey and Margalo, who become friends on the first day of fifth grade. Mikey and Margalo get into a fight with the boys in their class when they refuse to let Mikey play with them because she is a girl. Louis, the class bully, calls Mikey names such as "Porky" and "Blimpo." Louis' cousin Ronnie tells the girls that Louis chooses a new person every year to pick on. One year it was a girl he liked, the next a "smart nerdy boy." Louis calls Mikey a "stupid cow" and "Barbie" during soccer practice. The coach only warns Louis that he will get a yellow card if he does that during a game. Louis continues to get meaner. He steals one boy's cap and trips another. When Mikey tries forcing the team to pick between her and Louis, Louis loses his temper and cuts off Mikey' long braid. He gets suspended and reassigned to another fifth grade class. Rhonda, whom Mikey ignores a lot of the time, stands up for Louis and tries to get all the girls to turn against Mikey. Everyone in class asks the teacher if Louis can rejoin their class, even Mikey, who feels bad Louis was moved. When Margalo reasons that it is better to have two bossy students in the class to cancel each other out, Mikey angrily asks if Margalo is calling her a "bully." The girls fight again when they both want to run for class president. Mikey makes fun of Margalo's high mark on her spelling test and calls her "Miss Perfect Paper." The girls begin pushing and eventually a fist fight breaks out. The next day, without really resolving anything, they continue to work together on their school project. The two are brought closer together with the common enemy of Rachel. Margalo anonymously replaces Rachel's lunch with a dead squirrel and rotten fish because Rachel had said bad things about Mikey. The title "Bad Girls" is rather an overstatement. The girls are mean to each other at times but are hardly "bad."

Sixth grader Ricky V. Smootz tells people that the "V" stands for "very afraid" in *Cowboy Boy* (Proimos, 2003). He runs through a list of bullies he has endured from first and third grades. His friend tells Ricky that bullies can smell fear on him. Sixth grade presents a new bully, Keanu Dungston. Ricky gets in trouble with this mother because he is going to school without underwear. He does not tell her it is to avoid wedgies. Sure enough, he gets a super wedgie. The incompetent principal does not see Dungston giving students wedgies right in front of him. One wedgie victim get detention for crying in the hall. When Ricky calls his grandmother for advice, she tells him about his distant cousin, Crazy Enzio. The next day Ricky dresses up like Crazy Enzio in a cowboy outfit and approaches the bullies in the back of the school bus. They are going to pound him until he starts telling off-colored jokes. Ricky blackmails Dungston with a baby picture. Dungston confesses that he is actually relieved he does not have to play the "mean kid" anymore. When Dungston accidently runs into a locker and falls down, the kids at school think Ricky hit him. Dungston tells the kids that the cowboy had taught him a lesson and he was going to be nice now. Ricky takes on a new persona that gives him self-confidence to stand up to the bully. The bully also is relieved that he does not have to keep up his role as the school bully.

In the next two novels, bully victims use magic spells to ward off their bullies. What is unusual is that both books feature female lead characters. So many of the Harry Potter-type books are about boys. In *So You Want to Be a Wizard* (Duane, 2003), thirteen-year-old Nita is being chased by a group of bullies lead by Joanne. Nita has been beaten up and given a black eye by the group before. As Nita is hiding in the library, she finds a book on wizards. Just before she gets home, six girls jump her. Her parents are concerned but simply have her lie down with ice. Her mother looks away and sighs. Nita's younger sister volunteers to beat up Joanne since she has taken jujitsu class. Nita is horrified at the thought of her little sister taking on her battles. Nita refuses to have her father talk to Joanne's father, particularly since Joanne's father is rich and has a lot of power in the community. Nita tells her father that when she did fight back in the past, Joanne only got more kids to help beat her up the next time. As Nita reads the book on wizards, she develops special powers. Nita is able to make the pen Joanne stole from her disappear. After another beating, Nita calls out to Joanne that it will never happen again. Nita then jumps up and waves her arms, sending Joanne and her gang running away in fear. Nita then hones her wizard skills and goes on a great adventure slaying a dragon with her friend Kit. When Nita meets up with Joanne again near the end of the book, Joanne is alone. Nita tries a new tactic and asks Joanne to come to her house sometime to look at her telescope. Joanne makes a snide remark and keeps walking. Nita surmises that she has broken the cycle of anger and loneliness, at least for herself.

Three bullies torment twelve-year-old Millicent and her two friends in *Bully-Be-Gone* by Tacang (2006). The bullies call them names like "nerd" and "freak." The female bully, Nina, grabs Millicent by the collar. Nina later takes Millicent's friend's notebook of poetry and mocks it. Millicent invents a device that programs Nina's voice to say bad things about the librarian. The bullies flee the library when the librarian gets angry. Millicent creates a scent that neutralizes bullies. The scent works too well and the bullies fall in love with Millicent's friends. When Millicent tries to warn her friends about the scent, her friends get angry at Millicent for interfering. Millicent creates an anecdote and the bullies go back to normal and are eventually arrested because they are riding stolen bicycles.

The Revealers (Wilhelm, 2003) and *The Truth about Truman School* (Butler, 2008) are both stories about anonymous posts on the Internet that get students into trouble. The bully in *The Revealers* (Wilhelm (2003), Richie, singles out Russell to harass. Russell laments that he'd had friends in elementary school but now everyone changed and formed cliques as they entered middle school. He reads comic books as a way to imagine he can have super powers to overcome the bullies. Russell teams up with Elliot, another kid who gets bullied, and Catalina, a new girl who is shunned by the popular girls. They create an email forum for kids to share their bullying stories. Stories range from kids getting their things stolen or thrown in mud puddles to one boy who discloses that another boy had threatened to stab him with a switchblade. Even bullies send stories about how they enjoy "pounding" on other kids. One mean girl, Bethany, sets them up by sending an anonymous story about herself. The email contains an accusation that another girl wrote Bethany's paper in order to become a member of Bethany's group. Bethany manipulates her father, a lawyer, into threatening a libel suit. Russell, Elliot, and Catalina are required to write Bethany a letter of apology. Catalina is able to prove that Bethany wrote the email, however. Although she does not tell on Bethany, Catalina lets Bethany know that she is not afraid to stand up to her.

In Butler's (2008) *The Truth about Truman School*, Zibby and her friend, Amr, start an underground online newspaper when they get frustrated for being told what they could or could not write. The anonymous posts begin to target a popular girl named Lilly. Lilly, Zibby, and Amr were close friends in elementary school. Since then, Lilly joined a more popular group and left them behind. An anonymous student posts a picture of an overweight Lilly from elementary school. Students, including Lilly's friends, post insulting things on the photo. Soon there is an "I hate Lilly" page and a "Lilly's Lesbian Diary" page. When one of Lilly's former friends, Kylie, shows concern for what people are posting, Brianna, the ring leader, subtly threatens that it could happen to Kylie if she chooses Lilly over the group. Lilly eventually runs away and hides in an old tree house. When Lilly finally returns, she asks her parents to transfer schools. Trevor, a geeky boy whom Lilly used to pick on, apologizes for being the anonymous student who started the negative posts. Instead of getting angry, Lilly asks Trevor to forgive her for treating him poorly in the past. Zibby and Amr turn the Truth about Truman School into a closely monitored site where kids can discuss bullying instead of posting gossip. The story is not only about a website that got out of control, but reflects on bullying, retaliations, and the cost of being popular. The book really highlights the lack of anticipating or acknowledging the consequences of one's actions in the eighth grade. The intense need to belong is displayed by many of the characters, something that trumps empathy for others.

The Skin I'm In (Flake, 2007) is the story of Maleeka, a bright seventh grader with very dark skin who is struggling with bullies and mean girls. Maleeka bonds with her teacher, Miss Saunders, who is also teased and abused because of a skin condition. The leader of the mean girls, Charlese, pretends to be nice to Maleeka and lends her nice clothes to manipulate Maleeka into doing her homework and letting her cheat off her tests. Charlese lives with her overindulgent sister who rarely disciplines Charlese. A girl starts a fight with Maleeka when she mistakes Maleeka for Charlese, who was kissing the girl's boyfriend. Charlese bullies Maleeka into vandalizing Miss Saunders' classroom. Charlese frames Maleeka for stealing Miss Saunders' watch. She threatens Maleeka that she will beat her if she tells. She also calls Maleeka an "ugly, stupid black thing." Eventually Maleeka stands up for herself and Charlese is sent to live with her grandparents out of state.

The title character in *Indigo's Star* (McKay, 2004) comes back after missing school because of mono. The school bullies are eagerly awaiting Indigo's return. The gang targets Indigo because he tried to help another boy who was getting picked on. Indigo tries telling a teacher, who is of no help. Later, Indigo's sisters stand up to the bullies. The bullies turn their aggression to the new boy, Tom. Tom, although described as small, is not afraid to fight back. The bullies pull out Tom's chair as he sits down, causing Tom to hit his head. The bullies insinuated it was Indigo's fault. The teacher takes the bullies' word for it and warns Indigo that bullying will not be tolerated. When the bullies make fun of Tom, Tom pushes the leader, who falls down the stairs. The bully tells the teacher that Indigo did it. Later, the boys grab Indigo's little sister, Rose. Indigo comes to her aid and beats up the leader. The leader's two cronies do not follow the leader when he leaves the scene. The reign of terror appeared to be over. This book, like many others, points out adult ineptness and lack of teacher training regarding bullying.

In *Freak the Mighty* (Philbrick, 2001), Max and Kevin stand out because of their sizes. Max had a growth spurt and is unusually big for a boy his age. On the hand, Kevin suffers from a medical condition where he stopped growing. They are picked on by Tony D., who is 17 years old and a three- or four-time juvenile court attendee. He chases the two boys with a knife. Max, with Kevin on his shoulders, runs from Tony D.'s gang into a pond. When the boys get stuck in the mud, the gang begins throwing rocks at them. Luckily the police come to the boy's rescue. The next mention of Tony D. is at the end of the book when Kevin dies. A kinder, gentler Tony D. tells Max that it is a shame about Kevin. There is no mention of police action against Tony D. or the gang.

Hit Squad (Heneghan, 2003) is a dark novel about high school bully victims and their plan to get revenge. Mona and Shelley spit sunflower seeds in Birgit's hair. Birgit calls them "slobs." Angered by Birgit's response, one of Mona and Shelley's cronies, Jessie, pretends to be Birgit's friend to lure her into a closet to get some art supplies. The bullies hold Birgit down, put paper towels in her mouth, and spit on her. When the art teacher finds Birgit after the attack, the bullies are only suspended for one day. Mickey lives in a group home and just transferred to the school. Two male bullies demand Mickey's lunch. When Mickey resists, the bullies punch and kick him. A teacher, coming upon the scene, asks if anything is wrong. She thinks she saw a scuffle but takes no further action. In another bullying incident at the school, a boy named Joey is attacked in the boys' room because he is black. He is rushed to the hospital. Later Birgit asks Mickey and a couple of the football players to form a secret society, "the Hit Squad," to take the school back from the bullies. They recruit a large boy, Heck, from Mickey's group home. The hit squad kidnaps Mona and Shelley, the two girls who bullied Birgit. They tie up Mona, cut off her hair and put paint on her. Candy, a girl from the group home, questions Mickey about his involvement. She reminds him that his actions are no different than the bullies. Mickey and the boys watch as the bullies who attacked Joey are hassling a mentally challenged boy in the cafeteria. No one comes to the boy's aid. The Hit Squad chases the two bullies into a construction site. The members of the Hit Squad are going to let the bullies go, having scared them. However, Heck follows the bullies into the construction site. The beam Heck is standing on collapses. When Mickey begins to go after Heck, Birgit tells Mickey not to go after him since Heck is a "nobody." Heck is killed in the accident. Mickey feels remorse for seeking revenge and wanting to be in the "in crowd." This book is an example of an extreme revenge fantasy. It is similar to many of the revenge movies about bullying. The group sounded like a good idea at first; however, they appeared to enjoy the suffering of victims too much as they taught them a lesson.

Conclusion

Books would appear to be an effective vehicle for dispensing anti-bullying messages. Books have the advantage of allowing readers to process the information at their own pace, plus there is the expectation that books are written to educate as well as entertain. The significant number of children's books that address teasing and bullying currently on the market likely reflects the increased awareness of the problem.

The books on bullying and mean girls in this analysis tend to present more realistic and rational methods to handle bullies and mean girls such a talking to resolve the issue rather than using magical powers to combat the bullies. Books, unlike a vast majority of movies and television shows, include examples of helpful bystanders as well as competent and compassionate adults. This portrayal is in stark contrast to the incompetent adults that populate television and movies. Descriptions of additional books that give direct advice about to deal with bullying can be found in chapter 14.

13

Alternative Media

Bullying and mean girls have become popular themes not only in traditional media channels such as movies and television but in alternative media as well. This chapter covers a variety of other forms of entertainment, such as sports entertainment, video games, viral videos, comic books, and music lyrics and videos. New technology and an increase in bullying awareness have expanded the number and forms of messages adolescents are likely to receive regarding physical, verbal, and relational aggression. Together, the different formats illustrate the popularity of bullying and mean behavior as entertainment.

Professional Wrestling

In 2011, World Wrestling Entertainment (WWE) launched a promotion for the Be a Star bullying prevention program. They partnered with the National Education Association (NEA), Health Information Network (HIN), and the Creative Coalition to help create a positive and safe environment for kids regardless of their age, race, religion, or sexual orientation. WWE owner Vince McMahon's daughter Stephanie tours with the campaign, giving kids the tools to rise above bullying. The movie *That's What I Am* was co-produced by WWE Studios and includes one of their stars, Randy Orton. One of the bullies retaliates against a teacher by spreading rumors about the teacher's sexuality. Orton plays the father of the bully. Orton's character is homophobic and demands the teacher be fired. Unwilling to dignify the rumors, the teacher resigns but not before he teaches his students about being themselves.

Rosaline Wiseman (2011) criticized the alliance, accusing WWE productions of normalizing violence in their wrestling shows. She added that homophobia is the basis of masculinity in world of wrestling. She speculated that the organizations, such as the NEA and Creative Coalition, who partnered with the WWE for this project, have not seen the show in the last two decades. According to Jackson Katz, "WWE is one of the most culturally destructive and blatantly misogynistic businesses in the history of popular entertainment" (cited in Wiseman, 2011). Sut Jhally argued that the WWE is the opposite of anti-bullying. He compared WWE's role in an anti-bullying campaign to the pornography industry promoting abstinence (cited in Wiseman, 2011).

Gray (2011) wrote that he completely agrees with allegations that the WWE is hypocritical in its anti-bullying message. He pointed to examples of Jerry Lawler telling fat jokes about Vickie Guerrero or Jim Ross being humiliated about his health problems on stage. On the other hand, Jon Cudo (2012) claimed it is an unfair criticism to say that because WWE has characters on the show who bully, they cannot be affiliated with an anti-bullying campaign. He claimed that the bullies are heels, and therefore, are portrayed as bad characters doing bad things such as bullying. David Otunga participated in a Be a Star campaign. He, like many of the WWE wrestlers who are participating in the campaign, admitted he was bullied as a child. Otunga plays a heel (i.e., bad guy) in the ring. The Be a Star campaign appearances and PSAs do not mention the wrestlers' personae. Generally, the wrestlers are not allowed to break character in public. Producers do not want to break the illusion or to expose wrestling as "fake." Wrestler Mark Henry stated that the wrestlers' role is to entertain but they want kids to know that they do not bully in their everyday lives.

Christopher Shays (cited in Pena, 2012), political opponent of Linda McMahon, argued that McMahon should not be running for the US Senate because of her ties to the WWE. Shays specifically points to the "Kiss My Ass Club" and her husband's treatment of women in the arena. Connecticut Women against Linda McMahon for Senate used footage of WWE, particularly scenes of McMahon's husband, to demonstrate her lack of respect for women. In 2001, the McMahons set up a storyline where it looks as though Vince McMahon was having an affair with one of the female wrestlers, Trish Stratus. Stratus is portrayed as a gold digger, sleeping her way up the organization. In an episode of *WWE RAW*, Vince's daughter Stephanie slaps Stratus while a male wrestler slams her into the mat. Vince makes Stratus get down on all fours and bark like a dog. McMahon calls her "daddy's little toy" and warns her that "playtime is over." Vince ordered her to take off her clothes down to her bra and underwear. McMahon uses his daughter to help what he refers to as "cleaning up the mess." Stephanie puts Trish's head in a bucket of filthy water. One of the announcers, Jerry Lawler, excitedly yells, "Yes! Yes!" His co-announcer, JR, acts horrified and notes the humiliation.

In order to intimidate and humiliate his employees, Vince McMahon devised a Kiss My Ass Club. McMahon drops his pants and underwear in the ring and makes wrestlers, divas, announcers, etc., kiss his exposed behind. McMahon makes it clear to the audience that his employees are in danger of being fired or suspended if they do not comply. Even his own son, Sean, is forced to kiss McMahon's exposed behind. Instead of kissing McMahon's ass, "Stone Cold" Steve Austin hits McMahon in the crotch and beats him with a belt. The Rock also stands up to McMahon's bullying. When the Rock insists that McMahon kiss the Rock's ass, McMahon refuses and tells the Rock, "I am a certified billionaire who can buy and sell you and everyone in the arena." Stone Cold appears on the monitor and tells McMahon that his body guard, Kurt Angle, cannot help him since Austin is beating Angle up backstage. Stone Cold also threatens to beat up McMahon, too, if he tries to leave the ring before McMahon kisses the Rock's ass. Rick Flair, half owner of the company, tells McMahon that if anyone else comes to help him, they will be suspended. The Rock brings JR into the ring to have McMahon kiss his ass as retribution for McMahon bullying JR. However, the Rock stops JR. Next, the Rock brings out Trish to allow her to get her revenge; however, since McMahon looks happy about getting kissed by a diva, the Rock stops her as well. Lastly, the Rock brings out Rikishi. Rikishi is a large Sumo wrestler-type character. He gyrates and pulls his bottoms up, exposing his large, dimply cheeks. The Rock shoves McMahon's face into Rikishi's backside. The Rock declares the Kiss My Ass Club officially closed. The club resurfaces in later shows.

Women are also targets of bullying, from both men and other women in the WWE. Vicky Guerrero is a normal-sized woman compared to most of the ultrathin WWE divas. She has a screechy, high-pitched voice and screams her tag line, "Excuse me!" repetitively. The crowd purposely interrupts her and yells so she is unable to speak. The announcers' comments are mixed, one saying, "She doesn't deserve this," and the other saying, "I love Vicky but this is funny...." When she tells wrestler Jon Cena that she lost weight, he responds with, "Look around, I think you'll find it." She demands an apology from announcer Jerry Lawler. Lawler responds, "I can't help it if you are the only diva in the WWE whose bathtub has stretch marks." Cena adds, "Vicky is so fat, she wakes up in sections." They continue back and forth with fat jokes.

In an ongoing storyline in 2009, two WWE divas, Michelle McCool and Layla, harass another diva, Mickie James, about her "weight problems." Mickie James is thin and has a very athletic body, therefore, calling her fat is ridiculous. Michelle and Layla promise to make James' life a "living hell." Michelle and Layla take James' outfit from the locker room and rip it apart while she is in the ring. They make a video with a photo of James wearing a pig snout. The children's song "Old McDonald Had a Farm" is playing in the background, complete with oinking noises. They nickname James "Piggie James," and laugh when they make her cry. They tell her she needs extenders to get the title belt around her waist. When James is set to leave *Smackdown* for *RAW* (the WWE has two nights of wrestling and therefore breaks up their talent between the two shows), the mean girls have a "buh-bye Piggy James" party with a pig cake and balloons. Michelle scoops up pig cake and shoves it into James' mouth while a couple other divas hold James down. Michelle squeals like a pig as the mean girls dump a bowl of punch on James's head. They get her a trough of lettuce because it is calorie-free and a certificate to Jenny Craig's weight loss program. In an off-camera interview with Michelle McCool about the controversial storyline, McCool admits the organization received a significant amount of hate mail (Diva Dirt, 2011). McCool talks candidly about having to play a bully. She said it never got easier and they felt terrible having to do it. McCool credits Mickie for pulling it off.

Other targets of bullying include Goldust and Eugene. Goldust (AKA Dustin Rhodes, AKA Dustin Runnels) played various characters in his wrestling career. At one point he was dressed in a gold jumpsuit and a platinum blonde wig. His character had stereotypical homosexual tendencies and would grope his male opponents in the ring. He was the target of homophobic jokes and slurs by the announcer and fellow wrestlers. Years later, Rhodes was mocked when his character developed Tourettes-like symptoms. Eugene, a mentally challenged character in the mid-2000s, was bullied as well. In one scene, McMahon and his son, Shane, cover Eugene in green paint and give him a swirly, sticking his head in the toilet and flushing.

MTV's Bully Beatdown

Bully Beatdown is an MTV "reality" show featuring mixed martial arts fighter, Jason "Mayhem" Miller. Miller explains that he was picked on as a child and now his mission is to avenge bully victims. In each episode, a bully is confronted by someone bigger and stronger. The victims get the satisfaction of seeing their bully getting beaten without having to do it themselves. The bully is called out and put in a ring with a professional fighter. The bully starts with $5,000 and loses $1,000 for every submission hold. The money then goes to the victim. The studio audience is quite comical, chanting taunts at the bully. At the end of each episode, the bully almost always apologizes to his or her victim. The professional fighters often tell the victims at the end of the show to call them if they need additional help with the bully. In "Ryan: The Family Favorite," Alan reports his brother for bullying him. He claims Ryan pushed him down the stairs and put his head through a wall. Ryan boasts, "I'm the real bully, I'm the real man." As Ryan is matched with a professional fighter, Miller announces, "Time for retribution." Miller taunts Ryan from the stands between rounds. After the match, Ryan tells his brother that he is sorry and that he loved him. In the only female bully match I could find, "Two Girls and One Cage," Keiko complains that her coworker Amanda has been bullying her at work. Amanda announces, "I happily accept the term 'bitch.'" She is introduced as "the She Devil," as she blows kisses to the audience. Miller retorts, "Let's use less words and more physical violence." After Amanda is beaten by a professional kickboxer, she says she is sorry but adds with attitude, "Sorry enough." Amanda eventually hugs Keiko. The purpose of *Bully Beatdown* is to supposedly help victims get revenge. Many of the shows end with the bully repenting and apologizing. Although *Bully Beatdown* is obviously scripted, the message it sends is that the way to handle a bully is to bully the bully. The show perpetuates the hierarchy of physical size and portrays physical aggression as the only remedy.

Comic Books

Comic books have traditionally had bullying characters, from Bluto (AKA Brutus) from the Popeye comic strip to Moose from the Archie comics. Bluto was enormous compared to a pre-spinach Popeye and had a gruff beard. Moose is a jock who often bullies other boys, especially when he gets jealous of their attention to his girlfriend, Midge. The character Moose makes a transformation over the years from a dumb, bully jock to one of Archie's friends. Reggie, a friend of Archie's, is often one of Moose's targets for bullying, but because of his obnoxious character, he elicits little sympathy. He is notorious for pulling pranks and trying to steal other boys' girlfriends.

Comic-book heroes and superheroes are often bullied before they acquire or discover their powers. The bullying enhances the transformation from the wimpy character to become the superhero. The superheroes represent adolescent wish fulfillment. Readers can identify with the wimpy pre-hero and then fantasize about what it would be like to transform into a superhero with superpowers. The best example of the transformation from bully victim to superhero is Peter Parker, Spider-Man. On the very first page of the first edition of the Spider-Man comic-book series, Peter is portrayed as an outcast with the cool kids. He has a sweater vest, glasses, and poor posture as though lacking self-confidence. Flash Thompson, the high school jock, is the bully at Peter's school. Flash calls Peter "bookworm" and tells him to "get lost." Peter vows to "one day show them" (Lee & Ditko, 1962, p. 4). When Peter has to break his date with Liz to battle the evil character Sandman, Flash is there to steal her away. Peter loses his temper and threatens to "wipe that stupid leer" off Flash's face. Peter catches himself, worried that if he beats Flash it will give away his identity as Spider-Man. Now, even Liz thinks he is a coward as she drives off with Flash. When one of the teachers, Mr. Warren, finds Peter and Flash arguing, he makes the boys "settle their differences" in a boxing ring. Peter tries to pull his punches but knocks out Flash. Parker is also bullied by his boss, J. Jonah Jameson, publisher of the *Daily Bugle*. Jameson is a classic bully in the workplace, which carries over the bullying from Parker's high school days to adulthood. Again, Spider-Man needs to be careful not to blow his cover by standing up for Peter.

The next two comic books are targeted to a younger, adolescent audience. I chose one targeted to boys and one to girls for comparison. *The Knights of the Lunch Table* series by Frank Cammuso plays on the fantasy of Sir Arthur and the Knights of the Round Table. Arthur "Artie" King has no secret powers, just a vivid imagination, escaping to world of monsters. He and his friends, Percy and Wayne, are trying to maneuver their way through Camelot Middle School. *Knights of the Lunch Table: The Dodgeball Chronicles* (Cammuso, 2008) begins with Artie moving and starting at a new school. Artie's new friend, Percy, warns Artie about "the Horde." The Horde, headed by a boy named Joe, is a group of bullies who terrorize the school. When Artie suggests telling Principal Dagger that the bullies stole his lunch, Percy tells him that dealing with her is worse than dealing with the bullies. One of the teachers, Mr. Merlin, helps protect the boys from Principal Dagger. Joe is very upset when he finds out Artie's sandwich was filled with soap (a prank Artie's sister pulled on Artie). The boys try to outrun Joe but get tripped with a hockey stick by one of Joe's cronies. As Joe is about to hit Artie, Principal Dagger interrupts. She is not concerned about Artie's well-being but rather about Joe, the school's all-star dodgeball player. When Artie accidently trips Principal Dagger, she calls him "worm" and says he has a "wormlike presence." Artie is assigned a mysterious locker that no one has been able to open for years. The rumor is the locker is cursed. When Arthur is able to open the locker, Joe is furious. He is about to hit Artie when Percy challenges the Horde to a dodgeball game. Arthur exaggerated his skills and has bragged about being an "all-star" at his last school. The boys go to a large boy named Scott for help. Scott agrees to help in the dodgeball game if Arthur retrieves his father's Swiss Army knife, which Scott accidently dropped in the sewer. Scott's mother does not allow Scott to play. Artie brings a spider to the game, scares Joe, and wins the game.

Walker and Jones's (2009) comic book *Super Girl: Comic Adventures in the 8th Grade* deals with villains and mean girls. Twelve-year-old Kara is Kryptonian and has special powers. Her cousin Superman tells her she must learn about the culture of Earth before she can be Supergirl. He sends her to boarding school, gives her glasses as a disguise, and renames her Linda. Principal Pycklemeyer is very mean to her. When Linda accidently destroys the desk because of her super strength, the rest of her class laughs at her. She tries to warm up her food at lunch with her super vision but ends up setting off the sprinklers. Everyone laughs at her again. In PE class, she is pelted with volleyballs as the class laughs at her. For two weeks straight, she is laughed at. The kids call her "dorky" and "goofy" and claim that she looks like a monkey. The captain of the cheerleaders, Belinda, is especially mean to Linda. (Note: Belinda is Linda's evil duplicate.) Belinda pretends to be Linda's friend and tricks Linda into talking badly about others in the class as she records it. Belinda then plays the recording over the loud speaker during school. Linda befriends another new girl, Lena, who has a mind-control machine. Lena uses the machine to embarrass Belinda and the other cheerleaders by making them quack like ducks. Belinda tries to come between Lena and Linda by pretending to be friends with Linda. Lena is at first very jealous because she does not think Linda needs any other friends besides her. Lena eventually catches on to Belinda's plan to destroy her friendship with Linda and stands up to Belinda. When Lena finds out that Linda is from Krypton, she vows to destroy her. Lena is actually Lex Luther's sister, Superman's sworn enemy. Lena's memory is erased and Belinda is turned into a crystal statue. Linda and Lena go back to being friends, although it is puzzling whey Linda would want to be friends with someone who treated her so badly and was so jealous of Belinda.

Video Games and Apps

While traditional video games are primarily violent, there is seldom an ongoing relationship between two parties. Most games do not meet the definition of bullying where there is a significant on-going power difference. The videogame *Bully*, however, is specifically programmed to emulate real-life bullying. Smart-phone applications (apps) have also created games where users can either get revenge from a bully or be the bully themselves. In the videogame *Bully*, Jimmy Hopkins is dropped off at a boarding school called Bullworth Academy because Jimmy's mother has just remarried. Jimmy has also been expelled from every other school he has attended. The goal is for Jimmy to survive high school. He must fend off the bullies and manage the four cliques that make up the student body. Critics complain that players can earn points by terrorizing other students by physically or psychologically abusing them (Leapman & Copping, 2008). Players can dunk students' heads in toilets and fire catapults at teachers. Weapons range from baseball bats and slingshots to more practical joke items such as itching powder and stink bombs. A spokesperson for the company that makes *Bully* defended the game by stating that the purpose is not to necessarily be the bully (Leapman & Copping, 2008). Players can choose which path to follow. Jimmy is not allowed to commit violence against girls or smaller kids without severe consequences. When players fight, they can get into trouble with the police. Critics claim it encourages players to assault teachers and other students (Leapman & Copping, 2008). The critics fear the game will make bullying cool. The company claims the goal is to overcome bullies. It is left to the player to decide if they want to protect the weaker characters from the bully or to be the bully.

Similar to the *Bully* video game is *Mean Girls: High School Showdown*. Mean girls run the school so players must decide if they will retaliate using the same methods as the mean girls (i.e., "bully") or take the high road (i.e., "BFF"). A player selects one of four character types: slacker, nerd, rebel, or art freak. Skills available to combat the mean girls include low blows, butter up, charm, and dirty fighting. Producers market the game as a chance for players to relive high school drama.

The popularity of smart-phone apps has spawned an entire line of revenge games. For example, the goal of the *Supermarket Bully* is to throw grocery items and hit the bully for points. The mundane venue of a grocery store is perhaps a safe fantasy that is unlikely to be imitated. Extensive game play could perhaps make for a less civil environment or it could embolden targets to stand up for themselves. *The Bank Bully*, similar to *Supermarket Bully*, allows players to throw things at a bully in a bank. In the game *Recess*, the object is to hit the bully with a ball as he mocks the player. Players must protect their lemonade stand against bullies in *Slingshot Justice*. Players are provided a slingshot to help defend against wedgies. These games tout the satisfaction players can get by teaching the bully what it feels like to be the victim. Some of the apps, however, allow the user to go on the offensive and actually become the bully. The target can range from chickens (*Chicken Bully*) to stick men (*iBully*). *Library Nerd* is explicit in its enjoyment of acting like a bully. "Admit it, you've always wanted to throw random things to bother that geek who is always sitting reading at the library. Now you can!" ("iTunes preview," n.d.).

Other apps related to bullying range from safety to educational tools. *Learn to Deal with Bullies* and *Bully 911* promise users to teach them self-defense skills. *Bully Shield* is an app for parents and teacher to help create action plans to stop a child from being bullied. The *Bully Black List* feature not only allows users to block harassing messages and phone calls, but it also stores incoming phone numbers as evidence. *Bully Capture* allows users to record interactions with the push of a single button. The recording can be forwarded to parents, school officials, or even the police. Audio files can even be used to authenticate a bully's voice as legal evidence.

An issue with video games, particularly massively multiplayer online games (MMOG), is "griefing." MMOG allows players to interact while playing, either through text or audio messages. Griefers are online bullies who can harass other players and sabotage their games. Feldman (2007) defined "griefers" as "virtual thugs" who either target new players or one specific player with whom they have a vendetta. Feldman reports that griefers often travel in "gang-like packs," simultaneously targeting the same victim. According to Davies (2006), multiplayer online role-playing games differ from the average first-person shooter games and provide more opportunities for abuse. Online games offer voice-communication features so that players can hear each other while playing. There is a danger of communicating with strangers or as Silverman (n.d.) noted, children playing with adults who enjoy harassing and dominating younger players. In an extreme case, a gang of griefers raided a virtual funeral of a player who had died in real life. The griefers "killed" all the players who were attending the virtual funeral. Feldman (2007) advised players not to use their own name or adopt a provocative name. He also recommends players form watch groups to report online bullies. Griefers harass by leaving inappropriate voice and text messages or screaming or trash-talking while online (Wade, n.d.). Players can adjust privacy setting, mute abusive players, and file complaints with the game's producers. Banning online bullies is not cost effective for the game industry; therefore, game operators encourage players to form virtual societies so they can create and monitor their own rules and laws (Davies, 2006).

YouTube Videos

Video-sharing websites such as YouTube allow nearly anyone to upload videos with little screening or supervision. Videos that go viral on outlets such as YouTube can change the lives of the subjects. In 2002, Ghyslain Raza videotaped himself swinging a golf-ball retriever like a Star Wars light saber. Some kids found the video and posted it on YouTube. Popkin (2007) reported that the video is one of the most popular viral videos of all times with over one billion views. Because of the relentless teasing and bullying Ghyslain received because of the video, he dropped out of school and was treated in a psychiatric ward (Popkin, 2007). Pasternack (2010) called the incident the most "visible bullying in history." Raza's parents sued the families of the teenagers who posted the video and later settled out of court. Thirteen-year-old Rebecca Black's video "Friday" went viral with more than 112 million views to date. Countless parodies of the video were created and posted. Black received death threats, one post telling her to "go die in a hole" (Wright, Kazdin, & Knox, 2011). The bullying and teasing got so bad at school, Black's mother pulled her out and homeschooled her (Vena, 2011).

In another viral video that reached prominence, 16-year-old Casey Heynes loses his temper and slams Ritchard Gale onto the cement. Heynes claims Gale was bullying him until Heynes had endured enough. What was unusual about the scene is that the bully Gale was significantly smaller than Heynes. Without the context, it would appear that Heynes was the bully because of the size difference. Grant (2011a) accused the Australian media or turning the incident into a "schandefreude spectacle," where viewers took pleasure in seeing a "scrawny" 13-year-old boy being thrown onto the pavement like a "rag doll." The incident apparently spawned numerous copycat videos of bully revenge. The incident spawned a series of other videos known as *Locker Room Bully Beatdown*, in which vigilantes exact their revenge on camera. Bracetti (2011) posted an additional 12 videos on the website Complex Tech.com. Grant (2011b) commented that unlike movies or television, there is no context in these videos about who is the "good guy" and who is the "bad guy." The videos could potentially continue the cycle of violence that schools are trying to stop.

Music Videos/Lyrics

Music has long been a vehicle for communicating about social issues. Music videos reinforce messages with visualizations of the lyrics. The following song lyrics and videos specially reference bullying and mean girls. The artists range from country to kid pop to more mature rock and hip hop.

In the song "Mean," Taylor Swift sings to anyone who has made her feel like "a nothing." She sings that someday she will be successful and that person will only be mean. She sings about switching sides and pointing out faults. She talks about how those who claim she can't sing will be sitting in a bar, all washed up, and alone. The video shows a series of bully and mean-girl victims. One boy in a bowtie is getting hassled by the football team as they take his fashion magazine and muss his hair. Next, there is a girl getting laughed at by others. The mean kids throw food at her as she earns money for college by dressing in a star costume as promotion for a restaurant. The next scene is of a little girl who is shunned by some other little girls. She sits in a bathroom stall with her lunch tray on her lap. In the song lyrics, Swift acknowledges that the bullies were probably bullied themselves, but the cycle stops now. The video jumps to the future, where the boy is taking a bow on the runway of a fashion show, the high school girl is now a top executive, and the little girl is in the audience listening to Swift sing. The implication is that the little girl could easily be a young Taylor Swift.

In the video for "Don't Laugh at Me," Mark Willis sings alone in a dark playground. Images of children are interspersed, corresponding to the lyrics: a little girl with braces, a boy being bullied, etc. The song shifts to a homeless man being ignored and looked down upon by a man in a business suit. In the second half of the video, the mood changes and people are helping the less fortunate. In the Peter, Paul, and Mary version released the next year, many of the children have disabilities such as Down's Syndrome. The video ends with uplifting stills of people doing good deeds to help out those less fortunate. The lyrics describe not only being bullied for being short or fat but for being Muslim, lesbian, or poor.

Sugarland's "Mean Girls" is a commentary about how hateful mean girls are. The lyrics describe how mean girls make others cry, pull hair, and backstab. The song is very pessimistic in that mean behavior starts on the playground, gets worse in high school, and then continues into adulthood. To make matters worse, Nettles sings that mean girls beget more mean girls in a continuous cycle.

"How Do You Like Me Now?" by Toby Keith is a tale of revenge 20 years after he was humiliated by a mean girl when they were both in high school. The video shows how the subject of the song, a cheerleader, laughed at Keith as a teenager. As revenge, he confesses that he was the one who wrote her phone number and "for a good time call" on the 50-yard line of the football field. He rubs it in that she is now in a bad marriage. At the end of the video, Keith gets in a limo with his high school self and drives away.

The lead singer of country music group the Wilkinsons laments how life was simpler when she was in school in the song "Nobody Died." The video shows a boy being bullied on the playground. He is pulled into the principal's office. One girl stands up for him and offers him her coat after the bullies steal his coat. The boy comes back to school and pulls out a gun. In a struggle, one boy gets shot. There is a shrine on the shooting victim's locker. The bullied boy is shown sitting in an orange jumpsuit in a cell. It is unclear what the point of the song is beyond a yearning for a simpler time. It appears the song is an indictment of young people and their overreaction to the problems kids have faced for generations instead of the anti-bullying message of the other songs in this analysis. Nowhere in the song or the video does it explore the differences that could be attributed to the desperation of bringing a gun to school. Generally, country music lyrics are very constructive. It is surprising this song does not include a moral to the story.

Some of the pop music lyrics and videos are tailored specifically to a younger audience, the same age group that is likely to experience bullying. Michael and Marisa, who are both in their early teens, are very cute and very relatable to a young audience. The Eh Ohs is a kids' band from Canada. They are three guys with thick black-framed glasses and matching bowling shirts who sing fun and educational songs. Selena Gomez is a Disney star who played the lead role in the Disney Channel popular series *Wizards of Waverly Place*.

The lyrics to "Don't Bully Me" by the Eh Ohs include information about what listeners should do if they are bullied. The song advises listeners to report bullying behavior and emphasizes the role of bystanders. It also makes a declarative statement about the culture of bullying, stating that safety is every child's right.

Michael and Marisa's video for "The Same" begins with a girl looking for a place to sit in the cafeteria. She ends up sitting by herself as no one makes a place for her. As she walks down the hallway, girls whisper and point. The singer Marisa is featured in the video as a bystander. She laments about defying her friends. Once Marisa finally goes over and sits with the lonely girl, other kids join her. The song stresses the importance of bystanders. It acknowledges that it sometimes difficult to risk losing friends by taking a stand.

The video for "Who Says" begins with Selena Gomez in a fancy dress, singing during a photo shoot. She takes off her shoes and walks the streets of a somewhat rundown neighborhood. She takes a cab to an industrial park under a bridge. At home, she changes out of her fancy dress and takes off a layer of makeup. She runs to a beach and is surrounded by a group of girls of various levels of traditional beauty. She encourages girls to be themselves and not to aspire to some superficial ideal of beauty from a photo shoot. More specifically, Gomez sings about being made to feel insecure and not good enough by mean individuals.

Bullying is also a topic in more mature music. Songs by Radio Silence NYC and Rise Against about bullying specifically address gay and lesbian bashing. The Radio Silence NYC's "Renegade" video begins with the quote, "Six out of ten American teens will witness bullying at least once a day." The video features footage of the band performing in a small club interspersed with shots of a group of young people with a black makeup streaked across their eyes. One of the girls from the group is romantically involved with a girl without a black streak. The bullies find the girls together and physically take away one of the girls. The end quote reads, "Hatred is the enemy. Do something."

A teenage girl sees her locker covered in "dyke" stickers in Rise Against's video "Make It Stop (September's Children)." Some mean girls take her backpack and play keep-away with it. In another scene, a group of bullies hold a boy while a mean girl forces a kiss on him (the presumption is that the boy is gay). Another boy sits in the cafeteria where a group of bullies comes and spits in his food. (The way he runs away it is clear he is gay as well.) The girl goes home and pulls out a gun and puts it to her head. The kissed boy reaches for a noose. The cafeteria boy stands on a bridge. The reading of the names of teens who have committed suicide because of bullying is interspersed with video clips of a variety of individuals assuring their audience "it gets better." The cast includes It Gets Better founder, Dan Savage. The three bullied kids each flash to images of their successful futures. They all abandon their suicide plans. The video is extreme at times but also very hopeful. It specifically targets bullying of LGBT youth.

Many of the more mature songs include a revenge component where the victim strikes back. Jessie J.'s video of "Who's Laughing Now" begins with a little girl with black hair being harassed by a group of blonde girls in pink. They are pointing at and whispering about her. The girl is a clearly a younger version of the singer Jessie. Young Jessie works her way through the school wreaking havoc, spitting in the cafeteria food and spraying the blonde girls with a fire extinguisher. The bystanders are dancing behind her, cheering. The message of the song to viewers is if you are who you are, you will be successful and be able to get revenge someday. There does not appear to be any adults other than the teacher who is only shown in the first scene. In the lyrics, Jessie thanks her persecutors for the pain because it made her try harder to succeed.

Kelly Rowland in "Stole," sings about how the subject of the video used to be such a good boy. He sees his mother with a black eye, presumably from his father. He walks into the bathroom and kills himself with his father's gun. Rowland sings about how the boy had been bullied because he was smart. The video intersperses images of kids crying because of his death and flashbacks to kids bullying him. Playing a character in the video, she wishes she would have talked to him instead of turning away like the other bystanders.

In the video of "Thoughtless" by Korn, a boy walks down the hall where a group of jocks stop him and beat him up. Through special effects, anger starts to literally bubble under his skin. While swimming in a pool, the jocks push him under the water. To get revenge on the bullies, the boy hires an escort to take to the school dance to make them jealous. He then vomits so forcefully, that he knocks the other students down. The lyrics are full of vengeance and hatred with redemption at the end.

"No Love" by Eminem and Lil Wayne is about a boy who stands up to his bullies. The video begins with a small boy with a black eye. He is getting brutally hit with dodgeballs in gym class. He gets pushed around in the locker room and the school hallways. Lil Wayne raps about "legs being broken." The bullies attack the boy in the bathroom and dump his bookbag. Eminem joins in, singing that it is too late to apologize. When the boy gets home, his father yells at him. It looks like his mother is trying to comfort the boy, but the man pulls her away. The boy has posters of Lil Wayne and Eminem in his room. When the bullies push the boy down in the cafeteria, he finally hits back.

The video of "Why's Everybody Always Pickin' On Me?" by Bloodhound Gang appears to be a spoof of anti-bullying songs. The boy in the video is a younger, nerdier version of the lead singer. A popular girl approaches him and knees him in the groin. Some boys hassle him in the hall. At the end of the video, a group of men put him in a straight-jacket and push him down the stairs in a wheelchair. Everyone appears to be picking on him because of his acne, poor grooming habits, and bad fashion sense. He gets picked on for running like a girl and "sitting down to pee." The song ends with a warning to the bullies that he will go "berserk" like a postal clerk if they do not stop teasing him.

Conclusion

The examples in this chapter demonstrate the wide range of genres and media channels that include themes of bullying and relational aggression. New technology such as smart-phone apps allow users to report real-life incidents of bullying, while at the same time allowing users to pretend to be the bully in games such as *Library Nerd* or *Mean Girls: High School Showdown*. File-sharing technology allows anti-bullying campaigns such as It Gets Better to post inspirational videos for bully victims, while enabling users to upload embarrassing videos and post harassing comments and death threats on others' videos.

While the increased attention to the problems of bullyies and mean girls through a variety of channels can be beneficial, there is also a danger of overexposure of the bullying or mean-girl themes. Viewers can become desensitized to the messages or even worse, cynical toward the victims. Comedian Daniel Tosh spoofs the homemade videos featuring kids holding up flash cards with messages about how bad their lives are because of bullying. Tosh comments that he hates bullies almost as much as he hates bullying web videos. Tosh makes his own cards that read, "It costs $600 a month to keep my pool at 96 degrees" and "occasionally my shoulder hurts" to mock the overuse of the format. Anti-bullying campaigns are wise to strike a balance of messages.

14

Pro-Social and Anti-Bullying Messages

While media entertain viewers with portrayals of bullies and mean girls, media channels can also be used as a vehicle for change. The following section includes anti-bullying materials for adolescents, parents, and educators distributed through books, television, videos, and the Internet. A driving force of the anti-bullying movement has been celebrities and public figures who have lent their time, effort, and names to public service announcements and other programs.

Nonfiction Books: Children

Chapter 12 included an analysis of picture books and chapter books for children and adolescents. In this section, I included nonfiction books that provide young readers advice on how to handle bullies and mean girls.

Good-bye Bully Machine (Fox & Beane, 2009) was written using a machine as a metaphor. It references the power of the machine but also shows how a machine stops when it runs out of energy. The book identifies "sneaky" ways of bullying such as rumors and exclusion, often considered in the realm of relational aggression. It also addresses excessive teasing, which the authors refer to as "taunting." There is an inclusion of an interesting collage of phrases worded in the first person, for example, "If you don't tell, we won't stop." The first-person narrative is an unusual device in letting the bully's voice be heard. It gives readers the impression that they are hearing directly from the bully his or her motivation and strategy. The authors also include a discussion about how kids who are well liked, even by adults, can be bullies. This last section is particularly important since it is very difficult for victims when an adult does not believe the "nice" kid is a bully because he or she does not fit the bully stereotype.

How to Handle Bullies, Teasers and Other Meanies (Cohen-Posey, 1995), which is subtitled "A Book That Takes the Nuisance Out of Name Calling and Other Nonsense," emphasizes verbal as well as physical bullying and meanness. Cohen-Posey suggests turning insults into compliments or agreeing because it confuses and disarms the bully. The book teaches readers to find a "golden nugget," which means trying to get at the root of the bully's insult while leading the bully away from the initial prejudice. The author teaches readers to use "I" messages instead of "you" and "should" and advises readers to name their own feelings, whether it be fear or disappointment. Cohen-Posey directs readers to take more aggressive measures if the bully is physically violent. The book warns about using the correct tone, an often overlooked skill. The strength of the book is the inclusion of a significant number of examples of dialogue and worksheets to practice the new skills.

Published in the mid-1990s, *Dealing with Bullying* (Johnston, 1996) offers lists of reading suggestions for bully victims. The book contains some outdated or inaccurate information such as bullies are usually unhappy, and lonely, and have low self-esteem. Johnston advises readers who are victimized to walk away, tell the bully to leave them alone, or tell a grownup. The book also includes advice to readers if they are the ones bullying, which relieves the victim from full responsibility of handling the situation. Johnston also encourages bystanders to stick up for others. She tells the story of a playground bully who changed because other kids stood up for the target and later befriended the bully. The definition of a bully as a "person who teases, threatens, or hurts smaller people" leaves out some of the more severe aspects of bullying but perhaps is sufficient for a young person, kindergarten to third grade, the book's target audience.

Jakubiak's (2010) *A Smark Kid's Guide to Online Bullying* is one of the first books to address cyberbullying targeting younger users of technology. The book helps define what online bullying is and reasons why cyberbullies do what they do. It gives advice beyond ignoring the problem. It encourages the victim to not only tell a trusted adult but to collect evidence and work to stop the abuse by reporting the incident to the bully's internet service providers. Although the book is targeted to younger readers, it speaks at a mature level and acknowledges the computer savvy of young Internet users.

Talking about Bullying (Powell, 1999) is specifically targeted to first through third graders. It not only includes basic information such as what bullying is but also how bullying can make the victim feel. Powell emphasizes important messages, such as anyone can be the target of bullies. It also does a very good job of finding a middle ground between fighting back, which may be dangerous, and doing nothing, which lets the bully get away with their bad behavior.

The strength of *Why Do People Bully* (Hibbit, 2005) is that it explains that merely punishing the bully after the fact may provoke the bully to be even crueler. Although the book is written for children, this message is perhaps even more important for adults, particularly school officials. Advice to "tell an adult" is often too simplistic. Even young children know that there is a risk in telling. The book acknowledges that bullies are very good at being subtle, hiding their behaviors from adults and issuing threats for telling.

An excellent book for older readers is *Letters to a Bullied Girl: Messages of Healing and Hope* (Gardner, Buder, & Buder, 2008). It is a touching example of empathy and support from strangers. When two sisters read a local newspaper story about a girl, Olivia, being bullied in a neighboring town, they collected letters to help support Olivia. Olivia was being bullied because she was epileptic. Her bullies even created an "Olivia's Haters" page on the Internet. The letters the Buder sisters collected came from a range of writers from victims to bullies. The victims often wrote about being bullied for their looks, for being different, and for health reasons. The "Healing Words" section at the end of the book is particularly inspirational.

Television show host Dr. Phil is known for his anti-bullying efforts. His son Jay McGraw's book, *Life Strategies for Dealing with Bullies* (2008) and *Closing the Gap: A Strat-*

egy for Bringing Parents and Teens Together (2001) are targeted to older readers as well. McGraw covers the basics of causes and effects of bullying. He gives advice and offers strategies to victims and bystanders. He also addresses bullies directly. The book includes anti-bully pledges to be taken not only by students but parents and school faculty as well.

Hayley DiMarco (2008) has written a series of books on mean girls from a Christian perspective. In *Mean Girls: Facing Your Beauty Turned Beast*, DiMarco describes the book not as a self-help book telling girls to be brave and strong but rather as a way of life based on the Bible and a greater power. There are some self-empowerment messages in the book such as "don't make yourself a victim" (p. 57) and "don't be the easy enemy" (p. 81). DiMarco (2008) suggests readers ignore mean girls unless they feel God is telling them to confront the girl. She adds that the final tactic to combat mean girls is prayer. Readers are asked to see confrontation with mean girls as a chance to live their faith, to persevere, and to be closer to God. She recommends acting like Christ, who did not retaliate, made no threats, and entrusted himself to the Father. DiMarco even included a chapter called "Jesus Speaks to Mean Girls." The book gets pretty intense with a discussion on "dying to self" and giving oneself over to God. The concept of "dying to self" is a sophisticated concept that may be very difficult for her target audience to understand. The Bible passages are pretty deep and long range. DiMarco states, "Did you know God says that when you have angry or mean thoughts about someone, you get the same punishment as a murder?" (p. 106). DiMarco provides some context for the passage but it is rather a complex distinction for a girl in her early teens to grasp.

Mean Girls Gone: A Spiritual Guide to Getting Rid of Mean (DiMarco, 2005) is written in the form of a journal where blank pages are provided for girls to write their feelings. The book guides readers through a "journey" of their spiritual life and measures it via a self-inventory. Subsections of the book include a great deal of introspection: "Freeing Your Soul from the Bondage of Mean," "Healing from the Inside Out," and "Finding Inner Peace in the Face of Mean." The message DiMarco (2005) gives readers is that if their dreams are not tested, they will never truly be authentic. In *Frenemies: What to Do When Friends Turn Mean*, DiMarco (2010) once again uses Bible passages to guide young girls when someone close to them becomes the mean girl. She offers Jesus' relationship with Judas as the ultimate example of a frenemy. She gives advice about either gently guiding the friend back on track or, in extreme cases, to break up with the mean girl. One issue that is absent from the three DiMarco books is support from adults in the readers' lives. There is no mention of parents or a religious leader to help girls through this journey. The books appear to rely on the introspection of young readers.

Nonfiction Books: Parents and Adults

The premise of *Odd Girl Out* by Rachel Simmons (2002, 2011) is to educate parents, particularly mothers, about the world of girls. The premise of the book is that having once been a girl is not sufficient to understand the current dynamics of the girl world. Simmons does an excellent job of getting the reader to distinguish between the "reality of social order" and "intentional acts of meanness" (p. 304). Perhaps the most important, and potentially most controversial, item in the book is her advice to teach girls to be aggressive. She argues that aggressiveness will help in dealing with repressed feelings that come with girls who fear what Simmons calls "messy feelings" such as jealousy and anger. She is one of the few authors who address socialization in different cultures and how raising non-aggressive, "nice" daughters can put them at a disadvantage.

Rachel Wiseman (2003), in her book *Queen Bees and Wannabes*, educates parents and school officials by identifying trends in girl culture and naming the different roles they play, such as "queen bee," "sidekick," "floater," and "torn bystander." She notes that almost all girls are "pleasers" and "wannabes," which explains why girls would behave so differently in girl groups from the confident girls parents thought they raised. Wiseman focuses on how parenting styles contribute to social hierarchies. She gives options and advice to parents on how to talk to their daughters and, more importantly, how to listen. It is difficult to see how *Queen Bees and Wannabes* was the basis for the movie *Mean Girls*. The movie is rather callous in its comical portrayal of perpetrators and victims of relational aggression. Girls seeing the movie may miss the point since most of the characters are mean at some point and do not appear to be punished for their behavior. In the end, the mean-girl behavior lives on via the next generation of Plastics. The book is a much more thoughtful look at the intense pain and suffering caused by mean-girl behavior. The one thing that the movie *Mean Girls* does take from this book is the ways in which girls are mean—for example, exclusion and dividing loyalties.

Cheryl Dellasega and Charisse Nixon (2003) specifically address relational aggression in *Girl Wars*. Not only do they share stories of girls involved in relational aggression and their mothers, but they report research findings of experts, academicians, and organizations working to solve the problem. They offer solutions on how to handle a continuum of relational aggression from mild to severe. Dellasega and Nixon suggest teaching girls to be assertive instead of aggressive. They link aggression to low self-confidence; therefore, they advise parents to work on their daughters' confidence to help them stand up to mean girls for themselves and others. They also advise addressing the group and the group dynamics rather than singling out a "mean" girl. The last strategy they give specifically to mothers is to work to change the culture.

Carrie Goldman's (2012) daughter's bullying inspired her to write *Bullied: What Every Parent, Teacher and Kid Needs to Know About Ending the Cycle of Fear*. To her daughter's story she adds a section on kids who are at risk of peer victimization. Her advice for dealing with the issue ranges from creating a home that does not produce bullies or victims to changes in marketing toys and sexy clothing for children.

In Barbara Coloroso's (2008) *The Bully, the Bullied, and the Bystander*, she differentiates between bullying and normal childhood behavior, teasing and taunting, and flirting and sexual bullying. The last description in a list of twenty characteristics of who can be the target of bullying is simply a kid who is in the wrong place at the wrong time—basically anyone. Coloroso (2008) explains the effect of parenting styles and family dynamics on children's likelihood of becoming a bully or a target of bullying. She asserts that if parents identify their child as a bully, the family should discipline, nurture empathy, and monitor media use. She warns parents of bully victims not to minimize the problem, rush to solve the problem for their child, tell their child to avoid the bully or fight back, or confront the bully's parents alone. She also discusses how children can be turned from bystanders to witnesses and how parents can affect the climate in the school community.

In *The Everything Parent's Guide to Dealing with Bullies*, Deborah Carpenter and Christopher J. Ferguson (2009) address common myths such as, "Bullying is a normal rite of passage," "Kids need to learn to defend themselves," "Children who are bullied always tell an adult," "People are born bullies," and "Bullies are loners with no social skills" (p.

88). They also do an excellent job of addressing ideals of femininity and masculinity as part a culture where violence is acceptable, perhaps even expected. Carpenter and Ferguson (2009) represent a small minority of bullying experts who address bullying in books and movies and media effects from violent television and video games. They also incorporate theory, such as the social learning theory, where children are likely to imitate behaviors they see that are rewarded.

In *Raising Bully-Proof Kids: No More Jellyfish, Chickens or Wimps*, Paul Coughlin (2011) takes a Christian perspective. He claimes that Christian parents are raising some of the "wimpiest" kids and ignoring the "broadest counsel of God" (p. 17). He points to parents who think assertiveness is wrong, and thus they are raising overly compliant kids. Coughlin accuses some Christians of have a false image of Jesus as gentle and meek. He argues that Jesus was submissive to his Father's will, not the will of man. Coughlin advises parents to raise assertive children rather than aggressive or passive children. Coughlin (2011) argued, "There is no greater argument within the community that promotes not standing up to injustice and freedom-crushing than Jesus' much-quoted (and torturously ill-applied) statement that 'if someone strikes you on the cheek, offer the other also' (Luke 6:29 NRSV)" (p. 183). Coughlin interprets the "turn the other cheek" passage as a call for an individual to not retaliate. He argued that it does not mean an individual cannot stop abuse. He described countless churches as teaching passivity to children, including passivity toward bullying.

Television and Video Programming

The following programs provide useful information to adolescents, parents, and educators about aspects of bullying and bullying prevention and survival. The Cartoon Network produced a special called *Speak Up*. The special featured a mix of famous people, mostly athletes, and regular kids giving testimonials and advice to other kids. President Obama gives the opening statement. Contributions were made by a number of celebrities not usually seen in the media such as professional female athletes (e.g., Lisa Leslie, Venus Williams, and Hope Solo) and race car drivers (e.g., Jeff Burton, Joey Langano, and Trevor Bayne). Pro BMX rider Matt Wilhelm and teen actor Jackson Rogow both admit to having been bullied and then turning and bullying others. Alye Pollack, the "Words Do Hurt" YouTube video girl, adds her perspective.

I also included several lesser known outlets to demonstrate the range of the anti-bullying movement. *Fresh Take* is an educational program produced by Brigham Young University Television. Bully expert Dorothy Espelage reports an increase in the severity of bullying and adds that it is happening at a younger age. Espelage dispels myths and identifies bullying as a relationship problem. She assesses the programs that are and are not working in schools, particularly programs that fail to teach skills and do not address homophobic bullying. She warns about the difficulties working directly with the bully's parents because of defensiveness and the possibility that there is violence in that home. She suggests using the term "ally" rather than "bystander." The episode ends with footage of a successful school program where student ambassadors conduct role-playing workshops with other students.

A Place of Our Own is a Public Broadcasting Service program that deals with children's issues. The episode "How to Handle a Bully" featured a panel consisting of Pamela

Kisor from the Children's Center at Cal State LA, a childcare provider, and a mother of a bullying target looking for help. Kisor warns about using the word "bully" with preschoolers. She explains that children that young are not likely to have intentionality like an older child. At that young age, an aggressive child might not understand the consequences of his or her actions. The program also shows examples of managing aggressive behavior, such as something as simple as punching a pillow. Experts also demonstrate how to create a space for privacy to defuse aggressive situations. Unlike almost of all of the other programs, this episode focused on very young children. PBS is also one of the only outlets to air entertainment shows for preschoolers that deal with mean peers.

WHADDYADO is a syndicated educational series targeted to 13- to 16-year-olds that is meant to educate young viewers about what to do in various situations. The skits are only one and a half to three minutes long. The three segments that address bullying or mean girls are placed at the end of the show and are juxtaposed with stories about what to do if a bear attacks or a minivan runs into a ditch full of water. A piece on cyberbulling followed stories of a shark attack, a snow-covered snow boarder, and a house fire. However, the seriousness of cyberbulling is rather downplayed, "If someone hacks into your computer, they can make your life miserable." The segment only addresses computer hacking, which implies the culprit must be a computer geek. In the first scene, two attractive girls are getting a text. They look shocked at the content. The next scene cuts to a boy with severe acne and red hair sitting alone in a school computer lab. He says to himself, "That'll show her." It is not clear what prompted the boy to hack into the girls' systems. Dr. Suzy Goldstein from Childhood Solutions advises viewers that it may make them feel bad or uncomfortable if someone spreads rumors about them. She explains that the perpetrators are motivated by gaining attention and do not have enough going on in their own lives. She assures viewers that if they know who they are and have supportive friends and families, what other people say does not matter. The next time they show the girl on screen, she is smiling and laughing while holding her phone. After well publicized stories about cyberbullying and suicides, the segment seems quite underwhelming.

Another episode of *WHADDYADO* covers what their producers call "another type" of bullying such as malicious teasing, name calling, and exclusion. In the skit, two boys talk about a girl they do not like. They put a sticker on her back that reads "four eyes." The girl, who is wearing sunglasses, does not seem upset, just a little annoyed. She crumples up the paper and appears to go back to normal. Dr. Goldstein advises the target to first ignore the teasing. Then if the bullying continues, the target should ask for help from parents or school officials. She warns that threats cross the line. The illustration in the segment appears more comical than malicious. The last segment, which is about mean girls, begins with a group of girls talking about another girl. They giggle about how one of them wrote something about the other girl on the bathroom wall; however, they do not specify what was written. The mean girls call the other girl "disgusting." When the girl approaches them, they ignore her and tell her to go sit over by the garbage cans. Dr. Goldstein explains that it is not uncommon for girls to leave other girls out. It is how they make themselves feel good about themselves. She gives victims vague instructions to speak out and find better friends. While this illustration appears to be more intense than the previous segments, the advice is rather thin.

A group called Real Life Teens (2001) created an educational video called *Bullies & Harassment*. Interviews with students and school officials define bullying and give advice about how to deal with bullies. *Bully 911* is a self-defense program by Noel and Johnny

Gyro. They give mild, moderate, and major instructions to defend against physical bullying such as an arm grab or a choke so the victim can get away and seek help.

The Teaching Channel produced a series of educational videos on tackling the issue of bullying. The segment "Creating Rules and Rubrics to Prevent Bullying" addresses efforts by a principal of a Catholic school to create rules and rubrics to stop bullying. The plan includes teacher training that partners with the Olweus program. The video shows teachers struggling with developing a chart that designates the consequences depending on the offense because of the different types of bullying and levels of severity. The first step of their plan is to have the student fill out a reflection sheet to help him or her learn what they did wrong rather than an abstract punishment. The eighth graders lead discussions with younger students and help them create posters. In "Change Your Attitudes Toward Bullying: Be an Ally," students create t-shirts and bracelets to promote the idea of being an ally and not just a passive bystander. Each student is involved in six guided discussions. A group of eighth graders is selected for the leadership class doing workshops with other classes. The strategy is to have the kids speak to their peers. The leaders act out skits on topics including cyberbullying, after which there is a small group breakout session. The school counselor demonstrates a mediation session between students who are having a conflict. The counselor records the plan of action, which the students sign. The "Bully-Proof Your Child: Become a Solution-Coach" segment works closely with parents. The facilitator, Nicholas Carlisle, stresses listening skills. He advises the parents to think of the left hand as empathy and the right hand as action if a child comes to them with a bullying problem. Small groups of parents share their thoughts on different scenarios.

Multi-Media Campaigns

The Internet has proven to be an effective way to communicate information, especially to young people. Advice for parents and educators is available on a variety of websites, ranging from television-related websites, (e.g., oprah.com, ac360.blogs.cnn.com, and pbs.org) to "pop" websites (e.g., galtime.com, meangirlsnotcool.com, and askkids.com) to parenting and educational websites (e.g., parentfurther.com, webmd.com, greatschools.org, and commonsensemedia.org). "Ask Rosalind" is a feature on the Cartoon Network *Speak Up Special*'s website where Rosalind Wiseman answers kids questions about bullying from how to handle bullying from a friend to how to start a school anti-bullying group.

Arguably the most influential of the anti-bullying messages are being generated by the It Gets Better campaign and the Trevor Project. Author and sex advice columnist Dan Savage launched the It Gets Better campaign following the suicide of Billy Lucas, a 15-year-old boy who was bullied by students because they thought he was gay. The It Gets Better campaign and many other anti-bullying programs specifically focus on LGBT youth because of the high rates of bullying targeting this group. Sims (2004) reported that almost 90% of LGBT students are verbally or physically harassed or assaulted each year compared to 62% of straight students. Karki (2010) reported that gay and lesbian youth are three times as likely to make a plan to attempt suicide and five times more likely not to feel safe at school. Savage and his partner Terry Miller uploaded the first It Gets Better video September 21, 2010. Since then, more than 50,000 user-created videos have been added with an estimated 50 million views (It Gets Better Project, 2012). The goal is to give hope and show victims of bullying and harassment that life gets better with time. Although the program was initially designed to help gay and lesbian youth, it can be applied to all victims of bullying. Doyle (2010) argued that the project gives victims of sustained bullying an alternative to feeling like they are "unlovable freaks who bring bad treatment on themselves by virtue of existing."

There is a significant presence of celebrities and public figures in the uploaded videos. President Obama's It Gets Better video has been viewed over 1,360,000 times. Ellen DeGeneres' video is a close second with over 1,270,000 views. Casts of televisions shows such as *House* and *Pretty Little Liars* are featured in videos as are professional sports teams such as the Atlanta Braves and the San Francisco 49ers. Flock (2011) reported that the first three Republicans who recorded It Gets Better messages—Leonard Lance, Frank LoBiondo and Jon Runyan—did so even though each of them have opposed gay rights and voted against issues such as Don't Ask Don't Tell and gay marriage.

One NOH8 video focuses on how the political culture in the country is responsible for setting a climate for LGBT harassment because of what anti-gay legislation tells the youth about their worth: they cannot get married, they cannot serve openly in the military (at the time of the making of the video), they cannot donate blood, etc. Celebrity appearances include Kat Von D, Dave Navarro, Dr. Drew, Gene Simmons, and Jeff Probst. Perhaps the most notable contributor to the video is Cindy McCain, wife of Senator and 2008 Republican presidential nominee John McCain. GLAAD's Amplify Your Voice campaign features Mario Lopez, Sandra Lee, Tori Spelling and Dean McDermott, Lance Black, and Vinny Guadagnino from *Jersey Shore*. One of the more successful online campaigns is MTV's A Thin Line project. The project promotes the MTV Digital Rights Project, which includes online abuse. The project includes celebrities such as Snooki from *Jersey Shore* and Justin Bieber, who asks viewers to take small steps to help "dial down digital drama." Google Chrome's sponsored anti-bullying video has received nearly two and a half million views on YouTube. The montage includes It Gets Better founder Dan Savage, Chaz Bono, Lady Gaga, and Woody from the Disney movie *Toy Story*. An anti-homophobic-language "Think B 4 you Speak" campaign includes comments from NBA players, dissuading viewers from indiscriminately using the word "gay."

Television programs have incorporated the theme of bullying into individual episodes. *Extreme Makeover: Home Edition* producers teamed up with anti-bullying groups to make the episode "The Walker Family" a campaign rather than just another home makeover. The Walker family had experienced tragedy when Carl Walker hanged himself after being bullied at school. In addition to building a new house, producers of the show created a "Stand Together" website where viewers could post their picture in support. The show also teamed up with Cody Simpson who leads a Defeat the Labels campaign. Elmo and Big Bird make an appearance at one of their anti-bullying assembly. The Kardashian sisters add their support. Demi Lovato joined them at an event and sang her song, "Try to Tear Me Down." The reality series *The Little Couple* showed footage of Bill and Jen speaking to an elementary school about being picked on when they were children. Bill describes how he got teased for his surgical scars. Jen discloses that she often felt left out because she was a little person.

Even comedy shows have featured serious anti-bullying messages. Stephen Colbert, on his Comedy Central show *The Colbert Report*, featured a reply to the Religious Right's anti-anti-bullying. Colbert reports that, according to Gary Glen, the president of the American Family Association of Michigan, anti-bullying legislation is "just a Trojan horse for the homosexual agenda." Colbert's sarcastic response is, "It is well known that the homosexual agenda is just an insidious plot to keep gay teenagers from dying." Michigan's legislature added the statement, "This section does not prohibit a statement of a sincerely held religious belief or moral conviction." Colbert interprets the clause as, "Bullying is fine if you get a permission slip from God." He jokes, if someone gives a kid a swirly, that person can just say he or she is giving the kid a baptism. Colbert also jokes that Jesus acted like a bully when he threw the moneylenders out of the temple because they were the "mathletes." He adds the last supper was Jesus hanging out at the "cool kids" table. They restricted others from sitting with them even though there was plenty of room on the other side of the table. In a moment of seriousness, Colbert points out that the law that is supposed to protect gay teens from killing themselves is a statement that justifies that cruelty by appealing to God and the Bible.

Celebrities have made a significant impact on the anti-bullying movement from creating their own campaigns and videos to keeping the topic of bullying in the forefront of public discourse by sharing their experiences. Moved by the death of Tyler Clemente and other young people who have committed suicide because of bullying, Ellen DeGeneres is a staunch supporter of anti-bullying. DeGeneres uses her syndicated talk show to address the issue of bullying and garner support for the United against Bullying campaign. She hosted Tyler Long's family, one of the subjects of the documentary *Bully*, on her talk show *Ellen*. Big celebrities including Justin Timberlake, Selena Gomez, and Taylor Swift shared their experience of getting picked on and teased on her show as well. From Madonna to Drew Brees to Jeff Foxworthy to Kobe Bryant, celebrities and professional athletes joined DeGeneres to speak out on the topic on PSAs. Phil Graw also has included celebrities whom he adds to the conversation on his talk show, *The Dr. Phil Show*. Max Adler, the actor who plays the bully Karofsky on the television series *Glee*, appeared on the show "Bullies Beware." The two lead actresses in the movie *Mean Girls 2* came to discuss the movie on "Mini Mean Girls." Kristen Cavallari made an appearance on the episode "Bullying: The Power to Protect Your Child." She described her passion for bullying issues and her misrepresentation as the mean girl in reality shows such as *Laguna Beach*.

Lady Gaga launched her own foundation, named after her hit song "Born this Way," with the help of other big players like Oprah Winfrey. According to Thompson (2012), Gaga defines it not as a "foundation" but a "youth empowerment project." Various other celebrities have teamed up with anti-bullying groups. GLAAD PSAs feature celebrities from Shaq to Amy Poehler. Justin Bieber lent his support to the documentary *Bully* (2012), as did Nickelodeon teen star Victory Justice. Justice promoted a $20,000 competition on dosomething.org for fans to share stories of bullying (Rowley, 2012). Singer-songwriter Michele Branch and her husband Greg teamed up to fight bullying with Bully Proofed. The Broadway show *Wicked* partnered with Bully Bust. The producers of *Wicked* sponsored a "Defying Gravity" essay contest and donated proceeds from ticket sales of the show. Casts of ABC Family Network shows *Switched at Birth*, *The Secret Lives of the American Teenager*, *Pretty Little Liars*, and *The Lying Game* joined together to create Delete Digital Drama, which is a campaign to help end cyberbulling. The network also began a Twibbons campaign on Facebook and Twitter. A Twibbon is a digital bumper sticker users can post to show support. The ABC Family website included supplemental information that goes along with their movie *Cyberbullying*.

A significant number of celebrities have spoken out in the media about how they were picked on and bullied, ranging from comedian Margaret Cho to Linkin Park's lead singer Chester Bennington to rapper 50 Cent to Snooki from *Jersey Shore*. Zooey Deschanel reported that middle school girls spit on her ("Middle School Girls," 2012). Bullies tripped

Susan Boyle, called her names, and burned her clothing with cigarettes (Winfrey, 2010). Rebecca Black, famous for her "Friday" viral video, and Selena Gomez reported being forced to leave school. Because of the harassment by her classmates, Black was home-schooled her mother (Vena, 2011). Gomez was also homeschooled (Fuller, 2011). Most recently, Paris Jackson, daughter of Michael Jackson, reported being bullied in school ("Paris Jackson Suffers," 2012). Demi Lovato has been the most vocal about her experience as a bully victim. She has made appearances on *America's Next Top Model* and *Extreme Makeover: Home Edition* to promote her anti-bullying work. Lovato is a heavy supporter of *teensagainstbullying.org* and the Pacer Center. Young celebrities like Lovato and Miley Cyrus use Twitter to speak out against bullying.

Seventeen Magazine appears to rely heavily on articles featuring celebrities such as Demi Lovato, Miss Teen runner-up Audra Mari; and actors from ABC Family series. Lovato reported that the girls in her middle school started an "I Hate Demi" petition (Koday, 2011). Lovato (2011) wrote her own piece asking readers to join her fight against cyberbullying by taking a stand. Lovato was also featured in *People Magazine* ("Demi Lovato Opens Up," 2008). Lovato reported, in the interview, that she wants to use her fame to help other girls. Mari reported being called "Sasquatch" by a group of senior girls and told by kids in the bleachers to "go home" at a football game (Rosenfeld, 2011). At lunch one day, a girl threw a bag of food that horses would eat at her. Mari reported that she told her mother, who contacted the school, and the girl was later suspended. She recommended that girls should ignore the bad stuff and stay confident. She also suggested that if someone is being bullied, tell a trusted adult and not keep it inside. The magazine also published a link to ABC Family's Deleting Drama campaign (Gandhi, 2011). They also highlighted interviews with the actors who reported their experiences with bullying (Rosenfeld & Conte, 2011).

Several celebrities, including Kathy Griffin and Tim Gunn, have even admitted suicide attempts. Kathy Griffin (cited in Marikar, 2010) was most distressed by the apathy of an adult bystander. She reported that a man with a briefcase just walked by as she was getting beat up in a park. Gunn is now a big supporter of the Trevor Project, a confidential hotline for distressed GBTL youth. He cited his experience as a bullied youth and his understanding of the desperation as his motivation. In addition to Gunn, other gay youth such as Clay Aikin reported being bullied in school (McGraw, 2010). Chris Colfer from *Glee* reported that although he was not physically bullied, he was verbally bullied and called a "fag." Lance Bass admitted to bullying himself. He explained on the *Larry King Show* that he went along with the crowd because he wanted to fit in (cited in Mitchell, 2010). Because of his own insecurity in his sexual orientation, Bass made fun of gay people. Celebrity blogger Perez Hilton, a former closeted gay male, admitted he was a bully and was instrumental in outing Lance Bass and Neil Patrick Harris (Serjeant, 2010). He too is now an advocate of anti-bullying campaigns, specifically the harassment of gay youth. He has vowed to stop bullying on his blog (Serjeant, 2010) and has encouraged other celebrities and public figures to make supportive videos for the It Gets Better campaign. Hilton claims to have lost 200,000 Twitter followers because of his stance (Mitchell, 2010).

Public Service Announcements

A plethora of professionally produced public service announcements and homemade anti-bullying videos have racked up millions and millions of views in the past decade. Jonah Mowry's "What's Goin On" homemade video has received over 10 million views alone. Some of the most prevalent anti-bullying groups producing PSAs include the Trevor Project, Stop Bullying (stopbullying.gov), PACER National Bullying Prevention Center (pacer.org), and Noh8 campaign (noh8campaign.com). A search on YouTube of "anti-bullying PSA" netted 2,090 results and "anti-bullying videos" netted about 20,000 results. The following is an analysis of anti-bullying PSAs and videos with at least 100,000 views reported. Categories of videos emerged such as "stories," "messages," and "note cards."

STORIES

Many of the videos contain an upbeat and hopeful story. They portray models of positive behavior rather than preach to viewers. Many solutions to bullying focus on the intrinsic reward system of the bystander; in other words, they demonstrate how those who take action against bullies feel better about themselves. In "The Price of Silence," with 464,660 views, a boy is being threatened by a bully in a schoolyard. Students gather around and chant, "Fight, Fight Fight!" After about 30 seconds, a bystander steps forward and stands with the victim. As more students join the victim, the bully backs down. A cute girl smiles approvingly at the bystanders. The ending screen displays the tagline, "Stand up for a victim. I will remember you forever." In a similar video that demonstrates the power of the bystander, two male teens are caught holding hands by a group of bullies. The bullies taunt the boys later in class, saying "Who's gonna hold your hand?" One popular-looking boy stands up and tells one of the bully victims that he will hold his hand. Gradually everyone in the class, except the bullies, joins in holding hands with someone of the same sex. The two bully victims shyly smile at one another from across the room. In the final shot of the video, the two boys walk off holding hands, free from persecution. The video, sponsored by BeLonG, was produced in Ireland and to date has received almost a million views. Another video, which has received over 1,770,000 views and was produced by bullying.org, is the story of a group of bullies who make fun of a boy's red hair. The next time the bullies encounter the red-haired boy, they see an older red-haired boy sitting with his friends. When the older boy makes eye contact with the bullies, the bullies pass without teasing the younger boy. The younger boy walks away, confident and smiling. The message is very subtle in this video. The message is not that one look will necessarily stop bullying, but it does show that even small gestures can deter bullying.

MESSAGES

Whereas the "story" category of anti-bullying videos is uplifting, the "message" type videos portray more serious consequences of bullying. In "Words Hurt," sponsored by Ohio Commission DRCM, with almost a million views, mean girls are talking about another girl in a hallway at school. Each time the popular girls say something mean, the victim suffers from an invisible hand that slaps her and pushes her violently into the lockers. The message dispels the "sticks and stones may break my bones but words will never hurt me" myth. Another video that has less of a developing story but an interesting message is of a girl looking in the mirror. She looks confident and happy. Each time a hurtful word is said to her, however, the word appears written on her face. As her face fills up with the hurtful words, she becomes more and more distraught. It reiterated the "words hurt" message. The video has received three-quarters of a million views on YouTube. The next three videos are part of the MTV A Thin Line campaign, a site focused on the digital form of bullying. The videos are illustrations of what it would sound and look like if the negative, hurtful comments that were written online were actually said face to face. In the video entitled "Library," a boy is being harassed with names like "Princess" and other homophobic remarks such as, "Does your dad know how gay you are?" A female voice responds, "Everyone knows how gay he is." Another boy sitting near the bully target looks uncomfortable, but says and does nothing. A voiceover asks, "Will you stand up or stand by?" In the video "Cafeteria," kids are making fun of an overweight boy, Sam, as he is walking through the lunchroom. One girl snickers, "Someone needs to lay off the fries." A boy bumps into Sam and calls him a "lard ass." One of the boys shouts, "Forget to wear a bra this morning, Sam?" while the other kids just laugh. The video is followed by the tagline, "If you wouldn't say it, why would you type it?" The video "Tattoo" demonstrates how hurtful words can be permanent. A boy sits while getting a tattoo. He already has "loser," "freak," and "bitch" tattooed on his body. The boy gets a text message and informs the tattoo artist, "Looks like we are doing 'worthless' next." The voiceover warns, "There is a thin line between words and wounds." (Note: Because the videos appear on the a Thin Line website (www.athinline.org), view counts were not available.)

One video, created by Childnet International for Anti-Bullying Week, features a boy being bullied by a group of mean girls. Generally anti-bullying videos feature same-sex bullying. At first, the boy gets nasty texts from the girls. They call him on the phone and scream what are apparently nasty things to him (note: there is very little if any dialogue in the video). They send him hateful IM messages and create a website where they have photoshopped his picture to look like the teacher's pet. When he walks onto the school bus, the other kids laugh and chant "loser." After the boy's mother sees the messages, she goes to the principal. The end scene is of the mean girls watching out the window as a police officer approaches the school. Similar to the video critiqued by Wiseman (2011b) and Bazelon (2011), there is an ambiguity of the law enforcement officials coming for the girls. There appears to be immediate punitive consequences without any attempt at educational solutions or skills training of how the boy could have handled the situation before it got as far as it did. The video has been viewed over a quarter of a million times.

In the most extreme video in this analysis, a group of mean girls tell another girl they like her shirt. The girl thanks them and takes the comment as a compliment. Seconds later, the girl gets a hateful text seemingly from the mean girls. Blood begins to seep onto her shirt from her wrists. She collapses to the ground. There is a faint sound of sirens in the background. The vivid image of the blood is very disturbing and likely to turn off viewers. The video quickly jumps from one hateful text to suicide. The bully victim also appears to be powerless. She is surprised at the blood, making it appear as if her suicide attempt was inevitable. There is no reference to the producer and the video's sponsor is unknown. Wiseman (2011b) and Bazelon (2011) have criticized the use of suicide in anti-bullying videos.

There are at least two anti-cyberbullying videos that feature kids who are pressured by their peers to turn on a less popular person. The mean kids threaten the bystanders that if they hang out with "that loser," no one will like them either. The bystanders are in turn cruel to their friend.

Many of the videos look like MTV music videos that feature cover versions of hit songs from major artists. In one such video Ahmir, an R&B group, covers Pink's song "Perfect." The video focuses on an ethnically diverse group of bullies and victims. The video shows a supportive parent, teacher, and a group of friends comforting the bully victims. The video has over 1,500,000 views. Savannah Robinson, a 12-year-old girl, sings a version of Christine Aguilera's "Beautiful" while images of bullied kids are shown in the background. The video has received over a quarter of a million hits. Robinson was featured on Anderson Cooper's syndicated show *Anderson,* where she performed the song. A PSA entitled "Don't Bully Me" features a song by Corey Thornton, a Christian motivational speaker who looks more like a rapper than a choir boy. The message of the PSA is that the bully victim over time flourishes and enjoys life, while those who bully end up either in jail or homeless and begging on the street. The video has over 240,000 views.

NOTE CARD VIDEOS

Another extremely popular video style is the self-produced note card video. Bullied teens hold up cards with handwritten messages detailing their pain and suffering at the hands of bullies. There is generally somber music playing in the background. Although it appears the phenomenon began with Alye Pollack, Jonah Mowry's video is the most popular with nearly ten million views compared to Pollack's 671,000 views (note: there may be more than one posting of the video; therefore, it is difficult to get a truly accurate count). Another girl, Ellouise, created a similar video with roughly the same number of views as Pollack. One year later, Pollack released a follow-up video informing viewers that her life has gotten better. Each of these three young people thank others who have supported them through comments and video messages.

Public Service Announcements Critique

Wiseman (2011a) claimed that instead of an epidemic of bullying, the US is experiencing an epidemic of ineffective anti-bullying programs in schools and public service announcements. Wiseman (2011a) defined bad prevention programs and PSAs as including gimmicks (e.g., t-shirts and slogans), stereotyped situations, little or no racial diversity, no positive adult presence, and no skills or strategies. Two other important factors, according to Wiseman, are that ineffective PSAs ignore the fact that most bullies think they are justified in their actions. They see the victim as asking for it or starting the conflict. Bullies and bystanders often blame the victim, reasoning that if the victim would just act "normal" and not call attention to himself or herself, there would be no problem. Bullies may also see bullying as a method of survival; in other words, if they do not bully, they will be bullied. Another important factor, according to Wiseman (2011a), is that these programs or PSAs present suicide as a "natural consequence" of being targeted. They may also promote suicide as a "revenge fantasy" against the bullies.

Wiseman (2011a) mocked past PSAs as being outdated and using overly simplistic messages such as "Just delete the bad messages you get" and "If you wouldn't say it in person, don't send it online." These examples appear to represent mild cases, which are generally not considered cyberbullying. There is a danger of overreaction that takes away from the seriousness of true harassment. These responses do not address severe threats and comments such as, "I wish you would die" and "The world would be better off if you were dead."

Wiseman (2011b) reported that she gets particularly upset when the most powerful and influential corporations and government agencies in the world collaborate to make ineffective and even counterproductive PSAs. She warns against videos that rely on gimmicks and stereotypes and lack diversity. Bad PSAs present the prime motivation not to bully as punishment or guilt. Perhaps most importantly, PSAs should not present suicide as a "natural consequence" (Wiseman, 2011b). Wiseman argued that good anti-bullying PSAs should include realistic scenarios and provides skills proportional with the severity of the problem. They should also incorporate the role of the bystander and inspire bystanders to risk publicly supporting the target. The role of adults should also be made clear, acknowledging that sometimes adults are part of the problem.

One particular PSA produced by the American Bar Association drew the ire of critics. The video in question featured a girl who is repeatedly called a "fat pig slut" and commits suicide. The PSA ends with the class looking out the window and seeing the police arrive to arrest the mean girls. First of all, Wiseman (2011b) sees the PSA as outdated, comparing it to a 1980s after-school special. She accuses the producers of the PSA of portraying suicide as a revenge fantasy in which the bullies either feel guilty or are severely punished. She sarcastically questions where the girls are being taken, "to Mean Girl Prison?" Wiseman (2011b) also criticizes the lack of strategies or skills for victims to deal with bullying. She adds that it fails to represent the complexity of teen society. Similar to Wiseman's (2011b) argument, Bazelon (2011) launched criticism of anti-bullying PSAs. She warned about suicide contagion, a phenomenon in which vulnerable individuals see others' suicides as a solution to their problems. Bazelon (2011) described the PSA as the "perfect revenge" for bullying. The victim no longer suffers and the mean girls get punished. Bazelon (2011) called the video the "dark opposite" of the It Gets Better campaign.

Bazelon (2011) also criticized a similar video created by the Bergen County, New Jersey, prosecutors' office that shows a rope tied around a boy's neck being pulled tight around a bridge railing. Students had been whispering about the boy. The American Foundation for Suicide Prevention complained that the video "gives an overly-simplified understanding of the relationship between suicide and bullying which can lead other kids who are being bullied to see suicide as a solution" (cited in Bazelon, 2011). Instead of the intended goal of preventing cyberbullying, the PSA may unintentionally promote suicide. Bazelon (2011) also criticized the video for exaggerating the occurrences of cyberbullying making it appear to be normal or even expected.

Using suicide as a deterrent to perpetrators may likewise be ineffective. The cruelest bullies often do not appear to be upset by the suicide but in a sadistic way pleased at their accomplishment. There are numerous stories about "trolling" where bullies write obscene things on social networking pages of the deceased. According to Cullen (2010), the teens who bullied Phoebe Prince went on to "mock her in death." Phoebe Prince was a girl in South Hadley, Massachusetts, who hanged herself after severe bullying. Individuals posted derogatory comments on Prince's Facebook memorial site. One goal of cyberbullying is to dehumanize the victim. Suicide of a victim, whom the cyberbully may have never met, appears more like a death on a fictional television show or movie. Some made-for-television movies, in particular, include suicide attempts (e.g., *Betrayed at 17*, *Odd Girl Out*, and *Cyberbullying*). Even comedy movies such as *Better Off Dead* joke about suicide.

Conclusion

While there are many anti-bullying books on the market that target young children and adults (e.g., parents, school administrators), few address adolescents who are likely to be the most vulnerable to bullies and mean girls. The lack of inclusion in traditional print media, however, is not surprising, considering tweens and teens are likely to get information from nontraditional sources such as websites and Internet videos. Anti-bullying advocates have not only begun to use these venues to communicate messages but are also tapping into the celebrity-obsessed culture. Adolescents may be more likely to listen to a celebrity or public figure rather than an anti-bullying "expert" whom the adolescents may feel is preaching to them; however, anti-bullying campaigns need to be careful not to over-exploit the celebrity angle. Excessive celebrity confessionals can desensitize audiences or call into question the sincerity of the speakers.

15

Analysis and Recommendations

While the media industry is under no obligation to create pro-social messages for its users, it is important that bullying experts, parents, and school officials be aware of the lessons children and adolescents are learning from programming. This last section includes an analysis of overall trends of bullying and mean-girl portrayals over different media outlets and program genres. Several disturbing trends emerged. The final section offers advice to parents and educators about how to deal with the potentially negative effects of bully and mean-girl portrayals on adolescents.

Treatment of Social Classification

In an investigation of physical, verbal, and relational aggression, patterns emerged across media genres. Differences in portrayals were evident along gender and class lines throughout most genres of television and film. Bullying portrayals addressing race and sexual orientation were rare. When race and sexual orientation were included, they appeared in very specific subgenres: race in situation comedies and sexual orientation in television dramas.

GENDER

Bullying and mean-girl portrayals are heavily influenced by traditional definitions of masculinity and femininity. There is generally a clear distinction between portrayals of boys' and girls' aggression. Male bullies and victims are generally portrayed following traditional masculinity standards. Boys who bully generally fit the leather-wearing, buzz-haircut stereotype. Boy victims are stereotyped as less masculine (e.g., smaller in stature).

Parental roles are an important aspect in cases of bullying. Sitcoms of the '50s and '60s had strong paternal involvement in contrast to more modern sitcoms. Often the first thing the father does in these shows is teach his bullied son how to fight back. The parenting roles tend to closely follow the stereotypical script where the mother advises a non-violent resolution while the father tends to advocate for the "stick up for yourself" route. The father, however, often only expresses that view after the mother has left the room.

The father, while demonstrating a macho stance, at times appears afraid of his wife. Male victims are more likely being raised by a single mother. The lack of a strong masculine role model makes him vulnerable to bullying. In the "fight back" movies (e.g., *The Karate Kid*), an outside male must be called in to teach the boy the ways of being a man, which include how to fight.

Cross-gender bullying follows strict standards. In the girl-bully/boy-victim scenario, the boy is instructed not fight back or even defend himself. The boy must suffer black eyes and stolen backpacks in silence. He is reticent to tell anyone, with good reason because of the inevitable teasing that will ensue. In nearly every case, other characters laugh and taunt the boy for letting a girl bully him. In some cases, girls bully because they like the boy. This expression of love through physically aggressive behavior almost always results in a happy ending where the boy likes his female bully back and all is forgiven. There are few if any parallel examples of a boy liking a girl and bullying her. Another major threat to a boy's masculinity, nearly as bad as having a girl bully him, is having a girl defend him against a bully. When the girl, almost always his older sister, steps in, the boy's masculinity is questioned. Perhaps the worst-case scenario would be for the bully to be male and the girl to be the younger sister of the boy victim. The boy is harassed not only by the bully but his peers for his sister's intervention.

Male bullies appear fairly evenly in all different forms of media, across all genres. Portrayals of female bullies, on the other hand, are concentrated in television situation comedies and children's picture books. Reoccurring girl bullies are almost exclusively animated, young female characters such as 3-year-old Angelica in *Rugrats*, 9-year-old Helga in *Hey Arnold*, and elementary-school-age Bootsie Barker in the children's *Bootsie Barker* picture book series by Barbara Bottner.

Across all forms of media, females are more likely to engage in relational aggression than physical or verbal aggression. The one exception in this analysis is females in reality shows. I would argue that never before in the history of television have grown women been so physically abusive and verbally vile. Nearly every episode of *Bad Girls' Club*, *Basketball Wives*, and *Love & Hip Hop* begins with a recap of a fight from a previous episode. The physical fights generally break out, as the participants explain, because one or both parties feel "disrespected." A gesture such as putting one's hand in the face of another is a sign of disrespect and, therefore, cause for a physical attack. *Bad Girls' Club* appears to do away with the pretense of having a reason to fight. Members of the house apparently need no excuse or encouragement to start a physical altercation. Producers apparently plan for, and likely encourage fights, since large men in black t-shirts are at the ready to break up the physical altercations. Although fights are generally limited to stereotypical hair pulling, the women do occasionally connect with their fists.

Where bullying is represented by traditional masculinity standards, relational aggression or mean-girl behavior is closely linked to femininity. Mean girls in the media are almost exclusively portrayed as thin, pretty, and wealthy. She is the head cheerleader, the prom queen, and dating the quarterback of the football team. Simmons (2011) argued that because girls in real life are raised to be ladylike and not express anger or jealousy, they resort to indirect expressions of aggression. Portrayals of mean girls perpetuate that message. In a content analysis of teen movies, Behm-Morawitz and Mastro (2008) found that not only are female characters were more likely to be portrayed as socially aggressive than male characters, they are more likely to be rewarded than punished for social aggressive behavior. Television portrayals follow that model as well.

Mean girls are mostly present in movie comedies and television teen dramas. The cattiness of female adults has also extended to reality shows. Programming as seemingly innocuous as cooking competitions are rife with cruel and nasty adult mean girls. Catty behavior is also present in other female-focused reality competition shows such as *America's Next Top Model* and *The Bachelor*. The nasty attitudes and personal attacks are rarely addressed by the judges of these competitions. The incidents of relational aggression are actually used in promotions for the show. It appears the producers believe that bad behavior will attract audience members.

CLASS

Class is a major theme in media portrayals of bullies and mean girls. Media producers and writers tend to use class as an easily recognizable distinction between perpetrators and victims. Representations of class often break down along gender lines as most portrayals consist of upper-class mean girls and lower-class bullies. This trend holds true across programming targeting adolescents and adults. The classic background for a mean girl consists of wealthy, absent, and critical parents. The mean girl has been raised by nannies and taught to look down on others because of social and economic standing. Bullies' backgrounds are seldom divulged. When they are, they tend to come from dysfunctional families with abusive fathers and/or brothers and mothers who are too weak to stand up for their children.

RACE

Portrayals and documentaries often portray bullying and mean girls as a white, suburban or rural issue. Besides the comedy movie *House Party*, minorities are glaringly absent in film. The most prevalent portrayals of interracial bullying occur in television situation comedies. Of those portrayals, the most blatant example of interracial bullying appears in *Everybody Hates Chris*. Caruso, the white bully, calls Chris, the black lead character, racially charged names such as Kareem and Tito. Portraying Caruso as half-Italian and half-Irish, with red hair and freckles, gives license to his quick temper and love of fighting. The combination of true-to-life stories (i.e., the show is based on the life of comedian Chris Rock), comedic treatment, and a setting in the early 1980s makes the racial bullying seem less severe. The Tyler Perry sitcoms *Meet the Browns* and *House of Payne* include several portrayals of black-on-black bullying, as did classic 1970s sitcoms with minority casts such as *Good Times* and *Diff'rent Strokes*. There are almost no examples of a black bully and a white victim. In the few portrayals of girl bullies, bullies and victims are the same race except for episodes of *iCarly* and *The Bernie Mac Show* where the bully is black and the victim is white. With boy bullies, the opposite trend is apparent, in that white boys bully black victims but not the other way around. Perhaps the black bully/white victim is too threatening for audiences.

The rare portrayal of interracial mean-girl behavior is evident in the movie *Bring It On* and its subsequent sequels. Race is linked to wealth and geographical location. In the original *Bring It On* movie, the head of the inner-city squad is a well spoken African American girl, while her supporting cast of mainly black and Hispanic girls use street slang and make physical threats to the rich white girls. The rich white girls in turn are more snobbish and opt for verbal putdowns that emphasize the difference in class.

Producers of the shows *Basketball Wives* and *Love & Hip Hop* have taken the two strongest arenas of African American achievement, sports and entertainment, and turned them into a stage for shrill shouting matches and physical brawls. These shows not only perpetuate the stereotype of the angry black woman, they also reinforce the practice of having several children with different men outside of marriage. The men in these shows are very nonchalant about their four or five "baby mamas." (Note: the men themselves repeatedly use the term "baby mama" to refer to the mothers of their children.) This sub-genre of reality shows is drawing the ire of many critics who accuse the producers and casts of the shows of portraying black women in an extremely negative light. Turner (2008) criticized the portrayal of African American women on most reality shows as loud, domineering, and ready to pick a fight.

SEXUAL ORIENTATION

Of all the movies with bullying themes, *Curiosity of Chance* was only one that addresses homophobic bullying directly. No situation comedy addressed adolescent gays or lesbians with the exception of a *Will & Grace* episode that mentions Will being bullied as a teen because of his sexual preference. The one area where LGBT bullying is portrayed with any depth was television dramas. Portrayals of lesbian bullying are extremely mild and quickly resolved (e.g., *Pretty Little Liars*) with the one exception of a cyberbullied lesbian teen who commits suicide (e.g., *Harry's Law*). Gay teenage boy bullying is portrayed in both adult-themed shows (e.g., *Queer as Folk*) and teen shows (e.g., *My So-Called Life*). *Glee's* storyline of Dave Karofsky's tormenting of Kurt has received both praise for raising the issue and criticism for treating the topic too lightly at times. The writers and producers of *Glee* have also received criticism for giving unequal treatment to Santana's lesbianism. Critics argued that lesbians are more accepted and less stigmatized than gay males.

Stereotyping by gender and class appears in most media portrayals. Audience members can easily identify bullies, mean girls, and their victims with little effort on the part of writers and producers. There are very few differences between black and white bullies and victims. Similar stereotyped attributes are used as well as similar bullying and resolution tactics. It appears that most media genres avoid interracial bullying except for television sitcoms. Perhaps the comic effect makes the aggressive actions appear less threatening to the audience. On the other hand, there are virtually no comic portrayals of LGBT bullying in comedies, movies or television. Other than one movie, homophobic bullying only appears in a handful of television dramas. Producers appear to shy away from racial and homosexual bullying because of the controversy surrounding these themes.

Harmful Trends

Besides the standard patterns of gender, race, class, etc., often analyzed in media representations, some additional trends emerged that could potentially have a negative influence on adolescent viewers. One of the most obvious trends was the incompetence and bad behavior of adults in film and television. I also found one of the more troubling trends in comedies were mean-spirited teasing, particularly in adolescent-focused programming. A third trend that emerged was that a significant number of portrayals included unproductive strategies that lead to poor resolutions or no resolution at all. Bullying and mean-girl behavior is often portrayed as comical or, at the opposite end of the spectrum, taken to a dramatic extreme of murder or suicide. Many of these trends appear to create poor models of behavior and offer little in the way of helping adolescents learn to deal with bullies and mean girls.

BAD ADULT BEHAVIOR

Pepler and Craig (2009) identified adults not being aware or not being supportive as an important issue in bullying. Entertainment programming, aimed particularly at adolescents, often portrays adults as incompetent or uncaring. This subgenre of programming is perhaps the most influential to young viewers in learning about the consequences of actions. Because the adults are incompetent, oblivious, or just do not care, the adolescents must take matters into their own hands. On one hand, overcoming obstacles, such as lack of adult support, makes for a more dramatic finish to the television episode or film. On the other hand, this portrayal demonstrates to adolescent viewers that adults cannot be trusted. In almost every piece of anti-bullying literature I reviewed, the most consistent advice was for the victim to tell an adult. When adults are present to witness bullying in film and television, they often treat it as kids being kids and simply break up the bullying interaction rather than disciplining the perpetrators. Adults often use bullying and mean girl scenarios to nostalgically reflect back on their youth.

In *Ned's Declassified*, the only adult who seems capable of helping with the school bullies is the lunch lady. In the movie *Shredderman Rules*, the principal tells Nolan, the bullied character, that he should be thanking Bubba, his bully, for a "good life lesson." When Moody tries to make Clifford drink urine from a toilet in *My Bodyguard*, the principal gives Moody a one-day detention, saying there was "no harm done," and scolds Clifford for tattling. In *Salute Your Shorts*, Ug, the camp counselor, does nothing to protect Michael from the bully, Thud. Even after Thud hits Michael in the eye, knocking Michael to the ground, Ug does nothing. It is not surprising that the campers are very disrespectful to Ug. In "The First Day," the campers chant "Ug-ly." Many of these adults are bullies themselves. The gym teacher in *Diary of a Wimpy Kid* has the boys play a game called Gladiator, in which the large boys' goal is to tackle the smaller boys. In some of the sitcom episodes, the parents of the bully and the victim end up fighting instead of modeling productive anti-bullying solutions (e.g., *My Wife and Kids*, *The Fresh Prince of Bel Air*, *Alf*).

Even in the documentary *Bully* (2011), school officials look foolish as they often attribute bullying to simple conflict in which both parties have a role. The theater audience cringed as one assistant principal tells the bullying victim he is just as bad as the bully when the victim refuses to shake the bully's hand after an incident on the playground. Alex's parents were told by the assistant principal that the boys on Alex's bus who had hit and cursed at Alex were "good as gold."

Television and movie comedies occasionally portray adults as bullies (e.g., *Joe Somebody*, *Family Guy*). Television reality shows are rife with adults using similar bullying and mean-girl methods as adolescents. Participants name-call, gossip, and physically threaten each other. In an episode of *Bad Girls' Club*, a young woman tells her housemate to "go get yourself some dental floss and hang yourself, bitch." When describing shows that specifically feature female contestants, announcers often use expressions such as "the claws are coming out" or "cat fight." Even cooking competitions airing at 8 pm EST are full of foul language such as "bitch this" and "bitch that." Younger viewers do not even need to watch the full episodes because the promotions for the shows alone expose them to the inappropriate behavior.

TEASING AND MEAN HUMOR

Many situation comedies thrive on the disparagement of others, particularly of family members and so-called friends. The vicious teasing in sitcoms such as *Everybody Loves Raymond* has the potential to create a norm of disrespect. Laugh tracks signal viewers when material is supposed to be funny even when the reaction from the target being teased is largely negative. It may not be surprising that kids on a bus could be so cruel to their elderly bus monitor in upstate New York (see Karimi, 2012). Boys on the bus called their 68-year-old bus monitor a "fat troll" and asked if she was crying because she "missed her Twinkies."

Sitcoms targeting teens and tweens (i.e., those featured on Nickelodeon and the Disney Channel) give an interesting perspective on teasing and what it means to be a friend. Teasing in and of itself is not necessarily negative. Done in a good-hearted manner, teasing can bond individuals; however, these shows often express one-sided teasing. Oftentimes the sidekicks/teasing targets are portrayed as so dim, they are unaware that they are being teased (e.g., Screech from *Saved by the Bell*, Harper from *Wizards of Waverly Place*). Not only are the sidekicks victims of the joke, they are not bright enough to realize their mistreatment. Harper's naiveté and Screech's cluelessness make them acceptable targets. The audience has even more license to laugh at the expense of the sidekick. In addition, many of the lead characters in these shows are extremely disrespectful to parents, teachers, and principals.

Sitcoms targeted to adult audiences often use mean-spirited, disparaging humor even with the children on the show. In the series *Home Improvement*, the Taylors' family life is comical but hostile at times. The mother, Jill, does not shy away from the aggressive behaviors exhibited by her husband, Tim, and her two older sons. She calls her sons "obnoxious little pigs." The youngest son, Mark, gets the brunt of abuse from his two older brothers, Brad and Randy. The parents pay lip service to addressing the older boys' behavior; however, they follow up with few if any consequences. Outside the family, Tim is rather mean and disparaging to his sidekick Al. Tim makes fun of Al's weight, his mother's weight, his beard, and his flannel shirts. Tim is mean to Al because he can be. The characters of Al and Mark are bullied seemingly because of their passive nature. Tim is perhaps seen as comical rather than hostile because of his own ineptness.

UNPRODUCTIVE RESOLUTIONS

Television and movie dramas portray the resolution of bullying in one of several ways, few of which are constructive and positive. In some cases, victims take drastic measures, either attempting to hurt themselves or their persecutor. Some of the made-for-TV movies use attempted suicide as part of the story line to increase the dramatic effect of physical and relational aggression. In the made-for-tv movies *Odd Girl Out* and *Cyberbullying*, the main character attempts suicide but is unsuccessful. In *Betrayed at 17*, the main character runs into the street and is killed by a car. Bazelon (2011) warned about suicide contagion and that media representations may present suicide as a viable option to a vulnerable victims. Bully victims in dramas may also plot their revenge, such as the school shooting in the film *Heart of America*. Horror movies, including *Bully* (2001) and *The Final*, portray victims torturing their bullies in retaliation. An accumulation of these extreme reactions may create hysteria that is unrealistic and unproductive.

Media viewers are rarely exposed to resolution of a bullying or mean-girl situation perhaps because those endings lack the entertainment value of the extremes. In Swindey's (2010) analysis of youth-oriented movies, he found that the bully was in control for much of the movie except for the final scene when the bully either has a sudden epiphany and turns good or is abandoned by his or her sidekicks and the victim triumphs. Comical treatment may even encourage bullying and mean-girl behavior. Portrayals may actually glamorize the mean girl and her lifestyle. It is not hard to imagine a young girl leaving the theater after seeing the movie *Mean Girls* and not wanting to be a mean girl. The mean girls are beautiful, powerful, and, except for a brief moment of discomfort, successful.

Resolution in media portrayals often comes in the form of bullying the bully. Specific media such as professional wrestling and video games are geared toward punishing the bully by using the same tactics as the bully or mean girl used on his or her victims. Perhaps the ultimate bully-the-bully tactic is portrayed on the "reality" show *Bully Beatdown*. The premise of the show is bullies are put in the ring with professional mixed-martial arts fighters as their victims watch with amusement. For mean girls, victims often appear to fantasize not about reforming the mean girl but wanting to be the mean girl and have power over others. To get back at Regina in *Mean Girls*, Cady takes on the same strategies as Regina uses on her targets.

Many situation comedies end the episode with no resolution to the bullying storyline. Generally, the bully does not return to the series and no explanation as to why is given. Bystanders in almost all television and movie portrayals do nothing but silently witness the harassment or cheer on fights. Other than one episode of *Family Matters*, bystanders rarely stand up for the victim or tell an adult, not that the adult would be of any assistance as portrayed in these shows. Nelson (cited in Gray, 2006) argued that the mean and hateful things adolescents say, especially online, is because of their underdeveloped sense of empathy. They fail to anticipate the consequences. In media portrayals, there are often no consequences. The lesson portrayed in many of the television shows and movies analyzed is there will always be bullies so why bother fighting it. When the established bullies such as Reese from *Malcolm in the Middle* and Caruso in *Everybody Hates Chris* quit their roles as bullies, mayhem breaks out. A plethora of new bullies appear to try to take their place. The victims feel they have no other choice but to get the original bully back in power. In similar plotlines, Ned from *Ned's Declassified* and Bart from *The Simpsons* gain status as the reigning bully when they accidently injure the real bully. For example, they accidently hit the bully in the face as they are gesturing or trip the bully as they bend over to pick something up off the ground. In both cases, Ned and Bart strive to restore the bully to power because they are uncomfortable in that role. It appears from media portrayals that the struggle over social order is inevitable. As soon as one bully is expelled or a mean girl mends her ways, there is another to take his or her place. The movie *Mean Girls* ends as a new wave of Plastics makes its entrance.

BULLY BANDWAGON

In many instances, I found bullying was mislabeled in movie and television synopses and book summaries. Either the definition of bullying was simply too broad or, more likely, the term was misused for effect, to perhaps heighten the appearance of conflict and attract viewers. An overrepresentation of bullying and mean-girl portrayals may be harmful to society. Gillespie (2012) warned that too much emphasis on bullying will convince parents and students that they are powerless victims. Defining all bad behavior as "bullying" also may dilute the term and begin to trivialize those who are actually being bullied.

A rather unbelievable number of celebrities are disclosing stories about how they were bullied. There is an extensive list of celebrities who claim they were bullies, including 50 Cent, Ke$ha, and Snooki from *Jersey Shore* (see chapter 13). It may be comforting for bully victims to know that even popular, talented, and attractive people are bullied. On the other hand, there may be doubts to whether or not these celebrities really did get bullied or are just saying so for publicity. At times it appears the celebrities are pushed into naming their experiences as "bullying" by the interviewer who is anxious to get a good story. While many children get picked on, not every incident rises to the level of bullying. In interviews with Michael Jackson's daughter Paris and Olympic gold medalist Gabby Douglas, Oprah Winfrey appears to ask rather leading questions and perhaps unwisely elevates their experiences to bullying. One of the first questions Winfrey asked Paris Jackson was if she had ever been bullied. Jackson replied that some kids at her school tried bullying her but she would not let them. In the days after the airing of the interview, drastic headlines appeared in newspapers such as "Paris Jackson Reveals She Suffers Bullying at School" in *The Huffington Post* and "'I Was a Victim of Bullying': Paris Jackson Tells Oprah" in the UK's *Daily Mail*. Taylor Swift and Justin Timberlake discussed incidents of being picked on; however, if one listens carefully to the interview, it was Ellen DeGeneres who labeled their experiences as "bullying." Celebrities can appear hypocritical as well. Professional wrestlers bully in the ring and later participate in the Be a Star anti-bullying campaign. Tyra Banks is very open about how she was bullied as a child. While Banks features anti-bullying challenges on her show *American's Next Top Model*, her show promotes mean-girl behavior among the contestants (see chapter 10). Banks rarely addresses the relational aggression that goes on in her show among the contestants.

Advice for Parents and Educators

While it is unlikely the media industry will change its ways and portray bullies and mean girls in more productive ways, there are steps parents, school officials, and anti-bullying educators can take to help adolescents deal with bullies and mean girls.

Monitoring by Parents

Just as parents have been advised to monitor their children's consumption of sexual and violent programming, they are wise to pay attention to media portrayals of unhealthy and harmful social interactions. Young viewers may learn ineffective, even dangerous, ways of handling aggressive situations. Bullying and mean-girl victims may feel discouraged when they are unable to handle the situation as easily as in media portrayals. They may also feel their experiences are trivialized by comic portrayals. Media images of violent bullying or retaliation may create fear in young viewers regardless if they have experienced bullying or not. Parents must be careful not to assume programming on "child-friendly" networks such as the Disney Channel or Nickelodeon is going to be in their child's best interest.

INCLUSION OF MEDIA IN ANTI-BULLYING PROGRAMS

The influence of media on children's attitudes and behavior needs to be part of the anti-bullying programs in school. There is a great disparity between what the anti-bullying programs are teaching students and the representation of bullies and mean girls in programming directly marketed to that age group. The most striking example of the disparity is between the heavy reliance of adult involvement in anti-bullying materials and the absence of adults, or worse yet, the incompetence of adults, in media portrayals. Wiseman (2011b) and Bazelon (2011) warn that well-meaning groups creating anti-bullying PSAs may be trivializing the issue, or worse, inadvertently encouraging extreme solutions such as suicide. There is also the danger of overexposure of bullying messages that may begin to desensitize students, particularly if every hurt feeling is labeled "bullying."

MEDIA LITERACY COURSES

Schools are wise to teach media literacy courses for a number of reasons. Students should not only be made aware of how media portrays aggression in the form of violence and bullying but in terms of what media teaches about teasing and friendships. It is essential for children and adolescents to understand that the media industry is a business whose main goal is to attract viewers. Media producers rely heavily on stereotypes and exaggerations. They offer a fantasy world where even the "reality" shows are not real. Understanding of the media industry and skills in interpreting content are ways to decrease negative influences on young viewers.

Conclusion

Ruggles (2002) questioned whether or not Hollywood and other filmmakers have a responsibility to teach bullying prevention, tolerance, and an understanding of why bullies bully. While arguing that filmmakers have some responsibility, Ruggles (2002) suggested that it is not fair to expect movies to double as public service announcements. However, parents, educators, and anti-bullying advocates are wise to take media representations into consideration.

List of Programs by Chapter

1: Bullies and the Media

TELEVISION

The Adventures of Pete and Pete
Boy Meets World
The Craft
Diff'rent Strokes
Everybody Hates Chris
The Fairly Odd Parents
The Family Guy
Family Matters
Glee
Hey Arnold
Home Improvement
How I Met Your Mother
iCarly
The In Crowd
Kick Buttowski
Leave It to Beaver
Like Family
Malcolm in the Middle
The Middle
Ned's Declassified
Ned's Declassified School Survival Guide
Parker Lewis Can't Lose
Pepler and Craig
Phil of the Future
Phineas and Ferb
Ren and Stimpy
The Ren & Stimpy Show
Rugrats
Salute Your Shorts
The Simpsons
South Park

FILM

Back to the Future
The Breakfast Club
Little Rascals

Our Gang
The Outsiders
Pretty in Pink
Revenge of the Nerds
Some Kind of Wonderful
Teen Wolf
Weird Science
Zapped

2: Mean Girls and the Media

TELEVISION

A.N.T. Farm
Awkward
Beverly Hills 90210
Degrassi
Family Guy
Full House
Gilmore Girls
Gossip Girl
High School Musical
Little House on the Prairie
The Middle
90210
The O.C.
One Tree Hill
Popular
Saved by the Bell
The Secret Life of American Teenager
The Simpsons
South Park
Suburgatory
Suite Life of Zach and Cody
Wizards of Waverly Place

FILMS

American Girl Chrissa
Bad Girls from Valley High

The Clique
Confessions of a Teenage Drama Queen
Easy A
Heathers
Jawbreakers
Mean Girls
Mean Girls 2
Odd Girl Out
Saved
Sleepover
Thirteen

3: Film Bullies

About a Boy
Adventures of a Teenage Dragonslayer
Back to the Future
Bad News Bears
Bad Santa
The Benchwarmers
Better Off Dead
Billy Madison
The Bodyguard
Can't Buy Me Love
Carrie
The Chocolate War
A Christmas Story
The Craft
The Curiosity of Chance
D2: Mighty Ducks
Dangerous Minds
The Diary of a Wimpy Kid
Dickie Roberts
Dodgeball
Drillbit Taylor
The Fat Boy Chronicles
Field of Vision
Fight Back
The Final
The First Kid
Footloose
Former Child Star
Harry Potter
Heart of America
Hearts in Atlantis: The War
Heavyweights
House Party
How to Eat Fried Worms
The In Crowd
Joe Somebody
Just One of the Guys
The Karate Kid
Kenny & Co
Lean on Me
Learning Curve
Legendary

Let Me In
Lifted
Lucas
Max Keeble's Big Move
Meatballs
Mr. Woodcock
Napoleon Dynamite
Neverending Story III
The New Guy
The New Kids
The Outsiders
A Pig's Tale
The Prankster
P.U.N.K.S.
Revenge of the Nerds
Rocky V
Scarecrow
The Sensei
Shorts
Showdown
Shredderman Rules
Sidekicks
Simon Birch
Sky High
Sometimes They Come Back
Stand and Deliver
Stand by Me
Stephen King's It
Teen Wolf
Three O'Clock High
Tormented
The Toxic Avenger
A True Underdog Story
Twelve and Holding
The Waterboy
Zapped!

4: Film Mean Girls

American Girl Chrissa
Bad Girls from Valley High
Betrayed at 17
Bride Wars
Bring It On
Bring It On: All or Nothing
Bring It On: Fight to the Finish
Bring It On: In It to Win It
Camp Rock
Cheetah Girls
The Clique
Clueless
Confessions of a Teenage Drama Queen
Cruel Intentions
Cyberbullying
Easy A
The Fat Boy Chronicles

Fat Like Me
Heathers
Heavyweights
High School Musical
High School Musical 2
Holiday in the Sun
The Hot Chick
Jawbreaker
Mean Girls
Mean Girls 2
My Best Friend's Wedding
Never Been Kissed
Odd Girl Out
Pretty in Pink
The Princess Diaries
Queen Sized
Revenge of the Bridesmaids
Romy and Michele's High School Reunion
Saved
Sharpay's Fabulous Adventure
She Gets What She Wants
She's All That
Since You've Been Gone
Sleepover
Some Kind of Wonderful
Sorority Wars
Super Sweet 16: The Movie
Sydney White
Teen Spirit
Thirteen
To Be Fat Like Me
Valley Girl
Welcome to the Doll House
You Again

5: Television Bullies

A-Team
Adventures of Superman
All My Children
Anne of Green Gables
Bent
The Commish
Criminal Minds
CSI: Miami
Degrassi: The Next Generation
Doogie Howser, M.D.
Everwood
Flashpoint
Freaks and Geeks
Fringe
Glee
The Ghost Whisperer
Gunsmoke
Harry's Law
Jessie

Law & Order
Law & Order SVU
Less Than Kind
Life Goes On
Little House on the Prairie
Lincoln Heights
The Man Who Shot Liberty Valence
The Mentalist
Murder She Wrote
My So-Called Life
The O.C.
One Tree Hill
Picket Fences
Pretty Little Liars
Queer as Folk
The Rifleman
Ringer
Smallville
Supernatural
21 Jump Street
Ugly Betty
Veronica Mars
Walker, Texas Ranger
Without a Trace

6: Television Mean Girls

Anne of Green Gables
Beverly Hills 90210
Buffy the Vampire Slayer
Degrassi
Desperate Housewives
Dynasty
Freaks and Geeks
GCB
Gilmore Girls
Glee
Gossip Girl
Hellcats
The Hills
Huge
Jane by Design
Laguna Beach
Lincoln Heights
Little House on the Prairie
The Lying Game
Make It or Break It
Melrose Place
Melrose Place 2
90210
The O.C
One Tree Hill
Popular
Pretty Little Liars
Private
The Secret Circle

The Secret Life of the American Teenager
Ugly Betty

7: Television Sitcoms

The Andy Griffith Show: Opie and Bully
A.N.T. Farm: Pilot
According to Jim: Punch
Alf: Hit Me with Your Best Shot
Allen Gregory: Interracial McAdams
Allen Gregory: Pilot
Always Sunny: High School Reunion
American Dad: Bully for Steve
Are We There Yet: Fall of Troy
The Bernie Mac Show: Five Stages of Bryana
The Bernie Mac Show: The Main Event
Bewitched: Tabitha's First Day of School
Big Bang Theory: Pilot
The Big Bang Theory: The Speckerman Recurrence
Big Time Rush: Green Time
Boy Meets World: Back 2 School
Boy Meets World: He Said, She Said
The Brady Bunch: A Fistful of Reasons
The Brax Show: Bully
City Guys: Bully, Bully
Clarissa Explains: Bully
The Cleveland Show: Yemen
The Cosby Show: Mr Quiet
Dennis the Menace: The Bully
The Dick Van Dyke Show: Girls Will be Bullies
Diff'rent Strokes: Carmella Meets the Gooch
Diff'rent Strokes: Return of the Gooch
Diff'rent Strokes: The Fight
The Donna Reed Show: Weekend Trip
Don't Trust the B in Apartment 23
8 Simple Rules: School Nurse
8 Simple Rules: Secrets
8 Simple Rules: The Teacher's Lounge
Even Stevens: Hutch Boy
Everybody Hates Chris: Caruso
Everybody Hates Chris: Pilot
Everybody Hates Chris: Sausage
Everybody Loves Raymond: Bully on the Bus
Family Guy: The Kiss Seen Around the World
Family Guy: Tan Aquatic with Steve Zissou
Family Matters: In a Jam?
Family Matters: Requiem for Urkel
Family Ties: Designated Hitter
The Famous Jett Jackson: Something to Prove
Father Knows Best: Bud, the Boxer
Flash Forward: Dog Day After Lunch
Flash Forward: Skate Bait
Frasier: Bully for Martin
Frasier: Liar Liar
Frasier: Radio Wars
The Fresh Prince of Bel Air: Mother of All Battles
Friends: The One with the Bullies
Full House: Is It True about Stephanie

Gomer Pyle: Gomer Learns a Bully
Good Luck Charlie: Boys Meet Girls
Good Times: The Lunch Ripoff
Good Vibes: Pilot
Grounded for Life: All Apologies
Grounded for Life: I Right the Wrongs
Grounded for Life: Jimmy Was Kung Fu Fighting
Growing Pains: Fast Times
Hang Time: Fighting Words
Hannah Montana: School Bully
Happy Days: Richie Fights Back
Happy Endings: You Snooze, You Bruise
Hard Times of RJ Berger: Pilot
Home Improvement: Karate or Not, Here I Come
Home Improvement: What About Bob?
How to be a Gentleman: Pilot
I Hate My Teenage Daughter: Pilot
iCarly: iSam's Mom
iCarly: iTwins
iCarly: Make Sam Girlier
It's Always Sunny in Philadelphia: High School Reunion
Jessie: World Wide Web of Lies
King of the Hill: Bobby Goes Nuts
King of the Hill: Four-Wave Intersection
King of the Hill: Gone with Windstorm
King of the Hill: Hank's Bully
Leave It to Beaver: Lumpy Rutherford
Like Family: Bobby's Bully
The Little Rascals
Living Single: School's Out Forever
Lizzie McGuire: Lizzie Strikes Out
Lizzie McGuire: Sibling Bonds
Louie: The Bully
Malcolm in the Middle: The Bully
Malcolm in the Middle: Pilot
Malcolm in the Middle: Shame
Man Up! High Road is the Guy Road
The Middle: The Neighbor
Mr. Young: Mr. Witness
Moral Orel: Turn the Other Cheek
Mork & Mindy: Mork's Greatest Hits
The Munsters: Herman's Peace Offensive
My Brother and Me: The Big Bully
My Name Is Earl: Bullies
My Name Is Earl: O Karma, Where Art Thou?
My Three Sons: The Bully
My Wife and Kids: Snapping and Sniffing
Ned's Declassified: Bullies
Ned's Declassified: First Day
Ned's Declassified School Survival Guide: A New Grade/Dodgeball
The New Adventures of Old Christine: Popular
New Girl: Bully
100 Deeds for Eddie McDowd: "Tagged
Pair of Kings: Beach Bully Bingo
Parker Lewis Can't Lose: Pilot
The Partridge Family: This Male Chauvinist Piggy Went to Market

The Patty Duke Show: Big Sister
Phil of the Future: Double Trouble
Romeo! Season 1 Episode 4: Minimum Cool
Salute Your Shorts: Brownies for Thud Mackie
Saved by the Bell: The New Class: "Squash It"
Silver Spoons: 12 Angry Kids
The Simpsons: Bye Bye Nerdy
The Simpsons: Eeny Teeny Maya Moe
The Simpsons: Lisa Simpson, This Isn't Your Life
The Simpsons: Love Is a Many Strangled Thing
Small Wonder: Bully
South Park: Bass to Mouth
South Park: Butterballs
Step by Step: Bully for Mark
The Steve Harvey Show: Bully Call
The Steve Harvey Show: Don't Quit Your Day Job
Still Standing: Still Bullying
Suburgatory: Pilot
The Suite Life of Zack and Cody: Neither Speller Bee
The Suite Life of Zack and Cody: The First Day of High School
That's So Raven: Getting Out of Dodge
That's So Raven: Juicier Consequences
Tyler Perry's House of Payne: The Big Bang Theory
Tyler Perry's House of Payne: The Bully and Beast
Tyler Perry's House of Payne: Do the Fight Thing
Tyler Perry's House of Payne: Dodging Bullies
Tyler Perry's House of Payne: Worth Fighting For
Tyler Perry's Meet the Browns: Meet the Bully
Tyler Perry's Meet the Browns: Meet the Trouble-maker
The Wayan Brothers: I Do
Will & Grace: Bully Woolley
Will and Grace: Alice Doesn't Lisp Here Anymore
Will and Grace: Past and Present
Wizards of Waverly Place: Alex's Choice
The Wonder Years: Ninth Grade Man
The Wonder Years: Fate
The Wonder Years: Hiroshima, Mon Frere Yes Dear: Baby Fight Club
Yes Dear: Dominic's Buddy
Zeke and Luther: Plunk
Zoey 101: Defending Dustin
Zoey 101: The Great Vince
Zoey 101: Vince is Back

8: Glee's Bullies and Mean Girls

Glee

9: Documentaries and Talk Shows

FILM

Bullied
Bully

Finding Kind
Rats & Bullies

TELEVISION

AC360 Special Report
Anderson
Dateline NBC: My Kid Would Never Bully
Discovery Health: Mean Girls
The Dr. Oz Show
E! Bullying Special
Extreme Makeover: Home Edition
The 48 Hours Special: Words Can Kill
If You Really Knew Me
Investigation Discovery
Juvie
Kraze
Lifechangers
Not In Our Town: Class Actions
1 Girl and 5 Gays
Oprah
Oprah's Next Chapter
Saved: Temple Grandin
South Park
The Steve Wilkos
This American Life
Too Fat for 15: Fighting Back
What Would You Do?

10: Television Reality Shows

American Idol
America's Got Talent
America's Next Top Model
The Apprentice
The Bachelor
Bad Girls-Club
Basketball Wives
Bridezilla
Dance Moms
Dance Moms: Miami
Hell's Kitchen
Joe Millionaire
Kitchen Nightmares
Love & Hip Hop
Love & Hip Hop: Atlanta
Made
Master Chef
Mob Wives
My Super Sweet 16
Queen Bees
The Real Housewives of Atlanta
The Real Housewives of New Jersey
The Real Housewives of NYC
Remodeled
Restaurant Impossible
Say Yes to the Dress

The Simple Life
Tabatha Takes Over
Texas Women
The XFactor

11: Children's Programs

TELEVISION

Adventure Time
The Adventures of Jimmy Neutron
The Amanda Show
Anne of Green Gables
The Ant Bully
As Told by Ginger
Babar
Bali
Beach Bully Bingo
Bullies Are a Pain in the Brain
ChalkZone
Codename Kids Next Door
Danny Phantom
Davey and Goliath
Dino Squad
Doug
The Fairly OddParents
Fanboy & Chum Chum
Fat Albert and the Cosby Kid
Fish Hooks
The Grim Adventures of Billy and Mandy
The Haunting Hour
He's a Bully, Charlie Brown
Hey Arnold
Jacob Two Two
Jumanji: Animated

Kick Buttowski: Suburban Daredevil
Kid vs. Kat
Looney Tunes All Stars
Mad About
Matilda
Maya & Miguel
My Life as a Teenage Robot
Phineas and Ferb
Pippi Longstocking
Pokemon: Black & White
The Replacements
Rudolph the Red-Nosed Reindeer
Rugrats
Scaredy Squirrel
Sesame Street
Sponge Bob Square Pants
Tom and Jerry Tales
The Troop
Veggie Tales: Minnesota Cuke
You Can't Do That on Television
Yu-Gi-Oh!
Zexal

FILM

Aladdin
Annie
Beauty and the Beast
The BratzBabyz: The Movie
Cars
Chicken Little
The Lion King
A Little Princess
Toy Story
Toy Story 3

Bibliography

Adams, L., & Russakoff, D. (1999). Dissecting Columbine's cult of the athlete. *Washington Post*, p. A1.

The American Academy of Pediatrics. (2009). Policy statement—Media violence. *Pediatrics, 124*(5), 1495–1503.

Bandura, A. (1986). *Social foundations of thought and action: A social cognitive theory.* Englewood Cliffs, NJ: Prentice Hall.

Barboza, G. E., Schiamberg, L. B., Oehmke J., Korzeniewski, S. J., Post, L. A., & Heraux, C. G. (2009, January). Individual characteristics and the multiple contexts of adolescent bullying: An ecological perspective. *Journal of Youth and Adolescence, 38*(1), 101–121.

Baysinger, T. (2011). Survey: Realty TV affects how teen girls view themselves. *Broadcasting & Cable*. Retrieved from http://www.broadcastingcable.com/article/475160-Survey_Reality_TV_Affects_How_Teen_Girls_View_Themselves.php

Bazelon, E. (2011, April 4). How not to prevent bullying: Two anti-bullying videos that might do more harm than good. *Slate.com*. Retrieved from http://www.slate.com/articles/life/bulle/2011/04/how_not_to_prevent_bullying.html

Behm-Morawitz, E., & Mastro, D. E. (2008, April). Mean girls? The influence of gender portrayals in teen movies on emerging adults' gender-based attitudes and beliefs. *Journalism & Mass Communication Quarterly, 85*(1), 131–146.

Bennett. J. (2010). Everything I learned about women I learned from reality TV. *The Daily Beast*. Retrieved from http://www.thedailybeast.com/newsweek/2010/11/11/the-problem-with-women-on-reality-tv.html

Berk, B. (2012, November 10). The gay guide to *Glee*: Season 2, episode 6: "Never been kissed." *Vanity Fair*. Retrieved December 2, 2010. Retrieved from http://www.vanityfair.com/online/oscars/2010/11/the-gay-guide-to-glee-season-2-episode-6—never-been-kissed

Bjorkqvist, K., Lagerspetz, K., & Kaukiainen, A. (1992). Do girls manipulate and boys fight? Developmental trends in regard to direct and indirect aggression. *Aggressive Behavior*, 18, 117–127.

Bosworth, K., Espelage, D. L., & Simon, T. R. (1999). Factors associated with bullying behavior in middle school students. *The Journal of Early Adolescence, 19*(3), 341–362.

Boulton, M. J., & Underwood, K. (1992). Bully/victim problems among middle school children. *British Journal of Educational Psychology, 62*(1), 73–87.

Bracetti, A (2011). Sweet revenge! 12 videos of bullies getting owned by their victims. *Complex Tech*. Retrieved from http://www.complex.com/tech/2011/03/sweet-revenge-12-videos-of-bullies-getting-owned-by-their-victims/

The Bully Project. (2012). Bully now playing. *The Bully Project*. Retrieved from http://thebullyproject.com/indexflash.html

Bushman, B. J., & Huesmann, L. R. (2006). Short-term and long-term effects of violent media on aggression in children and adults. *Archives of Pediatrics & Adolescent Medicine, 160*(4), 348–352.

Cammuso, F. (2008). *Knights of the lunch table: The dodgeball chronicles*. New York: Scholastic.

Carpenter, D., & Ferguson C. J. (2009). *The everything parent's guide to dealing with bullies: From playground teasing to cyber bullying, all you need to ensure your child's safety and happiness* (186–193). Avon, MA: Adams Media.

Catty, evil black women have become the norm on reality TV. (2011). *Your Black World*. Retrieved from http://www.yourblackworld.com/2011/07/09/catty-evil-black-women-have-become-the-norm-on-reality-tv-should-black-women-accept-this/

Chan, S. (2010, October 4). In a wired world, children unable to escape cyberbullying [Blog]. *CNN, Anderson Cooper 360.* Retrieved from http://ac360.blogs.cnn.com/2010/10/04/in-a-wired-world-children-unable-to-escape-cyber-bullying/

Chang, L. (2005). Bullying increasing: First boys, now girls. *Web MD.* Retrieved from http://www.webmd.com/parenting/news/20051012-/bullying-increasing-first-boys-now-girls

Chory-Assad, R. M., & Tamborini, R. (2004). Television sitcom exposure and aggressive communication: A priming perspective. *North American Journal of Psychology, 6*(3), 415–422.

Cohen-Posey, K. (1995). *How to handle bullies, teasers and other meanies.* Madison, WI: Rainbow Books.

Coloroso, B. (2004). *The bully, the bullied, and the bystander: From preschool to high school—How parents and teachers can help break the cycle of violence.* Harper Collins: New York.

Coughlin, P. (2011). *Raising bully-roof kids: No more jellyfish, chickens or wimps.* Ada, MI: Revell.

Coyne, S. M., Linder, J. R., Nelson, D. A., & Gentile, D. A. (2012). "Frenemies, fraitors, and mean-em-aitors": Priming effects of viewing physical and relational aggression in the media on women. *Aggressive Behavior, 38,*141–149.

_____, Nelson, D. A.,Lawton, F., Haslam, S., Rooney, L., Titterington, L., Trainor, H., Remnant, J., & Ogunlaja, L. (2008, November).The effects of viewing physical and relational aggression in the media: Evidence for a cross-over effect. *Journal of Experimental Social Psychology, 44*(6), 1551–1554.

_____, Robinson, S. L., & Nelson, D. A. (2010, April). Does reality backbite? Physical, verbal, and relational aggression in reality television programs. *Journal of Broadcasting & Electronic Media, 54*(2), 282–298.

Craw, B. (2010, May 14). The '80s bully megacut: Shoves, wedgies, putdowns, and punches. [Video.] *The Huffingtonpost.com.* Retrieved from http://www.huffingtonpost.com/2010/05/14/the-80s-bully-megacut-sho_n_575350.html

Cullen, K. (2010, February 2). No safe haven for bullies. *Boston.com.* Retrieved from http://www.boston.com/news/local/massachusetts/articles/2010/02/02/nip_bullying_in_the_bud_at_home/

Davies, M. (2006). Gamers don't want any more grief. *The Guardian.* Retrieved from http://www.guardian.co.uk/technology/2006/jun/15/games.guardianweeklytechnologysection2

Dellasega, C., & Nixon, C. (2003). *Girl wars: 12 strategies that will end female bullying.* New York: Fireside.

Demi Lovato opens up about being bullied. (2008).

People Magazine. Retrieved from http://www.people.com/people/article/0,20230070,00.html

DiMarco, H. (2005). *Mean girls gone: A spiritual guide to getting rid of mean.* Ada, MI: Revell.

_____. (2008). *Mean girls: Facing your beauty turned beast.* Ada, MI: Revell.

_____. (2010). *In Frenemies: What to do when friends turn mean.* Ada, MI: Revell.

Doyle, S. (2010). Does "it gets better" make life better for gay teens? *The Atlantic.* Retrieved from http://www.theatlantic.com/entertainment/archive/2010/10/does-it-gets-better-make-life-better-for-gay-teens/64184/

Ebert, R, (2004). Review of *Mean Girls. Chicago Sun Times.* Retrieved from http://rogerebert.suntimes.com/apps/pbcs.dll/article?AID=/20040430/REVIEWS/404300306/

Espelage, D. L., Bosworth, K., & Simon, T. R. (2000). Examining the social context of bullying behaviors in early adolescence. *Journal of Counseling & Development, 78*(3), 326–333.

Feldman, E. (2007). Protect yourself against game griefers, online cyber-bullying. *Yahoo! Voices.* Retrieved from http://voices.yahoo.com/protect-yourself-against-game-griefers-online-cyber-473320.html?cat=19

Felmlee, D., & Faris, R. (2011, February). Status struggles: Network centrality and gender segregation in same- and cross-gender aggression. *American Sociological Review, 76*(1), 48–73.

Flock, E. (2011, September 26). New "It Gets Better" video features three Republicans with record opposing day rights. *Washingtonpost.com.* [Blog]. Retrieved from http://www.washingtonpost.com/blogs/blogpost/post/new-it-gets-better-video-features-three-republicans-with-record-opposing-gay-rights/2011/10/26/gIQAnHFzJM_blog.html

Fox, D., & Beane, A. (2009). *Good-bye, bully machine.* Minneapolis, MN: Free Spirit Publishing.

Fuller, B. (2011). Selena Gomez: "I was bullied every second" in school. *Hollywood Life.* Retrieved from http://hollywoodlife.com/2011/10/24/selena-gomez-bullied-in-school/

Gardner, O., Buder, E., & Buder, S. (2008) *Letters to a bullied girl: Messages of healing and hope.* New York, NY: Harper Paperbacks.

Gavin, G. (2011). What high schools and restaurant teach us about mean girls. *Miami Herald.* Retrieved from http://www.miamiherald.com/2011/03/05/2097339/what-high-schools-and-restaurant.html

Gentile, D. A., Coyne, S., & Walsh, D. A. (2011). Media violence, physical aggression, and relational aggression in school age children: A short-term longitudinal study. *Aggressive Behavior, 37,* 193–206.

Gentile, D.A. (2003). *Media violence and children: A complete guide for parents and professionals.* Westport, CT: Greenwood Publishing Group Inc.

Gerbner, G. (1998). Cultivation analysis: An overview. *Mass Communication & Society, 1*(3/4), 175–194.

Gini, G., & Pozzoli, T. (2006). The role of masculinity in children's bullying. *Sex Roles, 54*(7–8), 585–588.

Girl Scouts. (2011). New Girl Scouts research exposes the impact of reality TV on girls. *Girl Scouts.* Retrieved from http://blog.girlscouts.org/2011/10/new-girl-scouts-research-exposes-impact.html

Goldman, C. (2012). *Bullied: What every parent, teacher and kids needs to know about ending the cycle of fear.* New York: HarperCollins.

Gottheil, N. F., & Dubow, E. F. (2001). Tripartite beliefs models of bully and victim behavior. *Journal of Emotional Abuse, 2*(2–3), 25–47.

Grant, D. (2011). YouTube "bully" Richard Gale makes TV debut. *Salon.* Retrieved from http://www.salon.com/2011/03/21/richard_gale_bully_today_tonight/

Hadad, C. (2011, October 10). Schoolyard bullies not just preying on the weak [Blog]. *CNN.* Retrieved from http://ac360.blogs.cnn.com/2011/10/10/ac360%C2%B0-study-schoolyard-bullies-not-just-preying-on-the-weak/?hpt=ac_bn6

Harrison, L. (2004). *The clique.* New York: Little Brown.

Haxton, H. (2010, February 18). Cartoons, TV and pollies "create school bullies." *ABC News.* Retrieved from http://www.abc.net.au/news/2010-02-18/cartoons-tv-and-pollies-create-school-bullies/335914

Hibbet, A. (2005). *Why do people bully?* Oxford, UK: Raintree.

Hill, A., & Helmore, E. (2002, March 3). Mean girls, schoolgirls' ways of being cruel to each other are now so insidious and sophisticated that their victims can feel the devastating effects well into adulthood. *The Guardian.* Retrieved from http://www.guardian.co.uk/education/2002/mar/03/schools.uk

Holiday, E., & Rosenberg, J. (2009). Mean girls, meaner women: Understanding why woman backstab, betray, and trash-talk each other and how to heal. Orchid Press: Dallas, TX.

Hollingsworth, B. (2011, March 29). Mean girls use social networking site to torment victim. *The Examiner.* Retrieved from http://washingtonexaminer.com/opinion/columnists/2011/03/barbara-hollingsworth-mean-girls-use-social-networking-site-torment-victim

Huesmann, L. R. (1986). Psychological processes promoting the relation between exposure to media violence and aggressive behavior by the viewer. *Journal of Social Issues, 42*(3), 125–140.

_____. (2007). The impact of electronic media violence: Scientific theory and research. *Journal of Adolescent Health, 41*(6), 6–13.

_____. (1986). Psychological processes promoting the relation between exposure to media violence and aggressive behavior by the viewer. *Journal of Social Issues, 42*(3), 125–140.

Inglis, J., M. (2011, December 7). Rudolph the Red Nosed Reindeer and the bullying issue: A teachable moment. *Classroom Window.com.* Retrieved from http://classroomwindow.com/rudolph-the-red-nosed-reindeer-and-the-bullying-issue-a-teachable-moment/

iTunes preview. (n.d.). *Library Nerd.* iTunes. Retrieved from http://itunes.apple.com/us/app/library-nerd/id446208463?mt=8

Itzkoff, D. (2009, May 2009). Jane Lynch bring her inner mean girl to *Glee. The New York Times* [Arts Beat Blog]. Retrieved from http://artsbeat.blogs.nytimes.com/2009/05/18/jane-lynch-brings-her-inner-mean-girl-to-glee/

Jakubiak, D. J. (2009). *A smart kid's guide to online bullying.* New York, NY: Powerkids Press.

Jefferson, W. (2011, November 2). A tribute to '80s movie bullies. *Jezebel.com.* Retrieved from http://jezebel.com/5855695/a-tribute-to-80s-movie-bullies

Johnston, M. (1996) *Dealing with bullying.* Logan, IA: Perfection Learning.

Kaiser Family Foundation (2005, March). *Generation M: Media in the lives of eight- to eighteen-year-olds.* Presented for the Study of Entertainment Media and Health, Kaiser Family Foundation, March 2005, Washington, DC.

Karki, C. (2010). *Risk behavior and health condition of youth engaging in same-sex sexual behaviors: Analysis of the 2009 Wisconsin Youth Risk Behavior Survey (YRBS).* http://www.dhs.wisconsin.gov/aids-hiv/Stats/2009YRBSReport.pdf

Koday, D. (2012). Demi Lovato's mission: Stop bullying now! *Seventeen Magazine.* Retrieved from http://www.seventeen.com/college/advice/mission-demi-lovato

Kuhn, S. (2009, September 3). Life Stages. *Back Stage.com.* Retrieved from http://www.backstage.com/interview/life-stages

Kuntsche, E. N. (2004). Hostility among adolescents in Switzerland? Multivariate relations between excessive media use and forms of violence. *Journal of Adolescent Health, 34*(3), 230–236.

Kuntsche, E., Pickett, W., Overpeck, M., Craig, W., Boyce, W., & de Matos, M. G. (2006, December). Television Viewing and Forms of Bullying among Adolescents from Eight Countries. *Journal of Adolescent Health, 39*(6), 908–915.

Leapman, B., & Copping, J. (2008). Video game glorifies bullying, say critics. *The Telegraph*. Retrieved from http://www.telegraph.co.uk/news/uknews/1576078/Video-game-glorifies-bullying-say-critics.html

Lee, S., & Ditko, S. (1962). *The Amazing Fantasy*. New York: Marvel Entertainment.

Lee, E., & Kim, M. (2004) Exposure to media violence and bullying at school: Mediating influences of anger and contact with delinquent friends. *Psychological Reports, 95*(2), 659–672.

Lenhart, A. (2010). Cyberbullying 2010: What the research tells us. *Pew Internet*. Retrieved from http://www.pewinternet.org/Presentations/2010/May/Cyberbullying-2010.aspx

Lieberman, D. (2011). Report: Reality TV encourages "mean girl" behavior in teens. *Deadline Hollywood*. Retrieved from http://www.deadline.com/2011/10/report-reality-tv-encourages-mean-girl-behavior-in-teens/

Lipkins, S. (n.d.). Vulture culture: How we encourage bullying. *Justmommies.com*. Retrieved from http://www.realpsychology.com/content/gps-parents-and-teachers/vulture-culture-how-we-encourage-bullying

Marikar, S. (2010). 10 celebrities sticking up for gay teens. *ABC News*. Retrieved from http://abcnews.go.com/Entertainment/10-celebrities-sticking-gay-teens/story?id=11814018

McGraw, J. (2008). *Life strategies for dealing with bullies*. New York: Simon & Schuster.

_____. (2001). *Closing the gap: A strategy for bringing parents and teens together*. New York: Fireside.

Merrell, K. W., Gueldner, B. A., Ross, S. W., & Isava, D. M. (2008). How effective are school bullying intervention programs? A meta-analysis of intervention research. *School Psychology Quarterly, 23*(1), 26–42.

Middle school girls "spit in my face," Zooey Deschanel recalls. (2012). *MSNBC entertainment on today*. Retrieved from http://todayentertainment.today.msnbc.msn.com/_news/2012/01/17/10175357-middle-school-girls-spit-in-my-face-zooey-deschanel-recalls

Mitchell, J. (2010). Celebrities team up for anti-bullying campaigns. *PopEater*. Retrieved from http://www.popeater.com/2010/10/06/tim-gunn-ellen-degeneres-bullying-psa/1\

Moss, G. (2005). Teen mean fighting machine: Why does the media love a certain flavor of female aggression? In L. Jervis & A. Zeisler (Eds.), *BitchFest: Ten years of cultural criticism form the pages of Bitch Magazine* (44–48). New York, NY: Farrar, Straus and Giroux, Ltd.

Mueller, R. T. (1981). Sitcom morality: From Beaver to Ann Romano: It's the same old story. *Journal of Popular Film & Television, 9*(1), 50–55.

National Institute of Child Health & Human Development. (2012, July 12). Taking a stand against bulling. *National Institute of Health*. Retrieved from http://www.nichd.nih.gov/news/resources/spotlight/092110-taking-stand-against-bullying.cfm

National Institutes of Health Department. (2001). Bullying widespread in U.S. schools, survey finds. (National Institute of Child Health and Human Department press release). Retrieved from http://www.nichd.nih.gov/news/releases/bullying.cfm

O'Donell, J. (2011). Definition of mean girls. *About.com*. Retrieved from http://tweenparenting.about.com/od/tweenculture/g/MeanGirls.htm

Oesterle, J. (2010 June 10). 13 douchiest movie bullies [Review of movie]. *Mania.com*. http://www.mania.com/13-douchiest-movie-bullies_article_123131.html

Olweus, D. (1978). *Aggression in schools: Bullies and whipping boys*. Washington: Hemisphere Publishing.

Olweus, D. (2010). Understanding and researching bully: Some critical issues. In Jimerson, S. R., Swearer, S. M., & Espelage, D. L. (Eds.), *Handbook of bullying in schools: An international perspective* (9–33). New York, NY: Routledge/Taylor & Francis Group

Olweus, D. (2011). What is cyber bulling? *Hazelden Foundation*. Retrieved from http://owl.english.purdue.edu/owl/resource/560/10/

Paik, H., & Comstock, G. (1994). The effects of television violence on antisocial behavior: A meta-analysis. *Communication Research, 21*(4), 516–546.

Parent Further. (2011). Bullying and violence. *Parent further*. Retrieved from http://www.parentfurther.com/high-risk-behaviors/bullying?utm_campaign=parentfurther-search&utm_medium=search&utm_source=google&utm_term=bullying

Pasternack, A. (2010, June 2010). After lawsuits and therapy, Star Wars Kid is back. *Motherboard.Vice.com*. Retrieved from http://motherboard.vice.com/2010/6/1/after-lawsuits-and-therapy-star-wars-kid-is-back

Peitzman, L. (2012, November 10). How *Glee*'s gay-bullying plot misses the mark. *TV.com*. Retrieved from http://www.tv.com/how-glees-gay-bullying-plot-misses-the-mark/story/24522.html

Pellegrini, A. D., & Long, J. D. (2004). Part of the solution and part of the problem: The role of peers in bullying, dominance, and victimization during the transition from primary school through secondary school. In Espelage, D. L., & Swearer, S. M. (Ed.), *Bullying in American schools: A social-ecological perspective on prevention and intervention* (107–117). Mahwah, NJ: Lawrence Erlbaum Associates Publishers.

Pena, D. (2012). Attack ad launched toward Linda McMahon, ripped for past ties to WWE. *Wrestling Inc.* Retrieved from http://www.wrestlinginc.com/wi/news/2012/0912/556214-/linda-mcmahon/

Pepler, D., & Craig, W. (2009). *Bullying, interventions, and the role of adults.* Retrieved from http://www.education.com/reference/article-/role-of-adults-in-preventing-bullying/

Popkin, H. A. (2007). Surviving your inevitable online humiliation. *MSNBC.* Retrieved from http://www.msnbc.msn.com/id/20611439/

Powell, J. (1999). *Talking about bullying.* Oxford, UK: Raintree.

Relational aggression. (2011, September 21). Relational aggression, part 1: The clique. *Bullying Education.* Retrieved from http://www.bullyingeducation.org/2011/09/21/relational-aggression-part-1-the-clique/

Robinson, T., Callister, M., & Jankoski, T. (2008). Portrayal of body weight on children's television sitcoms: A content analysis. *Body Image, 5*(2), 141–151.

Rosenfeld, L., & Conte, A. (2011). ABC Family stars want you to delete digital drama. *Seventeen.* Retrieved from http://www.seventeen.com/entertainment/features/celebs-delete-digital-drama#slide-1

Rowley, M. J. (2012). Victoria Justice (Victorious) wants justice, not bullying. *MTV News.* Retrieved from http://act.mtv.com/posts/victoria-justice-wants-justice-not-bullying/

Salmivalli, C., & Voeten, M. (2004). Connections between attitudes, group norms, and behavior in bullying situations. *International Journal of Behavioral Development, 28*(3), 246–258.

Scharrer, E. (2001). Men, muscles, and machismo: The relationship between television violence exposure and aggression and hostility in the presence of hypermasculinity. *Media Psychology, 3*, 159–188.

School bullying. (n.d.). School bullying and teen bullying statistics. *Family First Aid.* Retrieved from http://www.familyfirstaid.org/bullying.html

Serjeant, J. (2010, October 13). Hollywood blogger Perez Hilton vows to quit bullying. *Reuters.com.* Retrieved from http://www.reuters.com/article/2010/10/13/us-perezhilton-idUSTRE69C16C20101013

Sharp, S., & Smith, P. K. (1991). Bullying in UK schools: The DES Sheffield bullying project. *Early Child Development and Care, 77*, 47–55.

Shrank, D. (2011, December 23). What *Glee* teaches about bullying. *Social Workers Speak.* Retrieved from http://www.socialworkersspeak.org/cheers-and-jeers/what-glee-teaches-about-bullying.html

Silverman, J. (n.d.). Is cyberbullying getting out of control? *How Stuff Works.* Retrieved from http://computer.howstuffworks.com/cyberbullying.htm/printable

Simmons, R. (2011). *Odd girl out: The hidden culture of aggression in girls.* Boston, MA: Mariner Books.

Sims, M. (2004, January 12). Largest ever study of anti-LGBT harassment in schools shows the problem in widespread, dangerous and preventable. *GLSEN.org.* Retrieved from http://www.glsen.org/cgi-bin/iowa/all/news/record/1444.html

Singer, D. G., & Singer, J. L. (2000). *Handbook of children and the media.* Thousand Oaks, CA: Sage Publishing.

Slee, P. T. (1995). Peer victimization and its relationship to depression among Australian primary school students. *Personality and Individual Differences, 18*(1), 57–62.

Smith P. (2004). Bullying: Recent developments. *Child and Adolescent Mental Health 9*(3), 98–103.

_____. (2004, November 3). Bullying: Recent developments. *Child and Adolescent Mental Health 9*(3), 98–103. Retrieved from http://stmaryseminars.tripod.com/sitebuildercontent/sitebuilderfiles/3smith.pdf

Smith, P. K. (2011). Bullying in schools: Thirty years of research. In I. Coyne & C. P. Monks (Eds.), *Bullying in different contexts* (36–59). Cambridge: Cambridge University Press.

Smith, P. K., Bowers, L., Binney, V., & Cowie, H. (1993). Relationships of children involved in bully/victim problems at school. In Smith, P. K., Bowers, L., Binney, V., Cowie, H., & Duck, S. (Eds.), *Learning about relationships, understanding relationship processes* (183–212). Thousand Oaks, CA: Sage Publications, Inc.

Smith, S. (2010, September 21). Cyber bully victims "isolated, dehumanized" [Blog]. *CNN health: The chart.* Retrieved from http://thechart.blogs.cnn.com/2010/09/21/cyber-bully-victims-isolated-dehumanized/

Social TV ratings. (2009). *Zap2it.* Retrieved from http://www.zap2it.com/tv/ratings/

Sporkin, A. (2012). Publishing industry has strong January revenue growth in print books and ebooks for all audiences. *Association of American Publishers.* Retrieved from http://www.publishers.org/press/62/

Swearer, S. M. (2008, December). Relational aggression: Not just a female issue. *Journal of School Psychology, 46*(6), 611–616.

Thompson, L. (2012) The real Dan Savage: The

bully against bullying. *NewsBusters*. Retrieved from http://newsbusters.org/blogs/lauren-thompson/2012/05/10/real-dan-savage-bully-against-bullying

Turner, L. (2008). The new mean girl: Black women on reality TV. *The Student Operated Press*. Retrieved from http://www.thesop.org/sotry/entertainment/2008/04/06

Twaddle, A. (2012). *Glee* on bullying: Gay v. lesbian. *The C.L.O.S.E.T blog: Communicate, listen, offer, share, & express thyself.* Retrieved from http://kajamsclosetblog.blogspot.com/2012/02-/glee-on-bullying-gay-v-lesbian.html

U.S. Department of Health and Human Services (2009) *Bullying: Children who bully.* Retrieved from http://www.education.com/reference/article/Ref_Children_Who_Bully/

Vena, J. (2011). Rebecca Black leaves school after bullying. *MTV.com*. Retrieved from http://www.mtv.com/news/articles/1668859/rebecca-black-bullying.jhtml

Wade, M. (n.d.). How to stop and prevent harassment on Xbox LIVE. *eHow*. Retrieved from http://www.ehow.com/how_4516224_stop-prevent-harassment-xbox-live.html

Walker, L. Q., & Jones, E. (2009) *Super girl: Comic adventures in the 8th grade.* New York: D.C. Comics.

Watson, S. (2011). Mean girls: How to deal with them. *WebMD.com*. Retrieved from http://teens.webmd.com/features/dealing-with-mean-girls

Wiseman, R. (2003). *Queen bees & wannabes: Helping your daughter survive cliques, gossip, boyfriends, and other realities of adolescence.* New York: Crown Publishing.

Wiseman, R. (2011a, April 23). What makes a good bullying PSA? *The Huffington Post.* [Blog]. Retrieved from http://www.huffingtonpost.com/rosalind-wiseman/good-bullying-psa_b_852489.html

Wiseman, R. (2011b, April 7). Worst bully PSA ever. *Rosalindwiseman.com.* Retrieved from http://rosalindwiseman.com/2011/04/07/worst-bullying-psa-ever/

Wiseman, R. (2011c). The NEA and WWE's new anti-bulling campaign. *Huffington Post.* http://www.huffingtonpost.com/rosalind-wiseman/devils-advocacy-the-nea-a_b_876366.html

Wright, D., Kazdin, C., & Knox, M. (2011, April 21). Rebecca Black, "Friday" singer, received death threats. *ABC News.* Retrieved from http://abcnews.go.com/Entertainment/rebecca-black-friday-singer-receiving-death-threats/story?id=13425921

Zimmerman, F. J., Glew, G. M., Christakis, D. A., & Katon, W. (2005). Early cognitive stimulation, television watching, and subsequent bullying among grade-school children. *Archives of Pediatric and Adolescent Medicine, 159*(4), 384–388.

Index